Aspen E. Brinton

Confronting Totalitarian Minds: Jan Patočka on Politics and Dissidence

KAROLINUM PRESS

KAROLINUM PRESS
Karolinum Press is a publishing department of Charles University in Prague
Ovocný trh 3–5, 116 36 Prague 1, Czech Republic
www.karolinum.cz

© Aspen E. Brinton, 2021
Cover and design by Jan Šerých
Set and printed in the Czech Republic by Karolinum Press
First edition

Cataloguing-in-Publication Data is available from the National Library
of the Czech Republic

ISBN 978-80-246-4537-7
ISBN 978-80-246-4519-3 (pdf)
ISBN 978-80-246-4539-1 (epub)
ISBN 978-80-246-4538-4 (mobi)

In memory of my father

Table of Contents

Acknowledgments

This book is a conversation as much as it is also about conversations. It was written with the hope that conversations about philosophical ideas can create moments of beauty, friendship, and transcendence within the everyday banality of an alienating world. Those who had conversations with me about this book, however short or tangential, made this book possible by creating such moments. I wish I could remember every conversation, though I cannot, and I realize that many may not even remember these conversations, even though I do. However limited and imperfect, I give thanks here to what I remember, to those who made this larger written conversation possible through a thousand smaller exchanges of words, ideas, exaltations, and questions: thanks to all the participants of the 2017 Patočka conference in Leuven and Brussels, and especially those who remember that late debate over yet another good Belgian beer about the last lines of *Heretical Essays*, including Anita Williams, James Dodd, Ian Angus, Emre San, Francesco Tava, Martin Koci, and Daniel Leufer; thanks to our 2017 ASEEES panel of Delia Popescu and Francesco and Martin again, where we had the opportunity to discuss Patočka's ideas and converse with an American audience about *The Socrates of Prague*; to Marci Shore and Ludger Hagedorn, for organizing a conference about totalitarianism and Central European philosophy, where conversations with Michael Gubser, Vladimir Tismaneanu, Omri Boehm, Krysztof Czyzewski, Irena Grudzinska-Gross, and Elzbieta Matynia, among many other distinguished guests, let us create a moment of solidarity in the midst of our political distress; to Jonathan Bolton, for several conversations, but most especially for that moment in Brussels that gave momentary light to impending darkness;

9

to David Danaher, for inviting me to converse with your students and colleagues about Havel and Patočka in Wisconsin; to Hana Fořtová, for many conversations about confusing Czech words, and for that wonderful mushroom-picking wander through the Bohemian countryside; to Pavel Barsa, for lingering late on the steps of the IWM for a conversation about the end of the left and right in modern politics; to Klaus Nellen, for listening over coffee to my account of becoming a dissident in a different totalitarian society, and for telling smuggling stories at Nachtasyl; to Kylie Thomas, for sympathy with the precarity of academia; to Walter Famler, for that long afternoon at Café Rathaus talking about Marcuse's hippopotamus, the dialectics of liberation, and life as a revolutionary; to Bill McKibbon, for answering my email the same day I sent it, and for coming to inspire my students to do better than their institution; to Holly Case, for organizing the twenty-first century Wiener Kreis, creating the Weltzentrum of conversational transcendence with the ongoing hospitality of Dessy Gavrilova and Ivan Krastev; to Alice and Yancy (and the other soldier) for that sublime conversation about what I should tell college students about war, and for your hospitality, friendship, and cat-sitting opportunities during nomadic times; to Ezgi, for so many conversations about life, writing, teaching, absurdity and all the political implications of that shared November morning in Vienna; to William and David, for letting *those* conversations end by naming the goldfish; to Julian, for picking up the phone that awful morning; to Avril, for picking up the phone that other awful morning, and for our writing 'vacation' that helped get this done; to Serena, for trusting me with a more pressing calamity; to Daniel, for making sure I kept laughing and dancing; to Alisa, for letting me be with you on a day of real creation; to Christian, for laughing through a deconstruction of the priestly class at a Warsaw tavern and for calling things by their proper name; to Laura Cronk, for all those extremely sane unscholarly conversations about what's important, and for giving me peace of mind knowing my loved ones were cared for while I traveled; to my sister, for the anti-conversational expletives at cancer and chemo; to Gerry, for listening yet again, and rising to the call so long beyond normal duty; to my aunt Ginna, for asking so many questions and for understanding that books and politics matter; to Jennifer and Mary, for coming out to hear the other side of the story that last cold December night in Boston; to those whose names I cannot say and the one 'no' voter, thank you for speaking truth to power on my behalf; to my students at Boston College who so quickly bridged the theory-practice nexus—you will always help me remember that all of us may someday become the practicum for our own ethical theories.

I owe ongoing thanks to my colleagues at VCU who took a chance on me and this Czech philosopher, and to Mark Wood and Motse Fuentes who made the future possible; I hope our conversations continue into the years ahead.

A special acknowledgement must go to Ludger Hagedorn, without whom many of the conversations already mentioned would not have happened, who supported this project with grace and humor, and who understood what it meant to practice Patočka's 'solidarity of the shaken' and Havel's 'power of the powerless' in the trying world of academia's politics.

More formally, the Institute for Human Sciences (IWM) in Vienna, Austria, supported this project with a residential fellowship to use their archive and complete the manuscript. My sincere and heartfelt thanks to Ludger, Mary, and Ana for everything they did to make the fellows feel welcome at the Institute. The Dean's Office at Boston College also provided financial support and research leave for this project.

This book was written through tumult—personal, professional, and political—and each conversation really did matter, and each moment of support, however small and despite the cliché, really did make a difference in bringing this book into existence. The final conversation that brought this book into print, with Michael Baugh, editor at Karolinum Press, included more living-in-truth than most normal conversations in academic publishing, and I will always be thankful for the unexpected yet conscientious response to the multifaceted tumult of this book's life-world. I would also like to thank Sydney Murray, Courtney Latourrette and Alexander Tyree for their assistance in the final preparation of the manuscript.

The prospectus for this book was the next thing I wrote after I composed and delivered the eulogy for my father's funeral, and so this is dedicated to his memory, but also in memory of all those who, like him, survived the destructiveness of war, experienced 'the front' in all its forms, and lived and died with war in their souls.

Preface

An umbrella opens. A tear gas canister explodes. Bodies march. A mural is painted. Someone addresses the crowd from atop a car. A mind goes blank at the sound of gunfire. Time stops. A body goes limp as the handcuffs are put on. Cameras livestream. Banners unfold. Riot police line up. Flags fly and are trampled. Images appear on a billion tiny screens. Crowds swirl. Articles are written. A Molotov cocktail is thrown. Appeals for help go viral. Commentators speculate. The bodies come and go, talking of history, hoping for freedom, trying to speak the truth about power and existential solidarity. They will return, and the questions persist: Why do they go? What if it all goes wrong? What will history say?

This book tries to illuminate dissident politics as something that *might* make human life seem more meaningful in the midst of the nihilism, despair, and existential crises wrought by modernity's political conundrums and calamities. By using Jan Patočka's ideas as lenses to examine the words of activists and dissidents across time and place, it seeks a glimpse at alternate forms of political thinking that might become antidotes to the totalitarianisms within our minds and political bodies. What is owed to Patočka in formulating these new (but also very old) questions should become clear in the chapters that follow, but what is owed to our contemporaries still working against the totalitarianisms of today should be the beginning, if only because it all must come back to these human confrontations with totalitarianism in the end. A few words to begin, then, from dissidents of the last decade, those who made headlines in recent memory, but who somehow also came to embody the ideas of this book.

Denise Ho is a spokesperson for the non-violent protest movement still ongoing in Hong Kong in 2020. She gave a speech at the Oslo Freedom Forum in 2019, describing the background to her life and activism:

The Umbrella Movement in 2014 proved to be a defiant move in a city where the majority of the population has always been so politically indifferent. Why were these young students courageously standing up to this giant machine, one that so many people were fearful of? Walking down the occupied streets of Harcourt Road, I remember seeing all these magnificent expressions of thought and creativity, something that I had never seen in my city. Graffiti, sculpture, art installations, small patches of farming, and our own posted mosaic version of the Lennon Wall, and even a temporary study hall... As a Hong Kong-born singer-song writer and a daughter of an immigrant mother who had spent her teenage years in Montreal, and also, the first female singer to have come out openly in Hong Kong, I had always felt out of place in this city... It was only until this moment, among the aspiring crowds of the Umbrella Movement, that I finally felt a real sense of belonging to this place where I have always called 'home'...

After my involvement in the Umbrella movement, I was banned from China... so I launched a campaign to crowd-sponsor my concert... I built my own system... and also improvised local tours in different districts of Hong Kong. We sang on trams and underground live houses and on sidewalks and even in local shops... By creating socially innovative art, music, and events, [and] by breaking rules and reinventing the game, I want to pass on this message to the younger generations. Create your own possibilities, even when all odds are against you... Fear grows in spaces where we feel alone, judged, and cut off. The key is to not get discouraged and intimidated by the bigger picture. But rather to look within and around ourselves, to find people with similar values and identify the possibilities that exist in our own spaces. By focusing on our everyday lives, on our skills and passion, we can and will reignite our courage... Do your best in what you do best... Live the life that you envision for generations to come. When the system does not provide for us, we take things into our own hands. Our fate is what we make of it. By reconnecting with ourselves we will reconnect with others. And finally, we will reconnect with our flexibility in finding answers as a humanity collective.[1]

---

1   Denise Ho, "Under the Umbrella: Creative Dissent in Hong Kong." Oslo Freedom Forum, May 27, 2019. Transcribed from video. https://oslofreedomforum.com/talks/under-the-umbrella -creative-dissent-in-hong-kong.

Extinction Rebellion, an organization that uses non-violent civil disobedience to highlight environmental problems related to climate change, describes its mission on its website:

Our world is in crisis. Life itself is under threat... We hear history calling to us from the future... It's a future that's inside us all—located in the fierce love we carry for our children, in our urge to help a stranger in distress... And so we rebel for this, calling in joy, creativity and beauty. We rise in the name of truth and withdraw our consent for ecocide, oppression and patriarchy. We rise up for a world where power is shared for regeneration, repair and reconciliation. We rise for love in its ultimate wisdom. Our vision stretches beyond our own lifespan, to a horizon dedicated to future generations and the restoration of our planet's integrity. Together, our rebellion is the gift this world needs. We are XR [Extinction Rebellion] and you are us.

This is the time. Wherever we are standing is the place... We have just this one flickering instant to hold the winds of worlds in our hands, to vouchsafe the future. This is what destiny feels like. We have to be greater than we have ever been, dedicated, selfless, self-sacrificial...

Time is broken and buckled, and seasons are out of step so even the plants are confused. Ancient wisdoms are being betrayed: to everything there was a season, a time to be born and a time to be a child, protected and cared for, but the young are facing a world of chaos and harrowing cruelty. In the delicate web of life, everything depends on everything else: we are nature and it is us, and the extinction of the living world is our suicide...

Each generation is given two things: one is the gift of the world, and the other is the duty of keeping it safe for those to come. The generations of yesterday trust those of today not to take more than their share, and those of tomorrow trust their elders to care for it... The contract is broken, and it is happening on our watch. A pathological obsession with money and profit is engineering this breakdown...

Tell the Truth is the first demand of Extinction Rebellion, using fearless speech, Gandhi's 'truth-force' which creates a change of heart...

Humans are by nature cooperative, and times of crisis can be times when life is lived transcendently, for a purpose beyond the self. No individual alone is fully human, as the African concept Ubuntu shows: our humanity results from being in connection with each other. Believing that there is no Them and Us, only all of us together, Extinction Rebellion seeks alliances wherever they can be found. We are fighting for our lives and if we do not link arms, we will fail because the forces we are up against are simply too powerful. We need you…

For our deepest longings are magnificent: to live a meaningful life, to be in unity with each other and with the life-source, call it the spirit, call it the divine, call it the still small voice, it doesn't matter what it is called or how it is spelled if it guides us in service to life…

This vision has a map. It is the map of the human heart. Believing in unflinching truth, reckless beauty and audacious love, knowing that life is worth more than money and that there is nothing greater, nothing more important, nothing more sacred than protecting the spirit deep within all life.

This is life in rebellion for life.[2]

"March for Our Lives," an organization in the United States started by secondary school students, works against gun violence. As written on their website:

Everywhere we look, gun violence is decimating our families and communities. Whether it's the mass shootings in shopping malls, concerts, schools, and places of worship, the retaliatory gun violence in urban neighborhoods haunted by the legacy of economic disinvestment, racism, and poverty, or the solitary suicides committed nationwide with increasing frequency, gun violence adds up: over 100 Americans die from it every day. 100 lives lost every single day. We started March For Our Lives to say, "Not One More." No more school shooting drills. No more burying loved ones. No more American exceptionalism in all the wrong ways. But we cannot do this alone.[3]

The Sudanese Professionals Association issued the "Declaration of Freedom and Change" in Khartoum on January 1st, 2019:

We, the people of Sudan across cities and villages, in the north, the south, the east, and the west; join our political and social movements, trade unions and community groups in affirming through this declaration that we

2 "Why We Rebel," Extinction Rebellion, curated by Jay Griffiths with XR UK Vision team, accessed January 4, 2020, https://rebellion.earth/the-truth/about-us/.
3 "Peace Plan: Conclusion," March for Our Lives, accessed January 30, 2020, https://marchforour -lives.com/peace-plan/.

will continue the course of peaceful struggle until the totalitarian regime is removed and the following goals are achieved: First: The immediate and unconditional end of General Omar Al Bashir's presidency and the conclusion of his administration. Second: The formation of a National Transitional Government. This transitional government will be formed of qualified people based on merits of competency and good reputation, representing various Sudanese groups and receiving the consensus of the majority... Third: Putting an immediate end to all violations against peaceful protesters, repealing of all laws restricting freedoms of speech and expression; and bringing the perpetrators of crimes against the Sudanese people to fair trials in accordance with accepted national and international laws.

By signing this draft declaration... we affirm that we will continue taking to the streets and leading the nonviolent struggle, until our demands are met. We call upon our brethren in the armed forces to take the side of the Sudanese people and to refrain from supporting Al Bashir by participating in the brutalizing and killing of unarmed civilians.[4]

In 2013, a group of protesters assembled in Istanbul to try to prevent the authorities from cutting down the trees in Gezi park. After protesters were abused by the police, a coalition formed to support the protesters by calling for democratic accountability. Together these groups issued a statement, "We are Taksim Solidarity. We are Here." These are excerpts from the statement:

Taksim Solidarity is comprised of 124 trade unions, political parties, community groups, sports club fan groups, and initiatives embracing diversity and expressing demands in a peaceful, democratic way. It is supported by environmentalists, artists, journalists, and members of the intelligentsia.

Taksim Solidarity's demand for a healthy urbanization and liveable city, merged with the cries of millions for more freedom and democracy, reflects a social sensitivity symbolized by Gezi Park. The creative genius of the young, the warm embrace of mothers, the power of the working

---

4   "Declaration of Freedom and Change," Sudanese Professionals Association, January 1, 2019, https://www.sudaneseprofessionals.org/en/declaration-of-freedom-and-change/.

classes and the loud and clear voices of women, the "we are here too" cries of the LGBT community and the revitalized oldies have come together to turn an irreversible page in the democratic history of this country... These spontaneous countrywide civil society initiatives have unfortunately been confronted with tear gas, water cannons, and rubber bullets. Four youths have lost their lives as result of violence by the police and their accomplices. How inhuman and incomprehensible is it that the government has still not shown any empathy with the families who have lost their beloved children?

Democratic demands can undoubtedly be met by democratic means. Our society needs an approach by the public administration perceiving the issues, demands, and expectations and taking steps for their solution. We are worried about the criminalization of democratic reactions and the treatment of everyone as guilty, as terrorists, and the use of police force pushing issues to intractability.[5]

Historian Marci Shore interviewed those who protested against the Ukrainian government of Victor Yanukovych in the winter of 2013–2014. These are a few moments from *The Ukrainian Night: An Intimate History of a Revolution*:

There were moments when Markiyan was certain the revolution had been lost. Yet he kept going back. Once someone asked why he was standing there freezing on the Maidan if he believed all was about to be lost? His only answer was that it was his choice.[6]

'I had not understood the moment when a person is ready to die. And there I understood it... it's a departure, a movement beyond the confines of the self, when you experience being with people who are ready to die for you, to make themselves vulnerable for you, to carry you if you're wounded... a willingness appears—it's a kind of rapture, a wonder at the possibilities given to man, and enormous gratitude towards others, simply

---

5   "We are Taksim Solidarity, We are Here!" July 19, 2013, https://www.taksimdayanisma.org /taksim-dayanismasi-biziz-biz-buradayiz?lang=en. With thanks to Ezgi Yildiz for a conversation about how 'solidarity' and 'civil society' translate into Turkish.
6   Marci Shore, *The Ukrainian Night: An Intimate History of Revolution* (New Haven: Yale University Press, 2018) 58.

a *Begeisterung* with generosity and devotion. And an experiencing of an enormous solidarity.'[7]

His shoulder had been battered, but he was not scared away, he stayed on the Maidan. 'Your mother must have been very upset,' I said. 'But she let you go back?' 'My mother was making Molotov cocktails on Hrushevskyi Street.'[8]

Tatiana Aleshka was on the streets in Minsk as ongoing protests emerged against the fraudulent reelection of Belorussian President Aleksandr Lukashenko in August 2020:

The city has woken up, and people have gone out into the streets to form a human chain of solidarity and to peacefully protest… It is impossible to fall asleep in a city where thousands of people remain behind bars for no reason, where they are humiliated, beaten, and mutilated with full impunity. It is impossible to fall asleep in a city overflowing with security forces, where you can be beaten or have your arm or leg broken, simply because you are waiting for information about your husband, brother, or daughter near the walls of a prison… Yet entirely peaceful protests and demonstrations continue in this city for the third day… The atmosphere is indescribable; words cannot do it justice… When you see it for yourself, when you stand holding flowers on the streets of the city, when you talk to strangers as if they are old friends, it can seem like there is hope… You feel happy to belong to such a people, to form a part of it! But you understand deep within you that they don't touch you only because the order hasn't been given… I myself, my friends and acquaintances, along with millions of people in the country don't need directions to come out to protests. We have had it up to here with life in Lukashenka's totalitarian state. We don't need a director to show us where and when to go and what to do.[9]

7   Shore, *Ukrainian Night*, 125. "Begeisterung" is not translated in Shore's text. The closest translation in this context might be something like exaltation or communion, but the German word also implies being overcome with a spiritual force or presence.
8   Shore, *Ukrainian Night*, 42.
9   Tatiana Aleshka, "For All Those Who Are Interested in Events in Belarus, and for All Those Who Are Asking What Is Happening Here," trans. Markian Dobczansky, IWM Chronicle from Belarus, August 18, 2020, https://www.iwm.at/chronicle-from-belarus/tatiana-aleshka -for-all-those-who-are-interested-in-events-in-belarus-and-for-all-those-who-are-asking-what-is -happening-here/. Originally posted in Russian on Facebook, August 15, 2020.

The Black Lives Matter movement in the United States responded to the videoed killing of George Floyd by a police officer, as well as the killing of many other African Americans by the police, with widespread and ongoing protests about racial injustice. Solidarity protests occurred around the world throughout the summer of 2020. These were the two main rallying cries shared by protestors globally:

"No justice, no peace."
"I can't breathe."

Introduction

*"Because no one can write about Plato
who has not had the Platonic worldview
opened up from inside oneself."*[1]
– Jan Patočka

In various Prague basements and living rooms in the 1970s, Czech philosopher Jan Patočka led seminars on the question of how philosophy might "help us in the distress... [of] the situation in which we are placed."[2] Patočka's own distress included being forbidden to teach publicly and living under conditions of censorship in Communist Czechoslovakia. Having retreated to private spaces to do his work, he confronted his situation by leading conversations with students and other intellectuals that

---

1   "So kann niemand uber Plato schreiben, wem nicht die platonische Weltsicht sich vom innen aufgetan hat." Jan Patočka in Eugen Fink und Jan Patočka, *Briefe und Dokumente 1933–1977*, ed. Michael Heitz, and Bernhard (München: Karl Alber, 1999), 95. (my translation)

2   Jan Patočka, *Plato and Europe*, trans. Petr Lom (Stanford: Stanford University Press, 2002) 1. The word "distress" here is a translation of the Czech *nouze*, which Patočka uses again at the end of these lectures to describe the general situation and condition of life at his historical moment. It can also be translated as "basic need," implying that a state of *nouze* is one where basic needs of food, water, and shelter are not fulfilled. Yet it is used in both a psychological and physical way relating to needs, and in some older usages refers to a situation where one's free will is taken away by the conditions of the situation, that is, a form of distress imposed from the outside and irremediable through individual action. Patočka is probably playing with all of these meanings together in choosing to describe philosophical reflection as something that can be done in a state of *nouze*, while acknowledging that the distress is produced from the constraints of the external situation. With thanks to Hana Fořtová for a clarifying discussion on this word.

were later compiled and translated as *Plato and Europe*.[3] Patočka believed that reading Plato in such a situation could begin to alleviate the distress he shared with his listeners.[4] In 1977, Patočka would be asked by Václav Havel to become one of the spokesmen for Charter 77, a group of dissidents that aimed to call out the Communist state's hypocrisy and human rights violations. The police interrogation that followed his involvement in Charter 77 would lead to medical complications and Patočka's death. His *Plato and Europe* lectures became some of his last philosophical work, one culmination of a life spent studying not just Plato, but also the work of Edmund Husserl, Martin Heidegger and the history of Western philosophy more generally.[5]

Patočka's turn toward political action in 1977 is the basis for probing the wider oeuvre of his philosophical work for insights into new ways of thinking that might change the way we frame *our* distress about our own political situations. This exploration asks whether Patočka's philosophical thinking can reveal insights valuable to all those in political distress in different times and places. Following the spirit of Patočka's philosophical project as it might be relevant to perennial ideas about political engagement and dissidence, the goal here is to reconstruct his ideas for a broader audience of dissidents, activists, and engaged global citizens, arguing that his insights are valuable for understanding dissident politics, as well as helpful for critically examining our ways of thinking about political theory.[6]

---

3 These lectures are 'compiled and translated' into a book, but the lectures were not originally written. As editor and translator Petr Lom explains: "*Plato and Europe* is a series of lectures Patočka delivered in the homes of friends after his last banishment from the academy just three years before his death. Thus what follows are transcribed, unedited conversations—left unedited and as literal as possible in this translation. The material is striking not only because it represents a high point of lifelong meditation, but also because of the urgency and unpretentious honesty it contains." *Plato and Europe*, xvi.

4 The conditions of early 1970s Czechoslovakia were distressful given the occupation of the country by Soviet forces in 1968 and the ensuing censorship and repression of independent culture. See Milan Šimečka, *The Restoration of Order: The Normalization of Czechoslovakia,* trans. A.G. Brain (London: Verso, 1984).

5 Patočka's *Heretical Essays in the Philosophy of History,* trans. Erazim Kohák, ed. James Dodd (Chicago: Open Court, 1996) was also written during this time and is seen as another culmination of his life's work. Translator Erazim Kohák writes that his first English translation was from "a barely legible typescript copy of the samizdat *Edice Petlice* edition of 1975, smuggled out of Czechoslovakia and too faint even for photocopying." (*Heretical Essays,* 156). *Edice Petlice,* "Padlock Editions," was the underground press run by Ludvík Vaculík. Subsequent versions after 1989 were circulated and used for the published English translation.

6 This argument builds upon previous commentaries about Patočka's role as a dissident. See: Alexandra Laignel-Lavastine, *Jan Patočka: L'Esprit de la dissidence* (Paris: Michalon Le Bien Commun, 1998); Aviezer Tucker, *The Philosophy and Politics of Czech Dissidence from Patočka*

To make this argument, Patočka's ideas are put into conversation with other dissident-philosophers, those perhaps more well-known: Václav Havel, Dietrich Bonhoeffer, Mahatma Gandhi, anti-nuclear activists, and global environmentalists. The justifications for these choices will be further elaborated in the chapters that follow, but in general these represent historical moments of dissidence that align conceptually with Patočka's main ideas, but also have familiar global resonances with wider audiences. By using these examples, the result is a series of textual 'conversations' designed to ask why it is that standing up against received opinions and established power structures might be worth our time. Why dissent? Why protest? Most people understand that sometimes dissenting can change political structures, but what about when it seems like nothing will change? What can we do when the powers of 'business as usual' are too strong and overwhelming? How is it that some people can carry on dissenting and protesting in conditions of hopelessness and difficulty, when others never think of even beginning such a risky task? Patočka's work can give us glimpses into the depth of these questions, and the dissident-interlocutors in each of these 'conversations' will add further insights when refracted through Patočka's categories.

Political Distress and Plato's Cave

Patočka chose to talk about political 'distress' in his underground lectures through the lens of Plato's ideas, and Plato's description of a prisoner leaving his 'cave' might be one of the earliest descriptions of a dissident in a philosophical text. The image has been rewritten countless times, and in some ways, it will be rewritten here yet again within this series of conversations. Plato's cave is not only one of the most iconic and persistent images from the history of Western philosophy, but it is also a story of both political and intellectual liberation: a group of

to Havel (Pittsburgh: University of Pittsburgh Press, 2000); Barbara J. Falk, *The Dilemmas of Dissidence in East-Central Europe* (Budapest: Central European University Press, 2003); Simona Forti, "The Soul as a Site of Dissidence," in *Thinking After Europe*, eds. Darian Meacham and Francesco Tava (London: Rowan and Littlefield, 2016) 57–74; Jiří Přibáň, "Resisting Fear: On Dissent and Solidarity of the Shaken in Contemporary European and Global Society," in *Thinking After Europe*, 39–56; Jonathan Bolton, *Worlds of Dissent: Charter 77, The Plastic People of the Universe, and Czech Culture under Communism* (Cambridge, MA: Harvard University Press, 2012); Jérôme Melançon, "Jan Patočka's Sacrifice: Philosophy as Dissent," *Continental Philosophy Review* 46, no. 4 (December 2013): 577; Emilie Tardivel, "La subjectivité dissidente. Etude sur Patočka," *Studia Phænomenologica*, no. 7 (2007): 435–463.

people sits chained in a cave facing a wall of images produced by the shadows of puppets, and those who are chained have come to believe that the shadows make up the full extent of their reality. This might represent all of us, Plato claims, unless we come to realize the ways we are all chained, in particular how the images around us continually entrap us and further our mental enslavement to others' ideas. We are duped, or so is suggested, unable to turn around to see the world outside the cave until we learn to think in a different way. Education of a certain sort can make us self-aware enough to begin to free us from our many caves, and Plato calls this form of education 'philosophy.'[7] This is not what we think of as professional philosophy today, nor is it exactly a 'philosophy of life' in the popular sense; instead, it is a certain way of structuring one's thoughts, a method of reasoning where one can come to see the shadows as shadows, and by seeing and thinking in a different way, get turned around and out of various caves of illusion and moving towards the sunlight of new realities.

When Patočka described the significance of Plato's philosophy for understanding the political distress of his situation, he remarked how "Plato himself forces the philosopher to return to the cave. Philosophers must return to the cave out of duty, even if they do not want to, because something like human life, that is, life where care of the soul is possible, is only realizable under these conditions."[8] Reading Patočka's lectures and his descriptions of Socrates-the-philosopher returning to the cave to help free others, one can imagine Patočka in the smoke-filled rooms of the Czech dissident underground, taking the role of the philosopher who is trying to help his non-philosopher audience figure out how to care for their souls and confront the stifling 'normalization' of totalitarian political conditions.[9] Given his circumstances, Patočka might have

---

7   See Books 6–7, "The Republic," in *The Collected Dialogues of Plato: including the Letters*, eds. Edith Hamilton and Huntington Cairns (New York: Pantheon Books 1961), 720–772.

8   As Patočka writes: "For Aristotle all of philosophy is within the Platonic cave. You know that Plato himself forces the philosopher to return to the cave. Philosophers must return to the cave out of duty, even if they do not want to, because something like human life, that is, life where care of the soul is possible, is only realizable under these conditions. For that reason they have to return to the cave; it is their duty, and should they resist, force must be used against them. Aristotle returns to the cave, but without violence." *Plato and Europe*, 189.

9   By 'normalization' I refer to several uses of the word: the period following the invasion of the USSR into Czechoslovakia in 1968 was generally known as the time of 'normalization,' where the political, social and cultural openings and intellectual ferment of the Prague Spring in 1968 were shut down after the invasion. One account of this political and intellectual process can be found in the work cited above, in addition to Milan Šimečka, *The Restoration of Order: The Normalization of Czechoslovakia*. The process of 'normalization' also has deeper

been living out the Socratic return to the cave, exercising his duty to use philosophy to illuminate the collective distress of his society and recover some modicum of humanity from a dehumanizing political situation. The rest of his *Plato and Europe* lectures elaborate what it means to 'care for the soul,' including the history of the idea, its political and existential consequences, and how caring for the soul can impart transcendence into mundane situations.[10] (See Chapter Two for a full description of 'caring for the soul.') Patočka wanted to use philosophy for elaborating what it meant to find a modicum of transcendence within history and political action; he then confronted his collective 'distress' by suggesting Plato and other philosophers might help us think beyond our entrapments and help us come to believe that we can (and should) make ourselves an active part of history's unfolding possibilities.[11] This history is 'heretical,' according to the title of another of Patočka's later works, *Heretical Essays in the Philosophy of History*, and within his heresies are various kinds of dissidence that will be elaborated in later chapters.[12]

In the more than two thousand years since Plato's parable about knowledge and ignorance entered into the human conversation about how to live a good life by thinking in a new way, this seductive allegory of the cave has inspired unending interpretations, some of which are clichéd, others helpful, and many obscure in their philosophical

philosophical references from Foucault's idea of normalization developed within *Discipline and Punish*, where he describes how institutions of all kinds—political, social, and cultural—force us to think in 'normal' categories and thus shut down critical thinking before 'not normal' thoughts are even formed. Michel Foucault, *Discipline and Punish: The Birth of the Prison*, trans. Alan Sheridan (New York: Vintage Books, 1995). Patočka (via Plato) asks us to see the world in a way that might prevent this normalization, where phenomena are encountered in their truthfulness, revealed under the terms of Heideggerian *aletheia*. This is rooted in the larger approach of phenomenological philosophy towards understanding how things appear in the world, and how those appearances change and are affected by time, place, and being. See Martin Heidegger, *Basic Writings*, ed. David Farrell Krell (New York: Harper Perennial, 2008). Also see Heidegger, *Being and Time*, trans. Joan Stambaugh (Albany: State University of New York Press, 1996).

10 For a technical philosophical analysis of the way Patočka interprets Plato throughout his wider oeuvre, see Filip Karfík, "Platons Bestimmung der Seele als Selbstbewegung," in *Unendlichkeitwerden durch die Endlichkeit: Eine Lectüre der Philosophie Jan Patočka's* (Würzburg: Königshausen and Newmann, 2008), 101–129 and M. Bernard, "Patočka and Plato: The idea of a politics of the soul," *Revue de métaphysique et de morale* 3 (2017): 357–370.

11 This is not the same thing as "historical progress"; see discussion of history below and in Chapter Two.

12 It is 'heretical' in a variety of senses, and there is scholarly debate about various senses of the 'heretical' in his work. See: Ludger Hagedorn and Yvanka Raynova, eds., *The Heretical Perspectives of Jan Patočka: 1907–1977* (Vienna: Axia Academic Publishers, 2018) Implicitly the structure of this book argues that it takes multiple senses of heresy to create a dissident, so various perspectives on Patočka's 'heresy' might be relevant and useful.

technicalities. Due to such interest and proliferation, however, no one has ever been able to assign the allegory of the cave to the mere past; it lives on indefinitely, and the cave reappears in the actions and ideas it has produced across different historical eras and within various cultures. In Plato's world, Socrates the philosopher was condemned to death for 'corrupting the youth' and 'believing in false gods'; in every age, people believe there is *something* that corrupts the youth, and every age and era has its 'gods' (literal and metaphorical) that can be denied.[13] Every new student who reads Plato must, therefore, reread the allegory of the cave into a present situation. Patočka's lectures in *Plato and Europe* were indeed such a rereading, and so too might this account of Patočka's thinking be yet another. To return to the cave to help others liberate themselves from false ideas, to undertake the practice that Patočka calls 'care for the soul,' and then to practice solidarity and dissident politics— these cannot be mixed together as identical kinds of thinking and action, but they are all interrelated ideas one can discuss alongside Patočka's life and thought. The way he philosophizes about these practices and evokes the potential interrelationship between philosophy and politics, I will argue, is the articulation of a particular vision of human life that should command our attention and thought.

Dissident Methods

'Dissident,' however, was not what Patočka called himself for most of his life, so this approach is not without some necessary caveats. While he wrote and studied topics not directly in line with the Marxist-Leninist orthodoxy of his Communist state, until Charter 77, he did not become actively involved in 'the politics of dissent' in the 'public sphere.'[14] Given

---

13 See Plato, "Apology" and "Crito," in *The Collected Dialogues of Plato*, 3–39.

14 This has led some to claim that the most important part of his work was not related to his dissidence. For example, Edward Findlay argues that it was a separate task. Edward Findlay, *Caring for the Soul in the Postmodern Age: Politics and Phenomenology in the thought of Jan Patočka* (Albany: State University of New York Press, 2002). More recently there has been emerging consensus that Patočka is not just a contributor to phenomenology, and more attention has been given to the political implications of his work. See: Ivan Chvatik, "Solidarity of the Shaken," *Telos 1992*, no. 94 (December 21, 1992: 163–166; Ivan Chvatik, "The Responsibility of the 'Shaken': Jan Patočka and his 'Care for the Soul' in the 'Post-European' World" in *Jan Patočka and the Heritage of Phenomenology* (Dordrecht: Springer, 2011), 263–279; James Dodd, *Violence* and *Phenomenology* (New York: Routledge, 2009); *The New Yearbook of Phenomenology and Phenomenological Philosophy XIV-2015: Religion, War and the Crisis of Modernity, A Special Issue*

the context of his situation, however, the argument here is that 'politics' was implied through and within any rejection of the official discourse and ideology of the Communist state, even if those who gathered together in alternative 'underground' spaces ironically called their actions 'anti-politics.'[15] Charter 77 famously claimed it was not political—perhaps ironically, or perhaps to lessen the brutality the signatories knew would be forthcoming from state authorities. Political dissidence was implied, however, by the circumstances of Patočka's writing and lecturing in the underground, especially when he chose to keep doing philosophy when he was not 'officially permitted' to be a professor in public at a university. His audience of students and intellectuals would have understood his underlying unorthodox and 'dissident' intention as he set about outlining their mutual "distress" using philosophy and holding an underground philosophy seminar. In his *Plato and Europe* lectures, Patočka assumed in his audience a common experience of repressive politics, and used philosophy to illuminate the cave of existence for that audience. By the end of these lectures, he suggested that caring for the soul was a way of moving toward potentials for the liberation of one's mind, even if one's body had to remain enchained due to the politics of the time. Patočka thought Plato represented the beginning

---

Dedicated to the Philosophy of Jan Patočka, vol. 14, ed. Ludger Hagedorn and James Dodd (New York: Routledge, 2015); *Über Zivilisation und Differenz; Tschechische Philosophen im 20. Jahrhundert: Klíma, Rádl, Patočka, Havel, Kosík*, ed. Luger Hagedorn, trans. Joachim Bruss and Markus Sedlaczek (Munich: Deutsche Verlags-Anstalt, 2002); Richard Kearney, "Poetics and the Right to Resist: Patočka's Testimony," *International Journal of Philosophical Studies* 2, no. 1 (1994): 31–44; Francesco Tava and Darian Meacham, eds., *Thinking After Europe*; Laignel-Lavastine, *Jan Patočka: L'Esprit de la dissidence*; Alexandra Laignel-Lavastine, *Esprits d'Europe: autour de Czeslaw Miłosz, Jan Potočka, István Bibó* (Paris: Calmann-Lévy, 2005); Melançon, "Jan Patočka's Sacrifice: Philosophy as Dissent," 577; James R. Mensch, *Patočka's Asubjective Phenomenology: toward a New Concept of Human Rights* (Würzburg: Königshausen & Neumann 2016); Cerwyn Moore, "Heretical Conversations with Continental Philosophy: Jan Patočka, Central Europe and Global Politics," *British Journal of Politics and International Relations* 11, no. 2 (2009): 315–331; Cerwyn Moore, "Jan Patočka and Global Politics," in *International Relations Theory and Philosophy: Interpretive Dialogues*, eds. Cerwyn Moore and Chris Farrands (London: Routledge, 2010), 46–59; *Jan Patočka: philosophie, phénoménologie, politique*, ed. Marc Richir and Etienne Tassin (Grenoble, France: Editions Jérôme Million, 1992); *Phenomenologies of Violence*, eds. Michael Staudigl (Leiden, Netherlands: Brill Academic Publisher, 2013); Francesco Tava, *The Risk of Freedom: Ethics, Phenomenology and Politics in Jan Patočka*, trans. Jane Ledlie (New York: Rowman and Littlefield, 2015); Tucker, *The Philosophy and Politics of Czech Dissidence from Patočka to Havel*.

15 For the way in which dissident communities framed themselves as practitioners of 'anti-politics,' see: Falk, *The Dilemmas of Dissidence in East-Central Europe*; George Konrád, *Antipolitics: An Essay*, trans. Richard Allen (New York: Harcourt Brace Jovanovich, 1984) and A. Brinton, *Philosophy and Dissidence in Cold War Europe* (London: Palgrave-Macmillan, 2016).

of European historical consciousness,[16] so he used lectures about Plato (among many other inspirations) to describe the shared distress of an historical moment; with Charter 77, he then stepped into history through his own political actions.[17]

Since his death, scholarly recognition from various disciplines, including mostly intellectual historians and philosophers, has emerged arguing that Patočka's political action was connected to his philosophical ideas.[18] I follow in agreement with the basic intuition of these scholars, building off their assertions and arguments about the political relevance of Patočka's ideas for the discipline of political theory. This elaboration for political theory seems necessary at this moment in time, as the majority of the scholarship in circulation about Patočka is not directly concerned with digging deeply into his political thinking, and is instead concerned with his contribution to the study of Husserl, Heidegger, phenomenology, and Czech history.[19] These commentaries do not necessarily approach

---

16   In *Plato and Europe*, Patočka asks: "What is the source of European history? What is at the birth of Europe? And our hypothesis is the thought in which is resumed all European reflexive effort hitherto, that is, the thought of the care of the soul. The thought of the care of the soul has its first formulation in the Platonic teaching," 212–213. In another place in the *Plato and Europe* lectures, he explains: "Through catastrophes, this heritage is kept alive, and this is why I suppose that perhaps it might be possible to dare to suggest the thesis that Europe—especially Western Europe—but even that other one, arose out of the care of the soul. This is the embryo out of which arose what Europe used to be..." *Plato and Europe*, 89. See also: R. Gasché, "Patočka on Europe in the Aftermath of Europe," *European Journal of Social Theory* 21, no. 3 (2018): 391–406.

17   Patočka's most explicitly political work includes the essays he wrote directly in response to the Charter 77 movement. These include "Obligation to Resist Injustice" and "What We Can and Cannot Expect from Charta 77," both in *Jan Patočka Philosophy and Selected Writings*, trans. Erazim Kohák (Chicago: Chicago University Press, 1989), 340–347. Other essays from this period include "On the Matters of The Plastic People of the Universe and DG 307." In *Sebrané spisy [Collected Works] vol. 12*. Praha: Oikoymenh, 2006: 425–427. Translated by Paul Wilson as "The Planetary Game," *Ethos*, Vol. 2, Nr. 1 (1986): 15. Reflecting on this last text in particular, Jozef Majernik has argued that Patočka's political turn was consistent with his commitment to the ancient Greek sense of the good life, in connection with a sense of what 'living in truth' as a philosopher meant to him in light of the problems of Communism: "Jan Patočka's Reversal of Dostoevsky and Charter 77," *Labyrinth: An International Journal for Philosophy, Value Theory and Sociocultural Hermeneutics* 19, no. 1 (2017): 26–45.

18   See note 14 above.

19   For recent work in phenomenology that analyzes Patočka's ideas of asubjective phenomenology, sense and perception, movement, embodiment and corporality, his critique of technology and his overall contribution to phenomenology, see: Renaud Barbaras, *L'ouverture du monde: Lecture de Jan Patočka* (Chatou, France: Les Editions de La Transparence, 2011); Renaud Barbaras, *Le mouvement de l'existence: Études sur la phénoménologie de Jan Patočka* (Chatou: Les Éditions de la Transparence, 2007); *Jan Patočka: Phénoménologies asubjective et existence*, ed. Renaud Barbaras, (Paris: Association Culturelle Mimesis 2007); *Jan Patočka and the Heritage of Phenomenology: Centenary Papers,* vol. 61, *Contributions to Phenomenology*, eds. Erika Abrams and Ivan Chvatik (Dordrecht: Springer, 2001); *The Phenomenological Critique of Mathematisation*

his work as if the political drama of his death had defined his life, and argue instead that his main contribution to contemporary philosophy is his work on phenomenology and its impact on Continental philosophy, and that his main contribution to Czech philosophy is his analysis of Comenius and Masaryk, important figures in Czech intellectual history.[20] In contrast to these more sustained conversations, the scholarship

and the Question of Responsibility: Formalisation and the Life-World, eds. Ivan Chvatík, Ľubica Učník and Anita Williams (Cham: Springer, 2015); Ivan Chvatík, "Jan Patočka's Care for the Soul' in the 'Nihilistic' World," (lecture at the 41st Annual Meeting of the Husserl Circle, New York, June 21–23, 2010), http://www.husserlcircle.org/HC_NYC_Proceedings.pdf.; Cristian Ciocan and Ivan Chvatík, "Jan Patočka and the European Heritage," *Studia Phænomenologica*, vol. VII (Bucharest: Romanian Society for Phenomenology and Humanitas, 2007): 9–15; Dragos Duicu, *Phénoménologie du mouvement: Patočka et l'héritage de la physique aristotélicienne* (Paris: Hermann, 2014); Filip Karfík, *Unendlichkeitwerden durch die Endlichkeit: Eine Lectüre der Philosophie Jan Patočka's* (Würzburg: Königshausen and Newmann, 2008); Eddo Evink, "Surrender and Subjectivity: Merleau-Ponty and Patočka on Intersubjectivity," *Meta: Research in Hermeneutics, Phenomenology and Practical Philosophy* V, no.1 (June 2013): 13–28; Simona Forti, *The New Demons: Rethinking Power and Evil Today*, trans. Zakiya Hanafi (Stanford: Stanford University Press, 2014); *Jan Patočka. Liberté, existence et monde commun*, ed. Natalie Frogneux (Argenteuil: Le Cercle Herméneutique, 2012); Michael Gubser, *The Far Reaches: Phenomenology, Ethics and Social Renewal in Central Europe* (Stanford: Stanford University Press, 2014); *Andere Wege in Die Moderne: Forschungsbeiträge zu Patočka's Genealogie der Neuzeit*, eds. Ludger Hagedorn and Hans Reiner Sepp, (Würzburg: Königshäusern and Neumann, 2006); Hagedorn and Dodd, *The New Yearbook of Phenomenology and Phenomenological Philosophy*; Hagedorn, Bruss and Sedlaczek, *Über Zivilisation und Differenz; Tschechische Philosophen im 20. Jahrhundert: Klíma, Rádl, Patočka, Havel, Kosík*, ed. Luger Hagedorn, trans. Joachim Bruss and Markus Sedlaczek (Munich: Deutsche Verlags-Anstalt, 2002); Giovanni Leghissa and Michael Staudigl, *Lebenswelt und Politik: Perspektiven der Phänomenologie nach Husserl* (Würzburg: Verlag Königshausen & Neumann, 2007); Sandra Lehmann, *Der Horizont der Freiheit: Zum Existenzdenken Jan Patočkas* (Würzburg: Königshausen and Neumann, 2004); Vladimír Leško, et al., *Patočka a novoveka filozofia* (Kosice, Slovakia: Univerzita Pavla Jozefa Safarika v Kosiciach, 2014); Vladimír Leško, et. al., *Patočka a filozofia 20. storocia* (Kosice: Filozifická fakulta UPJS v Kosiciach, 2015); James Mensch, *Patočka's Asubjective Phenomenology: Toward a New Concept of Human Rights*; Philippe Merlier, *Autour de Jan Patočka* (Paris: L'Harmattan, 2010); Christian Rabanus, *Jan Patočkas Phänomenologie interkulturell gelesen* (Nordhausen: Traugott Bautz, 2006); *Jan Patočka: philosophie, phénoménologie, politique*, ed. Marc Richir and Etienne Tassin (Grenoble: Editions Jérôme Millon, 1992); *Myth, philosophy, art, and science in Jan Patočka's thought*, eds. Miloš Ševčík and Vlastimil Zuska (Prague: Karolinum Press, 2014); Emilie Tardivel, *La Liberté au Principe: essai sure la philosophie de Patočka* (Paris: Librarie Philosophique Vrin, 2011); Ľubica Učník, "Esse or Habere. To Be or To Have: Patočka's Critique Of Husserl And Heidegger," *Journal of the British Society for Phenomenology* 38, no. 3 (October 2007): 297–317; Ľubica Učník, *The Crisis of Meaning and the Life-world: Husserl, Heidegger, Arendt, Patočka* (Athens: Ohio UP, 2016).

20   Patočka's works on the history of Czechoslovakia, Comenius, and his studies of T. G. Masaryk can be found in his compete works, volumes 9–12 and 21–22: Vera Schifferová, ed., "Komeniologické studie I," in *Sebrané spisy Jana Patočky*, vol. 9 (Prague: Oikoymenh, 1997); Vera Schifferová, ed.,"Komeniologické studie II," in *Sebrané spisy Jana Patočky*, vol. 10 (Prague: Oikoymenh, 1998), Vera Schifferová, ed. "Komeniologické studie III," in *Sebrané spisy Jana Patočky*, vol. 11 (Prague: Oikoymenh, 2003); Karel Palek and Ivan Chvatík, eds. "Cesi. Soubor textu k českému mysleni a český dějinám," in *Sebrané spisy Jana Patočky*, vol. 12 (Prague:

about Patočka's political ideas can seem, at least superficially, somewhat more episodic. While this account is meant to add one more fragment to the conversation about Patočka's political ideas already happening in European circles, it is also meant to try to cohere a line of conversation very much already in existence about the importance of politics in his work, therein generating more conversation about Patočka's ideas within comparative political theory, bringing in both global voices and Anglo-American political theory. Such an analysis might very well have fallen into obscurity given the lack of name recognition of its primary subject to these audiences, so it seemed important to put Patočka's ideas into conversation with more well known figures like Havel, Bonhoeffer, Gandhi and important activist voices from well-known historical and contemporary contexts. There are many other dissidents who might also belong here as relevant interlocutors, and choices of inclusion and exclusion are always difficult and costly; those chosen here are meant to be representative examples, never fully adequate to show every relevant aspect of Patočka's ideas, but hopefully evocative enough to promote further conversation and research.

By bringing together the viewpoints of various authors on the topic of dissident politics in order to illuminate the importance and applicability of Patočka's ideas, patterns emerged that inevitably went beyond the scope of Patočka's specific assertions. Perhaps controversially, I have chosen to analyze those general patterns of thinking and emerging forms of dissidence, especially in the concluding chapter. As there are many voices in the discussions that follow here, the reader should be forewarned that the conversations on occasion become more than the sum of their parts, and patterns of argument will sometimes go beyond a summary of what Patočka said or did not say. While the methodology of a scholarly philosophical commentary usually entails stopping at the border between what the philosopher said and what the commentator thinks (and the struggle to find that border with accuracy), the methodology of political theory

Oikoymenh, 2006); Vera Schifferová, Ivan Chvatik and Tomáš Havelka, eds."Korespondence s komeniology I. S přílohami o Chartě 77, norském vydání Kacířských esejů aj," in *Sebrané spisy Jana Patočky*, vol. 21 (Prague: Oikoymenh, 2011); Vera Schifferová and Ivan Chvatik, eds. "Korespondence s komeniology II," in *Sebrané spisy Jana Patočky*, vol. 22 (Prague: Oikoymenh, 2011). From different publishers: Jan Patočka, *Dvě studie o Masarykovi* (Toronto: Sixty-Eight Publishers, 1980); *Jan Amos Komenský (II). Nachgelassene Schriften zur Comeniusforschung* (Sankt Augustin: Richarz, 1984); Vladimír Jochmann, Pavel Kouba and Ivan Chvatík, eds. *Co jsou Češi? Malý přehled fakt a pokus o vysvětlení / Was sind die Tschechen? Kleiner Tatsachenbericht und Erklärungsversuch* (Prague: Panorama, 1992); *Schriften zur tschechischen Kultur und Geschichte*, Klaus Nellen, Petr Pithart and Miroslav Pojar, eds. (Stuttgart: Klett-Cotta, 1992).

entails building toward an argument with implications for praxis, that is, for how to do politics in the world based on a set of ideas. Philosophers might challenge this method as going out of bounds, yet political theorists would read a 'merely' philosophical commentary and ask: 'So what? Why does it matter for how we do things?' This account is an attempt at engaged political theory, and therefore it will sometimes move forward into the practical details of this author's own chosen examples of the problems Patočka only abstractly evoked.

Even if this method challenges the conventions of philosophical commentaries, the hope is to encourage readers to appreciate why the 'merely philosophical' debate about Patočka's works should be read and studied more deeply and thoroughly.[21] It is necessary to approach all dissidents' writings by first trying to understand the dissident's own self-understanding.[22] Who one is to oneself matters for what one does in the world. Patočka saw himself as a philosopher first and foremost. So, while this is a political-theoretic approach, it should lead back to philosophy and to Patočka's understanding of a 'philosopher' as someone responsible for turning others around in the cave through the right use of powerful ideas and arguments. Patočka's arguments shed light on how dissidence requires a certain understanding about what it means to act in the world through a philosophy of history, including how to dwell within that world while simultaneously transcending it. To understand this approach, the method of presentation calls for an integration of philosophy and historical thinking to illuminate politics, even if this is neither a history book nor exactly a philosophy book. As an attempt at political theorizing with philosophical texts, it might seem nonetheless *too philosophical* to some political theorists. If the main protagonist is indeed a philosopher, though, much of what is required to explain his existence and action is philosophical. The problem of what makes people (including philosophers) engage and act in the world politically, especially in the case of dissidence against perceived injustice in governmental systems, is still the main question at stake within these philosophical explorations.

The governments and political systems addressed in these dissident conversations can then include not just totalitarian Communist regimes,

---

21 See notes 14 and 19 above.
22 I have written more extensively about the importance of seeking the dissident's own self-understanding through a certain kind of hermeneutic investigation in another book. See Brinton, *Philosophy and Dissidence in Cold-War Europe* (London: Palgrave, 2016).

but also democracies, colonial empires, military dictatorships, and the world-governance attempts of technocratic international organizations. Injustice is possible within every kind of government, and so too is dissidence and political action always possible against those governments. The people who protest against unjust governments—in whatever time, place, political system, and culture—have something in common with one another, and this book is written to illuminate their actions, wherever they might be on Plato's trajectory (inside the cave or headed out of the cave already), and wherever they might be on their own trajectory of self-awareness vis-à-vis their historical situation, what Patočka calls "emplacement."[23] It is a complicated task to develop a sense of emplacement and self-awareness about 'where you are' in the course of history, but from the patterns that emerge in these conversations, it can be suggested that a sense of place and a sense of history are minimal prerequisites for being a dissident. Each interlocutor in conversation with Patočka in this account was deeply concerned with the *place* of human beings within history, as well as their own role in creating that history. These conversations reveal how we are placed within lives (and political systems) we have not chosen, and how our time and our place is put upon us, along with whatever distress that time and place create for us. Through the accidents of birth, however, we are nonetheless given

---

23 As Patočka explains in *Body, Community, Language, World,* trans. Erazim Kohák, ed. James Dodd (Chicago and La Salle: Open Court, 1998) (hereafter abbreviated "*BCLW*"): "There is one point, though, where we sensed a need to be more honest and specific than Heidegger. That was the phenomenon of our emplacement within things by our corporeity (such emplacement would make no sense for a purely spiritual being). Heidegger does not deny corporeity, he does not deny that we are also objectively among objects, but he does not analyze it further, does not recognize it as the foundation of our life which it is. Following Merleau-Ponty's analysis, we showed that the ongoing self-integration into the world, which makes us spatial and in space, takes place by means of our subjective corporeity which is horizontal, manifesting itself as corporeity in the strongest sense of the word." (*BCLW*, p. 176) See also his discussion of "self-localization" (*BCLW*, 47–48) and "self-placement" (*BCLW*, 53) and "self-retrieval from the world" (*BCLW*, 57). As he cites here, Patočka's ideas about 'emplacement' and 'corporality' have connections to his thinking about the works of Maurice Merleau-Ponty. See *Phenomenology of Perception*, trans. Colin Smith (London: Routledge, 2002). The political implications of embodiment for Patočka are suggested in a passage where he also challenges phenomenology to go beyond conceptions of the individual subject: "In addition to this I-Thou reciprocity, there exists another relation in the subject sphere of the world, a relation in which reciprocity and mutual presence do not matter, more of a relationship of a certain solidarity of various subjectivities, a relation of belonging and mutuality, not excluding reciprocity but not urgently or necessarily presupposing it, parallel but distinct from it—*the relationship of we...* The sphere of the we and of the you(all) are not exclusive but rather relative... It is not the phenomenon of the personal network, only observations towards one, its components. The all too ordinary we, you(all), that is a problem even phenomenology has barely begun to raise." (*BCLW*, 60–61)

occasional degrees of freedom to 'make something' of our historical moment. How to 'live within' that place in history where we find ourselves, to make something of it, and to do so truthfully, is a task of great political significance. It is also a task of considerable existential difficulty. Assuming Patočka was interested in helping others turn around and unshackle themselves from the constraints of cave-dwelling, evoking his ideas might help us think into existence moments of unshackling to overcome the existential and political inertia of our given place—and this moment—in history.

Unshackling this narrative from the strict traditions of philosophical analysis is necessary, or so I will contend, to respond to this particular moment in history.[24] As a playwright might consider putting famous characters who never knew each other together at a dinner party for a scene in a play, perhaps intentionally disturbing and disorienting an audience, each chapter that follows might be read as something of a posthumous heretical dialogue that imagines what might have happened had Patočka been able to be in conversation with these activist thinkers. This is done through staging dialogues about four of Patočka's key notions as they might be understood by his conversation partners: 'living in truth,' 'the care of the soul,' 'confrontation,' and 'solidarity of the shaken.' To clarify this structure of analysis, each of these concepts will be explained briefly here in the introduction, as each is also the central theme of a subsequent chapter. The notions of 'heretical history' and 'existential recognition' pervade various concepts and chapters, so the remainder of the introduction will sketch the ties between political dissidence, historical self-awareness, and transcendence in Patočka's work, as well as explaining briefly how 'existential recognition' might be one extension of this

---

24   Eric Manton describes the methodological situation created by Patočka's work vis-à-vis academic political science: "He wrote about the political events he was living through. Of course, his analysis of the historical events happening around him was not done in the style of contemporary political science. Patočka discussed different political programs, the nature of society, historical events, and the role of political opposition in authoritarian systems. But when writing about these subjects, he focused on a level much more fundamental than what is usually considered political science: Patočka analyzed these political topics *philosophically*. He concentrated on understanding the political from the ontological and phenomenological perspectives, looking at the historicity of human beings and the problematicity of Being, examining the existential angle on the role of the individual in society and human freedom, and he made ethical observations about the responsible manner of being for the authentic person who has little choice but to be some sort of dissident. To truly understand the significance of this combination, it is necessary to recall a different, original concept of political philosophy rather than what prevails in the academic world today." Patočka, *Living in Problematicity* (Prague: Oikoymenh, 2007), 71.

synthesis, that is, an extension of the patterns amounting to more than the sum of the parts.

'Living in truth' is a way of living, a way of seeking truth, and a way of being 'in' a place. Chapter One is a conversation and exegesis about how Patočka might have thought about 'living in truth,' how Václav Havel deployed 'living in truth' as one main pillar of his philosophically-informed dissidence, and how understanding Patočka and Havel on the idea of 'living in truth' can be helpful to dissidents in general as they seek to articulate new forms of political thinking. Havel was a playwright first (later a dissident and politician) who dedicated his most well-known essay, "The Power of the Powerless," to Patočka. They had actual conversations with one another, so this conversation is not entirely a hypothetical exercise, as the later chapters are. Examining Havel's writing in light of Patočka's ideas becomes an exposition of four layers of 'living in truth' that Havel and Patočka both approached from different angles of vision: the inward truth of the self, the truth of others, the truth of the political community, and truth as a recognition of objectivity's limits.

For Patočka and Havel both, the depth of the phrase 'living in truth' comes from the fact that it entails an analysis of 'living,' that is, 'how to live well?' as a classical philosophical and existential question. It also requires a certain idea of 'truth' in relation to living well, and one that goes beyond mere objective facts towards a recognition that individuals see the phenomenon of the world in important non-objective ways. The element of Patočka's thinking about 'living in truth' that is most relevant to dissidents, however, might be how he developed the 'in'—this particular preposition as the linkage between a mode of living and a mode of truth.[25] For Patočka, one has to try to move toward truth, strive to be

---

25 This "in" is in Czech "v," and like in English has a broad meaning that can construe 'in a place' quite broadly, i.e. in one's body, in one's soul, in one's town, in one's country, in one's time. For the sake of this formulation, all of these count as 'places.' For example, when Havel went about trying to describe what it meant to live in truth, he put the discussion directly into the context of the 'post-totalitarian' world of Communist countries. He was not trying to explicate an abstract universal totality in *Power of the Powerless*. He instead undertook to show what living in truth meant for the post-totalitarian states of Communist countries, and in going through that place and time, he managed to approach something universal about the human condition. But he had to start with the specific place. He specified a particular "in," a particular place, where his analysis was relevant, trying to show how humans can relate to that particular place in different ways, i.e. following a pattern of conformity, or instead choosing a mode of dissent. That context then helps the reader in other times and places to see that the ideas within his description are relevant to other times and places.

within it, and this makes truth necessarily *a place*. Humans are 'emplaced' in their world, and this place might be amidst truths or lies, and therefore one might be living in truth or living in lies.[26]

When truth becomes a place, rather than an abstract form or idea only possible through a limiting and restrictive definition, the life that 'truth' makes possible is not merely an individual life, but the individual is necessarily in a context, a structure, a community, a language, and a world. At the end of Patočka's Prague Spring lectures, entitled *Body, Community, Language, World*, he stated that he had tried to come up with a "conception of the world" that enables humans to "live in truth," and that humans can do this "because they are not indifferent to themselves and to their being."[27] We are, in other words, self-aware and reflective. He claims that the sort of human being who can relate to his or her particular context overcomes indifference and "is at home with itself," and has found a place, because he or she inhabits a certain "region of explicit relating," that is, a region where one can confront the world in an engaged way that avoids indifference.[28] Truth is this region—this place—to be found through actively (not indifferently) choosing how to relate to the world. 'Living' and 'relating,' however, never really get put into the past tense in a definitive way: to say that 'he lived in truth' or he 'related to the world,' in one way or at one moment, is not resonant with how Patočka developed his ideas. These are processes that are forever continuing and do not end, processes of continual motion towards a place that recedes past our line of sight. The retreating horizon then becomes, for Patočka, a place to 'live': "Horizons are not mere possibilities but are always already in part realized. To live in horizons means to broaden actuality immensely, to live amid possibilities as if they were realities."[29]

To make this somewhat more concrete, one 'place' where we find ourselves, which Patočka analyzes at some length in these lectures, is within our body, what he calls 'corporeity.' He remarks that "in their corporeity, humans stand at the boundary between being, indifferent to itself and to all else, and existence in the sense of a pure relation to the totality of

---

26 Patočka, *Body, Community, Language, World*, trans. Erazim Kohák, ed. James Dodd (Chicago and La Salle: Open Court, 1998), 172 (hereafter abbreviated "BCLW").
27 Patočka, *BCLW*, 177.
28 Patočka, *BCLW*, 177.
29 Patočka, *BCLW*, 35. Patočka worked with the idea of horizons from the beginning, commenting on Husserl's use of the concept. See *Le Monde Naturel Comme Problème Philosophique*, 94–96. For a comparative account of his idea of horizons, see: E. Evink, "Horizons and Others: Gadamer, Levinas, Patočka." *American Catholic Philosophical Quarterly* 84.4 (2010): 727–46.

all there is. On the basis of their corporeity, humans are not only the beings of distance but also the beings of proximity, rooted beings, not only inner-worldly beings but also beings in the world."[30] Thus we cannot ever really get all the way 'outside of ourselves' to a totally pure perspective on the 'outside' world because our bodies are here on earth in the world, in a context and in a place, the truth deriving in part (though not entirely) from that place. We can see ourselves moving towards the horizon and towards other places, though, so we are not fully 'rooted' as an object would be, like the 'rooted' tree that the metaphor comes from.[31] We are not motionless objects, but rather subjects of our lives-in-motion. Patočka's "living in truth," is not, therefore, merely a relativist approach to throw away the idea of absolute truth, but is rather a way of, as he claims, challenging the idea that humans are *only* "heirs of the absolute" where they think they "have a license to subjugate all reality, to appropriate it and to exploit it with no obligation to give anything in return."[32]

Such hubristic exploitation of the world is what Patočka wants to caution us against; a perspective where we believe we have *arrived at* the absolute truth puts us in danger of such hubris. So he claims that his method of 'living in truth' strives to conceive of human beings instead as *in motion towards* ideas of the absolute—as, after all, we can conceive of absolutes (like God or infinity)—but because our bodies are embedded and placed in the "rooted" world, humans must recognize that they are not the absolute, not the transcendent and the all-powerful universal entities we sometimes claim we are.[33] A theory of motion (based in part on Aristotle's ideas) precedes his conclusions about how humans live in

---

30 Patočka, *BCLW*, 170.
31 When Patočka outlines what he takes to be the 'three movements of human existence,' (see chapter 3), in a paradoxical sense the first 'movement' is "sinking roots or anchoring," which stops motion (*BCLW*, 248). The point of the second and third movement, especially the third, is to transcend this anchoring through further motion. By this account, we only ever remain partially rooted; if we become as rooted as an object, we lose some part of our humanity.
32 Patočka, *BCLW*, 178.
33 Patočka outlines how his own stance differs from Husserl's transcendental reduction; he states that the fullness of the transcendental reduction as defined by Husserl is not something we can ever fully accomplish; the transcendental reduction is one such absolute place with might strive toward, but unlike Husserl, he believes we can never in actuality pull ourselves entirely out of the world. (See "Edmund Husserl's Philosophy of the Crisis of the Sciences and His Conception of a Phenomenology of the 'Life-World" (1971) in Kohák, *Jan Patočka Philosophy and Selected Writings*, 223–238). Also using Heidegger, but also in part disagreeing with the full extent of Heidegger's thesis about 'being in the world,' Patočka attempts to carve out a place between Husserl and Heidegger's argument about where humans are "emplaced" vis-à-vis the everyday world and absolute transcendence. Whether he successfully accomplishes this task is a matter of some debate: see Tucker, *The Philosophy and Politics of Czech Dissidence from Patočka to*

the world in perpetual motion.[34] Humans are always in motion towards something for Patočka, going towards a place that they are not indifferent to, both in their minds and with their body.[35] Unlike a purely metaphysical theory of the absolute, though, for Patočka we never get 'there,' to an absolute place; life (and the mode of 'living well' that derives from these assumptions) is a life in motion towards a set of possibilities, and one of those possibilities is moving toward a transcendent absolute, but this is not the only possibility. He calls this approach to the world "living for the sake of," and such living is the hallmark of overcoming "indifference to the world."[36]

This might initially sound too abstract to be political. For any activist who has ever sought to recruit more people to an important political cause or movement, however, these ideas should resonate. Activists undertake a life where (at least partially) they must live *for the sake of* the cause, where they become part of a *movement* towards a new possibility, and they have conceived of that possibility through a thought process that must eschew indifference; they must *care* about what they are doing, and care enough to put themselves (including their bodies) in motion toward a goal that might never be reached in its total fullness. Overcoming the *indifference* of others who are around them—whether that is done with campaigns, petitions, marches or other methods of raising awareness—is for an activist or dissident what it means to fully live in the world as a moral human being. Through this mode of life, though, one recognizes that getting to a place of absolute perfection is likely impossible; one approaches a horizon, but with each forward step, the horizon regenerates itself a step farther away. A mere human being cannot make

---

Havel; Findlay, *Caring for the Soul in the Postmodern Age: Politics and Phenomenology in the thought of Jan Patočka*; Tassin and Richir, *Jan Patočka: philosophie, phénoménologie, politique*.

34 His theory of motion is based in part on Aristotle, though he does reject certain aspects of Aristotle and call for a radicalization of Aristotle's ideas. See *BCLW*, 143–147. More will be elaborated about the relationship between the human body, movement, and possibility in Chapter Three, illustrated with the example of Gandhi's body-politics. For Patočka's view on Aristotelian motion, see: Patočka, *Aristote, ses devanciers, ses successeurs*, trans. Erika Abrams (Paris: Librairie Philosophique J.Vrin, 2011).

35 A body concretely dies, but we do not know when we are going to die, nor do we know how our legacy will be lived after we die, so the horizons of the self actually continue beyond death. Patočka was influenced by Heidegger's idea of 'being-toward-death,' but while death mattered to him in a fairly Heideggerian way, he rejected certain parts of Heidegger's formulation he thought too individualistic. When the fact of death is meditated upon, it does usually change the way someone lives, that is, they can become concerned with how the next generation will see tradition, and how one person can leave a mark on the world.

36 Patočka, *BCLW*, 173.

the horizon stop retreating, and activists must continually ask themselves where they are going and whether they are living in truth, including the core questions from Plato's cave: what ideas (as shadows) have we received from our culture, society, parents, political systems, religion and history that we merely accept? Why do we not question these systems, these traditions, and this supposed wisdom of the ages? Where are we, and how do we move away from shadows to a new place of truth?

Even after the Velvet Revolution displaced the Communist governments with democratic ones, even after Havel had served multiple terms as president, and even as life for everyone in Czechoslovakia changed quite substantively, Havel was true to this sort of philosophical stance Patočka had outlined: he claimed the "existential revolution" towards living in truth was not completed, not over, and still had a long way to go:

> 'To live in truth' has its tradition in Czech philosophy but basically has biblical roots – it does not mean just the possession or communication of information. Because information, like a virus, circulates in the air so one person may absorb more and another one less. Truth, however, is a different matter because we guarantee it with our own self. Truth is based on responsibility. And that is an imperative that is valid in every age. Obviously, it takes slightly different forms today. Luckily, you don't have to hang portraits of a Havel, or a Klaus or a Kaczyński in the shop windows anymore and of course we no longer live under totalitarian pressure – but *that doesn't mean we've won*. We still need what I refer to as an 'existential revolution,' even though it might look different in different places.[37]

Each of the four dimensions of truth discussed in in the first chapter in conversation with Havel has within it some sense of motion; each truth is a type of place one can approach, but never quite arrive fully within. We do not ever fully win. But by looking at the world in this way, Patočka

---

37 Václav Havel, interview by Adam Michnik, "After the Velvet, an Existential Revolution?" *Central European Forum Salon*, November 20, 2008, http://salon.eu.sk/en/archiv/801. Havel's original description of an "existential revolution" in "Power of the Powerless" characterized it as a "way out" of part of the political problems of his day: "This as yet unknown way out might be most generally characterized as a broad 'existential revolution'... a solution cannot be sought in some technological sleight of hand, that is, in some external proposal for change, or in a revolution that is merely philosophical, merely social, merely technological, or even merely political. These are all areas where the consequences of an existential revolution can and must be felt; but their most intrinsic locus can only be human existence in the profoundest sense of the word. It is only from that basis that it can become a generally ethical—and, of course, ultimately a political—reconstitution of society."

suggests various ramifications for political undertakings, especially for dissident *movements*. Patočka's and Havel's ideas of 'living in truth' establish the foundation to generate a set of questions for activists and dissidents to continue probing various modes of indifference in the hearts and minds of other human beings. Questions of truth—as well as the questions generated in other chapters about care, solidarity, confrontation and recognition—might be able to sustain movement and *movements* toward possibilities. For those who are not activists and dissidents, the challenge posed by these questions is still highly relevant: how to *live* well, how to find *truth*, and how to find one's place *in* a world are questions necessary for everyone. Yet these are also questions that we cannot ever answer absolutely, questions that remain open infinitely and indefinitely, and questions that show us how to move towards possibilities.

Just as Havel asked dissident-activists to live in truth, going beyond just contemplating truth or formulating abstract truths, later chapters are also meant to show how to 'live within' the other ideas evoked by Patočka's texts, ideas that entail methods of how to act out 'truth' in the political world of particular moments in history. With that in mind, after dissecting the notion of 'living in truth' in the first chapter, the second will turn to the ideas of Dietrich Bonhoeffer, especially his writings from prison and the posthumously published fragments of his *Ethics*. A protestant pastor and theologian in Nazi Germany, Bonhoeffer had a keen sense of his place history, by both choice and necessity, but especially through his participation in a plot to assassinate Adolf Hitler, and then his arrest (and execution) by the Nazis. Writing in this context of historical urgency about the history of ethical thinking puts Bonhoeffer and Patočka on common ground. The comparison of their ideas helps to illuminate two perspectives on the 'care of the soul,' a Platonic cornerstone concept necessarily reworked in times of political urgency.[38] That urgency refracts back into more peaceful and sedate times with insights about to how to come to see oneself in light of history, philosophy, and a philosophy of history that allows for the 'care of the soul' within a community.[39]

---

38 For Patočka, the genealogy of his notion of care is both Platonic and Heideggerian; for Bonhoeffer it is arguably both Platonic and Christian. While the Platonic common ground is the starting point of part of this conversation between Patočka and Bonhoeffer, see Chapter Two for further elaboration of these distinctions, including how a comparison with Bonhoeffer brings out some of Patočka's latent theological concerns about Christian ideas.

39 Commentaries on Patočka's philosophy of history elucidate a complicated and unique vision influenced by many different thinkers. For a recent discussion, see: F. Karfík, "Jan Patočka

When Patočka aims the received tradition of Socrates back at contemporary philosophy and politics, he knows he must somehow explain how, two thousand years later, he himself as Jan Patočka is living in a totalitarian society extremely hostile to philosophers and the task of constantly examining. He is within a world where the Socratic method is very far from being sufficiently realized in everyday practice. He is not living in a context of 'progress,' as his 'today' is not necessarily better than his 'yesterday.' To begin to ask the Socratic question anew again, Patočka reads from Plato a possibility, a horizon he can see beyond, where Socrates' life does not end in martyrdom for truth, but where, because we have taken a Platonic stance toward caring for the soul, something different has happened:

> From the cultivating of our soul arises the possibility of forming the state, the community that is necessary so that a person like Socrates does not have to die... the question of the *polis* and its constitution, its constituting, is again the question of the soul, its character and its examination.[40]

Caring for the soul, in this view, is deeply political. Is a world possible where Patočka himself does not have to die after police interrogation, but also where those like Dietrich Bonhoeffer and Gandhi are not assassinated, and where we might not have to live within the possibilities of being vaporized by an atomic bomb or washed away as sea levels rise?[41] The process of envisioning such a world (and transcending today's everyday world through such thinking) is in itself caring for the soul, and involves searching for the obscured truths that society, tradition, and unthinking conformity have hidden from view. Once these necessary inward truths of the soul are uncovered from their concealment, we can live in a different way, in truth, and begin looking toward a different kind of state and community.[42] Care of the soul and living in truth are thus closely related and intertwined ideas.

---

a Problém Filosofie Dějin ke kontextu Kacířských esejů." *Reflexe* 50 (2016) and James Dodd, "Philosophy in Dark Times: An Essay on Jan Patočka's Philosophy of History," in L. Hagedorn and J. Dodd, eds. *The New Yearbook of Phenomenology and Phenomenological Philosophy XIV–2015.*

40 Patočka, *Plato and Europe*, 121.

41 These are the topics of subsequent chapters in this book.

42 Patočka derives his commentary about truth as un-concealment largely from Heidegger's analysis of truth as '*aletheia*'; for an examination of the Greek term, see Vladislav Suvák, "The Essence of Truth (aletheia) and the Western Tradition in the Thought of Heidegger and Patočka," *Thinking Fundamentals, IWM Junior Visiting Fellows Conferences* 9, no. 4 (2000): 1–18.

Bonhoeffer's vantage point puts Patočka's ideas into high relief, as his life demonstrates the depth and urgency of historical self-awareness and its relationship with transcendence. He reveals the way in which dissidence requires the combination of horizontal and vertical thinking, of thinking upward towards higher ideas at the same time as recognizing the consequences of one's 'emplacement' on earth. Havel wrote that 'living in truth' had "biblical roots," and on this he would agree with both Bonhoeffer and Patočka. The conversation between Patočka and Bonhoeffer therefore identifies three modalities of what I call earth-bound transcendence. Patočka claims that the 'care of the soul' has an ontological, a social-political and an existential dimension,[43] and therefore this chapter discusses three aspects of Bonhoeffer's thinking that are meant to further clarify Patočka's three-fold distinction: (1) Bonhoeffer's 'religionless Christianity' is an *ontological* idea challenging traditional religious belief structures through conceiving of the 'soul' at the intersection of divine and earthly, and paradoxically comparable to Patočka's challenge to metaphysics in his 'negative Platonism'; (2) 'sacrifice' is a *social-political* idea discussed by both Bonhoeffer and Patočka as a mode of care for the world; (3) a comparison of Bonhoeffer's idea of 'worldliness' (*Mundigkeit* in German) and Patočka's idea of 'amplitude' show how both are concerned with *existential* ideas that call for solidity of character and the ability to live within contradictions. The ontological, the social-political and the existential are integrated through 'care of the soul,' and these three examples begin to illuminate the consequences of this integration for human action.

Each of these ideas is also an example of combining a form of vertical thinking with a form of horizontal thinking, staying rooted to the earth while transcending the bounds of circumstances.[44] For a pastor

---

43 See Chapter Two; Patočka describes care of the soul as having three levels: "(1) The general philosophical teaching that brings the soul into connection with the structure of being; (2) a teaching about the life of the philosopher in the community and in history...[and thus] the center of all state life and also the axis of historical occurrence; and (3) the teaching about the soul as the principle of individual life... exposed to the fundamental experience and test... of death and the question of meaning." *Plato and Europe*, 180.

44 Patočka discusses the changing historical relationship in Western philosophy between what he calls "horizontal transcendence" and "vertical transcendence" in his essay "Intellectuals and Opposition," in *Thinking After Europe*, 7–22. Different kinds of intellectuals over the course of history (he focuses in this essay on the difference between intellectuals in Western Europe and Eastern Europe in 1968, but puts that into historical context) have focused on either too much vertical transcendence or too much horizontal transcendence, and he argues for finding an appropriate balance for the times.

and theologian, vertical thinking is easily demonstrated by the upward gaze toward God and divinity as a necessary stance for faith. Not all pastors, however, become politically engaged as Bonhoeffer did, so the other element of his thinking that created the ground for political action was horizontal, looking outward toward his community and his historical moment as a 'place' where living in truth and the care of the soul must also occur.[45] To care for one's community is to care for one's soul in light of both divinity and one's neighbors, at least in Bonhoeffer's view, and this has important structural analogies with Patočka's vertical thinking about the primacy of humanity's morality in combination with a horizontal view towards the importance of history, emplacement, and being-with-others. These stances are, in their internal logic, perhaps contradictory; they imply moving in two different directions at once. Instead of rejecting contradiction, however, this conversation between Patočka and Bonhoeffer attempts to show how embracing contradiction itself can be a mode of transcendence within the mundane urgency of empirical facts. To undertake the sacrifices necessary for political dissidence, one might have to hold in one's mind an idea of human beings as ontologically contradictory, and from that idea dissidence might arise more easily.

Both Patočka and Bonhoeffer, furthermore, were forced to write in the genre of unfinished books. Bonhoeffer's *Ethics* was incomplete at the time of his death; in *Letters and Papers from Prison*, texts that were hidden in the rafters of his house during the war were unearthed and published by someone else. Several of the most 'comprehensive' sources of Patočka's work are drafts of lectures or compilations of students' notes from his lectures (including *Plato and Europe* and *Body, Community, Language, World*). Like with Bonhoeffer's *Ethics*, this creates academic debate about ordering, intention, and translation.[46] Not being able to 'finish' a book due to the urgency of life's circumstances, and not being able to say

---

45 In the American context, Martin Luther King Jr. is also an example of this sort of approach to being a pastor and a minister. King would be a relevant comparison for the notion of sacrifice, given his assassination, but would differ from Bonhoeffer on religionless Christianity, turning toward a more traditional system of Christian ethics that Bonhoeffer questions. See Chapter Two.

46 On Bonhoeffer, see Clifford Green, *Bonhoeffer: A Theology of Sociality*, rev. ed. (Wm. B. Eerdmans Publishing Company, 1999), 302–303; Victoria Barnett, "The Bonhoeffer Legacy as a Work-in-Progress: Reflections on a Fragmentary Series," in *Interpreting Bonhoeffer: Historical Perspectives, Emerging Issues*, eds. Clifford Green and Guy Carter (Minneapolis: Fortress Press, 2013) 93–100. On Patočka, see: Ivan Chvatík, Pavel Kouba, Miroslav Petříček, «La structure des œuvres complètes de Patočka comme problème d'interprétation» in Tassin and Richir, *Jan Patočka: philosophie, phénoménologie, politique*, 223–230.

exactly what one would have said in a less fear-ridden environment—these were circumstances both writers shared. Manuscripts might have been confiscated by secret police; it was easy to be arrested for saying certain things and being too explicit in one's political statements would surely make the punishment worse. The written texts that come out of such circumstances are peculiar, making for a special kind of reading exercise. Examining these texts is not, as a professional philosopher might say, an exercise in 'systematic' study; the systems are not complete, and the author might not be aiming for anything systematic. Indeed, some of Patočka's and Bonhoeffer's writings are collections of fragments, potentially peppered with deliberate obfuscation and euphemisms, and while containing many finished and profound thoughts about politics, they are often lacking finished elaborations and applications of those thoughts.[47] Therefore this 'reading' of these texts is also sometimes an interpretation in search of applications that were never elaborated.[48] Especially in Chapter Two, the form of the argument may also follow the structure of the content, where from contradictory fragmented texts, we are meant to learn something about the contradictory and fragmented lives that are lived in the midst of complicated political landscapes. In the end, Patočka's idea of caring for the soul, where such care is the integration of the person, the community, and a sense of history, can illuminate these contradictions, but also show a way forward towards action.

In Chapter Three, Patočka's 'three movements of human existence' and his idea of *polemos* become the grounds for examining how confrontation (in its political and philosophical forms) can arise as a result of living in truth and caring for the soul, eventually setting up the possibility for seeking solidarity of the shaken (discussed in Chapter Four). By looking to Mahatma Gandhi's reflections on his campaigns in India and South Africa, and his development of satyagraha as a form of non-violent

---

47 Bonhoeffer published in his lifetime several complete major works that are not like this, including: *Sanctorum Communio: A theological Study of the Sociology of the Church; Act and Being; Discipleship; Creation and Fall.* See: *The Complete Dietrich Bonhoeffer Works* (New York: Fortress Press, 2014).

48 I use the word "application" here in a way self-conscious of Gadamerian hermeneutics, where the final stage of the process of interpretation, the intersection of horizons, and an attentive reading constitutes the application of that reading to a task of understanding the world. I have tried to push the methodology of "application" to be as broad and as deep as possible through the multiple and myriad 'conversations' with historical and contemporary voices and ideas; sometimes this goes beyond traditional Gadamerian hermeneutics. Hans-Georg Gadamer, *Truth and Method,* trans. Joel Weinsheimer and Donald G. Marshall (New York: Continuum, 2002), 307–311; 339–341.

resistance, Patočka's understanding of war, movement, and the structure of human existence are shown to be further extensions of living a life of sacrifice, amplitude, and problematicity. Following the structure of Patočka's 'three movements human existence,' the implications of each movement are more fully elaborated through application to moments in Gandhi's life and thinking.

Patočka's first movement, which he calls "the movement of sinking roots, of anchoring—an instinctive-affective movement of our existence,"[49] is discussed in light of both Gandhi's personal biography (his choice to start his movement on Tolstoy Farm in South Africa and his eventual return to his homeland in India) and the later development of a specific set of affective grounding and anchoring processes as a requirement for participating in the satyagraha movement: if satyagraha activists did not show themselves to be capable of controlling their own bodies and grounding their existence in practices of *khadi* (spinning cloth for one's own clothing) and *brahmachurya* (control of bodily functions and appetites), they were not allowed to undertake the 'work' of activism. As Patočka's 'second movement' of human existence concerns "the movement of our coming to terms with the reality we handle, a movement carried out in the region of human work,"[50] Gandhi demonstrates how a notion of work (including political work) can be valuable intrinsically, set apart from its final results, or 'fruits,' as Gandhi calls it. This paradoxical form of action that denies the importance of immediate results is essential for all activists to understand, as much of the work of activism does not bear immediate or tangible 'fruits.' Sometimes results are delayed; sometimes there are no results.

As Gandhi saw himself as a 'warrior,' albeit a nonviolent one, Patočka's 'third movement' of human existence is explored through examining the relationship between his idea of confrontation, or what he calls *polemos*, and the overall structure of Gandhi's life. As the first two movements are considered by Patočka to be incomplete without the third, and susceptible to forms of inauthenticity, the life of Gandhi demonstrates how the integration of the first and second movements creates a human existence that is, in Patočka's words, "the movement of existence in the true sense, the movement of self-achievement."[51] Gandhi's life then becomes a terrain to explore how political movements and confrontation

---

49   Patočka, *BCLW*, 148.
50   Patočka, *BCLW*, 148.
51   Patočka, *BCLW*, 151.

arise as the culmination of a certain modality of living philosophically, or 'living in problematicity,' as Patočka sometimes calls it.[52] Confrontation, or *polemos*, and its relationship to the third culminating movement of human existence then raise the difficult perennial question about the role of violence in human life and politics. This leads to a discussion of the last of Patočka's *Heretical Essays*, where he thinks through what the front-line experience of war (in particular World War One) tells us about human existence in contexts of violence. Patočka derives his usage of *polemos* from Heidegger, who borrowed it from its ancient Greek usage in Heraclitus.[53] In a basic sense, the word means 'confrontation,' but Patočka expands this to a larger conceptual framework to explain the relationship between conflict, the *polis*, and philosophy:

> It [*polemos*] is at the same time that which constitutes the *polis* and the primordial insight that makes philosophy possible. *Polemos* is not the destructive passion of a wild brigand but is, rather, the creator of unity. The unity it founds is more profound than any ephemeral sympathy or coalition of interests; adversaries meet in the shaking of a given meaning, and so create a new way of being human—perhaps the only mode that offers hope amid the storm of the world: the unity of the shaken but undaunted."[54]

It seems for Patočka that the idea of *polemos* unites the concepts of 'living in truth,' 'care of the soul,' and 'solidarity of the shaken.' This 'new way of being human' arises within 'the shaking of a given meaning,' which is to say that all questions must be thrown open, all dogmas challenged, and the 'unity' that remains is a group of human beings in the realm of freedom searching for truth. Engaging in this search is to 'live in truth,' but to live in truth via *polemos* is to understand one's weakness and the difficulty of a life situation, thus being willing to confront the situation and face up to one's responsibility for that situation. This is perhaps another way of both caring for the soul (individually), but linking that care to solidarity with others who are similarly shaken in positions of vulnerability.

---

52   Patočka, *Living in Problematicity*, ed. Eric Manton (Prague: Oikoymenh, 2007).
53   See Gregory Fried, *Heidegger's Polemos: From Being to Politics* (New Haven: Yale University Press, 2000), 26.
54   Jan Patočka, *Heretical Essays on the Philosophy of History*, trans. Erazim Kohák, ed. James Dodd (Chicago and La Salle: Open Court 1996), 43.

To put Patočka's ideas into conversation with Gandhi's thoughts on non-violence and satyagraha, therefore, will further elaborate the relationship between Gandhi's 'truth-force,' and the nature and origin of that 'force,' exploring whether Patočka's idea of *polemos* is useful more generally on the question of violence and non-violence.[55] This requires seeing *polemos* in light Patočka's earlier lectures in *Body, Community, Language, World*, where he theorizes the 'three movements of human existence' and the importance of corporality for understanding human existence. The 'third movement' for Patočka is the most important culminating construction of one's own human existence, and his definition of the third movement and his definition of *polemos* have too much in common to not wager a comparison and connection.[56] Gandhi helps illuminate this connection because his modality of confrontation depended on corporality, especially given his method of putting bodies in front of authorities and provoking violence, but also when he insisted on a non-violent mode of bodily confrontation by satyagraha activists.[57] Marches, sit-ins, fasting, celibacy and the Gandhian way of non-violent politics required the politicization of one's body and a willingness to use one's body in the name of political sacrifice. In order to do this, one needed significant philosophical instruction, and the mind and the body are not at all separate in this task; Gandhi is a challenge to Cartesian dualism, among other things.

Gandhi describes how a satyagraha activist must be trained in forms of bodily movement and stillness through the inculcation of the right ideas, including specific notions about humanity and the human relationship to oneself, to others, and to the world. Like Havel, Bonhoeffer, and Patočka, Gandhi also had a specific way of connecting horizontal and vertical thinking and placing the intersection at the core of his understanding of the human soul. Drawing on both Hinduism and Christianity, Gandhi has a vertical idea of 'love' that is meant to be a form of transcendence, but he calls on activists to be soberly earthbound in their relationships to their communities and to political action; spinning cloth

---

55 Mohandas K. Gandhi, *Gandhi: An Autobiography. The Story of My Experiments with Truth* (1927 and 1929; reprint Boston, MA: Beacon Press, 1993); Gandhi Heritage Portal, ed., *The Collected Works of Mahatma Gandhi*, vol. 1–100, n.d., https://www.gandhiheritageportal.org/the-collected-works-of-mahatma-gandhi.

56 See also James Dodd, "Polemos in Jan Patočka's Political Thought," in *Thinking after Europe*, Francesco Tava, Darian Meacham, eds., 77–94.

57 Tony Ballantyne and Antoinette M. Burton, eds., *Bodies in contact: rethinking colonial encounters in world history*, (Durham: Duke University Press, 2005).

from locally-grown cotton is done as part of a path of spiritual transcendence, and this is but one example. Gandhi's notion of sacrifice (drawn from the *Bhagavad Gita*), asks human beings to act in such a way to give up the fruits of their actions and focus on the action itself; this form of renunciation helps us understand Patočka's idea of a higher sacrifice as a way of doing things 'for the sake of nothing' in order to do something 'for the sake of everything.'[58] (See Chapter Two.) This renunciation of instrumental gains helps us understand how dissident politics is often done seemingly for the sake of no specific possible policy outcome, no specific material gain, and no specific want of territorial aggrandizement; rather, it is rather done for the intrinsic value of the action itself. From renunciation and through non-violence, action is thus sustained in circumstances of hopelessness.

The 'conversation' between Gandhi and Patočka is framed in terms of paradoxes that do not demand resolution, but rather evoke possibilities for new forms of responsible human action. Gandhi wants to start with emplacement and corporality, as does Patočka, and in doing so concludes that the space between public and private usually conceived of as necessary for effective politics is collapsed; the personal becomes political, but so too does the political become personal. Paradoxical as well, Gandhi demands we act for no specific set of ends or goals, renouncing the fruits of action, but therein creating a more powerful and more earth-shattering form of action than any instrumental or objective end-goal. The third paradox is perhaps the most helpful in asking new questions about the ambiguity at the end of Patočka's *Heretical Essays*: is he advocating and praising the violence of war, or is he, as Gandhi does, evoking the meaning and substance infused into life's third movement by taking up the task of being a warrior, where there are such paradoxical things as 'non-violent war' and 'non-violent warriors'? Together these three paradoxes illuminate Patočka's work as much as they point to the tensions and complications within the Gandhian approach to activism and dissidence. Gandhi managed a colossal feat of shaking the world apart, an unshackling and rupture that eventually destroyed the global

---

58 Patočka discusses sacrifice in "Dangers of Technicization in Science; Essence of Technology as Danger," in Kohák, *Jan Patočka Philosophy and Selected Writings*, 336–339. For secondary commentary, see: James Dodd, "Philosophy in Dark Times," in Hagedorn and Dodd, *The New Yearbook of Phenomenology and Phenomenological Philosophy*, 84–86, and Tava, *The Risk of Freedom*, 40–46; Claire Perryman-Holt, "Jan Patočka's Sacrificial Experience," in *The New Yearbook of Phenomenology and Phenomenological Philosophy*, 23–30.

political system of British colonialism, and managed to do so by provoking violence rather than inflicting it.

It is within Patočka's concept of 'solidarity of the shaken' where he comes closest to approaching the horizon of a political theory. What he means by 'shaken,' then, becomes the center of Chapter Four. To be shaken is to be aware of history, cognizant of one's emplacement, and to have a willingness to act in concert with others toward a new idea of political engagement. 'Solidarity of the shaken' both arises from, and creates, history:

> History arises from the shaking of naïve and absolute meaning in the virtually simultaneous and mutually interdependent rise of politics and philosophy. Fundamentally, history is the unfolding of embryonic possibilities present in this shaking.[59]

'Solidarity of the shaken' has several conceptual levels: it is a way of looking at history; it can be a vision for a community that is built on conscience; it also can become a way of inserting a moral-ontological vision into decisions about collective political action. As a result, a dissident would require 'solidarity of the shaken' as a way to come together with others who are, like we all are, in our states of human fragility and susceptibility to our environments, but nonetheless still willing to seek out new understandings of that world. Patočka suggests that this solidarity emerges from an acceptance of fragility and willingness to be 'shaken,' perhaps allowing us to imagine a kind of politics that allows for the care of the soul and living in truth.

To illuminate the conceptual and activist potentials in 'solidarity of the shaken,' Chapter Four argues that something about human history fundamentally changed when the nuclear bomb was dropped on Hiroshima and Nagasaki, and that this change relates to the solidarity and dissidence that characterized the 1950s and 1960s. Using several texts of activism from this era in the United States, Patočka's ideas about 'solidarity of the shaken' are explored in light of the possible destruction of humanity with atomic weapons. 'Solidarity of the shaken' in the context of atomic activism is a reflection on how general indifference might be transformed into action, and how this kind of solidarity might be a way of addressing the sort of indifference brought about by the paralysis of

---

59 Patočka, *Heretical Essays*, 77.

47

fear more generally. The nuclear cases of 'solidarity of the shaken' show how the awareness of death brought by war generates meaning, as such awareness creates moments of being "shaken" that transform both collective and individual lives towards possibilities of coming together in solidarity as a precursor to political action. The examined texts include Mario Savio's "The End of History," from the Berkeley Free Speech Movement (1964); Paul Tillich's "Shaking of the Foundations," (1955) a sermon on atomic weapons and prophecies of the Bible; the "Russell-Einstein Manifesto," (1954) on the problem of nuclear testing and scientific rationalism; and the "Port Huron Statement" of the Students for a Democratic Society (1962), a manifesto for a generation of atomic youth bracing for disaster and hoping for change.

All of these texts of dissidence reference the kind of human vulnerability created by the mere presence of the atomic bomb and its ability to obliterate existence in a matter of seconds, massively and collectively. Each dissident text, each in a different way, calls for a new form of solidarity to emerge in light of this situation, each identifying a new kind of 'distress' created by this particular fear of annihilation. Those who came together in their 'shaken-ness' to find solidarity in light of the of terror produced by the atomic situation were politically motivated in a way that aligns with some (though not all) of Patočka's ideas about 'solidarity of the shaken,' providing a terrain to explore the distinctions in Patočka's thinking and its relation to the 'heretical history' that gives rise to such shaking. In particular, Tillich's voice helps open the very question of 'foundations,' and whether or not there are traditional 'foundations' in Patočka's own thinking. This returns to the question that arose in regard to Bonhoeffer's insights, where the presence of both vertical thinking and horizontal thinking are necessary to act in a world where history itself might be near its end (given the possibilities for atomic destruction). This type of realization brought by the atomic situation might have forced us to begin living on anti-foundational grounding as our primary foundation, as Bonhoeffer's religionless Christianity asks us to live without traditional religious short cuts and excuses. This will surely shake apart certain aspects of tradition, but perhaps it will also force us to ask whether those traditions are merely projections on the wall of the cave, a question that will call us to a new form of forward movement toward confrontation with the world.

In the final chapter, the overall lessons and applications of living in truth, care of the soul, confrontation-as-*polemos*, and solidarity of the shaken are explored in regards to environmental activism. Patočka's ideas about the natural world and its relationship to science, technology and rationality are explored in light of his ideas about cosmic home-lessness, the three movements of existence, historicity, nihilism, and the politics of recognition. The ever-expanding activities and ideas of climate change activists and environmentalists are used as examples to illuminate how Patočka's ideas might represent a path towards a type of activism that can be sustained into a future of uncertainty and possible calamity for the earth and its inhabitants. 'Solidarity of the shaken' is explored as a possible modality of cooperation and being-together that might help address both modernity's nihilism and the problem of climate change and the earth's destruction.

The synthesis of these ideas then becomes an argument about one possible pre-political basis of activism inspired by Patočka's thinking: a mode of 'existential recognition' that might help those who are vastly different from one another recognize their common fate on the 'sinking ship' of the earth. If something like 'existential recognition' has already helped sustain environmental activism, if understood as connected to Patočka's solidarity of the shaken, it might also be capable of being one grounding for political cooperation across national borders and generations. While 'existential recognition' is not a term Patočka uses, as a derivative argument, this idea combines his concern about recognition articulated in the *Heretical Essays* with the general existential questions he asks throughout his work. While 'existential recognition' will remain a term in need of further exploration and research, the application of Patočka's ideas to environmental activism is meant demonstrate the fruit-ful theoretical and practical possibilities that might come from this and other synthetic integrations and applications of these concepts.

Heretical History and the Dissident Phenomenon

In 1977, a combination of ideas and events created a moment when Patoč-ka-the-philosopher stepped into politics, and thus into history, becom-ing Patočka-the-dissident. He was navigating his own concrete place in history while he was writing and lecturing about history in the general and abstract sense, interpreting history as both a type of ascent from the cave, a type of confrontation, and also a simultaneous descent towards death. *Heretical Essays in the Philosophy of History* (1975) raised all of these questions, as well as the question of history as the bridge between philos-ophy and politics. By the end of this account of Patočka's ideas, it will be argued that the activist or dissident comes to engage with the world by arriving at an understanding of how the 'normal' course of present history might be effectively (or heretically) derailed. Not all dissidence will fundamentally change history, and much dissidence is forgotten by formal and official historical research, but all dissidence will indeed change the way the dissident thinks about the world and lives within it. Seeing the world through the lens of 'heretical history' has an important role to play in inspiring human movement (if not physical, then intellectual) to turn around in Plato's cave, or in the philosopher's case, to move oneself to return to the cave out of a duty to educate others. One might need a heretical philosophy of history in one's own mind, so the actor-philosopher becomes capable of going against the accepted notions of history, whatever those notions may be within his or her time and place. Then, the dissident might become enabled to effectively rewrite the next chapter of history with those actions, if their situation provides such an opportunity. Patočka might have lived out and enacted a case of this phenomenon, both in his writings and in his actions, standing as a thematic model that other dissidents might imitate with their own variations.[60]

To follow the language of Patočka's own philosophical method of phenomenology rooted in Husserl's methods and questions, we could say that the *appearance* of the *phenomenon* of political action in his life becomes here the problem in need of *unveiling*.[61] Setting out to use phenomenology to do an analysis of international affairs, including a chapter on global activist movements, Ralph Pettman quips that "phenomenology is the lost continent of contemporary world thought... it is seen by analysts of international affairs as a mind-place which only the most intellectually adventurous or foolhardy enter and where the analytical equivalents of pre-historic monsters roam."[62] Patočka is a phenomenologist, and

---

60 This is not a direct causal chain; contingency is present at every juncture in Patočka's story. If one can at times see something that looks like a 'path' toward the moment of his politicization, the shape of it nonetheless depended on the chances of history within which Patočka's thinking happened. No account of Patočka's philosophy can be a tidy genealogical and linear account to explain the exact causes of his political actions; rather, a set of circumstances and a way of thinking came together. For a contrasting view of the conditions of politicization in Patočka's life, see: D. Leufer, "The wound which will not close: Jan Patočka's philosophy and the conditions of politicization." *Studies in East European Thought* 69, no. 1 (2017): 29–44.

61 For a general background on phenomenology and moral philosophy, see *Phenomenological Approaches to Moral Philosophy: A Handbook*, eds. John J. Drummond and Lester E. Embree (Dordrecht: Kluwer Academic Publishers, 2002).

62 Ralph Pettman, *Intending the World: A Phenomenology of International Affairs* (Melbourne: Melbourne University Press, 2008), 1.

most contemporary scholars and philosophers interested in his work are deeply absorbed in the conceptual debates deriving from the thought of Husserl, Heidegger, and Merleau-Ponty, among many others doing phenomenology.[63] Those political scientists interested in international affairs, if Pettman's tongue-and-cheek characterization has any truth to it, are often put off by the jargon of this world of 'phenomenology.' Three words from the tradition of phenomenology will be used throughout this analysis of Patočka's works (italicized above): *appearance, phenomenon,* and *unveiling.* These are hopefully not monstrously frightening, but it will help to say briefly what this method brings into question, and (hopefully) into the light.

Phenomenologists who have thought deeply about Husserl are concerned about whether and how far a person can step outside of one's own thoughts and world-view in order to understand the world beyond oneself, beyond one's own particular relation to that world, and towards the grasping of the views that others hold of the world, including (sometimes) the possibility of universal categories.[64] While Husserl argued that the method he called the 'phenomenological reduction' could be a way of training oneself to step most of the way outside of one's own body and historically-situated world, Heidegger and Merleau-Ponty argued (in different ways) that you cannot get 'all the way' outside yourself to a pure objective truth, so they turned toward examinations of how to dwell within the world and within your body in a truthful way. On this point (though not all), Patočka is closer to Heidegger and Merleau-Ponty than he is to Husserl's idea of a 'pure' reduction.[65] Parsing out these distinctions requires a complicated technical conversation about our ability (and often inability) to see the world accurately, as well as a debate about whether the thoughts inside of our heads are 'real,' including where those thoughts come from and how they influence our actions. The specifics of how the tradition of phenomenology approaches these questions (and the attendant jargon) are less important for this discussion than probing the assumptions behind asking this

---

63 See note 19 above.

64 One helpful place to start, if a more technical description is desired: Christian Beyer, "Edmund Husserl," *The Stanford Encyclopedia of Philosophy*, November 1, 2016, http://plato.stanford.edu /archives/sum2015/entries/husserl/.

65 Patočka, "La critique de l'objectivisme et le problème de la psychologie phénoménologique chez Sartre et Merleau-Ponty," *Les Temps Modernes* 55, no. 608 (2000): 222–234; Emre Şan, "Corporéité et existence: Patočka, Merleau-Ponty, Maine de Biran" *Studia Phænomenologica* 12, no. 1 (January 2012): 133–156.

question, because what gets 'unveiled' varies depending upon which philosopher is asking.

Patočka engages the question of the 'reality of thought' somewhere between Husserl and Heidegger. On the micro-level of one individual, Patočka and phenomenologists in general are sometimes concerned with how and whether one person can change his or her view of the world; on the macro-level of politics, this becomes for Patočka at the end of his life a question of whether one person can change the larger world by changing his or her own view of the world, that is, by changing the 'reality' of how one thinks about the world. This is *almost* the standard and somewhat clichéd question of whether one person can change the world, but it would be a mistake to equate the two questions as identical; Patočka does not seem to adhere outright to the conviction that one person can change the world. By his later lectures, one might say that there are too many questions embedded within that too-large question of changing the whole world, so he is asking about only part of that question, mainly about whether changing the way you think can change the way you see phenomena in the world and act in relation to those phenomena in your given horizon. Or as he frames it:

> We are always already somewhere in the whole of the world. This is the basis on which our active doing takes place. I do this and that within the framework of the possibilities I have seized. Acting always takes place in a particular stance and movement. The world placed us in a specific region, the world addressed us... the world addressed us in general, placed us in a certain context, now the need arises to take a stance with respect to the concrete particulars of the context. A region open in the awareness of how we are is a part of the phenomenon of the horizon.[66]

In a totalitarian society, it is rarely 'reasonable' to believe that one individual can change the whole system, so the context and place within which Patočka was thinking about wanting to change the world necessarily forced upon him qualifications and nuances. The world was addressing him in a certain context, and he sought to be aware of how his place shaped his view of his horizon. The wager that Patočka took (and that Havel agreed with, see Chapter 1) seemed to be that changing the way one thinks about the world does change something, even if that

---

66   Patočka, *BCLW*, 43.

'something' is not the whole world. Rather, changing a view of the world does change the way one is 'living,' and that can *unveil* a hidden 'truth' otherwise obscured behind various types of lies, habits, and the dishonesty of powerful social and political systems.[67]

As already stated, Patočka acknowledges that we cannot help but to read and experience the phenomena of the world while we are sitting in a particular moment in history, both in the quotidian sense of history's everyday events, as well as the 'heretical' sense of history being a philosophically structured way of thinking about time. Or as he puts it: "All un-situated truths are in the end abstractions from our human situation. They grow out of our encounter with something in our situation that we then consider for itself."[68] Our 'situation' is our momentary place in history. Striving to move toward truth within history can help us turn around in Plato's cave, especially if that truth can also show us how our choice to 'sit' in history via a particular way of thinking is indeed a choice, and that with a bit of 'heretical' philosophical education, we might change that choice, and thereafter decide to make moments in history (historical *phenomena*) look quite different through our own participation in those phenomena. Choosing to step into politics and engage in acts of dissidence, as Patočka did with Charter 77, is such a choice; it is the type of decision that can indeed change the course of history significantly, even if individual actions can sometimes do so only in small ways. But understanding oneself as part of history is no easy task of *unveiling* the world to oneself; chained as we are to our many shadows, illusions, and diversions, seeing political action and dissent as meaningful ways forward through life is a very particular (and sometimes peculiar) sort of choice, often quite risky, and forces us to make sacrifices.[69]

The events Patočka lived through were undoubtedly implicated in producing the *appearance* of his philosophy that can be characterized at times as fragmented, at other times as deeply pessimistic. Or in other words, his philosophy would be a different reading experience if he had lived in different times, and many of his thoughts and ideas might not

---

67 Patočka has been put into conversation with Foucault by several scholars: Simona Forti, *The New Demons: Rethinking Power and Evil Today,* trans. Zakiya Hanafi (Stanford: Stanford University Press, 2014); H. Vojtěch, *Změnit sám sebe. Duchovní cvičení Pierra Hadota, péče o sebe Michela Foucaulta a péče o duši Jana Patočky* (Červený Kostelec: Nakladatelství Pavel Mervart, 2010); Arpád Szakolczai, "Thinking Beyond the East-West Divide: Foucault, Patočka, and the Care of the Self," *Social Research* 61, no. 2 (Summer 1994): 297–323.

68 Patočka, *Plato and Europe*, 4.

69 For an analysis of risk in Patočka's writings, see Tava, *The Risk of Freedom.*

have appeared at all. To give just one local example (in addition to the global examples of the World Wars and the atomic bomb that Patočka references directly in *Heretical Essays*), no intellectual could really live through the *phenomenon* of the Prague Spring in 1968—when censorship laws were partly liberalized, free association became less criminalized, and intellectuals could practice their crafts in public (Patočka was able to lecture again for a short time at the university), and not be existentially devastated when the Soviet tanks arrived, censorship was redoubled, and the creative and artistic freedom passed away into what Václav Havel later called "post-totalitarian normalization."[70] 'Post-totalitarian' was a way of describing state repression that was often indirect, coercive, and couched in hypocritically benevolent terms; 'normalization' was the word used (ironically by dissidents) to describe the return to greater repression after the momentary but aberrational liberty of the Prague Spring.[71] So in this sense, historical events are phenomenon that appear in the world and provide an opportunity for the unveiling of truths about the world, and the history Patočka lived through mattered in framing his philosophy. In 1968, the truth was revealed that the power of the political state could not be quickly or systematically changed by citizen engagement, and the idea of 'socialism with a human face' was unmasked as merely a hopeful illusion, a shadow.[72] If the philosophical thinking that follows this historical event is fragmented, contradictory, or pessimistic, is this not appropriate and revealing? Historical conditions therefore matter in sorting out the relationship between philosophy and politics in any body of work, and Patočka after 1968 is but one example.

The method of phenomenology tries to avoid claiming that the same objective truth is revealed to all people who witness the same phenomenon in the world. This rests on the intuition (to perhaps over-simply) that different people see things differently, and objective, rationalistic, scientific understandings of the world cannot fully account for these differences. Husserl had raised the question in *Crisis of the European Sciences* about what happens when the hubris of scientific rationalism denies

---

70 See Gordon Skilling, *Samizdat and an Independent Society in Central and Eastern Europe* (Columbus: Ohio State University Press, 1989).
71 See note 4 above on normalization.
72 For a full account of the evolution of Marxist ideas in Eastern Europe, see Leszek Kołakowski, *Main Currents of Marxism: Its Origins, Growth, and Dissolution*, trans. P.S. Falla (Oxford: Oxford University Press, 1981).

elements of subjectivity and becomes dehumanizing; writing before the atom bomb and the Holocaust, this was a prescient question and insight.[73] History is a phenomenon, then, and not an object, as events and unfolding phenomenon are seen and described by different people in very different ways. As the conversations within this book aim to reveal, one basis for dissident thinking is coming to see 'history' as a phenomenon whose meaning one can change inside one's own life and thinking; one can choose to think differently about one's own role in history, and therefore come to act differently into history. When Patočka thought about 'politics' and his own place in history in light of Charter 77, like many other dissidents, he saw a role for himself in creating historical meaning, and he chose to act. (See Section IV, Chapter 5: 'Heretical metaphysics of historicity.')

What the phenomenon of Patočka-the-philosopher turned Patočka-the-dissident can explain, if we are brave enough to follow the "adventurous and foolhardy" methodology of phenomenology, is why there is dissidence when the objective, instrumental, and rationalistic world view would otherwise deliver to the potential political actor a message of deterrence at best, repulsion at worst. The potential dissident might say any number of things consistent with a 'rational' world view to refrain from getting involved in politics: "You will get yourself killed/imprisoned/tortured"; "You will not get anything from doing this"; "There is no 'rational' basis for thinking you can meet your 'objectives' with this method"; "This is against your 'self-interest"; and so on. Some types of dissidence require acting against one's own self-interest, against instrumental objectives, and in ways that do not look to other people as if they are 'objectively rational.' Why does this type of dissidence still happen, then? The dissident action in these cases—and Patočka's view of the world through the lens of phenomenology will help show this—has for these actors an intrinsic value, not an instrumental value; they do it because the act is valuable and meaningful in and of itself, not because they think it will get them some*thing*. Action is not entirely about the *thing* or object out there in the world that one wants to get, but can also be about the meaning of a phenomenon as it is conceived of internally, to oneself. This approach, however 'subjective' and perhaps 'just inside the head,' is very *real*. What is called in political science 'rational choice

73   Edmund Husserl, *The Crisis of European Sciences and Transcendental Phenomenology*, trans. David Carr (Evanston: Northwestern University Press, 1970).

theory' cannot explain the types of dissidence described here.[74] Phenomenology, however 'monstrous' its jargon, can explain it quite well.

If being historically aware and situated is one way of thinking that unveils the intrinsic value of dissidence, then Patočka also opens the terrain to look into the intrinsic *moral* value of dissidence. In some cases, a sense of history and a sense of morality can go together in moments of dissidence, though surely not all the time. While this is not an assertion backed by objective statistics, anyone who reads commentaries on Patočka has likely observed that one of the most frequently cited lines from his writings is about morality, from an essay he wrote about Charter 77:

> The point of morality is to assure not the functioning of a society but the humanity of humans. Humans do not invent morality arbitrarily, to suit their needs, wishes, inclinations, and aspirations. Quite the contrary, it is morality that defines what being human means.[75]

This is indeed Patočka at his most quotable, in part because this essay was about Charter 77 and the role of human rights in international politics, and as a spokesman for the Charter he necessarily had to distill his philosophical thoughts into something accessible to the public. This statement is consistent, however, with much of the complicated philosophy of his earlier lectures and essays.[76] In a commentary on Husserl, for example, Patočka challenges some of Husserl's ideas by arguing for a world-view that places moral concerns at the very center of human existence:

---

74 This is the basis of much of the work in sociology and political science known as 'social movement theory.' For one guide to a vast literature, see: Donatella Della Porta and Mario Diani, eds. *The Oxford Handbook of Social Movements.* Oxford: Oxford University Press, 2015.

75 Patočka, "Two Charta 77 Texts," in Kohák, *Jan Patočka Philosophy and Selected Writings*, 41.

76 The relationship of Patočka's thinking to the philosophical questions underlying modern ideas of human rights is discussed in James Mensch, *Patočka's Asubjective Phenomenology: Toward a New Concept of Human Rights* (Würzburg: Königshausen und Neumann, 2016). Patočka's involvement in Charter 77 is also related to his engagement with many other philosophical inspirations from both the Czech and German traditions, and this moment has been characterized as Patočka's "Kantian turn," discussed in: J. Čapek, «Le devoir de l›homme envers lui-même.» *Tumultes* 1 (2009): 351–370 and D. Leufer, "The Wound Which Will Not Close: Jan Patočka's Philosophy and the Conditions of Politicization." *Studies in East European Thought* 69, no. 1 (2017): 29–44. A philosophical-genealogical approach towards his work and subsequent politics is also undertaken in Francesco Tava, *The Risk of Freedom: Ethics, Phenomenology and Politics in Jan Patočka,* trans. J. Ledlie (New York: Rowman and Littlefield, 2015). Notable in Tava's argument are the influences on Patočka's dissident thinking from Eugen Fink, Emanuel Rádl, Bernard Bolzano, Karel Kosík, and T. G. Masaryk. See pp. 123–154.

This life-world is a world of good and evil, and its subjectivity is that of the drama of good and evil, the good and evil of an essentially finite being who cannot live except by projecting... ever knowing that this projection is accompanied by the shadow of the extreme possibility of not projecting at all.[77]

By "projecting," Patočka seems to mean that each human sends oneself into the world by imagining one's place in the world and interacting with others in the world, and 'the possibility of not projecting' is the possibility of death and withdrawal from the world. He goes on, after this assertion, to sketch what the world looks like within this drama of good and evil, the drama of morality:

It is a world where we can live, live in a community in which we can find a place and be accepted, enjoying the protection which enables us to take on the concrete task of defense and of struggle against what threatens us in the context of humans and of things alike. It is the world of embodied living beings who work and struggle, who approach each other and draw back, living in mutual respect; who communicate with the world of others by word and understanding... Corporeity, reciprocity, concrete spatiality which includes both the familiar and the foreign, language—those are the constant structures of that world. Finding a place, growing close to others, and renewing protective bonds is one of its fundamental circular movements...[78]

This might suggest that any political situation that Patočka would endorse would have to recognize and acknowledge something like this vision of the world. More to the point here, this is what the starting point of morality—or of looking at the world as a battle between good and evil—can create for human life. It can lead us to build communities, seek protection for the things that make us human, to work and to struggle, to find mutual respect and understanding from others in reciprocal ways. This all constitutes a movement, a movement around an infinite circular shape of human life being perpetuated, not ending, intrinsically valued unto itself. This is a vision of a certain sort of politics, and *almost*

77 Patočka, "Husserl on the Crisis of the Sciences and on Phenomenology of the 'Life-world," in Kohák, *Jan Patočka Philosophy and Selected Writings*, 236.
78 Patočka, "Husserl on the Crisis of the Sciences and on Phenomenology of the 'Life-world," 236.

a political theory. 'Almost,' because the reader has to see through the problem that this paragraph appeared not as the opening argument of a political treatise, but as an oddly inserted paragraph in a critique of Husserl.[79] The circumstances of history and the genre of theorizing are not unrelated: the censors might end up less offended with such a text (this is hardly an enthusiastic description of Communism at that time) because (one can merely speculate) they might have been too confused by the prior commentary on Husserl to keep reading this far into the article.[80] One historical moment demanded the hiding of heretical political ideas; another time's heretical history demands an unveiling.

One More Heresy

Before his arrest, and again from his hospital bed after he had been interrogated, Patočka penned several short essays explaining why he was getting involved with the dissident movement to protest against the Communist government. Two of them are translated as "The Obligation to Resist Injustice" and "What we can and cannot expect from Chart[er] 77."[81] These essays are his most accessible writing, justifying his political actions in readable prose for a wide general audience. He defends a thesis about the importance of human rights and human dignity. While he spent most of his life working through various complex philosophical problems in dense and technical language, at the point when he was able to present more accessible texts like these to the general public, endeavoring to explain the bridges he saw between philosophy

---

79 The title of the essay from where this quotation came is "Husserl on the Crisis of the Sciences and the Phenomenology of the Life-world." The reader casually flipping through a collection of Patočka's essays would never guess from this title that it might contain an articulation of a political vision, or that a sense of the 'good life' was the aim of its writing. In conditions of censorship and repression, the titles and the content of the essays are not always mutually illuminating; it was a lot more dangerous to write about politics than it was to write about Husserl's phenomenology, and that must be part of understanding the background of fragmented, incomplete and sometimes contradictory arguments in these texts.

80 This raises the possible applicability of the thesis put forward by Leo Strauss in *Persecution and the Art of Writing* (Chicago: University of Chicago Press, 1988). Patočka's notion of the "solidarity of those who understand" is taken up in later chapters to address this question, but inconclusively. Overall the argument proposed here is that a wide audience can understand the value and merit of Patočka's ideas, so even if some of the ideas Strauss has about writing in conditions of censorship are applicable, this is not a Straussian account of Patočka's work.

81 See Kohák's "Philosophical Biography," in Kohák, *Jan Patočka Philosophy and Selected Writings*, 127–131 and "Two Charta 77 Texts," 340–347.

and politics, his life was cut short because of his harsh interrogation by the police. The way Patočka's life ended is therefore one justification for the method of this analysis, as these circumstances raised various hypothetical questions that will never be answered definitively, but nonetheless have intrinsic value as questions in-and-of themselves.

The most basic question is about what might have happened had Patočka lived longer. What would he have said to other activists and dissidents that came after him, especially had he lived past 1989? Then there is the hypothetical political question: what if he had been able to speak more freely during his life? What if he had been able to have a conversation with other philosopher-dissidents, where would the conversation have gone? If he had been able to write a letter to Gandhi, to Dietrich Bonhoeffer as he sat in a Nazi prison, to the students protesting during the 1960s in the US—what might he have said? If these activists and dissidents wrote back, what might they have said to him? Would they have agreed or disagreed with each other about philosophical inspirations and questions of political and existential meaning? What conclusions, if any, could be drawn from these questions and conversations for the general task of illuminating the relationship between philosophy and dissident politics?

To imagine a conversation between Patočka and those he did not have actual dialogues with during his life is an exercise in hermeneutical interpretation, of reading texts in light of ideas in other texts, using one view to illuminate another view, the narrator mediating the exchange. Patočka's views and ideas can be found in texts now translated into various languages, so this is not a wholly imaginary conversation, even though only a 'textual' conversation. To enact and mediate this conversation, however, requires more than reading two books side-by-side. Those texts Patočka and his students left behind, as already mentioned, are not accessible to the general reader like his last essays about Charter 77, so they require some 'translation,' in the sense that translation is always an interpretation. Obscure philosophical language needs to be 'translated' into descriptions understandable by activists, dissidents, and those readers who might later become convinced to step into politics, or at least to turn around in the proverbial, metaphorical cave. This book claims to be such a translation: it is therefore also an act of interpretation, exegesis, and application.[82]

---

82 This is to say that the methods here are largely Gadamerian, with moments where the hermeneutics of suspicion must also necessarily be engaged. See note 48.

From this translation, these conversations are meant to demonstrate a way to recognize the unfolding of history in both political events and individual lives, therein recognizing what it means to become part of an historical community, as well as what it means to participate in a type of politics that goes against the prevailing norms and systems created by the complicated interaction of humans and their histories. Like Plato's dialogues, which on one level can be understood by the general reader, a back-and-forth questioning between Patočka and other dissidents and activists is meant to ask whether his ideas might help us see our own caves of illusion and confront our distress, especially our distress about matters of politics. No such dialogue will ever land precisely on Patočka's 'objective' intention and 'exact' meaning; this is not about reading his mind, but about reading his texts as ideas that are out there in the world, potentially able to challenge our illusions and passivity in the cave, should we choose to pay attention.

In light of these complications, this book will attempt to stay 'inside the cave' by avoiding the highly technical language used by the philosophers under which Patočka studied (Husserl and Heidegger) and those who now study his works (contemporary philosophers of phenomenology). This is a trade-off, impoverishing the discourse for some, enriching it for others. Such a reframing of the discourse about his work might be construed as going back down into the cave, to talk to those not yet accustomed to a philosophical method whereby one can pull oneself out of one's chains. But as any general reader who picks up Plato's *Republic* can attest, understanding the allegorical geography of Plato's cave and its relationship to a certain mode of thinking (perhaps 'philosophical' thinking) is not beyond the ability of a non-philosopher. Plato's dialogues progressively peel back layers of commonsensical ideas towards deeper understandings of the world, just as any good conversation with a person schooled in a different way of thinking can help one to see part of the world in a new way. Patočka willingly became a spokesman for a political movement, and the form and style of this analysis of his work is meant to reflect his role as a spokesman, which he took up only late in his life in a very abbreviated form. It was in that moment where he made his most ineffable impression on the world, earning the label of a 'modern Socrates.'[83] The accuracy of this label can be questioned, of

---

83 Marc Crépon, "Fear, Courage, Anger: The Socratic lesson," in *Jan Patočka and the Heritage of Phenomenology: Centenary Papers*, 175–186.

course, opening a discussion about the shape and durability of not just his legacy, but also toward the open question of whether his philosophy might be more enduring than his politics.[84]

For the reader or student of Patočka who feels such a journey requires putting too much trust in the simplifications and generalizations of this author, the footings of this supposedly more habitable house of words are meant to provide citations of technical philosophical readings, directing the reader towards important aspects of the academic scholarship about Patočka, some of which will inevitably challenge certain details of this presentation. The footnotes will therefore appear more cave-like to the general reader, but for the trained philosopher, these might be sufficient to hold up the structure of the argument. Or this method might not be enough. But that sort of debate is what will perpetuate the immortal yet historical dialogue into which Patočka placed himself alongside his activist and dissident companions when he opened Plato's cave and stepped into the political distress of his own time.

---

84 James Dodd, "Jan Patočka's Philosophical Legacy," in *The Oxford Handbook of the History of Phenomenology* (2018): 396.

Chapter One
Living in Truth:
in Conversation with Václav Havel

On the occasion of Václav Havel's death in 2011, the idea of 'living in truth' was celebrated as one of his main legacies as a playwright, a dissident, and a politician.[1] Journalists and commentators eulogized Havel's thoughts on 'living in truth' largely from his 1978 essay "The Power of the Powerless," dedicated to the memory of Jan Patočka and written in light of the harsh government reactions to Charter 77. While the eulogies did not necessarily agree that Havel fully managed to 'live in truth' throughout his time as a politician, the notion of 'living in truth' nonetheless framed his legacy as a dissident.[2] Havel's use of this idea was also partly inspired by Patočka's philosophical thinking and the tragedy of his death in 1977. 'Living in truth' was later evoked by dissidents around the world quite directly, including (to name only the two most famous) Charter 08 in China and Aung San Suu Kyi as she resisted the military dictatorship in Burma-Myanmar.[3] Within Havel's texts there are many direct and

---

1   *The Economist*: http://www.economist.com/node/21542169; *The Washington Post*: https://www .washingtonpost.com/opinions/Václav-havel-living-in-truth/2011/12/19/gIQATb204O_story .html; *Slate*: http://www.slate.com/articles/news_and_politics/foreigners/2011/12/vaclav _havel_dead_the_czech_leader_s_greatest_achievement_was_an_essay_the_power_of _the_powerless_.html; *Weekly Standard*: http://www.weeklystandard.com/blogs/vaclav -havel-and-living-truth_613534.html; Reuters/Sachs: http://blogs.reuters.com/amplifications /2011/12/20/the-power-of-living-in-truth/; *New Yorker*: http://www.newyorker.com/news /news-desk/postscript-vaclav-havel-1936-2011; *Huffington Post*: http://www.huffingtonpost .co.uk/2011/12/18/vaclav-havel-dead-the-quotes-died_n_1156201.html. Accessed 9/16/15.
2   Michael Ignatieff, "The Hero Europe Needed," *Atlantic Monthly*, March 2015; John Keane, *Václav Havel: A Political Tragedy in Six Acts* (New York: Basic Books, 2000); Michael Zantovsky, *Havel: A Life* (New York: Grove Press, 2014).
3   Havel nominated Suu Ski for the Nobel Peace Prize, which she won in 1991. Václav Havel, "A Rose for the Unfree," http://www.washingtonpost.com/wp-dyn/content/article

indirect insights about how dissidents and activists might engage the idea of 'living in truth' as it relates to political action, and this comparison of Havel's and Patočka's ideas about 'living in truth' aims to uncover and illuminate these ideas.

The idea that truth is something to be lived in the world—not just something thought, not just something written down, and not just the purview of professional philosophers and scientists—is an area of common ground shared by Patočka and Havel. Yet while Havel read Patočka's works and the two of them shared philosophical influences,[4] by comparing their ideas of 'living in truth,' this is not meant to argue that Patočka and Havel fully agreed, or that Havel merely put Patočka's ideas 'into practice.' This would overlook the possibility that given their conversations, there was likely cross-fertilization of ideas in both directions, especially in Patočka's last essays about Charter 77.[5] For Havel, philosophical categories were necessarily made more concrete by his efforts to substantiate ideas like 'living in truth' for the broader audience of Eastern European intellectuals, including those without access to the Czech samizdat in which Patočka was writing, and Havel's style is also more accessible to the general reader than Patočka's. In reading their two oeuvres together, there is a sense that Havel had an ability to riff off of Patočka (to use a colloquial phrase from jazz he might appreciate).[6] When Havel references Patočka directly, he takes the kernel of an idea and 'runs with it,' sometimes moving very much in his own direction. If

---

/2005/06/14/AR2005061401345.html; Aung San Suu Kyi Opening Speech "September 15, 2013, Prague Crossroads," http://www.forum2000.cz/en/projects/forum-2000-conferences/2013/panel-summaries/transcripts/speech-by-aung-san-suu-kyi-to-the-opening-ceremony/; "Charter 08: A Call for Change in China," 9 December 2010, http://www.bbc.com/news/world-asia-pacific-11955763.

4   See Michael Gubser, *The Far Reaches: Phenomenology, Ethics and Social Renewal in Central Europe* (Stanford: Stanford University Press, 2014). He traces the common heritage of phenomenology in Central Europe, Patočka and Havel included.

5   In the essay "Last Conversation," Havel details the degree to which he felt shy and intimidated in conversations with Patočka, up until a long conversation they had the day of the police interrogation that eventually led to Patočka's hospitalization and death: "My shyness began to dissipate only recently, as we came to be united by our identical views not only on certain matters around us but also on how to act, and—finally—by a bit of common work as well. In those exciting days Patočka all of a sudden ceased being merely a sort of deity and became more human for me, and, surprisingly, I was no longer afraid of relinquishing the posture of a devoted listener and adopting that of a partner... it was only then, too, that I began to realize fully the inconspicuous moral greatness of this man." Václav Havel, "Last Conversation," in Marketa Goetz-Staniewicz, ed., *Good-Bye Samizdat: Twenty Years of Czechoslovak Underground Writing* (Evanston: Northwestern University Press, 1992) 212.

6   For another example of such an analysis: J. Krapfl, "Boredom, Apocalypse, and Beyond: Reading Havel through Patočka," *East European Politics and Societies* 32, no. 2 (2018): 278–284.

the conceit of this book is that all dissidents should be given some access to Patočka's ideas in order that they might be able to riff off of those ideas, moving in directions of their own choice and necessity, then how Havel engaged with Patočka and 'ran with' notions of 'living in truth' is important for opening up the world of Patočka's thinking for those not immersed in the vocabulary of philosophical phenomenology.

Reading Havel's and Patočka's writings together makes it easier to see that under the larger umbrella of 'living in truth,' there are multiple possibilities for how forms of 'truth' can illuminate types of 'living,' and how these modes of living might relate to acting as a dissident. Focusing on four specific dimensions of Havel's and Patočka's visions of living in truth, I will explore (1) the inward truth of the self, coupled with the idea that unless you know yourself and the nature of your own soul, you cannot accurately grasp the nature of the world in general; (2) the truth of others, including the idea that you cannot define what is true without the help of others who came before you and who exist around you, and that truth therefore has a moral and ethical component; (3) the political truth, or the truth derived from relationships between people that enables action through a larger understanding of human groups and collectives;[7] and (4) truth as the necessary recognition of objectivity's limits, or the notion that the truth handed to us by science and objectivity might be incomplete, requiring a mode of living that recognizes how certain parts of the world cannot be objectively defined, such as spiritual meaning and subjectivity.

Each of these modes of truth implies a mode of 'living,' as well as a particular 'emplacement,' or an understanding of what the 'in' in 'living *in* truth' identifies as a 'place' (see Introduction). If these four types of truth should be sought out by dissidents, then there are also

---

7   This set of categories is built primarily out of my reading of Patočka's writings, but in *Power of the Powerless*, Havel also introduced the specific notion of 'living in truth' in a 'post-totalitarian society' as having four components: "In the post-totalitarian system, therefore, living within the truth has more than a mere existential dimension (returning humanity to its inherent nature), or a noetic dimension (revealing reality as it is), or a moral dimension (setting an example for others). It also has an unambiguous political dimension. If the main pillar of the system is living a lie, then it is not surprising that the fundamental threat to it is living the truth. This is why it must be suppressed more severely than anything else." These dimensions of "living in truth" that Havel identified are incorporated into the discussion here, albeit with slightly different categorizations for the sake of clarity in the narrative and for making connections to Patočka. All texts written by Havel are available and translated at the online archive of the Václav Havel Library, https://archive.vaclavhavel-library.org, with a corresponding document number. Unless otherwise noted, his work is cited hereafter as "AKVH." Havel, "Power of the Powerless," 1978 (AKVH 35781).

multiple types of 'places' where one can live in truth, if 'place' is construed as a much wider idea than merely being geographical, and something more like 'finding one's *place* in the world.' Any dissident could potentially put these modes of 'living in truth' into practice in their own world, in their own place, riffing or running off as needed. From another angle, elaborating these four modes of truth can also begin to show how Patočka offered a philosophical way to value dissidence intrinsically, not just instrumentally. Dissidence as something valuable and meaningful in itself, rather than just being valuable for what it can change in concrete politics, is a significant aspect of what a conversation between Patočka's and Havel's ideas might help to illuminate. These four modes of truth are each an example of that intrinsic value, each also demonstrating how seeking truth about these modes of living also might require something of a dissident attitude towards established norms. Such truth-seeking, and that attitude, are valuable in and of themselves, over and apart from whatever they might change about the world, politically or otherwise.[8] While 'living in truth' might not have been so eulogized alongside Havel had he not also led the Velvet Revolution and 'changed the world' through the 'success' of his dissident movement, the idea of living in truth offers more than just that legacy. The argument here is meant to suggest that each moment of 'living in truth' is a kind of revolution, intrinsically valuable in itself, and such moments can happen in both the small and large theaters of political and anti-political life.

The Inward Truth of the Self

For both Havel and Patočka, looking inward to find the truth of oneself is entirely *necessary* to begin the process of living in truth, but it is not *sufficient* to complete the process. Looking inward is the beginning, but it must be *for the sake of* eventually looking outward toward truths about the world in general, including the importance of history and the

---

8   Havel claimed he did what he did as a dissident even though it might not change a thing: "In other words, it is clearly a moral act, not only because one must pay so dearly for it, but principally because it is not self-serving: the risk may bring rewards in the form of a general amelioration in the situation, or it may not. In this regard, as I stated previously, it is an all-or-nothing gamble, and it is difficult to imagine a reasonable person embarking on such a course merely because he reckons that sacrifice today will bring rewards tomorrow, be it only in the form of general gratitude." Havel, "Power of the Powerless," 1978 (AKVH 35781).

politics of the day. Finding the inward truth of the self is a variant of the question of how to come to know oneself, an inquiry that has been at the center of Western philosophical discussions since at least as early as the ancient Greeks.[9] The inscription at the oracle of Delphi, "know thyself," became a question at the center of Plato's philosophy, and was therefore inherited by every philosopher who was heir to Plato and the Greek tradition. Patočka sees himself as part of this inheritance, and the task of 'knowing thyself' and 'caring for the soul' both accompany his reading of Plato, marking for him the beginning of the European philosophical tradition.[10] The suggestion that looking inward to find truths about the world as they might already exist in the structure of the individual soul is therefore an important part of Patočka's Platonic project, but as with each inheritor of the Greek tradition, this process of inward examination has local and temporal variation.

Patočka's ideas about the inward truth of the self are partially captured within his vision of 'caring for the soul.' This idea is at the center of his philosophical inquiry and also relates to his political action (see Introduction). While more will be elaborated in Chapter Two about the political implications of 'caring for the soul,' it is related to 'living in truth' in part because it contains a clear mode of self-examination, or in his own words, caring for the soul "manifests itself in three ways: in one way as the complete plan of existence, in another as the plan of a new political life, and in yet another as the clarification of what the soul is in itself."[11] When one asks the right sort of philosophical questions about oneself, therefore, caring for one's own soul can clarify something fundamental about our internal nature, our relation to the world, and our plan for political life. "The care of the soul," according to Patočka, "is something that transforms us internally, that at once makes us from instinctive and traditional beings, beings who look at what is normal in society and spiritually nourish themselves with this, into beings who

---

9   Patočka was necessarily embedded into the 'place' of Europe and European philosophical traditions, and he therefore turns towards the Greeks as his earliest inheritance and influence. In the context of globalizing political theory and political philosophy, however, it is important to note that there were many philosophical traditions around the world that pre-dated the Greeks and inevitably contained important ideas about inward self-examination. While such traditions, sometimes called 'indigenous philosophy,' are beyond the scope of this inquiry, it is important to acknowledge that the tradition of pinpointing the beginning of philosophy with the Greeks is a European tradition, not a global one, and the European tradition is particular, not universal.

10 Patočka, *Plato and Europe*, trans. Petr Lom (Stanford, CA: Stanford University Press, 2002).

11 Patočka, *Plato and Europe*, 86.

entirely reverse this course, who are constantly examining."[12] The linkage between thinking and action in this formulation is usefully suggestive: when we challenge the received traditions and what is 'normal,' not only does the way we 'spiritually nourish' ourselves change, but what we do and how we act changes: we reverse our course (our direction of motion) and do something differently, examining and questioning everything.[13]

'Living in truth' and the ability to care for the soul are therefore closely connected and interdependent ideas for Patočka: "What... makes humans just and truthful is their care for their soul... Care for the soul means that truth is something not given once and for all, nor merely a matter of observing and acknowledging the observed, but rather a lifelong inquiry, self-controlling, self-unifying intellectual and vital practice."[14] Deploying the idea of caring for the soul is thus an example of truth being a place beyond the horizon that is 'not given once and for all;' truth—and living within it—is a lifelong process and practice of both self-examination and worldly engagement. When Patočka defines what it means to think, 'cognizing,' he argues that that too begins with a forever-ongoing practice of trying to understand our own essence and our own character: "undoubtedly we cognize methodically and purposefully... it is not enough to open one's eyes, it is directed activity. And such directed activity has to naturally have its goal, which is obviously connected with our own character, with our soul, with what we are in our own essence."[15]

To point the Socratic method inward to our own souls, and to find our characters and essences, is for Patočka one way to care for our souls, but it is also a way to begin thinking anew about forms of community, politics, and relations with others:

---

12 Patočka, *Plato and Europe*, 120.
13 On the word "spiritual" in Czech, see David Danaher, *Reading Václav Havel* (Toronto: University of Toronto Press, 2015) chapter 4. Danaher has done a thorough ethno-linguistic analysis of Havel's use of the words "spirituality" and "spiritual" (*duchovnost* and *duchovní* in Czech) and concluded that these terms have a wider meaning in Havel's Czech than the traditional use of the words in English, encompassing both an intellectual and psychological state of the mind, at times not necessarily always connected to the strong religious connotations of the words in English. Patočka also had a much wider use of 'spirituality,' as argued in "The Spiritual Person and the Intellectual," in *Living in Problematicity*, ed. and trans. by Eric Manton. (Praha: Oikoymenh, 2007). See also: J. Homolka, "Jan Patočka's Non-Political Politics." *Acta Universitatis Carolinae Interpretationes* 7, no. 1 (2017): 130–146.
14 Patočka, *Heretical Essays*, 82.
15 Patočka, *Plato and Europe*, 202.

Socrates did not help himself, but he helps others. In what way can a philosopher who is in such dire straits help others? In a philosophical way, through the outline of a city where the philosopher can live, where the man who is to care for the soul can live, the man who is to carry out the philosophical thought that it is necessary to live and think on the basis of looking-in, nothing else but that. To create such a city is the world of his [Socrates'] successors... For this, a world of experience is needed; for this, a plan of what is truth is needed, an outline of all being...[16]

A "plan of truth" and an "outline of all being" are foundational to every sort of political philosophy, as well as existing within the everyday political practice of envisioning new 'cities.' Patočka wanted to think of a city where philosophers who examine the world in a Socratic fashion do not have to die, and where they could continue to ask questions and challenge traditions. While he believed that turning inward to find truth created a process that might enable a different sort of politics to happen, he also asserted that aiming toward "outward success" was not the goal or point of such thinking. Turning the intrinsic value of Socratic thinking into outward instrumental value did something to ruin it:

> The care of the soul is something completely internal. The care of the soul does not intend to teach some kind of outward success—let the sophists do that. The care of the soul is the intentional forming of the soul itself, forming into something unyielding and solid, into existence in this sense, because of the very fact that it is occupied with thinking.[17]

Here Patočka asserts the intrinsic value of a certain process of thinking, where turning inward forms the soul and changes its path, but where caring for the soul has to be intrinsically valued, separated from the concrete goals of 'changing the world' or outward success.[18] There is a tension here, of course, because Patočka can see in his mind a better world where 'Socrates does not have to die,' and he would surely like to arrive at such a world as a point of "outward success." Yet these statements about the fully internal nature of this process corroborate other statements (see below and in later sections) that such a world is probably impossible in Patočka's mind. Nonetheless, knowing what 'care of the soul' entails also

---

16   Patočka, *Plato and Europe*, 87–88.
17   Patočka, *Plato and Europe*, 86.
18   Compare Patočka's idea of "amplitude" as discussed in Chapter Two.

means knowing how that impossible world beyond the horizon must be improbably imagined for moral reasons. The ability to sustain this mental paradox becomes, especially in Havel's thinking, an entry into the morally ordered world of dissidence. Aware that such thinking might represent an experiential contradiction in everyday life, one needs to believe that one's soul—the amalgamation of our various internal truths—can sustain such a paradox. The ability to move one's thinking towards a place paradoxically in the world but also beyond the horizon of everyday life—that is, for Patočka, part of what it means to live in truth.

As described above, one of Havel's intellectual talents was to be able to take the core ideas of different philosophers, Patočka included, and 'run with' them in new directions. He and Patočka were going roughly in the same direction on the topic of examining the inward truth of the self: it is a potential salvation in the midst of humanity's crises. Havel's essays, speeches, plays, and his autobiography all pick up on this idea at different points. Finding truth within the realm of the soul and human conscience is a 'theme' in his writings insofar as there are too many specific examples to cite in limited space.[19] Therefore, what follows here are only a few emblematic examples, perhaps relevant to dissidents in general, as looking inward to find truth was necessary for Havel in order to motivate action, overcome fear, and to understand one's political place in the world.

In one of his first foreign speeches as president after 1989, for example, Havel implored the members of a joint session of the United States Congress to do a serious reckoning with their own search for inward truth:

The salvation of this human world lies nowhere else than in the human heart, in the human power to reflect, in human humbleness and in human responsibility. Without a global revolution in the sphere of human consciousness, nothing will change for the better in the sphere of our Being as humans, and the catastrophe toward which this world is headed, whether it be ecological, social, demographic or a general breakdown of civilization, will be unavoidable. If we are no longer threatened by world war or by the danger that the absurd mountains of accumulated nuclear weapons might blow up the world, this does not mean that we have definitively won. We are in fact far from definite victory.[20]

---

19   Havel will talk about one's 'conscience' more than he will use the word 'soul,' though he does not shy away from the 'soul' or notions of 'spirituality.' See Danaher, *Reading Václav Havel*.
20   Havel, "A Joint Session of the U.S. Congress," Feb. 21, 1990 (AKVH 35359).

To say that salvation lies in looking inward to the human heart with humbleness and responsibility, and that a change of consciousness (an inward modality of thinking) will constitute the next global revolution, Havel is indirectly questioning the utilitarian, economically-motivated, and power-laden world-view that penetrates most political bodies like the US Congress. There is even a tinge of (likely intentional) irony: Havel is standing in front of the leaders of the world's most powerful nation— the victor of the Cold War displaying full muscle in every economic, material, and military way—and telling them that the only way to change the world is through looking inward with humility to examine their own hearts. There is a difference between being naïve and being ironic; Havel was surely taken by some to be naïve in these assertions, but given the context of his previous writings, he was likely putting into practice ideas from his essay "The Power of the Powerless," and was doing so with a healthy dose of irony as he faced 'the powerful.' Even though at the moment of this speech he was a president and not a dissident, the power differential between Czechoslovakia and the United States was tremendous, and he was still the powerless one. Turning towards notions of self-examination and the reconstitution of the human heart, Havel evokes the idea that living in truth begins with oneself and looking inward. Telling the Congress that the US had not won a definitive victory (even when they felt they had), and that the crises would only continue (even though the major crises of the Cold War seemed to have ended at that particular moment), he challenged existing taken-for-granted 'truths' by first telling those in power to reexamine their inward self-deceptions.

Havel's admonitions about a continuing crisis turned out to be true, and this is perhaps not mere luck. Havel had never believed that capitalistic Western democracies were exempt from being implicated in a general crisis of governance in the modern world.[21] He spent a significant portion of his life dissenting against a Communist government, but saw both Communism and capitalism as problematic systems that both depended upon the same misuse of technological rationality (see part four, below).

---

21 One example from Havel's "Power of the Powerless": "This planetary challenge to the position of human beings in the world is, of course, also taking place in the Western world, the only difference being the social and political forms it takes. Heidegger refers expressly to a crisis of democracy. There is no real evidence that Western democracy, that is, democracy of the traditional parliamentary type, can offer solutions that are any more profound. It may even be said that the more room there is in the Western democracies (compared to our world) for the genuine aims of life, the better the crisis is hidden from people and the more deeply do they become immersed in it." Havel, "Power of the Powerless," 1978 (AKVH 35781).

His appeal to the inward truth of the human heart was justified in both East and West, both communistic and capitalistic systems, as he was trying to illuminate something about the way the individual person reacted to political power generally understood. He had long argued that the post-totalitarian system of the Communist states of Eastern Europe was just one variant of a wider problem, where the mode of political power that obscured the truth of the human heart and human responsibility "runs de facto through each person, for everyone in his own way is both a victim and a supporter of the system."[22] He also points out the overall effect this has on people in the context of post-totalitarianism:

> Not only does the system alienate humanity, but at the same time alienated humanity supports this system as its own involuntary master plan, as a degenerate image of its own degeneration, as a record of people's own failure as individuals. Yet, at the same time, each person is capable, to a greater or lesser degree, of coming to terms with living within the lie. Each person somehow succumbs to a profane trivialization of his inherent humanity, and to utilitarianism. In everyone there is some willingness to merge with the anonymous crowd and to flow comfortably along with it down the river of pseudo-life.[23]

To live in 'pseudo-life' was to fail at living in truth. The river of the anonymous crowd could exist anywhere there was a human political community—Communist, capitalist or otherwise.

Havel's famous example of this phenomenon was his hypothetical greengrocer, who had a sign in his shop window that read 'workers of the world unite.' In Havel's parable, the grocer keeps this Communist slogan visible in order to assure others of his proper conformity with the ruling ideology, and so that he will be left alone. But then Havel asks what might happen if one day he took it down. What would this mean? It would mean that one individual chose to look inward to find a different truth about his own self and his own behavior, and as a result, disrupted the system:

> He has shattered the world of appearances, the fundamental pillar of the system. He has upset the power structure by tearing apart what holds

22 Havel, "Power of the Powerless," 1978 (AKVH 35781).
23 Havel, "Power of the Powerless," 1978 (AKVH 35781).

it together. He has demonstrated that living a lie is living a lie. He has broken through the exalted facade of the system and exposed the real, base foundations of power. He has said that the emperor is naked. And because the emperor is in fact naked, something extremely dangerous has happened: by his action, the greengrocer has addressed the world. He has enabled everyone to peer behind the curtain. He has shown everyone that it is possible to live within the truth. Living within the lie can constitute the system only if it is universal.

To peer beyond the curtain of the self is also to peer behind the wider system that the self is within, the place that constitutes either the world of mere appearances, or the place that constitutes some reality, at least some partial truth. The language of hidden spheres and hidden truths runs throughout Havel's writings. This might be a partial riff off of Patočka, but also has connections with Heidegger's interpretation of the Greek word for truth, *aletheia*, which translates as something close to 'uncovering.' Heidegger developed notions of truth as un-concealment; philosophy for him was a way to uncover truths that were not readily visible, opening up the world and opening up human experience to the world. The green grocer is also something like the hypothetical figure of the philosopher in Plato's allegory of the cave, the one who tells the prisoners that the shadows on the wall are not reality, but are rather mere appearances created by fake objects and manipulated light. The green grocer figure in Havel's essay seems like an inspiration from a Plato-Heidegger-Patočka nexus of reading and thinking.

Whatever his sources, Havel is ultimately concerned with the political power of revealing the lie and deciding to live within the truth. It would not be quite the same thing if the green grocer came to the realization that the sign represented him being duped about his own propensity to lie to himself, but then decided to leave it in the window and do nothing. For Havel, the intellectual realization that the world is made up of shadows of untruth must be accompanied by responsible and humble (not self-serving) action that pulls back the curtain for oneself, but also for others: "Living within the truth, as humanity's revolt against an enforced position, is... an attempt to regain control over one's own sense of responsibility."[24] This means a sense of responsibility towards others, towards one's community, and towards the larger world. A dissident,

---

24 Havel, "Power of the Powerless," 1978 (AKVH 35781).

therefore, might be a person who can look inward to find the truth, but who also realizes (in humility) that she or he might be chained to the wall in a cave being duped and deceived by the world and its systems of social and political power. Looking inward is a way to question assumptions and recognize how it is possible to be living in a lie. Furthermore, following Patočka and Havel, it is necessary to be in dialogue with others to be able to question the entirety of a situation, to challenge assumptions and received beliefs, and to overturn supposedly universal knowledge and wisdom. Without other people, it is possible to remain unaware of the lie one is living. This is why for both Patočka and Havel both, 'living in truth' does not stop at the borders of the self, but must be linked to others through a sense of responsibility and through acting alongside others in communities, states, the world, and the cosmos.[25]

The Truths of Others

In acting alongside others through a sense of responsibility, 'truth' becomes part of a back-and-forth interaction with other people, where our observations about the world are tested against others' observations. The 'truth of others' therefore carries within it the assumption that articulating 'truth' is impossible without some sort of language (whether in words, visually, or musically) and that language was given to future generations by those within the communities of the past. If language implies an historically-situated community, and that community is necessary to exchange ideas and test truthfulness, then the truth of others is a necessary companion to knowing the self. In other words, one is much further away from 'truth' about the world when one is alone in a self-referential universe without other human beings.[26] However well one might 'know

---

25 See Part Two, below, for a further discussion of "co-acting." Patočka, *Body, Community, Language, World*, trans. Erazim Kohák, ed. James Dodd (Chicago and La Salle: Open Court, 1998) 135. Hereafter abbreviated *"BCLW."*

26 There is compelling research about what happens to prisoners in solitary confinement that corroborates this basic philosophical idea with biology, sociology, anthropology and the repeated testimonies of prisoners themselves. As Lisa Gunether argues (using the language of phenomenological philosophy to address a concrete social and political problem): "Persons who are structured as intentional consciousness but are deprived of a diverse, open-ended perceptual experience of the world, or who are structured as transcendental intersubjectivity but are deprived of concrete relations to others, have the very structure of their Being-in-the-world turned against them and used to exploit their fundamental relationality. This is the worst form of torture and the principle upon which all more determinate forms of torture are based."

oneself,' overcoming the pull of self-deception requires a community and a language that might constitute and encompass the self, but which are distinct from the self.

The bridge between the self and others, following Havel, requires a notion of the individual embedded into universality through participation in history:

> Historical experience teaches us that any genuinely meaningful point of departure in an individual's life usually has an element of universality about it. In other words, it is not something partial, accessible only to a restricted community, and not transferable to any other. On the contrary, it must be potentially accessible to everyone; it must foreshadow a general solution and, thus, it is not just the expression of an introverted, self-contained responsibility that individuals have to and for themselves alone, but responsibility to and for the world.[27]

For Havel and Patočka, the truth of others implies a moral relationship vis-à-vis others that underpins this responsibility "to and for the world."[28] As Havel described in his prison memoir, *Letters to Olga*:

> Human responsibility... has begun to appear... as that fundamental point from which all identity grows and by which it stands or falls... It is the mortar binding it together, and when the mortar dries out, identity too begins irreversibly to crumble and fall apart... the secret of man is the secret of his responsibility... I would say that responsibility for oneself is a knife we use to carve out our own inimitable features in the panorama of Being; it is the pen with which we write into the history of Being that story of the fresh creation of the world that each new human existence always is.[29]

Here Havel acknowledges the explicit relationship between the truth of the self and responsibility toward the world. The identity of the self will crumble and fall apart without taking responsibility for oneself in light

---

Lisa Guenther, *Solitary Confinement: Social Death and its Afterlives* (Minneapolis: University of Minnesota Press, 2013) p. xv.

27 Havel, "Power of the Powerless," 1978 (AKVH 35781).

28 The notions of responsibility in Havel's work have been detailed in the works of Delia Popescu and James Pontuso. James Pontuso, *Václav Havel: Civic Responsibility in the Postmodern Age* (Oxford: Rowan and Littlefield, 2004); Delia Popescu, *Political Action in Václav Havel's Thought: The Responsibility of Resistance* (Lexington Books, 2012).

29 Havel, *Letters to Olga*, trans. Paul Wilson (New York: Alfred Knopf, 1988) 145, 147.

of a larger context of the world, and unless one also takes one's place within history. In his speech to the US Congress, Havel takes this idea further:

> We still do not know how to put morality ahead of politics, science and economics. We are still incapable of understanding that the only genuine backbone of all our actions, if they are to be moral, is responsibility. Responsibility to something higher than my family, my country, my firm, my success. Responsibility to the order of Being, where all our actions are indelibly recorded and where, and only where, they will be properly judged.[30]

Trying to seek out the universal aspects of one's individual responsibility is a way of linking oneself with the larger context of 'the order of Being,' connecting oneself to history. To be responsible to others is to be moral, and to be moral is to have the right sort of relationship to other people, a relationship based on ideas of right and wrong, good and evil.

These sorts of moral relationships with other people, and an individual's ability to be responsible to others and to the world, became glaringly difficult in the context of the totalitarian society in which Havel and Patočka lived. With secret police infiltrating social institutions, expectations that citizens inform on one another to the police, and a pervading sense of mistrust and suspicion, what might seem now like a banal observation about moral responsibility, in that context became quite logistically complicated. This police presence was, for Havel, another example of the pseudo-life of untruth:

> Communist power walks though my bugged bedroom and distinguishes my breathing, which is my own private matter, from what I say, which the state cannot be indifferent to... The web of direct and indirect manipulation is a strait-jacket that binds life and necessarily limits the ways it can appear to itself and structure itself. And so it languishes, declines, wastes away. It is cheapened and leveled. It becomes pseudo-life.[31]

What most declined and wasted away in this situation was genuinely honest relationships with other people. Getting at the 'truth of others,'

---

30 Havel, "A Joint Session of the U.S. Congress," Feb. 21, 1990. (AKVH 35359).
31 Havel, "Stories and Totalitarianism," (1987) in *Open Letters*, 337–338.

therefore, became quite difficult, as these social and political circumstances left people isolated from one another, having lost their trust in the world.

Havel and many other dissidents understood the effects of this dynamic and actively sought to overcome the isolation. One tactic of social-political resistance, for example, was to defy the imposed isolation and gather together with other people in spite of legal and practical restrictions. Acknowledging that 'living in truth' was impossible without the company of other people, dissident enclaves created what they came to call 'civil society' and the 'parallel *polis*,' where a certain sort of conversation challenged the 'lies' of the Communist state, as well as other sorts of lies that individuals told themselves to tolerate the repression.[32] If the 'truth of others' had a 'place,' that place was civil society.[33] The seminars that Patočka gave in the living rooms and attics of dissidents' apartments and houses are an example of this sort of gathering of civil society. The ties of responsibility and solidarity created in these small communities were essential to the practice of dissidence, but also had intrinsic value as an activity unto itself.[34] Havel describes what this sort of 'parallel culture' consisted of:

---

32 For a more detailed examination of Havel's idea of civil society, see A. Brinton, "Vaclav Havel's Civil Society," in *Key Concepts in Václav Havel's Core Vocabulary: Analyses and Implications, eds.* David Danaher and Kieran Williams (Prague: Karolinum Press, forthcoming).

33 The use of the term "civil society" by dissidents in Communist countries inspired significant scholarly attention after 1989 to the idea of civil society. For a few representative examples, see: Jean L Cohen and Andrew Arato, *Civil Society and Political Theory* (Cambridge: MIT Press, 1992); Andrew Arato, *Civil Society, Constitution, and Legitimacy* (Landam: Rowman and Littlefield, 2000); Gideon Baker, *Civil Society and Democratic Theory: Alternative Voices* (New York: Routledge, 2002); Michael Bernhard, "Civil Society after the First Transition: Dilemmas of Post-Communist Democratization in Poland and Beyond," *Communist and Post-Communist Studies* 29 (1996): 309–330; Michael Edwards, *Civil Society* (Malden: Polity Press, 2004); Grzegorz Ekiert, *The State Against Society* (Princeton: Princeton University Press, 1996); Marlies Glasius, David Lewis, and Hakan Seckinelgin, eds. *Exploring Civil Society: Political and Cultural Contexts* (New York: Routledge 2004); Adrian Karatnycky, Alexander Motyl, and Aili Piano, eds. *Nations in Transit 1999–2000 Civil Society, Democracy, and Markets in East Central Europe and the Newly Independent States* (Washington, DC: Freedom House, 2001); Sanjeev Khagram, James Riker, Kathryn Sikkink, *Restructuring World Politics: Transnational Social Movements, Networks, and Norms* (Minneapolis: University of Minnesota Press, 2002); Juan J. Linz and Alfred Stepan *Problems of Democratic Transition and Consolidation: Southern Europe, South America, and Post-Communist Europe* (Baltimore: Johns Hopkins University Press, 1996); Guillermo O'Donnell and Philippe C. Schmitter, *Transitions from Authoritarian Rule: Tentative Conclusions about Uncertain Democracies* (Baltimore: Johns Hopkins University Press, 1986); Robert D. Putnam, ed. *Democracies in Flux: The Evolution of Social Capital in Contemporary Society* (Oxford: Oxford University Press, 2002) and *Making Democracy Work: Civic Traditions in Modern Italy* (Princeton: Princeton University Press, 1993); Ernst Gellner, *Conditions of Liberty Civil Society and its Rivals* (New York: Penguin, 1994).

34 Brinton, *Philosophy and Dissidence in Cold War Europe.*

What exactly is a 'parallel culture'? Nothing more and nothing less than a culture, which for various reasons will not, cannot, or may not reach out to the public through the media which fall under state control. In a totalitarian state, this includes all publishing houses, presses, exhibition halls, theaters and concert halls, scholarly institutes, and so on. Such a culture, therefore, can make use of only what is left—typewriters, private studios, apartments, barns, etc.[35]

Another Czech dissident, Martin Palouš, described the effect of these gatherings on those dissidents who met in these spaces to seek out a different kind of social interaction through living in truth:

> They have given priority to the life of the community and have set aside the comforts of private life. As a result, they have seen the benefits that the existence of a genuine public sphere bestows upon individuals as well as the entire community. They also recognize the threat to society, the danger of social paralysis, that stems from the government's attempts to deny the public sphere its freedom. The decision to enter the parallel *polis*, then, should not be seen as a retreat from the world: it is a decision to move to the very center of the crisis besetting our country. Individuals take this step because they believe that only through personal initiative and personal participation can they overcome the crisis.[36]

To recognize one's personal crisis as a constituent part of a political crisis is not a turn of thought that comes naturally in all times and places, but in this context, it was this mode of thinking that created a parallel culture where trust could be renewed, where some truth could be spoken aloud between a few people, and as a result, some kind of community could be created over and against the pressures of the bureaucracy, state power, and the repressive apparatus of Communist politics.

While Havel spoke explicitly about how the structure of repression limited social interaction and living in truth, Patočka did not engage in this type of direct confrontation until he joined Charter 77. Prior to that, Patočka approached the problem of the 'truth of others' through the philosophical problem of intersubjectivity, following the traditions of continental philosophy in general and Husserl in particular. While

---

35 Havel, "Six Asides," in *Open Letters,* 276.
36 Martin Palouš, "The Parallel Polis after Twelve Years," *Cardozo Studies in Law and Literature* 2, no. 1 (Spring, 1990): 59.

'intersubjectivity' has been theorized through many technical philosophical lenses, in more colloquial terms, intersubjectivity consists of that which passes between two subjects, two human persons who are not objects, and 'intersubjectivity' allows them to develop between them a meaningful type of understanding, communication, and interaction. Patočka might say that living in truth is not possible without the subjectivity of others dynamically interacting with the subjectivity of the self. He bases part of his critique of Heidegger, for example, on his inadequate understanding of intersubjectivity:

> This Heideggerian delimitation of the world is incomplete. We need to add that this understanding (understanding itself, its possibilities) takes place in the mode of co-being. Encountering inner-worldly existents is an encounter which involves other beings who exist in the mode of co-being.[37]

In order to co-exist with other human beings, in other words, we have to figure out how to understand our existence in light of how others understand their ability to be "in the mode of co-being" with us. This is a dialogical process, a back and forth between my 'me' and your 'you,' where no one arrives at a clear understanding of others immediately. Yet through attempting to understand someone different from us, there can eventually be meaning in both the struggle and the sacrifice required of seeking intersubjectivity. Ultimately the outcome of this 'co-being' depends upon a sense of responsibility, as Havel also outlined. This idea becomes perhaps most clear in Patočka's justification for joining Charter 77:

> Our people have once more become aware that there are things for which it is worthwhile to suffer, that the things for which we might have to suffer are those which make life worthwhile, and that without them, all our arts, literature, and culture become mere trades leading only from the desk to the pay office and back. We know all that now, not in the least thanks to Charta 77 and all it has meant.[38]

Signing Charter 77 in the midst of totalitarian repression is something that for the preceding several decades seemed intrinsically terrifying and

---

37 Patočka, *BCLW*, 135.
38 Patočka, "Two Charta 77 Texts," (1977) in Kohák, 346.

impractical for the majority of the population. Havel once quipped that "the dissidents were... an isolated handful of suicidal maniacs who might enjoy the tacit admiration of the public but could not expect any visible help from it."[39] So what Patočka might mean here, when he says, "we know all that now... thanks to Charta 77," is that the intrinsic benefits of associating with others in solidarity were not fully evident or obvious before the act itself was undertaken. The value revealed itself only through the action, and this action entailed "the need to accept even discomfort, misunderstanding, and a certain risk."[40] Patočka can retrospectively see meaning created from this action, from this risky co-being, and therein life is made worthwhile by having come together with others, by having suffered, and by having done something more than going "from the desk to the pay office and back." Overcoming those deadening instrumental routines of everyday life forced upon us by circumstances might therefore be one of the intrinsic values of "Charta 77 and all it has meant."

While fully dissecting Patočka's nuanced ideas of intersubjectivity would require a separate analysis, especially given that the philosophical origins of his particular views of intersubjectivity are influenced by a wide range of complex thinkers, what is important in the context of understanding his ideas of 'living in truth,' perhaps more superficially, is how he conceived of intersubjective relations as central to the philosophical pursuit of knowledge about both the self and the wider world. Again, to know oneself was not enough for him, but nor was it enough to merely seek knowledge of the external objective world; one might find partial pieces of empirical facts with such pursuits, but one would never find truth. To cultivate the process of 'living in truth,' Patočka suggests that one needs conversation, a dialogical exchange with others who are willing to *intersubjectively* challenge embedded cultural, historical, and political ideas *together*.

The Politics of Truth and the Truthful Political Life

The third type of truth through which Patočka and Havel can be put into conversation, in addition to the truth of the self and the truth of others, is 'political truth.' While it is possible to see in this term an oxymoronic

---

39 Havel, "Testing Ground," (1989) in *Open Letters*, 374.
40 Patočka, "Two Charta 77 Texts," (1977) in Kohák, 343.

jest, given the presumed dishonesty of politics in many spheres, it is used here to suggest that merely apprehending the 'truth of others' might not always be enough to create a grounding for political action *on behalf of others*. Following Havel, by accepting the possibility of a 'political truth,' one can ask whether there is such a thing as a type of truth that creates possibilities for collective political action. This is an important question for dissidence, as it is conceivable that one might embrace intersubjective truths about others and gather together with them in civil society organizations, but nonetheless still find it impossible to take political action together with others. Living in truth *politically* therefore implies a certain type of action for Havel, also implying the necessity for pre-political ideas that overcome the fears and distastes surrounding politics. Acknowledging the reality of pervasive politics hovering around the self and one's relationship with others is also therefore necessary in order to live in truth, as whatever world one 'lives within,' Havel assumes there will always be politics at stake, sometimes hidden and sometimes overt.

Telling the truth is a difficult thing to do in any politicized space, however. Havel (and Patočka as well) would probably say that the path to political truth begins by knowing yourself as well as others in truthful and moral ways, but that it is also necessary to actively seek to unveil the truth about the relationship between morality and power as it exists in one's own political world. When Havel gave one of his first speeches as president, he declared that he had not been elected in order to continue lying to the people of Czechoslovakia.[41] As his presidential tenure wore on, he was held up against his own criteria of 'living in truth' as a way of critiquing his dishonesties and obfuscations.[42] Yet even if he did not live up to his own ideals, in his writings and speeches, he articulates a vision of what it might mean if politicians and citizens did in fact strive to tell the truth. By arguing that such a thing as 'political truth' exists, it implies that both politicians and citizens should be responsible to one another to tell the truth, and sometimes citizens therefore must be willing to make sacrifices to tell the truth in uncomfortable and dangerous circumstances.[43] When a dissident speaks out against an established power structure

41 Václav Havel, "New Year's Address to the Nation. January 1, 1990." Reprinted in *Art of the Impossible: Politics as Morality in Practice,* trans. Paul Wilson (New York: Fromm International, 1994).

42 See John Keane, *Václav Havel: A Political Tragedy in Six Acts* (New York: Basic Books, 2000); Michael Zantovsky, *Havel: A Life* (New York: Grove Press, 2014).

43 For a full discussion of Patočka's ideas about sacrifice, see Chapter Two.

by using moral arguments, for example, they develop a different kind of 'political truth' than someone who accepts preexisting power structures as 'right' or 'moral.'

What poses the greatest danger to forms of political truth for both Havel and Patočka hinges on not just the problem of totalitarianism, but also on other 'absolutist' structures in multivalent forms, especially those that cultivate 'automatism,' or following along automatically with social and political processes. In spaces of automatism and absolutism, both political truth and a willingness to make sacrifices become more difficult, in part because critical thinking is eclipsed by thinking that is overly automatic, perhaps fearful, and therefore unreflective. While in everyday political discourse 'absolutism' usually means a form of government with a single ruler who is not subject to the checks and balances of other powers or a democratic body politic, for both Havel and Patočka, 'absolutism' was a way of thinking and acting that could appear in any political world, democratic or non-democratic. During Havel's tenure in (democratically-elected) political office, he observed absolutism all around him, solidifying his prior suspicion about how this form of thinking creates immoral politics.

Patočka never addressed absolutist politics so directly as did Havel, but his philosophical work contains deep suspicions about absolutist thinking in general, especially in the realms of science, technology, and mechanization. Patočka's critique of absolutist thinking goes back to the foundations of philosophy, to metaphysics and to questions of whether or not we can arrive at the 'absolute Good' and 'absolute Truth.'[44] When Patočka sets himself apart from Husserl, it is Husserl's ideas about the road to absolute knowledge (the transcendental reduction) that he rejects.[45] While Patočka's path away from Husserl's absolute knowledge at first follows Heidegger's critique of Husserl, Patočka also then departs from Heidegger, primarily for his inability to recognize that the fundamental problem of the "natural" world is "one of good and evil."[46] Therefore Patočka's contribution to this philosophical debate within phenomenology is also a contribution to a debate about absolutism and

---

44 Patočka elaborates this idea in several places. See *Plato and Europe*, 89; and "Negative Platonism: Reflections concerning the Rise, the Scope and the Demise of Metaphysics—and Whether Philosophy Can Survive It," in *Philosophy and Selected Writings*, ed. and trans. E. Kohák (Chicago: University of Chicago Press, 1989), 175–206.

45 Patočka, *BCLW*, 106–107; 110–111; 119–120; 174–175.

46 Patočka, "Husserl on the Crisis of the Sciences and on Phenomenology of the 'Life-world," in Kohák, 236–237.

the constitutive role of morality in everyday human life, a question Havel repeatedly evoked about politics. Going against the absolutist thinking that endangers morality and political truth, therefore, requires conceptions of good and evil, the moral and the immoral, but it also requires tempering the potential absolutism in moral categories themselves.[47] This paradox is key to understanding Patočka's view of the world, but whether or not the paradox can be sustained in other forms of dissident politics depends in part upon what it might mean to live in truth politically according to Patočka's vision.

Some of Patočka's paradoxical but politically-relevant thinking, to take a metaphorical detour to illuminate this tension, occurs on the tightrope he constructed between Husserl and Heidegger and between their specific philosophical forms of relativism and absolutism. In a technical, logical, and philosophical sense, he could be said to be falling off this tightrope at various moments, as the interpretation of an analytical philosopher might point to something like the 'inconsistency of his grounding arguments' as a logical and technical reason to condemn his contradictions (and declare this thinking as a weakness and potentially a failure). Yet for a political theorist trying to make sense of dissidence, even if Patočka might be contradictory, his perspective is rather helpful in solving certain puzzles of political action. On a tightrope, it is impossible to balance unless one stays in motion, and it is Patočka's theory of motion that provides a way to understand why a form of politics suspended between absolute morality and anti-absolutist thinking might be possible in practice.[48] Philosophy and caring for the soul, as described above, are processes of perpetual motion for Patočka; as he puts it: "philosophy is reflection. At the moment when reflection breaks through, when people awaken, this does not mean they stop falling back into slumber. They will live in myth again."[49] This implies that philosophy will have to wake them up again, prompting them to continue again to care for their souls in a new age, collectively perpetuating a moving process onward into eternity. To keep at this task and to keep going, motion and

---

47 This is a heretical inversion of the usual claim that in philosophical method, notions of good and evil are only possible with an underlying belief in absolute truth; see further discussion in Chapter Two about 'negative Platonism.'

48 Patočka endorses 'the absolute' only in the case of morality. When talking about the need for universal human rights in the Charter 77 documents, he states: "We need, in other words, something that in its very essence is not technological, something that is not merely instrumental: we need a morality that is not merely tactical and situational but absolute." In Kohák, 340.

49 Patočka, *Plato and Europe*, 88.

momentum are necessary, and as Patočka describes it: "This [the care of the soul] is the attempt to embody what is eternal within time, and within one's own being, and at the same time, an effort to stand firm in the storm of time, stand firm in all dangers carried with it, to stand firm when the care of the soul becomes dangerous for a human being."[50]

Tightropes are indeed quite dangerous, and if motion is required to prevent falling, then Patočka sees Socrates as trying to navigate between eternal absolutes and the storms of the day by staying in motion. This (moving) 'position' (therefore not a fixed position) requires personal sacrifice in order to stay upright, but it is also a vision where philosophy and politics are, according to Patočka, structurally analogous: "Just as in acting politically humans expose themselves to the problematic nature of action whose consequences are unpredictable and whose initiative soon passes into other hands, so in philosophy humans expose themselves to the problematic being and meaning of what there is."[51] Both philosophy and politics are predictably unpredictable, sharing a structure of the eternal return of the same recurring problematicity. So Patočka asks:

Is not Nietzsche's search for eternity [in the eternal return of the same], his attempt to leap from history into what is beyond time, proof that it is absolutely necessary to reiterate care for the soul even under new circumstances?... We have to say what is, again, over and over, and always in a different way, but it always has to be the same thing![52]

At the risk of mixing metaphors, one might be able to say that the philosopher who steps into the political arena is Sisyphus on a tightrope—Sisyphus for the need to march through the eternal return of the same, and on a tightrope for the need to balance between the needs of today and the imperatives of eternity. This would help illuminate Havel's comments in a speech just after 1989:

The pressure of exhilarating events... abruptly vanished, and I found myself standing bewildered, lacking the inner motivation for anything at all, feeling exhausted, almost irrelevant... Everyday reality was back... We had simply been tossed into the current and forced to swim. It seemed to us that only now could we begin to appreciate fully the weight of the des-

---

50 Patočka, *Plato and Europe*, 87.
51 Patočka, *Heretical Essays*, 63.
52 Patočka, *Plato and Europe*, 90.

tiny we had chosen. That realization brought with it a sudden, and under the circumstances seemingly illogical and groundless, sense of hopelessness… at the deepest core of this feeling there was, ultimately, a sensation of the absurd: what Sisyphus might have felt if one fine day his boulder stopped, rested on a hilltop, and failed to roll back down. It was the sensation of a Sisyphus mentally unprepared for the possibility that his efforts might succeed, a Sisyphus whose life had lost its old purpose and hadn't yet developed a new one."[53]

Havel's expressions of being overwhelmed as a politician at the beginning of his presidency seem to be a response to what Patočka called the task trying to 'stand firm in the storm of time.' Having before been able, as a writer, 'to embody what is eternal within time,' Havel finds himself needing to reconstitute his sense of purpose and possibility beyond himself and 'the everyday' as a politician. He had to find a new way to step outside of his immediate horizon, and such a reconstitution of the self was an exhausting and overwhelming task.

Havel did, though, find a solution to his personal paradox. By the time of his speech to the US Congress, he advocated that intellectuals in general should get involved in politics in an effort to help bring about a moral reconstitution of society and humanity. Those reluctant to lose their 'independence,' ought to, he argued, think of independence in light of other people, not just themselves. "If the hope of the world lies in human consciousness, then it is obvious that intellectuals cannot go on forever avoiding their share of responsibility for the world and hiding their distastes for politics under an alleged need to be independent. It is easy to have independence in your programme and then leave others to carry out that programme. If everyone thought that way, soon no one would be independent."[54] He then went on to point out to the Americans that their own founders were intellectuals. In speaking of the US Constitution, he referenced Thomas Jefferson: "What gave meaning to that act… was the fact that the author backed it up with his life. It was not just his words, it was his deeds as well."[55]

Through his involvement in Charter 77, Patočka chose to back up his ideas with his life. A political life that rejects absolutism is underpinned

---

53 Havel, Speech at the Salzburg Festival, July 1990, in Havel, *The Art of the Impossible: Politics as Morality in Practice*, 49.
54 Havel, "A Joint Session of the U.S. Congress," Feb. 21, 1990. (AKVH 35359).
55 Havel, "A Joint Session of the U.S. Congress," Feb. 21, 1990. (AKVH 35359).

85

by two central tasks for Patočka: one must figure out how to live in a world of good and evil as a moral human being, and while doing that, one must also acknowledge one's particular place in history, the "storm of time," eventually aspiring to participate in the historical process of shaking apart the structures of given meaning and tradition.[56] Each of these tasks requires moving towards a horizon of problematicity, of questioning everything 'given' as potentially a 'problem' to be confronted. Patočka's individual search for the truth of his own being and his theorization of the importance of co-being and intersubjectivity combined through a willingness to question authority that was necessarily political: the inward search for truth, the truth of others, and the truthful political life came together as elements of a more comprehensive notion of 'living in truth.' This synthesis can be seen in *Plato and Europe*, for example, when Patočka discusses how to understand the crisis of the self in light of more general social and political crises:

> The situation of my crisis certainly is connected to other situations through which I am brought into relation with the situations of others... in the end, the situation of all individuals is incorporated into some kind of general situation or, better said, into the entire human situation. And so to reflect upon what we are in—about our situation—ultimately means to reflect how mankind's situation appears today. To philosophize, I think, means to meditate within the entire situation, and to be its reflection."[57]

The purpose of reflection and philosophy, by this account, is to be able to put oneself into a context of universality that includes the presence of others, to look at those relationships critically, then "*to be* its reflection," to embody it and take responsible action.

Havel expressed similar aspirations in his essays and speeches as he tried to articulate his notions of political truth, often self-reflectively using himself as an example of a larger phenomenon within 'the human situation.' In a speech to the French Academy, for example, he told

---

56 Phenomenology itself, the method of investigating the world, is also identified by Patočka as avoiding absolutism: "Phenomenology is a method which can never become a metaphysics. It cannot be the gateway to an absolute thesis. Theses are for it always only occasions for investigating the conditions of the possibility of their givenness. Such inquiry is non-absolute, non-definitive as every thesis. Theses are phenomena of being, not phenomena of themselves." *BCLW*, 120.

57 Patočka, *Plato and Europe*, 3.

a rather philosophical story about his own impatience with post-Communist political reforms:

> I longed desperately for at least some of these problems to be resolved so that I could cross them off the list and put them out of the way... I found it difficult to accept the fact that politics, like history itself, is a never-ending process, a process that never allows us to say something is definitively over. It was as though I had forgotten how to wait, to wait in the way that has meaning... I succumbed to precisely the thing I had been critical of: the destructive impatience of contemporary technocratic civilization. This grows out of a vain ratiocentrism and assumes erroneously that the world is nothing but a crossword puzzle to be solved, that there is only one correct way, the so-called objective way, to solve it, and that it is entirely up to me whether I succeed or not. Without even being aware of it, I too succumbed to the perverted notion that I was the master of reality, that the only task was to improve reality according to some existing recipe, that it was entirely up to me when I do it, and thus there was no reason not to do it right away. In short, I thought time belonged to me.[58]

He then goes on to reflect on the general problems of "contemporary technocratic civilization" and the widespread impatience with what he calls the "sense of time." "The world, Being, and history have their own time," he concludes, and the politician must react to this flow with a certain kind of patience: "He must have the will to open events to the possibility of manifesting themselves as they really are, in their essence. His actions cannot derive from impersonal analysis; they must come out of a personal point of view, which cannot be based on a sense of superiority but must spring from humility."[59] This language echoes Patočka's method of seeking self-awareness through a phenomenological analysis of one's humble place in the world, doing so both within and above the 'storm of time.'

The problem that Havel evokes in this moment of self-examination, the "destructive impatience of contemporary technocratic civilization," is related to the human inability to see 'absolutism' for what it is, as well as the difficulty of finding the truth of others in a way that does justice

---

58 Havel, "A Speech by Mr. Vaclav Havel [at] the Academy of Humanities and Political Science," October, 27 1992 (AKVH 36020).
59 Havel, "A Speech by Mr. Vaclav Havel [at] the Academy of Humanities and Political Science," October, 27 1992 (AKVH 36020).

to our humanity as it arises within political communities. "Technocratic civilization" and the science that created it, therefore, must be made into a moment of problematicity, to use Patočka's formulation. As the next section attempts to show, turning what is 'taken for granted' into a 'problem' requires a particular type of dissident thinking, especially when it comes to the power of science and technology to change the way we think. This will become important in dissecting how science is used (or dismissed) in political debates about climate change in the final chapter as well.

The Crisis of Science and Objective Truth

Phenomenology, the school of philosophy that most influenced both Havel and Patočka, begins with the premise that the phenomena of the world—everything that we see, hear and touch—cannot display its full truth to us at first glance. When we initially apprehend something, what we see is not necessarily what is there or what is true. Phenomenology assumes that what we see is mediated by many layers of our own consciousness, language, cultural learning, and history. The task of phenomenology is to peel back these layers to approach the truth of the phenomenon (see Introduction). Patočka described Husserl's approach to phenomenology as "a method of exceptionally fecund unveiling of things that are not normally thematized because of their trivial nature."[60] Phenomenologists like Husserl and Patočka were therefore concerned with examining what has been taken for granted, looking at it in a new way, applying a certain method of inquiry that unveiled the hidden truth of things, and thereafter saying something new about familiar phenomena. Husserl's last work, *On the Crisis of the European Sciences*, applied this phenomenological method of inquiry to a method of inquiry, that is, to science itself. His wager was that we had come to take the method of scientific inquiry for granted, that science was within all of our life processes in a such a way that we had stopped seeing its influence, and that it had so changed the way we thought about the world that science itself had become too familiar to be seen and critiqued in any meaningful way.

---

60   Patočka, "Husserl on the Crisis of the Sciences and on Phenomenology of the 'Life-world," in Kohák, 232.

Husserl's method of inquiry (itself influenced by science) sought to unveil the inner workings of how we come to know things in the world; the mechanics of his method are less important here than the fact that Patočka carried on his legacy of questioning the presuppositions of the scientific world-view and its impact on human beings and humanity in general, though not fully embracing Husserl's methodology.[61] Patočka also characterized Husserl's work on science as somewhat prophetic:

[The] Husserlian theory of modern science is nothing other than a reflection on the perils of fruitfulness, on the ruses of genius, on the irrationality which rationality itself engenders—not, to be sure, necessarily, yet not wholly accidentally, either. (Might not this shadowy side of rationality, this negative aspect of science, lie at the roots of certain specific evils that not only occasioned the catastrophe that Husserl sought to prevent with his reflections but that, unfortunately, are also still very much with us?)[62]

Husserl was writing in the 1930s; Patočka's samizdat works and lectures from the 1960s and 1970s take up the continued relevance of Husserl's questions about science; Havel's essays and speeches take up this theme from the 1970s into the 1990s. Havel shared many of Patočka's suspicions about technological rationality, and also seemed sympathetic to Heidegger's adaptation of the same question, which became a critique of technology as the product of science.[63] Husserl could see, as Patočka commented, the coming catastrophe of science and technology a decade before it came to full fruition in the concentration camps and atomic bomb.[64] (See Chapters Three and Four.) This prescient understanding

---

61 Patočka, *An Introduction to Husserl's Phenomenology*. trans. Erazim Kohák, ed. James Dodd (Chicago, Open Court 1996); see also James Dodd, *Crisis and Reflection: An Essay on Husserl's Crisis of the European Sciences* (Dordrecht: Kluwer Academic Publishers, 2004).

62 Patočka, "Husserl on the Crisis of the Sciences and on Phenomenology of the 'Life-world," in Kohák, 226.

63 Patočka, "Husserl on the Crisis of the Sciences and on Phenomenology of the 'Life-world," in Kohák, 242. For Havel, this is "the crisis of contemporary technological society as a whole, the crisis that Heidegger describes as the ineptitude of humanity face to face with the planetary power of technology. Technology—that child of modern science, which in turn is a child of modern metaphysics—is out of humanity's control, has ceased to serve us, has enslaved us and compelled us to participate in the preparation of our own destruction. And humanity can find no way out..." Havel, "Power of the Powerless," 1978 (AKVH 35781). See for reference: Martin Heidegger, *The Question concerning Technology* (New York: Harper & Row, 1977).

64 In the wake of World War Two, following this line of thought was by no means limited to Husserl's followers and Heidegger; the social and political philosophers of the Frankfurt School also meditated deeply on this question. While doing a genealogical description of the relationship between phenomenology in Husserl and Heidegger and the Frankfurt School is

continued to matter for Patočka throughout his own work, and Havel's suspicions about 'techno-science' also motivated his inquiries into the idea of 'living in truth.' Both believed that science and rationality could sometimes get in the way of 'truth' and 'the good life.'

Becoming suspicious of science, objectivity, and rationality in our time has become even more complicated than it was for Patočka and Havel. Science and technology are familiar, quotidian, and so embedded into our lives that questioning the presuppositions of the scientific method (outside specialized philosophical circles) is at worst a kind of heresy that will be misunderstood, and at best yields accusations of being a neo-Luddite and phobic of technology.[65] Both Havel and Patočka would argue, however, that we cannot 'live in truth' without being willing to question the predominance of the 'technoscientific' world-view by unveiling the dynamics of power behind such a view. Neither Patočka nor Havel, however, would go so far to say that, thereafter, we then must necessarily condemn the science itself. The point is not to delegitimize scientists and their work, but to undertake the exercise of unveiling, to ask serious questions about what is behind the veil of normalcy supporting the everyday habitual legitimacy of world-views about science.[66] From where they wrote and developed their ideas, from within a totalitarian state that claimed its legitimacy from a rationalized rule-based world-view sometimes even called 'the science of Marxism,'[67] it was perhaps somewhat easier to see the perverse logics of an understanding of the world where science turns people into objects, rationality objectifies us, and something

---

beyond the scope of this analysis, interesting and comparable critiques of science and rationality appear in different forms in the work of Theodore Adorno, Max Horkheimer, Hannah Arendt, Erich Fromm, and Herbert Marcuse. Frankfurt School notable books include Horkheimer and Adorno, *Dialectic of Enlightenment*; Herbert Marcuse, *One Dimensional Man*; Hannah Arendt, *The Human Condition*; Erich Fromm, *Escape from Freedom*.

65 The critique of the 'technocrats' by many populist political parties might be one new place where this discourse has opened up again, and this is a form of dissidence against an absolutist world-view where the 'technocrats' claim to have only one right answer to all political questions. Populists have responded with another absolutist view that delegitimizes technocracy in the name of an exclusionary vision of 'the people.' Neither view would count as 'living in truth' under the frame of this discussion, as both deny the possibility of 'the truth of others' and intersubjectivity, the basis of pluralism. See: Jan Werner-Müller, *What is Populism?* (Philadelphia: University of Pennsylvania Press, 2016).

66 The field of Science and Technology Studies, now represented by established university departments, takes up Husserl's charge in a variety of fruitful ways, crossing the boundaries of academic disciplines to unpack the complicated repercussions of such questions.

67 For a summary of how Marx used ideas of 'science' in his work, and some of the surrounding debates, see Paul Thomas, *Marxism & Scientific Socialism: From Engels to Althusser* (New York: Routledge, 2008).

about our humanity, subjectivity, and moral consciousness comes to be lost in the process of making life technological and 'scientific.'[68]

This is not to say, however, that this is a set of concerns that ended with the end of totalitarian societies built on the politics of objectification and the 'science of Marxism.' Havel is adamant that this was not just a problem of Communist systems, and often argued that the same objectifying rationality of techno-science plagued free democracies, and was perhaps even more veiled, more hidden, and more pernicious, largely because it was taken-for-granted in democracies that science is a savior and problem-solver.[69] Havel experienced this directly within his own social and political circumstances during *and after* Communism. As described above, when he turned his own lens of phenomenological analysis on himself in his moment of impatience, he saw *in himself* "the destructive impatience of contemporary technocratic civilization."[70] This impatience was pervasive for him even in places where people are self-conscious and reflective, and even when they know how scientific rationality restricts our mode of thinking. Special effort, therefore, was required to unveil the degree to which science alters our humanity.

The core concern of Havel and Patočka is that rational scientific world-views are without a conscience and do not have a way to delineate

68 Havel, "Politics and Conscience" in *Living in Truth,* ed. Jan Vladislav (London: Faber and Faber, 1986) 142: "As the apex of it all, man has constructed a vision of a scientifically calculable and technologically achievable 'universal welfare,' that need only be invented by experimental institutes while industrial and bureaucratic factories turn it into reality. That millions of people will be sacrificed to this illusion in scientifically run concentration camps is not something that concerns our modern man unless by chance he himself lands behind barbed wire and is thrown drastically back upon his natural world. The phenomenon of empathy, after all, belongs with that abolished realm of personal prejudice which had to yield to science, objectivity, historical necessity, technology, system, and the apparat—and those, being impersonal, cannot worry. They are abstract and anonymous, ever utilitarian, and thus ever a priori innocent... So, too, the totalitarian systems warn of something far more serious than Western rationalism is willing to admit. They are, most of all, a convex mirror of the inevitable consequences of rationalism, a grotesquely magnified image of its own deep tendencies, an extreme offshoot of its own development and an ominous product of its own expansion. They are a deeply informative reflection of its own crisis."

69 "This planetary challenge to the position of human beings in the world is, of course, also taking place in the Western world, the only difference being the social and political forms it takes. Heidegger refers expressly to a crisis of democracy. There is no real evidence that Western democracy, that is, democracy of the traditional parliamentary type, can offer solutions that are any more profound. It may even be said that the more room there is in the Western democracies (compared to our world) for the genuine aims of life, the better the crisis is hidden from people and the more deeply do they become immersed in it." Havel, "Power of the Powerless," 1978 (AKVH 35781).

70 Havel, "A Speech by Mr. Vaclav Havel [at] the Academy of Humanities and Political Science," October, 27 1992 (AKVH 36020).

moral bearings for individuals or communities. Adherence to rational scientific views exclusively, and holding an absolute ardent 'faith' in science, can therefore be morally dangerous and dehumanizing, as a mechanistic world-view calls for the automation of human action and decision-making. Havel's term for this process in "Power of the Powerless" is 'automatism:' "The automatism of the post-totalitarian system is merely an extreme version of the global automatism of technological civilization. The human failure that it mirrors is only one variant of the general failure of modern humanity."[71] During his time in political office, he continued to see this problem manifesting itself in the bureaucratic processes of everyday politics, economic policy considerations, and everywhere within the reasoning of 'experts' that came into his life as a president. He pushed back against this tendency he saw around himself, but was continually frustrated by it:

> It is impossible to avoid projecting scientific knowledge into specific decisions, including decisions of the economic and political variety. Yet two things must always be kept in mind. In the first place, scientific knowledge can serve life, but life is certainly not here merely to confirm someone's scientific discoveries and thus serve science. And in the second place, science may be a remarkable product and instrument of the human spirit, but it is not itself a guarantee of a humane outcome. A familiar example: science can lead people to discover atomic energy, but it cannot guarantee that they will not blow each other up. Clearly, nothing can get along without the participation of powers as unscientific as healthy common sense and the human conscience. Not even economic reform.[72]

In the same set of essays where he wrote this passage (*Summer Meditations*), Havel also reflected on the fact that journalists had started to ask him whether his time in political office had convinced him that 'living in truth' was a naïve idea, requiring a revision after his transition from dissident to politician.[73] Havel rejected that question, and wrote about how he had become even more convinced of the need to live in truth and retain moral foundations and human conscience, in a large part because of what he saw happening within bureaucratic and political structures.

71 Havel, "Power of the Powerless," 1978 (AKVH 35781).
72 Havel, "What I Believe," in *Summer Meditations*, trans. Paul Wilson (New York: Vintage Books, 1993) 67.
73 Havel, *Summer Meditations*, 10.

Keeping a watchful eye on "the destructive impatience of contemporary technocratic civilization" was what he thought every politician ought to be doing.[74]

Havel also knew that the problem of scientific rationality diluting moral conscience was out there on the horizon, a problem toward which one could move with the possibilities of new questions, but that it was not a problem that could be fully solved anytime in the near future. The habits of thinking derived from technocratic civilization were deep and lasting, and the power of future technologies and scientific discoveries were still unknown in their potential effects. It was common for Havel to use environmental destruction as one example in these discussions. In his speech to the US Congress, he links the problem of science to a form of modern hubris vis-à-vis the environment:

> We are still under the sway of the destructive and thoroughly vain belief that man is the pinnacle of creation, and not just a part of it, and that therefore everything is permitted. There are still many who say they are concerned not for themselves but for the cause, while they are demonstrably out for themselves and not for the cause at all. We are still destroying the planet that was entrusted to us, and its environment. We still close our eyes to the growing social, ethnic and cultural conflicts in the world. From time to time we say that the anonymous megamachinery we have created for ourselves no longer serves us but rather has enslaved us, yet we still fail to do anything about it.[75]

Havel believed the problem could be addressed, even if he knows the momentum of technology will outpace our ability to imagine humane responses to such "megamachinery" (see Chapter 5). He was echoing in this speech what he had already written in "Power of the Powerless:"

> If a better economic and political model is to be created, then perhaps more than ever before it must derive from profound existential and moral changes in society. This is not something that can be designed and introduced like a new car. If it is to be more than just a new variation of the old degeneration, it must above all be an expression of life in the process of transforming itself. A better system will not automatically ensure a better

---

74 Havel, "A Speech by Mr. Vaclav Havel [at] the Academy of Humanities and Political Science," October, 27 1992 (AKVH 36020).
75 Havel, "A Joint Session of the U.S. Congress," Feb. 21, 1990 (AKVH 35359).

life. In fact, the opposite is true: only by creating a better life can a better system be developed.[76]

Here he is expressing a form of 'living in truth' which arises by thinking through the problem of "a better life," or the perennial philosophical question of what it means to 'live a good life,' and linking it to the question of rethinking old models of 'automatic' politics. Figuring out political relations with others is not a process like designing a new car, but rather a moral and existential question, and the hubris of a technological approach will, he believes, at some point reveal its inhumanity.

Through the lens of Husserl, Patočka offers an explanation for why such technocratic approaches will necessarily come to haunt us:

> Thus the world comes to be equated with an aggregate of physicalist structures (not physical only, but objective and efficacious and consistently mathematically construed), with a few remaining islands of subjective translations of secondary appearances. This, as a view, both extremely effective and extremely flat and tedious, has absolutely nothing to say to concrete human beings, as this complete draining of all meaning, raised to the status of ultimate... provokes reactions like irrationalism and mysticism, a reversion to action free of a rational basis, a flight to the realms of make-believe or to the sphere of pure feelings and mere corporeity.[77]

In other words, something in the human soul will revolt against excess rationality and all that is "effective and efficacious and consistently mathematically construed," and this will produce excess in the opposite direction. "Mere corporeity," only being concerned with the body, is a rejection of higher order moral and transcendent concerns. "Mysticism," "make-believe," and the "sphere of pure feelings" are dangerous places to make politics. The rise of nationalist movements after the collapse of Communism might be one example; the methods of religiously-motivated terrorism might be another; populist movements that attack the 'technocratic elite' while circulating in conspiracy theories of 'make-believe' might also be explained in this light.

Living in a Communist society, Havel and Patočka had access to something those in Western democracies do not: an example of what

---

76 Havel, "Power of the Powerless," 1978 (AKVH 35781).
77 Patočka, "Husserl on the Crisis of the Sciences and on Phenomenology of the 'Life-world," in Kohák, 230–231.

happened when an ideology based on rationalism and historical determinism (scientific Marxism) attempted to put itself into practice in the everyday lives of human beings by claiming to control every aspect of life 'scientifically.' This drained much of life's meaning, while outwardly claiming to be the ultimate and absolute 'scientific' truth; Communism had a 'rational' explanation for the way history had unfolded, it described specific 'mechanics' to show how human beings have interacted with one another throughout the centuries, and it offered a 'formula' for how our supposedly rational-choosing selves should 'operate' in social and political circumstances. There was a blueprint for everything, and that flat and tedious world led to a dehumanized existence under the philosophical ruse of a scientific method. As will be seen in later examples, transcending tedious everydayness is often what it means to be a dissident, and within Patočka's ideas there are resources for how to unveil the manifestations of one's manipulation by a techno-scientific system that pretends to know you better than you know yourself.[78] As Patočka explains:

> Science, the vital foundation of our life as a community, without which mankind could simply not survive in the industrial age, lies at the same time at the roots of the emptiness of modern life, of its anonymization, of the draining of all tangible meaningfulness in a bottomless abstraction. That which makes life possible by supplying us with the means of living at the same time strips life of all higher reasons for living, leaving us alone in the face of the chaos of instincts and of traditions devoid of any but merely factual cohesion. Today we might put it even more strongly: the very practical advantages bestowed by science have become problematic, the emptiness of life has become almost tangible with the absurd possibility of a negation of all life, brought about by a destructive power surpassing all that humans can construct and produce positively.

> Having first furnished the instruments of suicide to a Europe which, with its monopoly on rational civilization, had for two centuries exercised a virtually complete mastery over the globe and had identified itself with humanity as such, this power has today created a setting for an age of megasocieties which is now beginning to unfold before our eyes, an

---

78 The online world of marketing algorithms comes to mind as one possible further contemporary exploration of this line of thought.

age characterized by growing anxiety and by the frequent refusal of the younger generations to participate in it.[79]

These passages are, in part, Patočka summarizing some of Husserl's ideas, and in part an extended response to the destruction of the World Wars, but he is also extending and applying the core of those ideas to his own time. He does not specifically elaborate which "younger generations" are refusing to participate, but given that this essay was written in 1971, he was likely referencing the activism in his own country during the Prague Spring in 1968, but perhaps also the student protest movements in both Europe and the United States at the same time (see Chapter Three).

Havel and Patočka are also suspicious of 'techno-science' because they saw how these modalities of rationalized technocratic thinking do not seem to lead to action, nor to individual human agency, nor to meaningful social bonds, nor to a sense that one can change the world. Instead, science and technology send the message to the average person that there are large, impersonal, automatic systems that are too big for any one person to face off against and attempt to influence. This rationalized world-view, therefore, further emasculates and pacifies populations already subject to political and social controls. When Havel thinks of a solution, he turns to discussing how "a change will have to derive from human existence, from the fundamental reconstitution of the position of people in the world, their relationships to themselves and to each other, and to the universe."[80] When Patočka comments on what he thinks Husserl did not understand about finding a solution to the problem, he asks a question: "Can a concept of our life-world as a world of good and evil lead us to that [solution]? Perhaps so, if it can show us something real that is capable of bearing something like a life-fulfilling meaning, valid not only subjectively but, so to speak, in itself."[81] Turning to a world-view where good and evil matter (in Patočka's case) and a world where people are fundamentally responsible to themselves, other people, and the universe (in Havel's case) is turning toward a certain type of political world. Writing from within his attempts to create a renewed political

79   Patočka, "Husserl on the Crisis of the Sciences and on Phenomenology of the 'Life-world," in Kohák, 232–233.
80   Havel, "Power of the Powerless," 1978 (AKVH 35781).
81   Patočka, "Husserl on the Crisis of the Sciences and on Phenomenology of the 'Life-world," in Kohák, 237.

world, Havel connects his critique of techno-science with his belief in the politics of human responsibility:

> The only thing that worries me is the depersonalization and dehumanization of politics that has come about with the progress of civilization. An ordinary human being, with a personal conscience, personally answering for something to somebody and personally and directly taking responsibility, seems to be receding farther and farther from the realm of politics. Politicians seem to turn into puppets that only look human and move in a giant, rather inhuman theatre; they appear to become merely cogs in a huge machine, objects of a major civilizational automatism which has gotten out of control and for which nobody is responsible.[82]

While humans may think the power of scientific objectivity gives them control of the universe, in fact it is not the unlimited and complete power it can seem; furthermore, if the sort of power one seeks in politics tries to match that illusion of power with absolute knowledge, for Havel and Patočka, this sort of politics will dehumanize its subjects, turning them into objects. The political mode of 'living in truth,' therefore, is a combination of knowing oneself, knowing one's own community, and realizing that one's place in the universe might go beyond what techno-science has determined mechanistically. These ideas evoke a kind of politics based on the power of those who know the limits of their power. This sense of politics will appeal to those who, with humility, look towards horizons of possibility, and to those who can restrain themselves from speeding towards hasty technological or technocratic fixes.

Living in Truth as a Dissident

Given this wariness toward automatism and absolutism in politics, neither Havel nor Patočka would argue that there could be a genuine 'political science,' or a study of politics where the outcomes were predictable and regimented in a frame that resembled 'techno-science.' There is, however, common ground underneath their beliefs that might be said to represent something like a political *theory*. The various elements of living in truth discussed here could be part of a theoretical vision: seeking the

---

82   Havel, "Speech: The Onassis Prize for Man and Mankind," May 24, 1993. (AKVH 35480).

inward truth of the self and the truth of others in a civil society are necessary precursors to political action, as is being able to see the troubling implications of a society organized around a techno-scientific world-view. These ideas are general enough to be applied to a variety of political contexts both contemporary and historical, and thus have innovative theoretical content.

One moment where this possible theoretical synthesis can be glimpsed is in Havel's 1984 essay "Politics and Conscience." Despite the relationship that Havel and Patočka had with each other, the cases where Havel cites Patočka directly are relatively few. One such instance is worth quoting at length from "Politics and Conscience," as it shows how Havel thought about the political and theoretical implications of Patočka's ideas:

> It is becoming evident that wholly personal categories like good and evil still have their unambiguous content and, in certain circumstances, are capable of shaking the seemingly unshakeable power with all its army of soldiers, policemen and bureaucrats. It is becoming evident that politics by no means need remain the affair of professionals and that one simple electrician [Lech Walesa in Poland leading the Solidarity movement] with his heart in the right place, honouring something that transcends him and free of fear, can influence the history of his nation... Under the 'rule of everydayness' we have to descend to the very bottom of a well before we can see the stars... When Jan Patočka wrote about Charter 77, he used the term "solidarity of the shaken." He was thinking of those who dared resist impersonal power and to confront it with the only thing at their disposal, their own humanity. Does not the perspective of a better future depend on something like an international community of the shaken which, ignoring state boundaries, political systems, and power blocs, standing outside the high game of traditional politics, aspiring to no titles and appointments, will seek to make a real political force out of a phenomenon so ridiculed by the technicians of power—the phenomenon of human conscience?[83]

In some sense, this essay is Havel's full tribute to Patočka, even more than "Power of the Powerless," which was directly dedicated to him. "Politics and Conscience" is a description of what Havel calls "anti-political" politics, a type of politics based on the ideas already described here:

---

83   Havel, "Politics and Conscience," in *Open Letters,* 271.

turning inward toward the human conscience to find truth, acting in solidarity with those who similarly understand the predicament of human isolation and the destructive power of techno-science, and putting truth and morality into practice in order to transcend the 'everydayness' of a stultifying totalized existence.

While more is elaborated in Chapters Four and Five about Patočka's notion of 'solidarity of the shaken,' what is illuminating about Havel's use of the idea in this passage is that he understands a mode of solidarity as a precursor to an *international* community that would identify itself around a way of thinking about human conscience and morality. Patočka writes that the "solidarity of the shaken is the solidarity of those who understand,"[84] and then Havel takes this notion and expands it globally, relating political action to the connection between the truth of oneself and the truth of the world. For Havel, the 'place' of truth in this sort of 'living in truth' is the bridge between the personal and the global; the "international community of the shaken" connects the individual's recognition of his or her 'shaken' truth with global solidarity. While Patočka never gets this specific, with his extrapolation, Havel manages to presage what became after 1989 the phenomenon of 'global civil society,' that is, the world-wide network of NGOs, international organizations, and citizen's groups that expanded exponentially at the end of the Cold War.[85] This was something like an "international community of the shaken," and the contemporary climate change activism discussed in the last chapter is put forward as another illustrative example, demonstrating part of Patočka's 'global' appeal. There is something within all of these ideas that can indeed cross state boundaries, question the power blocs of state sovereignty, and do so in the name of human conscience.

Havel never wrote a systematic political theory treatise, nor did Patočka, but it might be possible to say that Havel's writings have left behind such a thing that can be called 'Havelian politics.'[86] As this conversation has hoped to demonstrate, that view of politics and the world

---

84 Patočka, *Heretical Essays*, 134–136.
85 The publication that best tracked this phenomenon from 2001 until 2012 was the "Global Civil Society Yearbook," based at London School of Economics, http://www.gcsknowledgebase .org/.
86 Some commentary on Havel's political thought and political life: Aviezer Tucker, *The Philosophy and Politics of Czech Dissidence from Patočka to Havel* (Pittsburgh: University of Pittsburgh Press, 2000); David Danaher, *Reading Václav Havel* (Toronto: University of Toronto Press, 2015); Marketa Goetz-Stankiewcz and Phyllis Carey, eds., *Critical Essays on Václav Havel* (New York: G.K. Hall and Co., 1999); John Keane, *Václav Havel: A Political Tragedy in Six Acts* (London: Bloomsbury, 1999); James Pontuso, *Václav Havel: Civic Responsibility in the Postmodern Age*

has much affinity with Patočka, demonstrating that Patočka is himself, in his philosophical thinking, creating a bridge between the personal and the global, the philosophical and the political. If this might be Sisyphus on a tightrope, it might not be the place for everybody, just as the police interrogation room where he spent some of his last days is not for everybody. Yet there is a framework here for moving forward on that tightrope: for dissidents and activists both historical and contemporary, his ideas can add depth, meaning, and purpose to our understanding of politics. The historical and contemporary examples that follow are chosen to show moments in time where Patočka might have recognized his own dissident sensibility in the political actions of others.

(Oxford: Rowan and Littlefield, 2004); Delia Popescu, *Political Action in Václav Havel's Thought: The Responsibility of Resistance* (Lexington Books, 2012).

Chapter Two
Care of the Soul:
in Conversation with Dietrich Bonhoeffer

In the years leading up to his execution by the Nazis, theologian Dietrich Bonhoeffer had been working on a book he never finished. The fragments were posthumously published and edited by his close friend Eberhard Bethge as *Ethics*.[1] We learn from these writings what it was like for Bonhoeffer to think about ethical questions during a time when everyone was, he observed, "oppressed by a super-abounding reality of concrete ethical problems."[2] This was a complicated task, as World War Two in Germany shone light onto humankind's ability to be 'ethical' and 'unethical' in an exceptional way, and for Bonhoeffer it was possible to "ask whether there have ever before in human history been people with so little ground beneath their feet—people to whom every available alternative seemed equally intolerable, repugnant and futile."[3] The ethical paradoxes of this moment in history echoed moments previously imagined for Bonhoeffer mostly within dramatic fiction:

---

1   *The Complete Dietrich Bonhoeffer Works, Volume 6: Ethics*, New York: Fortress Press, 2014. The texts have been sequenced and arranged differently by various editors in different volumes and translations. Bethge edited and compiled the first German editions. For a description of the various scholarly efforts to understand and compose this posthumous text, see Clifford Green, *Theology of Sociality*, 302–304.

2   Bonhoeffer, *Ethics*, 64. This is quoted from the 1955 edition, edited by Eberhard Bethge. Trans. Neville Horton Smith, (New York: Macmillian, 1955). This is a publication which is separate from *The Complete Works*, where *Ethics* also appears. It is specified below which of the different translations of *Ethics* I am using. The history of the translation and compilation of Bonhoeffer's *Ethics* is not so different than the complications of turning Patočka's samizdat editions into the complete works. See: Ivan Chvatík, Pavel Kouba, Miroslav Petříček, «La structure des œuvres complètes de Patočka comme problème d'interprétation» in Tassin and Richir, *Jan Patočka: philosophie, phénoménologie, politique*, 223–230.

3   Dietrich Bonhoeffer, *Letters and Papers from Prison*, enlarged edition, ed. Eberhard Bethge, trans. Reginald Fuller and Frank Clark (New York: Touchstone, 1997) 3.

Shakespeare's characters walk in our midst. But the villain and the saint have little to do with systematic ethical studies. They emerge from primeval depths and by their appearance they tear open the infernal or the divine abyss from which they come and enable us to see for a moment into mysteries of which we had never dreamed.[4]

Bonhoeffer could see into the cosmic abyss tearing open around him, so he set out to reconcile evidence from these "primeval depths" and "mysteries" with his desire to add to theological and philosophical theories about "systematic ethics."[5] The context of his life gave him the hard case; his theories were forced to respond. Bonhoeffer's work was interrupted by daily ethical dilemmas of dramatic life-or-death consequence, including his imprisonment for supporting an unsuccessful assassination attempt on Hitler's life,[6] resulting in his book *Ethics* being left incomplete after his execution in 1945.

In both his actions and his writings, Bonhoeffer opens possible grounds for a dialogue with Patočka's ideas about why it is worth dissenting against injustice in hopeless circumstances, and why it is worth risking one's life in order to live in truth. As the title of this chapter suggests, 'the care of the soul' is at the center of the structure of thinking that Patočka and Bonhoeffer might share. While Patočka's idea of the 'care of the soul' is a multifaceted concept, what Bonhoeffer and Patočka have in common is a notion of 'care' and a notion of 'the soul' where one finds truth by looking upward and outward at the same time. In other words, the task of 'caring for the soul' requires examining the world by looking upward vertically to 'higher' things (for Bonhoeffer towards God, for Patočka towards transcendence in history) and also looking outward horizontally to daily life and the world of human phenomenon, examining how people make their lives, interpret their world, and face death together in communities.[7] It might be the case that all dissidents

---

4   Bonhoeffer, *Ethics*, 64.
5   Bonhoeffer, *Ethics*, 64.
6   David Gides, *Pacifism, Just War and Tyrannicide: Bonhoeffer's Church-World Theology and his Changing Forms of Political Thinking and Involvement* (Eugene: Pickwick Publications, 2011).
7   Examining the intersection of the horizontal and vertical aspects of life is nothing new to philosophy; it is as old as the difference between Plato and Aristotle, as depicted in Rafael's painting that shows Plato pointing upward and Aristotle with his hand horizontally outstretched. In an article taking up the philosophical technicalities of the horizontal and vertical in Patočka, Michael Staudigl argues that it is not caring for the soul where this intersection is most salient and important, but rather within Patočka's three movements of human existence. See "Human Existence and the Vertical Life," in L. Hagedorn and J. Dodd, eds. *The New Yearbook of*

everywhere have to engage in some variant of looking upward and outward at the same time.

As a dissident living in complicated times, Bonhoeffer is also representative of a hard case of a different sort, as he was a Christian who turned to violent methods considered unchristian, as well as being a religious leader who turned toward the politics of the world rather than looking exclusively towards heavenly pursuits. As a result, reading Bonhoeffer requires attending to certain contradictions; his life and way of thinking then seem to necessitate a theory about the structure of dissidence that should be able to explain such an embrace of contradiction, Combining upward and outward thinking, as I will argue throughout this chapter, can look contradictory on the surface, as it did in Bonhoeffer's case, but this framing might also be deeply practical for kindling a deeper sense of dissidence through a self-awareness of self-contradiction. Reading Bonhoeffer in light of Patočka shows that being able to think in two different directions at once is central to the task of caring for the soul, as it reveals and makes explicit the tensions involved in understanding a certain human relationship to the world, as well as opening the possibility of translating a bidirectional vision of the world into historically meaningful action. An understanding of contradiction is at the center of seeing why this structure of thinking is important for any dissident; part of that bidirectional 'structure' can only 'stand' by being in tension with itself, and from that tension emerges a type of action that is 'spiritual' and 'political' at the same time, rising *above* the human world in order to live more authentically *in* the human world. To get above the world while living within it might require some mental acrobatics, but on this account, such thinking is necessary to care for the soul, both one's own soul and that of the community.[8]

To make such generalizations about Bonhoeffer's work, as with Patočka's oeuvre, requires attending to the diversity of texts and writings they authored, including relying on their 'unsystematic' and unfinished

Phenomenology and Phenomenological Philosophy XIV—2015: Religion, War and the Crisis of Modernity, a special issues dedicated to the philosophy of Jan Patočka (New York: Routledge, 2015). The connection between the third movement and horizontal and vertical thinking is also discussed in Chapter Three in the case of Gandhi.

8   For more in-depth commentaries on Patočka's idea of care of the soul, see: Martin Cajthaml, *Europe and the Care of the Soul. Jan Patočka's Conception of the Spiritual Foundations of Europe* (Nordhausen: Verlag Traugott Bautz; 2014); James Mensch, "Caring for the Asubjective Soul," in *Thinking After Europe*, Tava and Meacham, eds.; James Mensch, *Patočka's Asubjective Phenomenology: Toward a New Concept of Human Rights* (Würzburg: Königshausen und Neumann, 2016).

works that emerged out of complicated political circumstances. In such unsystematic works, it is sometimes only possible to see the borders around empty spaces where a more structured theory might have arisen in an environment with less political urgency and repression, where the authors might have had the time and space to complete their works, among other conveniences they did not always have.[9] This openness (perhaps incompleteness) in their work, however, can be a resource and not a limitation, as what follows can be seen as the architectural plans for a certain type of house, usable by multiple future builders and even more future inhabitants. From the architectural structure shared by Patočka and Bonhoeffer, one can draw ample space for many different ideas of future dissidence to be built and to dwell within, and from this, a provisional vision might emerge for examining modes of dissidence receptive and attentive to local environments, as not all dissidence looks (or should look) the same.[10]

If there were four concepts of truth at stake in the conversation between Patočka and Havel, then what follows here might be thought of as three areas where Bonhoeffer and Patočka would find common ground for a conversation about why 'care of the soul' should be included in any dissident's approach to the world. The structure of this analysis will therefore follow Patočka's assertion that caring for the soul has three components:

> (1) The general philosophical teaching that brings the soul into connection with the structure of being; (2) a teaching about the life of the philosopher in the community and in history... [and thus] the center of all state life and also the axis of historical occurrence; and (3) the teaching about the soul as the principle of individual life... exposed to the fundamental experience and test... of death and the question of meaning.[11]

---

9   See discussion of these types of text in the introduction.

10 Patočka was aware of Bonhoeffer, and mentions him once as a student of theologian Karl Barth (*Sebrané spisy Jana Patočky*, Vol. 2, "Češi," ed. Karel Palek and Ivan Chvatík, 347), and mentions Barth a couple other times (as indexed in his complete works). A more specific study of Patočka's writings in this area would be necessary to fully illuminate whether there is any deeper engagement with Barth worth analyzing.

11 Jan Patočka, *Plato and Europe*, trans. Petr Lom (Stanford: Stanford University Press, 2002) 180 (abbreviated hereafter *PE*); Eric Manton, on the political implications of these three forms: "Patočka agreed with the classical concept of political philosophy, in which the soul correlates with society. Patočka talked about how Plato dealt with the issue of the soul on three levels: the ontological, the political, and the existential... All three levels and precisely their interconnection is the political. Already from his earliest writings, Patočka presents his

Philosophically, these three ways of caring for the soul might represent the ontological, the social-political, and the existential understandings of the world. Following this pattern, three aspects of Bonhoeffer's thinking will be put in conversation with Patočka: religionless Christianity (an ontological idea), sacrifice (a social-political idea), and worldliness (*Mundigkeit* in German) (an existential idea). The goal of discussing these ideas is to show how a general ontological vision of the world forms the basis for a social-political vision that engages an existential concept of the self, the combination rendering the soul cared for through both action and thinking. Or, in more simplified terms, this conversation shows how general ideas about the cosmos can influence politics through changing one's conception of oneself. The notions that 'I must dissent,' or 'I must make sacrifices for my community,' or 'I must get involved in politics' can often have a pre-political basis in theological and philosophical ideas. Only certain theological and philosophical ideas, however, give rise to such thoughts and corresponding actions. Bonhoeffer's ideas of 'religionless Christianity,' 'sacrifice,' and worldliness (*Mundigkeit*) are examples of ideas that give rise to action, and each has an analogue in Patočka's thought. Each will be described briefly here, and then elaborated upon the sections below with further examples.

Firstly, Bonheoffer's idea of 'religionless Christianity' and Patočka's idea of 'negative Platonism similarly demand a thought-process that moves upward and outward at the same time. Bonhoeffer's idea of the soul is underpinned by theistic beliefs (vertical thinking), but is also deeply rooted in the world (horizontal thinking); he looks upward to a Christian god, but he also questions not just the 'institutionalized religions' that failed to act ethically in Nazi Germany, but also rejects 'religious' ideas that ignore the urgency of the here-and-now by promoting self-deception and passivity. Patočka's concept of the soul has a similar bidirectional structure. His notion of the soul is Platonic, but it is Platonic in a 'negative' sense, where human experience is defined by a stance of questioning that allows one to look upward and transcend the given world, but for Patočka, one must also reject the absolute notions of Platonic forms in light of the ontological condition of being placed within history, including the task of attending to the uncertainty

---

understanding of politics as concerning the historical person living philosophically within the world. Hence he focused from the beginning on an interpretation of politics that encompassed the classical multi-level, holistic view of that which is political." Manton, *Living in Problematicity*, 71.

of the retreating horizon of the future. These two paradoxical stances about 'the structure of being' show two very different ways of combining upward and outward thinking, stances that might seem oxymoronic, but which in fact might be deeply important for political praxis.

Secondly, both Patočka and Bonhoeffer thought deeply about sacrifice, and what proper, good, and justified sacrifice might entail. For both, the willingness to sacrifice one's life (as well as undertaking the lesser sacrifices of everyday comforts that politics can demand) had origins in a notion of care for the world—a care that went beyond care for any particular thing, person, or idea, but was rather for the whole structure of society, politics, and history. To give up part (or all) of oneself to care for the world requires believing that one's role in that lived (outward) world is sustained by a higher (upward) force that might require the ultimate voluntary sacrifice of oneself and one's place within the 'axis of historical occurrence.' Thinking through the sacrifice necessary for dissidence, therefore, requires rethinking the relationship between the self and the community on both horizontal and vertical axes, necessarily reaching toward an understanding between the care of the soul and the care for the world.

Thirdly, Patočka and Bonhoeffer also share a sense that caring for the soul and thinking through the difficult and intractable problems of the self and the world makes one a tougher, stronger, and more solid person, even if such thinking can alienate one from the 'common life' through a forceful insistence on overcoming illusions and self-deception. In one essay, Patočka will call this character trait 'amplitude,' and Bonhoeffer will refer to something similar as maturity and worldliness [*Mundigkeit*]. Both call for an overcoming of childish illusions and everyday platitudes through a more rigorous approach to truth. This character trait, and the corresponding 'principles of individual life,' permit a kind of thinking that gives one the courage to act within history, and thus opens the possibility of the transformation of history through action. As both claim in a somewhat Nietzschean way, cultivating this maturity in oneself requires an existential stance that combines the ontological sense of caring for the soul and the social-political sense, intertwining the three components of Patočka's idea of caring for the soul (as quoted above).

These three areas of overlap between Patočka and Bonhoeffer lead toward an argument about what caring for the soul in times of political urgency might look like, reiterating Bonhoeffer's question about whether Shakespearean heroes and villains may or may not help us understand ethical action. 'Care of the soul' in the prior chapter was characterized as one component of living in truth: one cannot live in truth without caring for one's soul, particularly in regard to the task of knowing the inward truth of the self, so caring for the soul is one basis of all that comes after, in both the search for truth and the action it might underpin. Caring for the soul, however, is revealed here as more than just an inward subjective truth, for if one does not care for the soul, Patočka might say, it is difficult to figure out how to live in truth, how to create communities of solidarity, or how to do all the other things necessary to care for the world by supporting things like Charter 77 and assassination attempts on the Hitlers of the future.

To follow the house metaphor used earlier, if modes of truth (as discussed in Chapter One) might be the architectural layers at the foundation, modes of caring for the soul might be the next layer, making up the rooms that require a shared grounding, but subdividing that ground into particular areas of dwelling. This is not an entirely tidy floor plan, and these do not map precisely onto the modalities of living in truth already outlined, but they are additions to the larger architecture at stake in the whole account, that is, about constructing a vision of what it means to 'think like a dissident' in light of Patočka's ideas. Bonhoeffer, as a thinker and as a dissident, is a *partial* illumination of the potentials of this structure of thinking. If they were to have a conversation, Patočka and Bonhoeffer would not agree on the all the details of the complete architectural plan, but this is an attempt to show how they might agree on the necessary inclusion of these 'rooms,' or these areas of thinking where upward and outward visions would come together in caring for the soul. Such architecture might be, as Patočka describes, related to how "our mental development is not, figuratively speaking, a mere change of the objects in our living space, but rather movement from room to room, during which horizons into the indefinite open up from all sides."[12] In the spirit of this architectural notion, this is a movement from room to room meant to open up the horizons of experience from multiple sides.

---

12 Patočka, "Life in Balance, Life in Amplitude," in *Living in Problematicity*, ed. and trans., Manton, 36.

The Soul as "a Structure of Being": Religionless Christianity and Negative Platonism

If Patočka's notion of a soul might also be a certain sort of architectural plan out of which can be built multiple conceptions of what counts as a human being, he chooses to combine the Christian conception of a soul with the idea of 'care of the soul' from ancient Greek philosophy, while also attentive to Heidegger's concept of 'care.'[13] What emerges is a set of claims about how the care of the soul arises through a certain way of looking at the relationship between life, death, humanity, and the world-in-crisis. In Patočka's own words, the care of the soul is "a constant conversation of the soul with itself and with others;"[14] it is a desire to "be in unity with one's own self;"[15] it "is incredible work, the work of a whole life;"[16] it is one point where the major differences between Plato and Aristotle can be reconciled;[17] it is the beginning of the spirit of European history, symbolized by a certain way of doing philosophy, history and politics;[18] it is "inseparable from care for death which becomes the true care for life";[19] the soul that is cared for can become "that within us which is related to that un-perishing and imperishable component of the whole which makes possible truth and in truth... an authentically human

---

13 For scholarship on the role of Christianity in Patočka's work, see: Jacques Derrida, *The Gift of Death*, trans. David Wills (Chicago: University of Chicago Press, 1995); Eddo Evink, "The Gift of Life: Jan Patočsky and the Christian Heritage," and L'ubica Ucník, "Patočka's Discussion with Dostoevsky on the Future of Science and Christianity" and Nicolas deWarren, "The Gift of Eternity," in Hagedorn, L. and J. Dodd, eds. *The New Yearbook of Phenomenology and Phenomenological Philosophy XIV—2015;* Martin Koči, *Thinking Faith After Christianity: A Theological Reading of Jan Patočka's Phenomenological Philosophy* (Albany: State University of New York Press, 2020) and "The Experiment of Night: Jan Patočka on War, and a Christianity to Come." *Labyrinth: An International Journal for Philosophy, Value Theory and Sociocultural Hermeneutics* 19, no. 1 (2017): 138–155; Ludger Hagedorn, ""Christianity Unthought"—A Reconsideration of Myth, Faith, and Historicity," in *The New Yearbook for Phenomenology and Phenomenological Philosophy*, 49–64.

14 Patočka, *Plato and Europe*, 137.

15 Patočka, *PE*, 189.

16 Patočka, *PE*, 189.

17 While there are many places in Patočka's work where he discusses the relationship between Plato and Aristotle, in the last lecture in *Plato and Europe*, he does a comparison arguing that they are less divergent than previously caricatured. See 195–223. Here he also describes the difference between horizontal and vertical thinking.

18 Patočka, *PE*, 212–219; Jan Patočka, *Heretical Essays on the Philosophy of History*, trans. Erazim Kohák, ed. James Dodd. (Chicago and La Salle: Open Court, 1996) 79–93; see also Paul Ricoeur's introduction to *Heretical Essays* on this point, pp. vii-xvi.

19 Patočka, *Heretical Essays*, 103. (Hereafter abbreviated *HE*)

being";[20] and "because care of the soul is possible, the state is also possible and the community is also possible."[21] All the details of these rather ambitious claims cannot be elaborated here, but this is all to say that Patočka sees the 'care of the soul' as the center of *something*, and perhaps the center of *everything*.

When Patočka says that the care of the soul is part of the "structure of being," he suggests that it is integrated into his vision of how humans relate to the universe and their place within that universe. This ontological sense of 'care of the soul' emerges in Patočka's discussion of the status of metaphysics in his 1955 essay "Negative Platonism: Reflections on the Rise, the Scope and the Demise of Metaphysics—and whether Philosophy Can Survive It."[22] 'Negative Platonism' is key to understanding how Patočka sees ideas about freedom, history, and philosophy through a Platonic lens, but also how his own conception of thinking allows for the combination of upward and outward thinking as a basis for seeking truth and caring for the soul. He claims his reading of Plato (a partial embrace and a partial rejection) can do the following:

> [I]t preserves for humans the possibility of trusting in a truth that is not relative and mundane, even though it cannot be formulated positively, in terms of contents. It shows how much truth there is in man's perennial metaphysical struggle for something elevated above the natural and the traditional, the struggle for the eternal and the supratemporal, in the struggle, taken up ever again, against a relativism of values and norms— even while agreeing with the idea of a basic historicity of man and of the relativity of his orientation in his context, of his science and practice, his images of life and the world.[23]

This is his conclusion to the essay "Negative Platonism," the culmination of his argument about how modern philosophy can no longer take metaphysics seriously (after Heidegger especially), and how scientific positivism does not take adequate account of the historicity of human beings, but how nonetheless there must be a way forward found so we

---

20 Patočka, *HE*, 93.
21 Patočka, *PE*, 121.
22 Patočka, "Negative Platonism; Reflections on the Rise, the Scope, and the Demise of Metaphysics—and whether Philosophy Can Survive It," (1955) in Erazim Kohák, *Jan Patočka Philosophy and Selected Writings* (Chicago: University of Chicago Press, 1989) 175–206.
23 Patočka, "Negative Platonism," in Kohák, 206.

do not slip into 'relativism of values and norms,' so morality can still be possible.

Patočka wants to retain firm normative ground as a basis for making moral claims, as his conception of a person is deeply intertwined with morality.[24] To do this, he turns to the Socratic model and characterizes it in a negative way, where the 'negative' part of 'negative Platonism' derives from taking on the world through questioning, negating that which is there already. From there, the impossibility of pure metaphysics and limits of positivism can be superseded by a very old idea, which is the negation (that is, overturning) of assertions that are mundane or mistakenly taken for granted. This leads to the higher 'supratemporal' idea of rigorous questioning. The model for this is Socrates:

> So Socrates, in contrast with the ordinary mode and direction of life, reaches a new level on which it is no longer possible to formulate objective, factual, positive assertions but in which, for all his mastery of life, he moves entirely in a vacuum. He formulates his new truth—since the problem of truth is what is at stake—only indirectly, in the form of a question, in the form of a skeptical analysis, of a negation of all finite assertions.[25]

If one thinks of "finite assertions" as relating to the horizontal and limited world of everyday life, commonplace observations, and the taken-for-granted world where we think we know the truth (but actually do not), then Socratic questioning is a path towards freedom for Patočka, because once everything about the everyday, mundane, and finite life is questioned, it opens up life to the possibility of verticality and to the possibility that there must be something more that is outside this mundane world, something beyond everydayness. To access this other world through questioning and negation is to experience freedom:

> Wherein does the experience of freedom consist? It is the experience of dissatisfaction with the given and the sensory, intensified by the growing awareness that the given and the sensory is neither all there is, nor definitive. For that reason, too, 'negative' experiences are decisive for the experience of freedom, showing as they do that the content of passive experience is trivial, transient, and insubstantial.[26]

---

24 As previously quoted in the introduction. "Two Charta 77 Texts," in Kohák, 341.
25 Patočka, "Negative Platonism," in Kohák, 180–181.
26 Patočka, "Negative Platonism," in Kohák, 193.

What he calls the "struggle" for the "supratemporal" and the eternal is a process of questioning in order to open space for "dissatisfaction with the given and the sensory," where one begins to mistrust and question what is received passively, absorbed from the environment, and is probably therefore "trivial, transient and insubstantial." What is important for this process of questioning, however, and what sets Patočka apart from traditional metaphysics, is that he accepts and embraces the historicity of the questioning, as well as the historicity of the language in which such negation and questioning is to happen: each age will ask its negative questions in a different language. Each age will have a way of questioning the trivial and mundane that will set it apart from the universalism of metaphysical assertions. So this sense of vertical thinking not only acknowledges the horizontal historicity of human life, but embraces it and requires it: unless we figure out the language of questioning that can reveal and unmask the banalities of sensory experience and probe more deeply into questions of the eternal and the supratemporal in any given age, the negative questioning will not reveal the world, and will not unveil the larger truths of a given situation, and therefore will not open the path towards human freedom.[27]

The political implications of this set of ideas are particularly relevant for dissident politics. To be able to question the given and traditional institutional structures—governments, churches, political systems, social conventions and the like—one has to be able to step outside of the mundane realities that these institutions create, including stepping outside of standardized language. Everything one has taken for granted about social institutions throughout one's life has to be potentially negated, put into question, and opened to overturning. Patočka takes this so far as to ask the practitioner of negative Platonism to challenge the structure of reality itself, as the power to do this is the power to gain one's own freedom:

It [negative Platonism] is first and most basically the power of de-objectification and de-realization, the power from which we derive all our ability to struggle against 'sheer reality,' the reality that would impose itself on us as an absolute, inevitable, and invincible law... Here the capacity of

---

27 The band the Plastic People of the Universe was an example of this 'language' difference: what they were doing was essentially a Socratic exercise, but their language was necessarily historical and situational. See Timothy Ryback, *Rock Around the Bloc: A History of Rock Music in Eastern Europe and the Soviet Union* (New York: Oxford University Press, 1990).

negation breaks forth in all its forms, from a mere acknowledgement of what is not and what contradicts itself to the trust to break up what exists, to desecrate what considers itself sacrosanct, to condemn the actual in the name of that for which we long and which is not.[28]

This method is a multi-staged process, where one will first question traditional notions of reality and objectivity, and in gaining power from this process, a stronger form of negation allows the unmasking of the sacrosanct. The person capable of doing this, however, is not a god or divine in any way, not outside of everyday life; even though capable of pulling themselves toward the vertical world and outside of the horizontal world, they are very much human, and therefore "historical":

> A historical being leans on the past, using it to open up the horizon of the given, with its help overcoming the given and the present. He can do that, however, only if the power of dissociation is available to him, the power of liberation from the purely objective and given.[29]

The political import of this stance implies that understanding one's own place in history (the 'given') is part of what gives one strength to stand up to given realities (the 'purely objective'), to question the sacrosanct, and to deconstruct the supposedly given objective realities as potentially false and contingent.

The process of questioning in Patočka's negative Platonism, then, can be applied in a scenario where the sacrosanct, the given realities, the established objectivities, and the whole horizontal world can be seen as historical, and in being seen as historical, can be questioned as contingent and constructed. This is not, however, as Patočka claimed, only producing a truth that is "relative and mundane," or in other words, questioning all things into oblivion and relativity. Rather, there is an implicit claim that the process of questioning itself holds together a form of living and acting that is as solid as it is transcendent. The Socratic process is itself firm, consistent, truthful, valid across the ages, normatively rigorous, and non-relative. The struggle toward elevation is the supra-temporal and eternal element of the process—the vertically-oriented movement pulling the horizontally situated mind out of the fray of

---

28 Patočka, "Negative Platonism," Kohák, 200.
29 Patočka, "Negative Platonism," Kohák, 199.

everydayness—but simultaneously being able to do this because human beings are in history and aware of the process of historicity shaping their own lives. Awareness of this historicity is therefore necessarily entwined with vertical notions of the supra-temporal, not contradictory to it or in opposition to it.

"Eternity and historicity" is the title of one of Patočka's essays, and in it he elaborates this dynamic beyond the sketch he gives in "Negative Platonism."[30] In the usual structure of philosophical categories, 'eternity' is separated from 'history' because by definition something eternal is not bound by time, and by definition, something historical is indeed bound by time. Patočka is challenging this antinomy and simplicity, however, pointing to a more complex relationship. This has significant political consequences, because if history and eternity are not at odds, by situating oneself within both, a human being can transcend the world while remaining within it, or in more political language, one can take action to change history in order to shape one's own time, while also speaking to the timelessness of an historical legacy that approaches eternal recurrence. Political action directed toward building something to last far beyond one's own historical moment has moral and normative solidity because building towards eternal ideas, even when knowing such goals will never be reached concretely in one's own lifetime, can potentially overcome instrumental self-interest with reasoned moral concern.[31] A process of questioning is essential to this, as is a mix of eternity and historicity. In order to find the language of questioning in any given time and place, and the corresponding relation to timelessness, negative Platonism points to the timelessness of negation itself as a process of non-relative thinking. Without negation first, without eternal Socratic questioning being shaped and sculpted for the particular historical time, dissidence is not possible.

If Bonhoeffer were presented with Patočka's negative Platonism, he would likely extrapolate to his own situation by suggesting that taking a Socratic approach to religion was part of being both a good theologian, a good Christian, and good citizen. Bonhoeffer's writings evoke how the divinity of man in history (in the form of Christ) not only constitutes one's responsibility to his neighbor through concrete actions, but

---

30 Patočka, *Éternité et historicité,* trans. Erika Abrams (Paris: Éditions Verdier 2011).
31 The anti-monarchical political dissidents who wrote the US Constitution had this quality—as does constitution-writing in general, as well as environmental activist movements (see chapter 5).

that all action in historical time can potentially transcend time. Bonhoeffer turns to God's presence in time within the Christian story to ground his ethical claims, and he might therefore read 'eternity and historicity' as a partial retelling of an Augustinian vision of history, where the earthly and the heavenly realms are intertwined until the end of time.[32] Patočka would not disagree with Bonhoeffer on the first part of this formulation, but he would not go so far to suggest that 'negative Platonism' depends upon the end-point of the Augustinian vision, as Patočka's argument does not rest upon the revelation of God at the end of time (whereas for Bonhoeffer and Augustine it would).[33] The fixed metaphysics of the theistic tradition is not part of the logic Patočka uses, especially in "Negative Platonism" where he discusses the end of metaphysics. At other places in his work, he engages the Christian tradition and European legacies of the Christian structure of thinking, but generally he does so within an ongoing series of questions, not with final answers.[34] So this is not to suggest that he and Bonhoeffer would have the same vision of the integration of the horizontal and the vertical, of upward and outward thinking, but rather to try to describe how they both seek to integrate horizontal and vertical forms of thinking within structural similarities. To compare these structures is to illuminate further why negative Platonism and what Bonhoeffer calls 'religionless Christianity' are both ontological modalities of caring for the soul.

The structural parallels of these two processes of thinking, even if aiming at different destinations (or a perpetually retreating horizon in Patočka's case), show how the intertwining of history and eternity creates a modality of dissidence that can enable actions not otherwise thought possible. Bonhoeffer was himself a case of overcoming various forms of impossibility and overcoming the potentially irreconcilability of the horizontal and the vertical. Bonhoeffer's thinking required going against religion (in the form of certain religious institutions and practices), against the laws of the state (what he took to be an unjust state), and against commonly held and unquestioned 'ethical' assumptions (those

---

32 St. Augustine of Hippo, *City of God*, trans. H. Bettenson (London: Penguin, 2004).
33 For a cautionary tale about inserting Augustinian logic into current politics, see William Connolly, *The Augustinian Imperative: A Reflection on the Politics of Morality* (New York: Sage Publications, 1993). For a much more optimistic argument about why Augustinian logic belongs in the discussion of world politics, see Reinhold Niebuhr, "Augustine's Political Realism," in Robert McAfee Brown, ed. *The Essential Reinhold Niebuhr: Selected Essays and Addresses* (New Haven: Yale University Press, 1986).
34 See note 13 above on Christianity in Patočka's work.

that produce passivity and indifference to others).[35] These three 'here-sies' in Bonhoeffer's writings were not unconnected to the fact he was living through a time when religious institutions, the law, and common ethical practices were all failing miserably to confront the Nazis. While his case was somewhat exceptional, it was not entirely exceptional: this overcoming of impossibility is at the core of all dissidence, and Bonhoeffer shows how the Christian ontological conception of care of the soul is one modality of such overcoming. It relies on history because within his theological vision, without history the Christian story is itself impossible. As Bonhoeffer explains:

> History does not become a transient vehicle, but through the life and death of Jesus Christ it does for the first time become truly temporal. It is precisely in its temporality that it is history with God's consent. Consequently, when we ask about the historical inheritance we are not asking the timeless question about those values of the past which the validity is eternal. Man himself is set in history and it is for that reason that he now asks himself about the present and about the way in which the present is taken up by God in Christ.[36]

Thus, for Bonhoeffer, the intertwining of the temporal and eternal is within the history of Christ, and "that alone is what enables man to set his eyes upon God and upon the world at the same time. This place does not lie somewhere out beyond reality in the realm of ideas. It lies in the midst of history as divine miracle."[37] This sense of history rests logically for Bonhoeffer on the corresponding Christian belief that man and God are reunited through the Second Coming of Christ at the end of time, but as a theologian, this is not what Bonhoeffer expends most of his energy analyzing and writing about.[38] The end of time is not very present in his thinking, but the actual historical events of his own time, and his own ability to recognize divinity in history, is what is at stake throughout *Ethics* and *Letters and Papers from Prison* (and arguably his

---

35 Bonhoeffer's view of the ethical errors of standard Christian thinking are discussed below.
36 Bonhoeffer, *Ethics*, 89.
37 Bonhoeffer, *Ethics*, 69.
38 As Paul Ricoeur argues: "Every moment of Bonhoeffer's thought is to lead us, as he says, on this side of death, for the seriousness of a life resurrected here and now." Paul Ricoeur, "The Non-religious Interpretation of Christianity in Bonhoeffer," in Brian Gregor and Jens Zimmerman, *Bonhoeffer and Continental Thought: Cruciform Philosophy* (Indianapolis: Indiana University Press, 2009) 175.

earlier works too, especially *Sanctorum Communio*[39]). He was concerned with how to act within *this* history and *this* moment, *this* situation of Nazi Germany, and asked what a Christian vision could do in the midst of the dramatic life and death events tearing apart the fabric of traditional religion, ethics, and politics. As a result, he does not read Christ apocalyptically, but rather horizontally, as to what he was in the world of historical time:

> Christ did not, like a moralist, love a theory of good, but He loved the real man. He was not, like a philosopher, interested in the 'universally valid,' but rather in that which is of help to the real and concrete human being. What worried Him was not, like Kant, whether 'the maxim of an action can become a principle of general legislation,' but whether my action is at this moment helping my neighbor to become a man before God. For indeed it is not written that God became an idea, a principle, a programme, a universally valid proposition or a law, but that God became man.[40]

This is the unification of the horizontal and the vertical within man himself, the intersection running right through the soul of a human being, where that soul has the willingness to care for others within the community. Therefore, the ontological sense of 'care of the soul' for Bonhoeffer, like for Patočka, relies upon a conception of being and human existence where the horizontal and the vertical intersect, necessarily combining these ideas with a conception of social-political life. A soul that is cared for will care for its community, and in the Christian vision, the shorthand for this is "loving my neighbor."

This idea underpins Bonhoeffer's idea of "religionless Christianity." Ostensibly this is a contradiction in terms, as Christianity is a religion, so how could it be without religion? Yet looking through what he called the "abyss torn open" in Nazi Germany, Bonhoeffer is able to separate out what he takes to be the practices in Christianity that corrupt the soul, and those that nourish it, critiquing both institutional and spiritual modalities of religious existence. He does not merely adopt

---

39 Clifford Green makes the argument that the view of sociality that Bonhoeffer presented in *Sanctorum Communio*, his dissertation and first book, remained infused in the rest of his work throughout his life; this sociality is characterized by what Bonhoeffer calls 'communities without a telos.' Dietrich Bonhoeffer, *Sanctorum Communio, (The Communion of Saints)*, (New York: Harper and Row, 1963) 61; Clifford Green, *Bonhoeffer: A Theology of Sociality*, (Wm. B. Eerdmans Publishing Company; Revised edition, 1999).

40 Bonhoeffer, *Ethics*, 85.

the commonplace notion that one can be 'spiritual but not religious,' but applies a method like Patočka's Socratic questioning to observe the failings of 'sacrosanct' institutions that were unable to uphold the core ethical principles of Christianity during Nazism. Part of this comes from Bonhoeffer's simple empirical observations: Christian institutions (both Protestant and Catholic) were ineffective at standing up to the 'objective reality' and 'everydayness' created by the Nazis. While some church officials were able to 'see through' to the potential horrors of Nazi politics, very few were willing to stand up and 'act through' this belief towards a fuller articulation of truth by doing something to stop the atrocities.[41] Fear had shut down the process of Socratic questioning, and in Bonhoeffer's world, 'religion' was at least partly to blame. There was a higher and a purer form of belief and truth that he claimed led him to become involved in the Hitler assassination attempt, and he called this 'religionless Christianity.'[42]

Writing in Berlin's Tegel prison in 1944, Bonhoeffer describes the beginnings of this formulation, though he did not live long enough to fully elaborate all the implications. From fragments in his letters, one can discern that Bonhoeffer set the erroneous parts of 'religion' in contrast to 'faith,' and asserts that "the 'religious act' is always something partial; 'faith' is something whole, involving the whole of one's life."[43] The partiality of religion leads to the concept of 'religionless Christianity' via Bonhoeffer's definition of 'true' faith:

---

41 There is a large literature on the issue of both Protestant and Catholic churches cooperating with the Nazis. Two representative examples: Robert Erikson, *Complicity in the Holocaust: Churches and Universities in Nazi Germany* (Cambridge: Cambridge University Press, 2012); Doris L. Bergen, *Twisted Cross: The German Christians* (Chapel Hill: University of North Carolina Press, 1996).

42 Bonhoeffer: "God is the beyond in the midst of our lives. The church stands not at the point where human powers fail, at the boundaries, but in the center of the village... I am thinking a great deal about what this religionless Christianity looks like, what form it takes, and I'll be writing you more about it soon." *DB Complete Works* Vol. 8, 367. This concept and passage is also discussed in Victoria Barnett, "Bonhoeffer's Understanding of Church, State and Civil Society," in Nielsen, Wüstenbrg, Zimmermann, eds. *A Spoke in the Wheel: The Political in the Theology of Dietrich Bonhoeffer* (München: Gütersloher Verlaghaus, 2013) 366–368.

43 Bonhoeffer, *Letters and Papers from Prison*, 362. See also *DB Complete Works* Vol. 8, 372–373, "A few more words about 'religionlessness'...What matters is not the beyond but this world, how it is created and preserved, is given laws, reconciled, and renewed. What is beyond this world is meant, in the gospel, to be there for this world—not in the anthropocentric sense of liberal, mystical, pietistic, ethical theology, but in the biblical sense of the creation and the incarnation, crucifixion and resurrection... At the moment I am thinking about how the concepts of repentance, faith, justification, rebirth, and sanctification should be reinterpreted in a 'worldly' way—in the Old Testament sense and in the sense of John 1:14."

It is only by living completely in this world that one learns to have faith. One must completely abandon any attempt to make something of one-self, whether it be a saint, or a converted sinner, or a churchman (a so-called priestly type!), a righteous man or an unrighteous one, a sick man or a healthy one. By this-worldliness I mean living unreservedly in life's duties, problems, successes and failures, experiences and perplexities. In so doing we throw ourselves completely into the arms of God... That, I think, is faith; that is metanoia; and that is how one becomes a man and a Christian... I'm glad to have been able to learn this, and I know I've been able to do so only along the road that I've travelled.[44]

The road he had travelled was soon to end in his execution, and so within his thinking there is an attempt to reconcile the 'abyss' that his world had thrown open with a certain theological-ethical vision, and the result is rather paradoxical:

When we speak of God in a 'non-religious' way, we must speak of him in such a way that the godlessness of the world is not in some way concealed, but rather revealed, and thus exposed to an unexpected light. The world that has come of age is more godless, and perhaps for that very reason nearer to God, than the world before its coming to age.[45]

The idea of 'coming of age' (*Mundigkeit*) is discussed further below, and is intertwined with the idea of religionless Christianity, as it takes a rather mature and solid stance toward the world to deal with its god-lessness; it also requires a particular way of thinking (and an embrace of paradox and contradiction) to take godlessness as the nearness of God.[46] For Bonhoeffer, part of caring for the soul and caring for the world is to maturely recognize that God is not there in the daily grind of life.[47]

---

44 Bonhoeffer, *Letters and Papers from Prison*, 369–70.

45 Bonhoeffer, *Letters and Papers from Prison*, 362.

46 Bonhoeffer, *Letters and Papers from Prison,* 327: "the attack by Christian apologetics on the adulthood of the world I consider to be in the first place pointless, in the second place ignoble, and in the third place unchristian. Pointless, because it seems to me like an attempt to put a grown-up back into adolescence, i.e. to make him dependent upon things which he is, in fact, no longer dependent, and thrusting him into problems that are, in fact, no longer problems to him. Ignoble, because it amounts to an attempt to exploit man's weakness for purposes that are alien to him and to which he has not freely assented. Unchristian, because it confuses Christ with one particular stage in a man's religiousness, i.e. with a human law."

47 "Man is summoned to share in God's sufferings at the hands of a Godless world. He must therefore really live in the godless world, without attempting to gloss over or explain its

Bonhoeffer admonishes his readers not to think of God as a 'stop gap measure,' or something to call upon in troubled times to fix things. He characterizes such petitioning prayer as one mistake of 'religion' that goes against proper 'faith.'[48] For Bonhoeffer, the proper reason to pray is not to ask God to remedy the problems of your own life, but rather one prays to help oneself to recognize that it is one's own responsibility to deal with those problems, and in so dealing, one exhibits (true) faith that the problems were put there for reasons known only to God. Then, the human task is to respond, to take responsibility, exercise free will, and to act.

'Religion' can prevent this sort of action, or lead it astray, when it relies on ethical principles that are not adequate for confronting the difficulty of the circumstances. As he sets out to confront Nazi evil with his ideas of systematic ethics, Bonhoeffer identifies six ways of trying to be ethical (derived from erroneous 'religious' understandings) that fail us in urgent times: being too "reasonable" and therein avoiding any confrontation; falling into moral fanaticism by claiming the purity of the will in self-righteousness; isolating oneself from others by claiming to be uniquely devoted to one's own conscience; relying only on concepts of duty to the church, state, and higher authority; claiming the wisdom of 'free' responsibility by choosing a 'lesser' evil and falling into tragedy when in fact one does not have knowledge of relative evil; and finally, claiming to be virtuous through withdrawal into private spaces away from public evils.[49] After explaining these failings in greater detail,

---

ungodliness in some religious way or other. He must live a 'secular' life, and thereby share in God's sufferings. He may live a 'secular' life (as one who has been freed from false religious obligations and inhibitions). To be a Christian does not mean to be religious in a particular way, to make something of oneself (a sinner, a penitent or a saint) on the basis of some method or other, but to be a man—not a type of man, but the man that Christ creates in us. It is not the religious act that makes the Christian, but participation in the sufferings of God in the secular life. That is metanoia: not in the first place thinking about one's own needs, problems, sins, and fears, but allowing oneself to be caught up in the way of Jesus Christ, into the messianic event, thus fulfilling Isa. 53." Bonhoeffer, *Letters and Papers from Prison*, 361–62.

48   In a commentary about this concept in Bonhoeffer's work, Paul Ricoeur notes: "one appeals to this 'God' in the boundaries of experience and when the resources of experience have been exhausted, or when it fails. It is therefore truly the *deus ex machina*, that is, that to which one has recourse in order to wrap up an unresolved intellectual situation. But, says Bonhoeffer, the human being has come of age in the sense that he has learned to grapple with all of the important questions without resorting to his 'God' as a working hypothesis... the 'God' of the gaps in the world is also the 'God' of the limit experiences of the human being: death, sin, suffering. But we are approaching the day when these ultimate questions of humanity are also resolved without the 'God' of metaphysics." Ricoeur, in *Bonhoeffer in Continental Thought*, 161.

49   Bonhoeffer, *Ethics*, 65–67.

Bonhoeffer will admit that "reason, moral fanaticism, conscience, duty, free responsibility and silent virtue, these are the achievements and attitudes of a noble humanity."[50] Yet living through times of great evil led him to conclude that these are ethical and religious deceptions, and that stronger ethical tools were needed to confront the situation. "The great masquerade of evil has played havoc with all our ethical concepts. For evil to appear disguised as light, charity, historical necessity, or social justice is quite bewildering to anyone brought up on our traditional ethical concepts."[51] So an understanding of 'religionless Christianity' can be seen as one step in the development of these new ethical tools.

As Bonhoeffer's *Ethics* was left unfinished, so too was a full elaboration of 'religionless Christianity.' In a letter near the time of his death, he states that he will "be writing you more about it [religionless Christianity] soon."[52] There was no time for enough additional letters to fully explain it. Yet from the sketch he gives, his doubts about the structures of thinking inherited from traditional religious practices are reasonably clear, as is the subdivision between practices of 'faith' and 'responsibility' on the one hand, and those of 'religion' on the other. To use Patočka's Platonic terms to describe Bonhoeffer, the ineffective ethical practices he condemns are no longer capable of caring for the soul, and should be subjected to the rigorous critique of Socratic questioning. A religion-based Christianity is concerned with caring for the institution of the church, whereas 'religionless Christianity' is something that would be capable of caring for the soul through questioning traditional institutional practices and unmasking the hypocrisy of religion in times of political urgency. While he was not able to fully elaborate the mechanisms for practicing such an approach to human spiritual engagement, he was clear about the needed result of this mode of thinking and dissidence:

> Thinking and acting for the sake of the coming generation, but being ready to go any day without fear or anxiety—that, in practice, is the spirit in which we are forced to live. It is not easy to be brave and keep that spirit alive, but it is imperative.[53]

---

50 Bonhoeffer, *Ethics*, 68.
51 Bonhoeffer, *Letters and Papers from Prison*, 4.
52 Bonhoeffer, *DB Complete Works*, Vol. 8, 367.
53 Bonhoeffer, *Letters and Papers from Prison*, 15.

If one approaches the problems of the world not as tasks to avoid, but rather as a set of problems and questions that are put there in order to be confronted and addressed by human action and responsibility, this requires an ontological frame of religionless-ness, where there are not hard and fast rules predetermined for every situation, and where waiting for the end of time and Second Coming is an excuse: "Mere waiting and looking on is not Christian behavior. The Christian is called to sympathy and action, not in the first place by his own suffering, but by the sufferings of his brethren, for whose sake Christ suffered."[54] Fulfilling this vision requires overcoming the ways traditional religion trains people to think and to act passively; having Augustine's steadfast patience until the end of time is irresponsible in some cases.[55]

That dissidence requires a framework of responsibility seems somewhat obvious, but the ways such responsibility is cultivated in particular human communities is nuanced and complicated. Christianity without religion and Platonism without metaphysics are both, in a technical sense, contradictions; as tools of dissidence in totalitarian worlds, religionless Christianity and negative Platonism are examples of a combination of simultaneous upward and outward thinking that produce ripe ground for meaningful action that can transcend circumstances while also living within those circumstances. Bonhoeffer's ontological vision is a framework of problematicity and responsibility, as is Patočka's idea of negative Platonism, where it is the responsibility of the Socratic questioner to care for the soul by confronting and questioning human existence. This ontology of problematicity is shared by Bonhoeffer and Patočka, and leads them both to a mode of political thinking that requires acting "for the sake of the coming generation," not for the sake of immediate personal and instrumental interests. To care for the soul, therefore, requires thinking of the world through a framework of questioning the horizontal world, but it also requires the upward and vertical vision of something higher.

Yet even if Patočka and Bonhoeffer share the horizontal vision of questioning, they part ways on the upward-looking vertical goal of such questioning. In the end, Bonhoeffer finds his hope from a deeply Christian framework where he believes God will impart ultimate meaning on the full depth of evil he is living through.[56] Patočka's stance on the

---

54 Bonhoeffer, *Letters and Papers from Prison*, 13–14.
55 Augustine, *City of God*, 1.
56 Bonhoeffer, *Letters and Papers from Prison*, 11: "I believe that God can and will bring good out of evil, even out of the greatest evil. For that purpose he needs men who make the best use

ultimate grounding of the meaning of human existence is much more fluid; at times it is rooted within history, where eternity and historicity are intertwined to give meaning to a retreating horizon, but not always.[57] There is some sense of hope within Patočka's linkage of truth, care, and solidarity through the probematicity of history, but it is much more tenuous and contingent than Bonhoeffer's vision of a 'true' and 'religionless' faith in God. Both, however, nonetheless share a similar sense of the social-political consequences of caring for the soul: they are both willing to justify sacrifices made for the 'sake of coming generations.'

If negative Platonism is related to the ontological basis of caring for the soul, what Patočka called "the general philosophical teaching that brings the soul into connection with the structure of being," then there are two other components he identifies that are connected to that, "a teaching about the life of the philosopher in the community and in history" and "the teaching about the soul as the principle of individual life." These aspects of caring for the soul are the social-political and the existential aspects, respectively, and are interrelated with one another, as well as with the ontological grounding and the structure of being. Following the prior argument that negative Platonism is an ontological form of caring for the soul, in that it provides a framework to probe the structure of being in a philosophical way that does not imply a fixed metaphysics, then both the social-political and existential aspects of caring of the soul will be extensions of that ontology. In other words, the approach of the philosopher to community, history, and politics is going to be a mode of questioning as well, a Socratic endeavor to unite the horizontal and vertical aspects of being through the capacity for negation and questioning.

The existential aspect of caring for the soul will require the individual, in light of his social-political community, to then turn that mode

---

of everything. I believe that God will give us all the strength we need to help us resist in all times of distress. But he never gives it in advance, lest we should rely on ourselves and not on him alone."

57   In Patočka's last essay before he died, "On Masaryk's Philosophy of Religion," he stated that the "phenomenology of meaning" was the horizon he wanted to further explore, a horizon not adequately addressed (in his eyes) by Western philosophy. Patočka sketched a way forward through this question by a rather labyrinthine account of Dostoevsky, Nietzsche, Masaryk, Kant, and Heidegger. This essay of Patočka's, as well as several useful commentaries about it, can be found in L. Hagedorn and J. Dodd, eds., *The New Yearbook of Phenomenology and Phenomenological Philosophy XIV—2015,* 93–199. Also see: J. Majernik, "Jan Patočka's Reversal of Dostoevsky and Charter 77," *Labyrinth: An International Journal for Philosophy, Value Theory and Sociocultural Hermeneutics* 19, no. 1 (2017): 26–45.

of questioning upon the self, and the "soul as the principle of individual life" is turned into a set of questions. In the end, one cannot have a proper existential view of the self and the individual soul unless one also places oneself in an ontological framework and a social-political framework. Caring for the soul is not, as has already been discussed, a mode of withdrawal from the world; it is a way of embracing the world within the self and the self within the world. When applying Patočka's ideas to the case of Bonhoeffer, it is therefore somewhat impossible to separate out the existential and the social-political aspects of caring for the soul. What follows, therefore, is an integrated discussion of the ideas of sacrifice, amplitude, and 'worldliness' (what is characterized above as the social-political and existential aspects of caring for the soul in Bonhoeffer's and Patočka's works).

This combining of ideas can be justified by reflecting upon praxis: in order to engage in sacrifice in the political arena, one has to have a certain existential understanding of oneself first. Both Patočka and Bonhoeffer invested considerable time and effort in caring for their souls in an existential sense before they stepped into politics and exercised their ideas of sacrifice. While they were engaged in politics, their sense of themselves and the existential aspect of caring for their soul was surely deepened and extended, but their presence in politics in the first place depended upon first attending to pre-political existential difficulties. This pattern, or so I will argue, holds for most dissidents in most times and places; there is an existential transformation first, and politics comes after.[58] Patočka might have listed the order incorrectly when he defined the three elements of caring for the soul. The third (existential aspect) might be placed before the second (political aspect), in no small part because in his life, he lived 'care of soul' in the order argued for here: the existential came before the political. The same was arguably true for Bonhoeffer.

Amplitude: The Soul and the City in Sacrifice

After Nazi Germany occupied Czechoslovakia, Patočka wrote an essay entitled "Life in Balance, Life in Amplitude."[59] The two forms of life he describes in this essay led him toward the goal of developing

---

58 I make the same argument here: A. Brinton, *Philosophy and Dissidence in Cold War Europe*, 2016.
59 Eric Manton, ed. *Living in Problematicity*, 32–43. (Hereafter abbreviated "*LIP*")

a "philosophy of amplitude."[60] The mode of life he rejects, a 'life in balance,' corresponds to a set of philosophical and social-political assumptions he sees as having culminated in German National Socialism, Stalinist Russia, and in certain aspects of technocratic utopianism still present in capitalist Western democracies.[61] "Balance" is a short-hand for "living from the ready-made,"[62] "the common life," "the calm of ordinary harmony," the "frenzy of work and activity," the "necessary, diligent, reasonable everyday finitude" that also pretends to be "a guarantee of a happy ending, a guarantee of the reasonable and practical purposefulness of living."[63] This sort of 'balance' of the 'finite' life does not recognize the 'depth' of a 'spiritual' life, nor does it allow us to "test our possibilities," to develop our freedom, to live in truth, or to understand history. "Life in amplitude," rather, is the type of existence that does indeed allow us to do these necessary things.[64] At the core of a 'life of amplitude' is the ability to acknowledge that human beings cannot be socially engineered into a big happy ending. Rather, life is full of unexpected, problematic, and unpredictable forces that must be embraced and confronted in order to properly exercise our human freedom:

> Living in amplitude means a test of oneself and a protest. In amplitude, Man is tested by exposing himself to extreme possibilities that are mere abstract, distant possibilities for the common life, and protests against those that are usual and obvious... Man reaches amplitude under the fascinating impression of the boundaries that encircle his life. He must face these boundaries, if he searches for truth. If we want truth, we are not allowed to look for it only in the shallows, we are not allowed to be fas-

---

60 Patočka, (Manton), *LIP*, 42.
61 An interesting comparison that follows a similar structure might be Eric Fromm's essay "The Prophets and the Priests," where he distinguishes a similar existential stance towards the legacy of Nazism and Stalinism, but with different categories. Fromm, *On Disobedience, Or Why Freedom Means Saying 'No' to Power* (New York: Harper Perennial, 2010) 13–40.
62 Patočka, (Manton), *LIP*, 40.
63 Patočka, (Manton), *LIP*, 38–39.
64 E. Manton characterizes Patočka's view of 'balance' as follows: "All human activity has harmony, balance, and happiness as its orientation. Human beings may be incomplete and imperfect, but this will be remedied by the appropriate measures of education and social organization. Patočka criticizes this attitude for its closed concept of Man, its tendency to resist and suppress (even violently) anything that is not 'normal,' to ignore or discount anything that shakes this balanced picture of life, and to see society as basically a technical problem that can be solved through rationality or a necessary historical development. He attacks this attitude for its deterministic approach to the concept of Man and all social activity." *Living in Problematicity*, 73.

cinated by the calm of ordinary harmony; we must let grow in ourselves the uncomfortable, the irreconcilable, the mysterious, before which the common life closes its eyes and crosses over to the order of the day.[65]

This is a description of a life that is not easy to live, a life that demands effort and engagement with oneself and the world. This is also a deeply political vision, connecting the search for truth to a protest that overcomes the 'calm ordinary harmony' advertised and promised (but rarely delivered) by utopian political projects. The concept of 'amplitude' from this early essay arguably reappeared later in different forms in Patočka's work, including the notion of *polemos* or confrontation (see Chapter 3), which he sets off against a contrast to "the forces of the day" in *Heretical Essays*.[66] In this earlier essay, the 'order of the day' is connected to the 'life of balance' that one must 'protest' against, and this is one moment of his explicit advocacy for protest. 'Amplitude' is also arguably an important component of Patočka's "third movement of human existence," an idea he developed in both his Prague Spring lectures and *Heretical Essays*, where the third (and final) movement of one's life should, in Patočka's vision, entail a certain confrontation with history that opens the soul to the shaking apart of given meanings of the world, opening the social and political ground for 'solidarity of the shaken' (see Chapters Three and Four). If his essay on amplitude (and the Nazi invasion) was an occasion for Patočka to set the goal of developing a "philosophy of amplitude," then there is a way to argue that he succeeded in developing such a philosophy, even if from this starting point in the 1940s, the 'philosophy of amplitude' split into several different projects, some more political than others.[67]

A case can be made that Bonhoeffer was a good example of what 'living in amplitude' entailed for Patočka. As one commentator put it: "Though he would not have liked to be called a bruiser, one can safely say that in Dietrich Bonhoeffer we have a strong personality, a powerful man, who shared—by nature and nurture—Nietzsche's dislike of spineless and half-hearted life."[68] Indeed, Patočka's idea of amplitude requires

---

65 Patočka, (Manton), *LIP*, 39.
66 Patočka, *Heretical Essays*; for his discussion of "forces of the day," see 119–137.
67 The aspiration to 'face the boundaries' that 'encircle life' is arguably the core of his phenomenological project (and is a response to Heidegger, Husserl and Merleau-Ponty) that was often not political, but concerned with the ontological level of caring for the soul—see above.
68 Fritz de Lang, "Aristocratic Christendom: On Bonhoeffer and Nietzsche," in Eds. Brian Gregor and Jens Zimmerman, *Bonhoeffer and Continental Thought: Cruciform Philosophy* (Bloomington, IN: Indiana UP, 2009) 75.

a dislike of spinelessness, and Patočka used Nietzsche as one of his examples of someone who approached one version of amplitude, though he does qualify that statement with a discussion about the spiritual aspects of amplitude that might diverge from a pure Nietzschean position.[69] What amplitude allows for, in both Patočka and Bonhoeffer's cases, is an idea of sacrifice that might require being something of "a bruiser," but it is a stance that also requires caring for the soul of both the individual and the community, intertwined together. Caring for one's own soul, then, can be a way to make oneself into a more solid being of amplitude, a being that can then participate in the politics and history of a community.

'Solidity' is part of Patočka's description of what caring of the soul does: "The care of the soul is the intentional forming of the soul itself, forming into something unyielding and solid, into existence in this sense, because of the very fact that it is occupied with thinking."[70] What makes the soul solid, in this view, is a mode of thinking, and as argued above, a mode of thinking that starts with 'negative Platonism.' Amplitude is also itself a mode of thinking about the world apart from 'the common life' and the unquestioned assumptions of 'the given' and 'the day.' Bonhoeffer would characterize a related mode of existing-through-thinking as *Mundigkeit*, or mature worldliness.[71] This approach undoubtedly helped him justify his involvement in the attempt to assassinate Hitler. This was an act of amplitude, embracing the uncomfortable, the irreconcilable, the sinful, and the unpredictable. One of the mysteries that the abyss opened up to him in the face of Hitler, then, was that in certain contexts one had to 'sin' to be 'ethical,' and at the same time, it might be necessary to be 'unethical' in order to avoid a systematic existential sin against life itself.[72] Getting oneself killed in order to try to kill Hitler

---

69 Patočka, "Life in Balance, Life in Amplitude," (Manton), LIP, 40. Nietzsche is referenced here.
70 Patočka, *Plato and Europe*, 86.
71 Bonhoeffer also probably had in mind Immanuel Kant's use of the word's opposite, *Unmundigkeit*, in the first sentence of his "What is Enlightenment?" "*Unmundigkeit*" is the word usually translated as 'tutelage' or 'immaturity.' Kant's essay argues that 'enlightenment' is freedom from one's "self-incurred immaturity or tutelage." So "*Mundigkeit*" is the state of not being under tutelage and being able to overcome being immature.
72 Bonhoeffer on the question of illegality and righteousness: "It is not necessarily hypocrisy if the declared aim of political action is the restoration of the law, and not mere self-preservation. The world is, in fact, so ordered that a basic respect for ultimate laws and human life is also the best means of self-preservation, and that these laws may be broken only on the odd occasion in case of brief necessity, whereas anyone who turns necessity into principle, and in doing so establishes a law of his own alongside them, is inevitably bound, sooner or later, to suffer

might have constituted 'sin' in a traditional understanding, but if faith and purity of the heart are 'true Christianity' for Bonhoeffer, then religionless Christianity is the grounding for an act of sacrifice that validates God-given freedom through exercising the freedom to give one's life for others. Bonhoeffer's execution, and the sacrifice of himself for the sake of his community (and arguably the world), required the intertwinement of the existential and the political, where caring for the soul leaves it more unyielding and solid.

Sacrifice and Pseudo-sacrifice

To turn to the details of Patočka's and Bonhoeffer's respective ideas of sacrifice, it is perhaps most illuminating to focus on the political-existential question raised by sacrifice: How does a willingness to sacrifice make caring for one's soul and one's community more possible? Both Patočka and Bonhoeffer suggest that contemplating sacrifice reveals the qualities of a person and their relationship with the surrounding world; there has to be a volition in the person to act, but also a world that seems to demand such sacrifice. But then the two points are related: a person of 'amplitude' will hear the call for sacrifice; a person of 'common life' and 'balance' will not. In some ways, these two different types of people live in two different worlds, even as neighbors. While Patočka and Bonhoeffer would agree on this much, to see the divergences from this common ground, it is useful to look at how each sees the difference between 'real sacrifice' and other forms of 'pseudo-sacrifice,' as well as how each uses a discussion of sacrifice to illuminate what the soul of a human being is, indirectly illuminating how to care for that soul.

For Patočka, there are several ways a person can engage in a form of pseudo-sacrifice that is not the authentic and real path of genuine sacrifice: one can romanticize it (and see it as the solution to the world's problems, rather than as a phenomenon that demonstrates the tragic nature of the universe); one can do it for the sake of a material thing or a particular person (rather than doing it for everyone and no one, for all of Being); one can do it in the context of an inauthentic human institution, like involuntary participation in an army at war, or for the

---

retribution. The immanent righteousness of history rewards and punishes only men's deeds, but the eternal righteousness of God tries and judges their hearts." *LPP*, 11.

sake of reputation and living on past one's own death (as opposed to doing it as a way of being-toward-death authentically, in recognition of the absolute end of one's life as the primary goal, rejecting the need of immortality).[73] Overall, 'real sacrifice,' which Patočka is calling 'repeated sacrifice' in this particular lecture (because it maps onto a particular past understanding he is mirroring) is about authentic protest:

> The entire mode of acting needs to be understood as a protest, not against individual concrete experiences but, in principle, against the understanding by which they are borne. From this perspective, the repeated sacrifice is something no longer concerned with positive content.[74]

If one is concerned with the "positive content" of a sacrifice, one is sacrificing for a particular thing: a country, a family, or a religion. This is not fully authentic sacrifice because it is not strictly voluntary, or it is self-serving in some way (a mother sacrifices for her child so part of herself may live on in the world), or it requires false romanticizing or deification (the sacrifice required of some religions, for example). Voluntary self-sacrifice for the whole of the world seems to be Patočka's (rather high) standard for genuine sacrifice, and he argues this by claiming that true sacrifice is quite literally sacrifice for nothing, no-thing whatsoever, but rather for the entirety of Being:

> Sacrifice acquires a remarkably radical and paradoxical form. It is not sacrifice for something or for someone, even though in a certain sense it is a sacrifice for everything and for all. In a certain essential sense, it is sacrifice for nothing, if thereby we mean that which is no existing particular.[75]

---

73 Patočka, "The Dangers of Technicization in Science according to E. Husserl and the Essence of Technology as Danger according to M. Heidegger," also called the "Varna Lecture," in Kohák, 337–339. For a discussion of Patočka's notion of sacrifice, see James Dodd, "Philosophy in Dark Times: An Essay on Jan Patočka's Philosophy of History," in L. Hagedorn and J. Dodd, eds. *The New Yearbook of Phenomenology and Phenomenological Philosophy XIV—2015* and Francesco Tava, *The Risk of Freedom: Ethics, Phenomenology and Politics in Jan Patočka,* trans. Jane Ledlie, (New York: Rowman and Littlefield, 2015) 73–76.

74 The rest of this passage, while enigmatic, suggests the possibilities for inauthenticity being overcome through moving beyond a technical-rational understanding of the world (a common theme in Patočka's writings, see Introduction and Chapter One): "The repetition of sacrifice presupposes a voluntary self-sacrifice, just as in the case of naïve sacrifice, but not only that. For if in this repetition the central point is the overcoming of technical understanding of being which is the basis of the non-acknowledgement and vanity of sacrifice, then the naïve stance with respect to sacrifice will no longer do at all." Patočka, "Varna Lecture," in Kohák, 338.

75 Patočka, "Varna Lecture," in Kohák, 339.

This might be slightly less daunting to think about if this last word, 'particular,' is thought of in contrast to a 'universal,' and that Patočka's mode of 'proper' sacrifice is 'proper' because it is connected to universal Being, to the whole world and everyone in it. His contrast seems to be between particularity and universality, between sacrifice for the sake of one person or an immediate instrumental cause (a particular thing), and sacrifice for the sake of no thing, for 'nothing' as the opposite of 'something' that is merely a thing, an object.[76] An ideology, a religion, and a country are still 'things,' so this notion is different than dying for the sake of an idea, which would probably count as an excess romanticizing of sacrifice for Patočka. The test of genuine sacrifice is that it does not have some particular finite aim, but is (however grandiose it sounds) a sacrifice for the whole of humanity, a sacrifice for everything and everyone.[77] This echoes, then, both the Socratic idea of the philosopher returning to the cave (and risking death) to educate those who are entrapped by false ideas, as well as the Christian idea of God sending Christ to die for everyone, for all of humanity and all human sins. Neither martyr engaged in sacrifice for a 'thing,' but rather for an intangible that was for, with, and a part of *everyone*.

The way Patočka explains this mode of sacrifice is rather cryptic, and in one paragraph following his assertion about 'sacrifice for nothing,' he evokes the Christian idea of sacrifice alongside the Socratic language of 'turning away from everydayness':

> Such an understanding of sacrifice might basically be considered that in which Christianity differs from those religions which conceived of the divine always as a power and a force, and of a sacrifice as the activity which places this power under an obligation. Christianity... placed at the center a radical sacrifice... and rested its cause on the maturity of the human being. The divine in the sense of the suprahuman, the suprahuman in the sense of turning away from ordinary everydayness, rests precisely in the radicalness of the sacrifice. Perhaps it is in this sense that we need to seek the fully ripened form of demythologized Christianity.[78]

---

76 Dodd, "Philosophy in Dark Times: An Essay on Jan Patočka's Philosophy of History," in L. Hagedorn and J. Dodd, eds. *The New Yearbook of Phenomenology and Phenomenological Philosophy XIV—2015*.

77 Tava, *Risk of Freedom*, 73–76.

78 Patočka, "Varna Lecture," in Kohák, 339. For a further commentary, see: Martin Koci, "Sacrifice for Nothing: The Movement of Kenosis in Jan Patočka's Thought," *Modern Theology* 33, no. 4 (2017): 594–617.

If "turning away from everydayness" is what negative Platonism allowed ontologically and epistemologically, then an "understanding of sacrifice," together with the "maturity of the human being" (like Bonhoeffer's *Mundigkeit*), comes together in a call for seeking "demythologized Christianity." There is not enough in this particular passage to sort out whether this "demythologized Christianity" and Bonhoeffer's 'religionless Christianity' are analogous, but undoubtedly there is an echo of structural similarity: what passes as 'normal Christianity' no longer shows the "fully ripened" form of faith, and in that absence, something else must be sought by those 'mature' enough to see the problem.

For Bonhoeffer, the Christian mode of sacrifice on the cross is his primary reference point, so the way he thinks through the issue might help illuminate some (though not all) of what Patočka elusively evokes. Bonhoeffer's reflections are less cryptic; he begins by clearing some conceptual ground before he justifies and describes his own actions as a proper sacrifice that avoids pseudo-sacrifice. On the most basic level, Bonhoeffer admonishes his readers that they do not have to become entirely Christlike and that they do not have to be gods to understand the importance of sacrifice:

> We are certainly not Christ; we are not called upon to redeem the world by our own deeds and sufferings, and we need not try to assume such an impossible burden... but if we want to be Christians, we must have some share in Christ's large-heartedness by acting with responsibility and in freedom when the hour of danger comes... Mere waiting and looking on is not Christian behavior. The Christian is called to sympathy and action, not in the first place by his own sufferings, but by the sufferings of his brethren, for whose sake Christ suffered.[79]

Even after establishing this difference between humble Christ-like human action and the actual sacrifice of a god, Bonhoeffer still had to wrestle with the commandment 'thou shall not kill' and relate it to both the attempt to kill Hitler, as well as the structural reality that engaging in a plot to assassinate Hitler was very likely to get himself killed, and might be viewed as a form of suicide. If Havel could ironically quip that dissidence in Communist Czechoslovakia was done by an "isolated handful of suicidal maniacs," then Bonhoeffer could say the same, but entirely

---

79   Bonhoeffer, *Letters and Papers from Prison*, 14.

without irony and almost without contingency.[80] If he got caught, he would be killed, and he wrote about this reality while in prison waiting to be executed. This seemed suicidal by one conception, but Bonhoeffer argued against conceiving of his action (and that of his co-conspirators) as a form of suicide.

Bonhoeffer uses the term self-murder (*selbst-mord*) for suicide to avoid conflation with the German word for self-inflicted death (*selbsttötung*):

> Self-murder is a human effort to confer ultimate meaning on a life that, in human terms, has become meaningless. The involuntary shudder that grips us when confronted with the fact of self-murder is not because it is so reprehensible, but because the eerie loneliness and freedom of such a deed, which can affirm life only by destroying it. If we nevertheless must say that self-murder is reprehensible, we can do so not before the forum of morality [*moralität*] or of humanity, but only before the forum of God. The self-murderer is guilty before God alone, the creator and lord of the person's life... Freedom toward death, which is given in human natural life, is misused when it is not used in faith with God.[81]

For Bonhoeffer, the problem with self-murder (suicide) is that it denies faith in God by trying to confer ultimate meaning on life through an act of human freedom that goes against God; the assumption for a Christian is that God has already given meaning to life. The point of life, then, is to reconcile one's own existence with God's meaning, which given Bonhoeffer's particular theology, is defined by the Christian notion of freedom, where being able to be free means one is free in God's freedom. In this light, Bonhoeffer defines self-murder (suicide) as a failed attempt to give selfish meaning to one's one particular life through a lonely solipsistic act. In contrast, sacrifice (in the form of 'self-inflicted death') is meaningful for Bonhoeffer because it is also an act of freedom, but this freedom is God-given and has the possibility of being a death-for-others:

---

80   While the one contingency his family seemed to be holding out for was that the Allies might defeat Germany before he was executed, he was executed (along with many other political prisoners) when it became clear to the Germans that they were about to be defeated. See Christiane Tietz, Trans. Victoria J. Barnett, *Theologian of Resistance: The Life and Thought of Dietrich Bonhoeffer* (New York: Fortress Press, 2016).

81   Bonhoeffer, *Complete Works,* Vol. 6 *Ethics,* 198.

Only because human beings are free for death can they give up their bodily lives for the sake of higher good. Without the freedom to sacrifice one's life in death there would be no freedom for God, and there would be no human life... The freedom to risk and to give one's life as a sacrifice is the counterpart of the right to life. Human beings have freedom toward death and the right to death, in the sense of sacrifice, but only when the good sought through sacrifice, and not the destruction of one's own life, is the reason for risking one's life.[82]

Here he seems to argue that good can be sought through sacrifice and it can be an acceptable action. If human life is defined as a life that is "free for death," then sacrificing one's life for others is an exercise of this freedom. Both suicide (self-murder) and sacrifice have an 'eerie freedom,' but sacrifice lacks the sense of loneliness that suicide has, because it is done in a context with others and for the sake of others. While only a tentative wager at judgment is possible, meeting Bonhoeffer's standard for avoiding pseudo-sacrifice would be easier to achieve than Patočka's standard, as justifying the action is more accessible: dying for the sake of others does not mean for Bonhoeffer, as it seems to mean for Patočka, dying for the sake of both everyone and no one at once. "Others" for Bonhoeffer might mean neighbors, countrymen, and family; it might also mean the others of 'the world' and 'of Being,' but such an all-encompassing conception does not seem to be strictly necessary for him.

This difference in ideas is paralleled by a tricky question about the relationship between the ideas articulated in the texts they wrote, and the fact that both Patočka and Bonhoeffer chose to sacrifice themselves for political causes. Were they examples of their own theories? Bonhoeffer, sitting in prison writing while waiting to die, is perhaps much more directly 'justifying' his own actions with his textual arguments, explaining why he was doing what he was doing. Patočka, writing an essay about sacrifice many years before the actual event, an essay that pretends to be about Husserl, is a more distant linkage. The prelude to Patočka's death was a case of chronic bronchitis he decided to ignore in order to participate in political activities alongside Havel and other Charter 77 members. He was sick the day he happened to be arrested, interrogated for many hours, exhausted, and then hospitalized as complications set

---

82   Bonhoeffer, *Complete Works*, Vol. 6 *Ethics*, 196–197.

in before he died.[83] Getting out of bed that morning and 'going anyway,' an action of setting aside concerns for immediate self-preservation, was the moment where the existential and the political came together for Patočka, but he never had the chance to write a self-analysis of that dramatic day, so the connections between his actions and his theories can only be inferred. By Patočka's criteria in the earlier essay, one's actions must reach far beyond personal consequences and local circumstances to be 'proper sacrifice,' where the action is not about oneself, but about the world. Being able to set aside the consequences of the action from the action itself, as will be further discussed in the case of Gandhi, might be one important aspect of Patočka's 'sacrifice for nothing' that is more widely applicable. In Bonhoeffer's case, there is still *something* rather than *nothing*, in that destroying Hitler, following God, and doing it for his 'neighbor' were all 'consequential' in a way that getting out of bed sick, with what would later turn into pneumonia, was in itself quite inconsequential, but because of how events unfolded, came to represent a type of 'everything' through the hindsight of history.

Nonetheless, Patočka's standard of sacrifice for nothing (as articulated in his writings) might be so high that only Socrates and Christ would "count" as "real sacrifice," and someone like Bonhoeffer might, following Patočka's theory, only be a close approximation (or partial failure) that illuminates how difficult the standard might indeed be. In the hour of his actual sacrifice and becoming involved in the assassination plot, Bonhoeffer knew Hitler's impact was entirely global, and he could see that his own sacrifice might be good for everyone in general, but not good for prolonging his life in particular. In the way that Patočka's notion of caring for the soul is "inseparable from care for death which becomes the true care for life,"[84] Bonhoeffer also recognized his actions as a form of caring for his soul through a preparation for a certain sort of highly thoughtful death:

---

83 Ivan Chvatík, "Jan Patočka and the Possibility of Spiritual Politics," in *Thinking after Europe*, eds. Tava and Meacham, 29–30: "Patočka was confined to bed by the acute symptoms of chronic bronchitis, and it must have been clear to him that by accepting their offer he would overexert himself. But it was no common imprudence on his part. Patočka's act was in perfect agreement with what he had already learned, lectured, and written about over several years: namely, that political life is 'ever seeking the opportunity for action, for possibilities that present themselves; it means a life in active tension, one of extreme risk and unceasing upward striving [i.e. upswing] in which every pause is necessarily already a weakness for which the initiative of others lies in wait.'" Chvatík is quoting *Heretical Essays*, 38.

84 Patočka, *HE*, 103.

Fundamentally we feel that we really belong to death already, and that every new day is a miracle. It would not be true to say that we welcome death… [as] we should like to see something more of the meaning of our life's broken fragments. Nor do we try to romanticize death, for life is too great and too precious. Still less do we suppose that danger is the meaning of life—we are not desperate enough for that… We still love life, but I do not think that death can take us by surprise now. After what we have been through during the war, we hardly dare admit that we should like death to come to us, but not accidentally and suddenly through some trivial cause, but in the fullness of life and with everything at stake. It is we ourselves, and not outward circumstances, who make death what it can be, a death freely and voluntarily accepted.[85]

This is an articulation of how to care for the soul according to Bonhoeffer: love life's broken fragments, integrate the reality of death into life, freely and voluntarily accept and embrace the end of life, and adopt a notion of the human condition where one chooses to create meaning out of the tensions and contradictions of experience. The actual moment of one's death becomes a culmination of a lifetime of thinking and preparation that gives structure and meaning to the task of caring for the soul as one lives towards accepting human mortality.

As he was dissenting against the powerful leader of a state that had been turned into a death-machine, death was a possibility for Bonhoeffer at any moment as he wrote. Patočka also believed that caring for the soul was a complicated process moving toward the end of death, and as quoted above, to care for the soul meant preparing for death in the right way. This 'being-toward-death,' however, while it might have been partially inspired by the Heideggerian concept,[86] where Heidegger argues that the meaning of a life can be conceived through contemplating one's own death, for Patočka and Bonhoeffer, sacrifice as a way of being-toward-death was not just about their own death and personal meaning, but about their connection to the life and death of the whole community.[87]

---

85 Bonhoeffer, *Letters and Papers from Prison*, 16.
86 Heidegger, *Being and Time*, §53. Bonhoeffer takes up Heidegger's being-toward-death in his early work, *Act and Being* (*DB Complete Works*, Vol. 2, 148).
87 In discussing sacrifice, this is one place where Patočka uses Heideggerian categories against Heidegger. Heidegger defined 'being-toward-death' as central to his system of understanding, but claimed that one could only truly be concerned with one's own death, not the death of others, and that 'sacrifice' did not make sense. For Patočka, sacrifice for Being (that is the entirety of all beings and their world) made sense as a way of overcoming objectification,

Patočka finishes his analysis of sacrifice in the Varna lecture with a global claim: "radical sacrifice is the experience... [that] might lead to a transformation in the way we understand both life and the world—a transformation capable of bringing our outwardly rich yet essentially impoverished age to face itself, free of romantic underestimation, and thereby to surpass it."[88] On this measure, Patočka's sacrifice is an action that upholds the procedure of negative Platonism for the sake of the whole "age"; it gives rise to the constant questioning that in turn gives rise to a new transformation that can surpass old understandings. Patočka's sacrifice is then the bridge between an ontological understanding of the world based on negation and questioning and an existential understanding of caring for the soul. Still, the existential precedes the political. Without an existential awakening and a certain metanoia or conversion in the way one sees the world, the difficulties and inhibitions of 'sacrifice for nothing and everything' cannot be surmounted. One must think and exist in a certain way first, and from this a dissident's 'care of the soul' follows, and only after that does the politics of sacrifice seem possible.

Truth, Sacrifice, and Caring for the Soul as a Dissident

When Patočka speaks of sacrifice, he seems to be seeking out the possible relationship between sacrifice and finding truths of human existence, claiming that the rational-technological world might be unable to explain the paradoxical dynamics of sacrifice, and therefore self-sacrifice might also be an appearance of some deeper truth about the human condition. When sacrifice appears in the world, this framework suggests that we should pay close attention to what is being said. While not specifically named in his lecture containing these ideas about sacrifice, Patočka's thoughts should be read in the context of the philosophy student Jan Palach, who in 1968 died after lighting himself on fire to protest the invasion of Czechoslovakia by the Soviet army.[89] The event both made sense and made no sense: a college student was frustrated and depressed

---

dehumanization, and a lack of authenticity (that is, Heideggerian problems). See M. Heidegger, *Being and Time*, Trans. J. Stambaugh (New York: SUNY Press, 1996), 231–246; § 50–53.

88 Patočka, the "Varna Lecture," in Kohák, 339.

89 For a discussion of the wider context of Palach's self-immolation and self-immolation in general, see: A. Brinton, *Philosophy and Dissidence in Cold War Europe*.

enough about the political conditions of the world to take his own life. But such are the "uncomfortable, the irreconcilable, [and] the mysterious"[90] aspects of living in amplitude. As Patočka writes:

> Amplitude is where Man leaves behind him the everyday level of the usual life of enchantment, the level of sober untruth that veils the vision before the true heights and true dangers of our existence—there towards which Man heads with a calm expression and before which our timid finitude flees... The philosophy of amplitude is one that is conscious that life must in each moment bear the entire weight of the world and accepts this duty. The philosopher does not want to look for and construct artificial paradises that transform the human future, and does not want to awake banal hopes.[91]

In light of Dietrich Bonhoeffer's writings and life story, Patočka's ideas about amplitude suggest that the social-political and existential aspects of caring for the soul are not only deeply intertwined, but mutually constituting. Amplitude, and Bonhoeffer's idea of *Mundigkeit* or worldly maturity, can become that which makes the very high standard of sacrifice possible for the 'mere' human being, that is, for those of us who are not Socrates or Christ. A dissident can move between this idea of amplitude and the idea of sacrifice as long as they "accept a certain duty" and understand the "weight of the world."

In a colloquial sense, when Bonhoeffer and Patočka stepped into politics, they sacrificed themselves for a good greater than themselves, a cause higher than any mere object, in part for the sake of acting on the basis of principle. They did this at a time when others around them could only see the high instrumental costs of dissident action. Having undertaken such a sacrifice and participated in history as they did, they are not necessarily remembered as if their bodily sacrifices and deaths were 'for nothing' in the common sense—what they did has been ascribed meaning retrospectively by historians, and thus they are celebrated in the narratives of the twentieth century's wars. It must be remembered, however, that while both Nazism and Soviet Communism were defeated, at the time of these writings of Patočka and Bonhoeffer the outcomes of history were not self-evident; that their actions would be given 'meaning'

---

90 Patočka, (Manton), *LIP*, 39.
91 Patočka, (Manton), *LIP*, 38–9.

was not clear to them or a foregone conclusion for those around them. Germany might have won the war; Charter 77 might have disappeared into historical obscurity without 1989. As dissidents, Patočka and Bonhoeffer had to, in the fullness of their maturity and *Mundigkeit*, remove themselves from the instrumental-rational paradigms of their own times that prescribed ultimate ends, reject those ends and purposes as tenuous and uncertain, and come to believe in the intrinsic value of what they were doing. Only then could their actions approximate something that resembled what Patočka calls being for the sake of 'no particular thing,' but for everything in general, for everybody—that is, every human body that exists in time and history. They had to act, however, within a concrete vision of history and with respect to their own place within it; they had to recognize that their time had come to do something for the sake of everything, even if practically-speaking, it might amount to "nothing."

Patočka began his *Plato and Europe* lectures by asking his semi-illegal students to think about how philosophy could help them in the 'distress in which they found themselves' (see Introduction). Patočka repeats the word "distress" at the end of these lectures, pointing out how Plato and Aristotle were practicing philosophy as a way to "reconcile oneself with the fundamental distress of life."[92] This was not academic scholarly philosophy, Patočka claims, but they were engaging in 'philosophy' and advocating for 'caring for the soul' because they were concerned about the fact that "we do not know how to act and that we [nonetheless] have to, and that no one will take this responsibility from us and that we cannot take it away from ourselves to lighten it."[93] To care for the soul, then, in the terms of the Platonic cave, is a way of turning oneself around to face the world's somber realities and deeper truths, just as much as it is about going back inside the cave to face death by helping others (and thus going against the world's norms by becoming a dissident). Not unlike the chained inhabitant of Plato's cave, it also might take a whole lifetime of thinking (thus philosophy) to care for the soul and prepare oneself for going into the cave to help others turn around and care for their souls, as Socrates did, only to face liberation and death at the same moment.[94]

---

92 Patočka, *PE*, 219.
93 Patočka, *PE*, 219.
94 See Plato's *Apology* and *Crito* for the narration of how Plato conceived of Socrates' life as trying to get others out of the cave and dying for his actions. Patočka makes a series of distinctions about how a Platonic return to the cave is not the same thing as an Aristotelian return to the

Whatever Bonhoeffer's thoughts were as he was taken onto a scaffold to be hanged, no one will ever know, and as Bonhoeffer himself might say, only God can know the purity of the human heart.[95] He knew he was using violent 'unchristian' methods to be a 'Christian' committed to minimizing harm in the world, and we know from his writings that this contradiction did not deter him.[96] He had a structure of thinking that allowed him to live and take action within that contradiction; he did not think around contradiction, but with and within it. He believed that the law of the state was not the final judge, and he also knew that religion was not the final judge, as his religion gave him the dictate to 'turn the other cheek,' which he refused to follow. What he advocated instead was something which on the surface seems like an oxymoron (religionless Christianity), but in the dire circumstances of Nazi Germany, it made more sense to Bonhoeffer than both the religion and the politics of the day.[97] If we use Patočka's categories to describe Bonhoeffer's mode of 'contradictory' thinking, we see that Bonhoeffer had developed a way to 'care for his soul' in the midst of "intolerable, repugnant and futile" circumstances.[98] If his letters from prison are an accurate indication, he never regretted his decision to act and he went to the scaffold with the sense he had done the right thing, that his sacrifice had been done to care for the world, and that he had acted in full human maturity, *Munidgkeit*,

---

cave (*Plato and Europe*, 215–216), pointing out how Aristotle goes into the cave 'without force' and that for him the cave is a much richer, freer place than it is for Plato. He also seems to suggest that Aristotle combines both vertical and horizontal movement in his conceptions, whereas Plato limits human freedom by suggesting the only sort of motion is vertical motion. Both Bonhoeffer and Gandhi combine vertical and horizontal movement in their dissidence; see Chapter Three for discussion of Gandhi.

95 Bonhoeffer, *Letters and Papers from Prison*, 11: "The immanent righteousness of history rewards and punishes only men's deeds, but the eternal righteousness of God tries and judges their hearts."

96 Bonhoeffer, like Patočka, also rejects the romanticized reasons, the selfish reasons, and the aspiration for immortal grandiosity that can be reasons for suicidal behavior, but he recognizes how difficult it is to tell the difference in real life between sacrifice and pseudo-sacrifice: "Because the boundary between the freedom to sacrifice one's life and the misuse of this freedom for self-murder can often barely be perceived by the human eye, there is no basis for judging the single deed... it would be shortsighted to equate every form of self-inflicted death [Selbsttotung] with self-murder. When killing oneself is a conscious sacrifice of one's own life for others, judgment must at least be suspended, because here we have reached the limit of human understanding." Bonhoeffer, *Complete Works* Vol. 6, *Ethics*, 200.

97 The Catholic church had signed a concordat with Hitler; the Protestant Church supported pockets of resistance; individual Christians responded in as many different ways (from outright resistance to complicity to passivity) as the general population. See note 41 for two references on the roles the churches played during the Nazi era.

98 Bonhoeffer, *Letters and Papers from Prison*, 3.

in doing so. He also shows how the structure of 'caring for the soul' must rest on a foundation of what has already been described in the prior chapter: living in truth.

Like Patočka and Havel, Bonhoeffer sees truth as having multiple layers and demanding action in the world. For understanding the structure of dissidence in his writings, however, the truths Bonhoeffer understands about his world need not be identical with all dissidents. No situation of dissidence is ever identical with another. So even though it is factually accurate to say that he would not have done what he did without the 'truth' that was his faith in the Christian God, his theology (that is, the substance of his truth through the lens of religious ideas) is not the total contribution at stake here. His Christian faith became the building materials that Bonhoeffer chose to use, but the design of his thinking (the structure of that truth) could have been built with other materials. As I hope will become clearer in comparison to other activists in later chapters, no particular God or religious tradition has a monopoly on becoming a part of the structure of effective and sustained dissidence. Bonhoeffer's use of Christianity, however, illuminates part of the structure of dissent more generally as it relates to 'religious' ideas, and this can help all dissidents connect 'truth' to political action, the vertical to the horizontal, whether that truth is God-given or not.

Such a caveat is necessary, because to compare these two thinkers has its own sense of being 'heretical' to professional philosophy and theology. Devoutly Christian theological projects like Bonhoeffer's are not often compared to phenomenological projects like Patočka's that challenge universal metaphysics; so, in one way, this analysis itself rests on a contradiction. While I do not mean to oversimplify the very serious differences between them, that they were both dissidents who can teach us something important about the relationship between sacrifice and caring for the soul nonetheless matters. The similarities reveal a way of understanding modalities of political community in the midst of crises, as well as giving a glimpse into the human potential to live in truth in dark times. To look outward and upward, then, is necessary for dissidence, but notions of 'upward' can vary just as much as the time, place, and historical moments in one's 'outward' horizontal vision will necessarily vary. The structural analysis of dissidence should therefore be able to connect robust and complete understandings of both types of variation. So, even though Czechoslovakia in the 1970s was not Germany in the 1940s (two horizontal variations), the presumptions of Bonhoeffer's Christianity and Patočka's phenomenology (two vertical variations) were also far from identical. The point here is that each would recognize part of his own *structure* of thinking in the other, even though there is very different content holding together and making up that structure.[99]

Of those structural similarities, it can be seen that Patočka and Bonhoeffer both came of age through the abstractions of theology and philosophy in idealized and systematic forms, both trained quite formally in the academic conventions of their disciplines during their youth. But then they were both swept into the drama of twentieth century Europe's massive and complicated wars, and both chose quite deliberately to enter the messy world of ethical dilemmas, politics, and the unpredictable risks and unsystematic results of their actions. Neither emigrated: Patočka had several opportunities where he could have left Prague for Western Europe, and he declined to take them.[100] Bonhoeffer was studying at Union Theological Seminary in New York when World War Two began, and deliberately chose to depart for Germany, even though he could have sought safety in America.[101] Politics opened up their lives to risk and to sacrifice, linking lives previously concerned with primarily abstract categories with practical urgencies in an historical moment. Each chose to walk a narrow path between the impossibility of the circumstances and the possibilities for ethical action in their own community. The ideational abstractions of their philosophical and theological thinking, when confronted with certain political dilemmas, seemed to allow both to recognize that abstract systemizing could be escapism, and that action had

---

99 As has been pointed out above, there are other limitations of this comparison where it is necessary to emphasize the difference between structural similarity and substantive similarity: substantively, the times in which Patočka and Bonhoeffer found themselves were quite different from one another, and their deaths were also distinct. The sacrifice of Patočka's life as an indirect result of medical complications after harsh police interrogation for being the spokesman for Charter 77 is not in the same as Bonhoeffer's execution by the Nazis for actively participating in an assassination plot. The injustices, persecution and oppression suffered by the victims of the Nazis was also on a different scale than what was suffered in Warsaw pact states during Soviet occupation. No two historical moments will ever directly align substantively; all structural analogies have these limits, but the claim here is that it is nonetheless necessary to find similarities and patterns in dissident actions to be able to understand a more general human phenomenon.

100 Patočka's direct political involvement in dissident activities came only very late in his life (see Introduction). The suggestion here is that much earlier in his life (at an age comparable to Bonhoeffer) he chose not to emigrate, and to stay in Czechoslovakia; this was a 'passive' political decision, but of substantive political and existential importance. Many philosophers and writers from Eastern Europe chose to leave and seek exile and greater freedom in the West; Patočka did not do this. Sometimes doing nothing amounts to everything, to use the terms from above, where sacrifice for nothing amounts to everything.

101 Reinhold Niebuhr, "Death of a Martyr," *Christianity and Crisis*, no. 5 (June 25, 1945): 6–7.

to become responsibility, and responsibility action. Responsible action arises somewhere in the crossroads between upward thinking and outward thinking, and forward visions are made possible by caring for the soul in both life and death. It made no sense to Bonhoeffer to wait until someone else did something about Hitler; he saw it as his responsibility to try to do something, even if failure and disappointment were extremely likely. This may or may not have made him a 'bruiser,' but it surely did make him a dissident with whom Patočka would be able to converse.

Chapter Three
Confrontation as *Polemos*:
in Conversation with Mahatma Gandhi

In Philip Glass's opera *Satyagraha*, Mahatma Gandhi's life is depicted in three movements. In Act One, Gandhi receives his inspiration from the ancient Hindu text of the *Bhagavad Gita* and the mythical battle of Krishna and Arjuna; then he founds Tolstoy Farm in South Africa to work the land as a spiritual exercise; then he re-grounds his life in a vow of sacrifice.[1] In Act Two, Gandhi translates his work on the farm into the work of political protest after he is violently attacked, concluding: "If I were not to do my work these worlds would fall to ruin and I would be a worker in confusion."[2] In Act Three, Gandhi confronts the world with his satyagraha movement, beginning the Newcastle March in South Africa; in the last lyrics he recites 'The Lord': "Whenever the law of righteousness withers away and lawlessness arises, then do I generate myself on earth. I come into being age after age and take a visible shape and move a man with men for the protection of good, thrusting the evil back and setting virtue on her seat again."[3] The opera is performed in

---

1   *Satyagraha Libretto*, (chorus, end of act I). Vocal text by Constance DeJong; adapted from the *Bhagavad Gita;* Book by Philip Glass and Constance DeJong. Kanopy and Arthaus Musik, 2016. Originally produced by Arthaus Musik in 1983. https://www.metopera.org/metupload/ Satyagraha_libretto.pdf

2   *Satyagraha, Libretto*, Act II. One review claims the opera has no plot: Kate Dobbs Ariail, "Philip Glass' *Satyagraha*: Sounds Are Beautiful, but Stamina Is Required," http://www.indyweek. com/arts/archives/2011/12/06/philip-glass-satyagraha-sounds-are-beautiful-but-stamina-is-required. This review praises the overall impact of the movement: "Visually the work seduces and thrills. The movement is magisterial, mythic, infused with changing energies by the colors of light, props and costumes. You don't really have to 'make sense' of the scenes: Just go with the flow of energy. 'Satyagraha' means 'truth-force,' and the truth is in the music as well as the visual and kinetic aspects of the opera."

3   *Satyagraha Libretto*, act III.

Sanskrit, the language of the ancient Hindu text of the *Bhagavad Gita*, and the verse is adopted from this same text in combination with Gandhi's writings. The libretto is only two pages long.[4] When staged, it is the movement of the bodies and the visuals that communicate the overall meaning; the words are minimalist poetic and musical accompaniment, but are not meant to create a linear 'plot.' The opera depicts not so much a 'story,' but a 'life' and the meaning of its existence in three movements.[5]

To recall Patočka's discussion of the three movements of human existence (see Introduction), there seems to be some resonance with the structure of Glass's *Satyagraha* worth considering:

> If we are to explain the movement of our existence... we need to appeal to a triad of movements which presuppose and interpenetrate each other and whose basic relations need to be examined phenomenologically: (i) the movement of sinking roots, of anchoring—an instinctive-affective movement of our existence; (ii) the movement of self-sustenance, of self-projection—the movement of our coming to terms with the reality we handle, a movement carried out in the region of human work; (iii) the movement of existence in the narrower sense of the word which typically seeks to bestow global closure and meaning on the regions and rhythms of the first and second movement.[6]

If Patočka asks about the structure of movement necessary for a human life of engagement and meaning, then Glass's illumination of Gandhi's life in three movements shows something important about how Patočka's thinking can inform understandings of political movements. Glass explains Gandhi first through depicting a movement of sinking roots and grounding, then through the movement of coming to terms with a certain mode of human work, and then forward to a third movement of confrontation with the world that seeks to give larger meaning to existence. As so many contemporary non-violent political movements owe to Gandhi at least partial inspiration, then the overlap of Glass's artistic

---

4   *Satyagraha Libretto*, (chorus, end of act I). Gandhi was a prolific writer and his complete works are comprised of 100 volumes of roughly 400–500 pages each. https://www.gandhiheritageportal .org/the-collected-works-of-mahatma-gandhi. The contrast of this to the two pages of Glass's operatic representation of his life is notable for the difference.
5   Reviews of the performances of *Satyagraha* in newspapers tend to advise viewers to read up about Gandhi before the performance or in the program notes, as the structure and presentation assumes fairly detailed knowledge of Gandhi's life. See reviews cited above.
6   Patočka, *BCLW*, 148.

vision, Gandhi's life, and Patočka's philosophy can speak to something important about the existential aspects of activism and dissidence, in particular how political action can arise from living through the rhythms of these three movements. Approaching Patočka's "third movement" with Gandhi's life in mind is particularly illustrative:

> The third movement is the movement of existence in the true sense, the movement of self-achievement... the first two movements are movements of finite beings which self-realize fully within their finitude, wholly plunging into it and therein surrendering themselves to the rule of a power—of the Earth. The third movement is an attempt to break through our earthliness. Not by inventing illusions: rather, detachment from particulars brings us to a level on which we can integrate finitude, situated-ness, earthliness, mortality precisely into existence... Existence, in the sense of the third movement, is... a task for all of life in its integrity.[7]

This abstract description could map onto Gandhi's life, but also onto the life of many dissidents who have given themselves over to the task of protest and a life of amplitude (see previous chapter on 'amplitude'). If philosophy seeks to describe abstractly a set of categories that can illuminate individual lives and worlds by connecting particularities to generalities, then seeing Gandhi as a case of Patočka's third movement of 'breaking through our earthliness' is to show the general applicability of Patočka's philosophy to all who turn to dissident politics as a way to move through life. While the scale of Gandhi's operatic story seems quite literally larger than life, the three movements of existence, at least in Patočka's formulations, can help us narrate acts of resistance on a scale applicable to everyone's life, the small writ large through the common ground of philosophical categories. Through the 'three movements of existence,' Gandhi's life becomes comparable to everyone's life.

To characterize the unfolding of human life in three movements represents Patočka building on prior tropes: the human experience of birth, life, and death is a three-fold reality, and the general influence of Christianity's tripartite structure of the divine also makes three-act plays feel familiar. There is something that starts it all, there is something that ends it all, and then there is the question of how to categorize everything in between. The beginnings and endings, and the borders

---

7   Patočka, *BCLW*, 151.

where the beginning ends and the end begins, become the interesting substance of many three-fold structures. In Patočka's case, he was significantly influenced by Hannah Arendt's distinction between labor, work and action, as well as the three-part arguments of other philosophers.[8] Given that Glass interpreted Gandhi's life in a three-act framework that seems to align loosely with the categories put forward by Patočka as 'the three movements human existence,' this must be taken as part of a larger reflection of something already there in human experience, not as a causal or interpretive claim linking Glass to Patočka in any particular way. The point is not that Glass read Patočka, or that Patočka was thinking of Gandhi when he wrote *Body, Community, Language, World*. Rather, as Patočka and Glass thought through the structure of human existence—one interpreting and celebrating a famous activist, one thinking in abstract philosophical categories about the way to understand human life—they landed on similar ways to explain a tripartite structure already there in the world. It can therefore be asked if Glass, Gandhi, and Patočka would agree that "worlds would fall to ruin" were it not for human action being able to reach the culmination of something like Patočka's 'third movement of human existence.'

Glass's opera *Satyagraha* is also helpful for putting Gandhi and Patočka into conversation because Patočka understands the third movement of human existence through the metaphor of music:

A movement of this kind is also a *dynamis*, a possibility being realized... something that is not yet present and that can take the given into itself and forge it into a unified meaning. That again is reminiscent of a melody in which every component, tone, is part of something that transcends it; in every component something is being prepared that will form the mean-

---

8   Arendt, working with inspiration loosely from Aristotle, claims in the *Human Condition* that political action is the highest form of human action, higher than both 'work' and 'labor.' She distinguished between 'work,' which left something behind in the world (a work of art, a work of literature, a work of architecture) with 'labor,' the repetitive tasks done to maintain daily bodily life. Neither of these for Arendt came to the level of the *vita activa* symbolized by political action, which revealed the identity of the actor, allowed for engaged democratic participation, and built the community. Patočka evokes Arendt in developing his own theory of action and movement, but he moves in a somewhat different direction, and addresses politics much less directly. Given that Patočka knew Hegel's work quite well, and translated his *Phenomenology of Spirit* into Czech early in his career, it would also be possible to see here echoes of Hegel's three-fold conception of consciousness, where there is a developmental progression from consciousness to self-consciousness to reason. Patočka would reject the end point of Hegel's drive toward absolute spirit, however, in a way that he would not object outright to Arendt's view of action.

ing and nature of the composition, but it is not a movement of something that exists already at the start. While the composition is being performed, its overall meaning remains to some extent futural, still being formed. Just as a polyphonic composition is a movement of movements, so the movement of our existence unfolds in a series of relatively autonomous sequences which modify each other and affect each other.[9]

Music is an act of human expression where movements (in musical scores) and acts (in operatic scores) can be performed in very different ways given the time, place, musicians, and directors shaping the production. The meanings created by the combination of the score and the performance, furthermore, as in the case of certain modes of political activism, are constructed through choices about how to perform the same libretto differently, variations following themes but remaining variations.[10] The performance is meant to be intrinsically valuable in and of itself, read as its own work of artistic creativity and expression; the 1980 premiere of *Satyagraha* and a 2011 Met Opera performance are different works of art, but based on the same text.[11] The interpretation of the score by directors, actors, and musicians, despite the common code of the libretto shared between the performances, is what makes the art complete and whole, what moves an idea into reality. Glass's two-page libretto cannot tell us very much about the force of Gandhi's existence until it is performed, perhaps as a person's genetic code cannot write the history of a life.

Something similar holds for the kind of 'acts' practiced by Gandhi and conceived in Patočka's three movements: life as movement and movement as life create polyphonic compositions aimed at both the present and the future. To find 'unified meaning,' the movement has to be performed to connect the present to the future. Much of what

---

9 Patočka, *BCLW*, 147. See also *Natural World as a Philosophical Problem*, where Patočka uses music to talk about the fluidity of the interpretation of language. The attempt to analyze music that we do not understand, that is "beyond the pale of our acoustic," is instructive for thinking about language translation (*BCLW*, 45). When explaining Bergson's theory of movement, Patočka cites his use of the metaphor of tones and melody (*BCLW*, 144–5) but then critiques Bergson for being less profound than Aristotle on the issue of movement.

10 The politics of performance and the performance of politics is a topic in political theory. Two examples: Judith Butler, *Notes Toward a Performative Theory of Assembly* (Cambridge, MA: Harvard University Press, 2015) and Elzbieta Matynia, *Performative Democracy* (Boulder: Paradigm, 2015).

11 The opera premiered in 1980 in the Netherlands and there were later performances in many countries. For a full history, see http://philipglass.com/compositions/satyagraha/.

Gandhi did was political performance on the stage of history, political theatre that interpreted the meanings of sacrosanct texts through his movement, including both his political 'movement' in the larger social sense, and the micro-movement of his own body in the most local sense. (More on this below: Gandhi's way of putting his body in other people's way was a form of political movement.) If Patočka's theory of three movements is thought of as the stages of a bodily life performance that is always in perpetual motion-unto-death, a libretto always in need of being performed anew in evolving contexts and expanding horizons, then Patočka and Gandhi in conversation reveals key paradoxes that can illuminate the connection between philosophy and dissidence as two types of movement.

Following the three-fold structure of human existence as conceived by Patočka, three paradoxes of Gandhi's life and ideas will be discussed here to provide illumination of Patočka's philosophical categories: (1) the vision of corporality articulated by Gandhi's insistence on collapsing the traditional borders between public and private by grounding politics in bodily existence (related to the first movement of anchoring); (2) the paradoxical way that Gandhi conceives of human work as needing to 'deny the fruits of action' and focus on means rather than ends (this being a mode of 'work' related to the second movement); (3) and in terms of the third movement, Gandhi paradoxically conceives of 'non-violent war' as the proper mode of confronting (and therein transcending) the given structures of human existence to find a more truthful and more authentic "self-achievement" through movement that "breaks away from our earthliness." The discussion will conclude with an analysis of how Patočka's third movement is an example of the intersection of the horizontal and vertical modalities of life discussed in Chapter Two (suggesting that Bonhoeffer and Gandhi have much in common as well), and therefore the third movement is also a modality of what Patočka calls *polemos*, a specific form of confrontation drawn from the ideas of Heidegger and Heraclitus.

Throughout his discussions of the three movements, Patočka insists that "each of those three movements is always a movement *shared*."[12] This shared aspect of the three movements hints at important political implications: one does not move through the world alone on this vision, and for Gandhi and Patočka both, the third movement necessarily happens

---

12   Patočka, *BCLW*, 149. Patočka's emphasis.

in a social and political context alongside others. The struggle to reveal the shared truth of this contested world is at the center of *polemos*, the confrontation that Patočka sees as the intersection of politics and philosophy, and "that which constitutes the *polis* and the primordial insight that makes philosophy possible."[13]

The First Movement: Sinking Political Roots and the Body

As he describes the first movement, Patočka begins by taking up the question of how to think about one's own human body philosophically: "Having a body at our disposal is at the same time the basis of life and an understanding of its most basic possibility."[14] That we could not be human without having a body seems rudimentary, but in the context of the philosophical inheritance of Descartes, where "I think, therefore I am" was traditionally the underlying assumption, the importance of the body and its corporality for defining what it is to be 'human' was marginalized in the history of western philosophy until the twentieth century. Pushing against this, Patočka is placing himself in a conversation trying to rectify this marginalization of the body as a philosophical category.[15] He uses the framework of movement to emphasize the "fundamental corporeity of our existence."[16] He goes on to point out how, "in our self-movement, we understand that we move a body and that its guidance depends on us. If we did not understand that, then all our higher mental life, all lived experiencing over and above that, would become impossible. So it is not just that movement belongs to existence, rather, existence is movement."[17] Therefore the first movement of coming to be human is what he calls "sinking roots or anchoring," and it requires that we recognize both our corporeity, but also "that aspect

---

13 Jan Patočka, *Heretical Essays on the Philosophy of History*, trans. Erazim Kohák, ed. James Dodd (Chicago and La Salle: Open Court 1996) 43.
14 Patočka, *BCLW*, 144.
15 This is to say he is responding to and building off the work of Maurice Merleau-Ponty. See: Maurice Merleau-Ponty, *Phenomenology of Perception*, trans. Colin Smith (London: Routledge, 2002); *The Primacy of Perception and other Essays on Phenomenological Psychology, the Philosophy of Art, History and Politics* (Evanston: Northwestern University Press, 1964); *The Visible and the Invisible: Followed by Working Notes*, ed. Claude Lefort, trans. Alphonso Lingis (Evanston: Northwestern University Press, 1969 [2001]).
16 Patočka, *BCLW*, 144.
17 Patočka, *BCLW*, 144.

of existence which is our situation (that we are always already set into a world)."[18] The first movement therefore entails acknowledging that we came to exist somewhere by the accidents of our birth, and this "instinctual-affective sphere totally and continuously co-determines life in all further spheres."[19] In this view, while there are certain aspects of our body and our place in the world we can transcend and move beyond, our body and our given (un-chosen) situation will always determine certain aspects of our life. Patočka knows that instinctually everyone knows this on some level, but becoming aware of all of the various implications of our 'emplacement' (as discussed in the Introduction[20]) is the first step to move toward self-awareness and a more 'authentic' existence, where transcending our bondage to the 'earthliness' of our situation becomes possible.[21]

This is why the first movement does not actually entail moving: to 'sink roots' and 'anchor' requires being still. Gandhi's life helps to clarify what this paradox aims at articulating. Born in colonial India, as a young man Gandhi travelled to the UK to be educated as a lawyer. As he wrote about in his autobiography, he dressed himself as an Englishman, attempted to take up habits that made him respectable to those in positions of power, and sought 'normal' legal work. He travelled to South

---

18 Patočka, *BCLW*, 148.
19 Patočka, *BCLW*, 148.
20 As quoted previously: "We are always already somewhere in the whole of the world. This is the basis on which our active doing takes place. I do this and that within the framework of the possibilities I have seized. Acting always takes place in a particular stance and movement. The world placed us in a specific region, the world addressed us... the world addressed us in general, placed us in a certain context, now the need arises to take a stance with respect to the concrete particulars of the context. A region open in the awareness of how we are is a part of the phenomenon of the horizon." Patočka, *BCLW, 43.*
21 There is a kind of Schrödinger's Cat problem with the first movement: once you observe and describe it as the first movement, implying that being in the first movement is a state of being naïve and not fully authentic, by the mere fact of your observation and reflection on the issue, you can no longer be "in" the first movement, and it ceases to exist for you. The person "in" the first movement does not know it; he or she is naïve and living a merely bodily existence unreflectively. To discuss the "first movement" of Gandhi's life and the importance of the body, therefore, is to discuss how he did indeed live naïvely for a time, but then transcended the body by reflecting philosophically on the body, circling back to reflection on the first movement as a springboard toward the third. In *Plato and Europe*, Patočka acknowledges the challenges of this circle in general: "Our reality is always situational, so that if it is reflected upon, it is already different by the fact that we have reflected. Of course the question is whether by reflection reality is improved... a reflected-upon situation—in contrast to a naïve situation—is to a certain extent a clarified one... but we will not get to the heart of the matter without reflecting...If we reflect, then, upon our situation, we can change it, and change it into an enlightened, self-conscious one. This enlightening is on the way to truth about the situation." (*PE*, 2). So, like the cat, observing it can nullify one understanding of it.

Africa as part of that work.[22] All of this would be, on Patočka's framework of movement (and Gandhi's later self-understanding), moments of an *inauthentic* existence, because Gandhi had not become fully aware of the degree to which his colonized existence was 'anchored' and 'rooted' in a very different place than where he thought he was 'existing.' Later in his political campaigns for Indian home-rule (Swaraj), he not only took off the British clothing and insisted on spinning his own cloth as a boycott to the British textile industry, but the idea of "home-rule" took on a corporal and political importance simultaneously.[23] Satyagraha required bodily and corporal discipline as a prerequisite for political action; participants in the struggle for (political) independence had to show themselves to be (existentially) independent of their corporeal desires.[24] He required satyagrahis (the activist followers of satyagraha) to do purification rituals before they acted politically, and he himself made a vow of celibacy as an exercise of bodily control.[25] There was never any separation of public and private in all of this: overeating, copulating, and lack of personal discipline in private disqualified someone for Gandhi's politics in the public sphere.[26] This was done with the acknowledgement that one's lack of control of the body was a source of potential violence; the 'instinctual-affective' body was anchored in violence, and therefore considerable work had to be done to break through the earthliness of

---

22 Mohandas K. Gandhi, *An Autobiography. The Story of My Experiments with Truth* (Boston: Beacon Press, 1993) 42–140.

23 Gandhi, *An Autobiography*, 50–51.

24 "We experience every moment of our lives, that often while the body is subject to our control, the mind is not. This physical control should never be relaxed, and in addition we must put forth a constant endeavor to bring the mind under control. We can do nothing more, nothing less. If we give way to the mind, the body and the mind will pull different ways, and we shall be false to ourselves. Body and mind may be said to go together, so long as we continue to resist the approach of every evil thought." M.K. Gandhi, *From Yervada Mandir: Ashram Observances*, trans. Valji Govindji Desai. (Ahmedabad: Jinanji Desai, 1991 [1930]) 19. These quotations are from a translation of *From Yeravda Mandir* available alongside the *Complete Works of Mahatma Gandhi* on the Gandhi Heritage Portal, www.gandhiheritageportal.org. The Complete Works are hereafter abbreviated "CWMG" followed by volume number then page number.

25 "Chastity is one of the greatest disciplines without which the mind cannot attain requisite firmness. A man who is unchaste loses stamina, becomes emasculated and cowardly. He whose mind is given over to animal passions is not capable of any great effort." (in *Hind Swaraj*, CWMG X: 52) The difficulties of getting early followers to take these requirements seriously is discussed in Gandhi, *An Autobiography*, 469–474 and in Gandhi, *From Yeravda Mandir* (Ahmedabad: Navajian Trust, 1991) 14–27. Part of this 'duty' of chastity was to obey orders like a soldier. For a commentary on this aspect of his activism, see: Veena R Howard, *Gandhi's Ascetic Activism: Renunciation and Social Action* (Albany, NY: State University of New York Press, 2013).

26 Farah Godrej, "Nonviolence and Gandhi's Truth: A Method for Moral and Political Arbitration," *The Review of Politics*, 68, no. 2 (Spring 2006) 287–317.

this bondage to overcome the body's instincts towards violence.[27] Once he developed this more 'authentic' understanding of his anchoring and became self-aware of the fact he was trapped in what Patočka would call a first-movement frame, Gandhi took pains to move onward toward transcending the problems given to him by his emplacement in a world governed by British colonialism. This did not happen all at once.

While initially he 'projected' himself into the world of work as a lawyer and not an activist ('work' is a second movement category for Patočka, see below), Gandhi later overcame his initial denial of his actual anchoring and rooting as a colonized Indian. He did this by doing the opposite of denying his roots: he returned to India from South Africa, understanding that his "instinctual-affective sphere totally and continuously co-determines life in all further spheres."[28] He believed he had to cultivate this in order to transcend it; he had to be 'home' (rooted, anchored) before he could do political work that was able to transform the inauthenticity of the first movement of his existence as a passive colonial subject.[29] In doing this, Gandhi comes to understand the relationship between 'the place' of his body and 'the place' of his accidental birth as coterminous and codetermined. He is placed in his body as much as he was emplaced within colonial India, and the movement of life cannot escape these facts. To use his body in political actions in the public sphere, to make his body the place of politics, was a way to ground politics locally and turn existence into movement by moving his body toward political confrontation, just as much as going 'home' back to India was a movement of political confrontation.[30] This confrontation

---

27 When Patočka elaborates instances of the third movement in history, his description of Buddhism sounds something like Gandhi's tactics: "The third movement is an attempt at shaking the dominance of the Earth in us, shaking of what binds us in our distinctiveness... we shall restrict ourselves to only two examples of this attempt at shaking the rule of the earth in us... one from the sphere of Buddhism, the other from that of Christianity... In Buddhism... domination is thirst, needs, appetites to fill the emptiness within us. Thus to break with the earth, we try to break with need, to extinguish need and thirst..." Patočka, *BCLW*, 160–161. The relationship with the earth articulated in these passages changes and shifts somewhat in Patočka's later work, see Chapter 5.

28 Patočka, *BCLW*, 148.

29 The second movement has an additional feature relevant to Gandhi. As Patočka describes it: "as soon as the movement of self-extension becomes dominant, the sphere of instinctual affective movement is repressed and forgotten. That is a special mode of non-understanding, of being in untruth." *BCLW*, 158.

30 Given the discussion in the previous chapter on sacrifice, suicide, and the political relationship to the body in Bonhoeffer and Patočka, it is pertinent to include here one passage where Gandhi comments on this relationship: "Should we commit suicide? Even that is no solution, if we believe, as we do, that so long as the spirit is attached to the flesh, on every destruction

is arguably part of what would make up his third movement, (more on this below) but in order to get there, he had to go back and reflect on the first movement and re-anchor himself self-consciously in his body and homeland.

If 'home rule' applied to both the body and the body politic, then Gandhi's idea that truth was something never absolutely attained by any mere mortal human meant that both the body and the body politic became grounds for his 'experiments with truth.'[31] In order to find the truth, he believed various and multiple ideas and principles had to be tested through everyday practices and daily actions; he thus experimented with his body and his politics, often changing and correcting course when an experiment went awry.[32] Satyagraha was one such experiment. In Hindi, *satya* means 'truth' and *graha* means 'force.' Gandhi continually reiterated the distinction between his satyagraha and the English term 'passive resistance.' To him, what he was doing was not passive, and it was not about reacting to an outside force through resistance, but rather depended upon developing that force inside oneself that would be able to push forward through life by an impetus toward truth. The truth was both in the body and in the movement.[33] Gandhi's tactics observed from the outside look very passive: limp bodies blockading roads, fasting and refusing to eat, sit-ins, etc. There is a stillness and inertness to some of these tactics, but there is a considerable amount of motion and action in the inward stance necessary to stay still (and do nothing)

---

of the body it weaves for itself another. The body will cease to be only when we give up all attachment to it. This freedom from all attachment is the realization of God as Truth. Such realization cannot be attained in a hurry. The body does not belong to us. While it lasts, we must use it as a truth handed over to our charge. Treating in this way the things of the flesh, we may one day expect to become free from the burden of our body. Realizing the limitations of the flesh, we must strive day by day towards the ideal with what strength we have in us." Gandhi, *From Yervada Mandir,* 11–12.

31 "But it is impossible for us to realize perfect Truth so long as we are imprisoned in this moral frame. We can only visualize it in our imagination. We cannot, through the instrumentality of this ephemeral body, see face to face Truth which is eternal. That is why in the last resort one must depend on faith." Gandhi, *From Yervada Mandir,* 7–8.

32 Gandhi, *An Autobiography*, pp. xxvi-xxvii. He explains why he has called his life a series of 'experiments' in the introduction to his autobiography.

33 In some of his later writings he also equated truth with God: "The word Satya (Truth) is derived from Sat, which means 'being.' Nothing is or exists in reality except Truth. That is why Sat or Truth is perhaps the most important name of God. In fact it is more correct to say that Truth is God, than to say that God is Truth... Sat or Satya is the only correct and fully significant name for God. And where there is truth, there also is knowledge which is true. Where there is no Truth, there can be no true knowledge... Devotion to this Truth is the sole justification for our existence. All our activities should be centered in Truth. Truth should be the very breath of our life." Gandhi, *From Yervada Mandir,* 1–2.

when confronted violently.[34] In both stillness and motion, Gandhi's tactics require bringing the body to the political field, in its full mass and weight, to stand between opposed forces while refraining from reacting violently.

From where Gandhi was standing, his 'emplacement' within the violent and discriminatory colonial worlds of South Africa and India, Gandhi could articulate with "body language" (quite literally) how non-violence was moral action in and of itself, enacted through 'truth' and 'force' together. Gandhi's moral-political language is therefore contained in the motion of the body: by placing the body in a stance of confrontation vis-à-vis others who were willing to do violence, he and his campaigners were able to articulate the moral claim that the violence was wrong.[35] His way of living in truth began *and ended* with nonviolence, what he called 'ahimsa.'[36] Nonviolence was a contrast to the violence and the ethos of instrumental gains within the colonial state, as well as the instinctual violence of the untrained body, and therefore nonviolent action (given the structure of satyagraha) contained its own purpose and meaning. Even if no legal or political gains were ever made beyond the emphatic stating of moral claims through physical movement (sit-ins, blockades, and marches), something moral had still been *done*. Or, in Patočka's terms, Gandhi had transcended the first (and second) movements of life, but could not have done so without acknowledging and using the rooted corporeity of the first movement.

---

34 Patočka might appreciate this stillness, as he argues that "even a thinker meditating must assume a certain physical posture; even quieting down, negation of movement and dynamism, even interrupting the immediate thrust toward things, are physical accomplishments." *BCLW*, 43.

35 Faisal Devji, *The Impossible Indian: Gandhi and the Temptation of Violence* (Cambridge, MA: Harvard University Press, 2012).

36 Bhikhu Parekh explains the paradoxical spiritual origin of Gandhi's idea of nonviolence: "He takes over the Hindu concept of *ahimsa*, finds it passive and negative and turns to the cognate Christian concept of love to help him understand and redefine it. He realizes that love is an emotion, compromises the agent's autonomy and builds up attachments to the world, and so he redefines it in the light of the Hindu concept of *anasakti* or detachment. Gandhi's double conversion, his Hinduisation of the Christianized Hindu concept, yields the fascinating concept of a non-emotive, serene and detached but positive and active love, and a non-activist life of action. Although the concepts contain tensions, they are highly suggestive and beyond the reach of either tradition alone." *Gandhi's Political Philosophy: A Critical Examination* (Notre Dame: University of Notre Dame Press, 1989), 195. Parekh's characterization of Gandhi's technique of philosophical and spiritual synthesis in this case leads him to a wider generalization: "In each case he sets up a creative dialogue and sometimes an imaginative confrontation between the relevant traditions and not only combines what strikes him as their valuable insights but also occasionally generates wholly new concepts. Even when his 'discoveries' are unconvincing, his intellectual and moral 'experiments' are invariably stimulating." 196.

Using one's body in this way requires a very specific non-Cartesian understanding of one's relationship to one's own (potentially pained and discomforted) flesh; it requires the ability to understand one's own body in a political way, and as Patočka might argue, to also understand the body in a philosophical way.

The Second Movement: The Work of Life Without Its 'Fruits'

In describing the second movement, Patočka is concerned with how work and productivity shape the quality of our existence. This movement is necessary to live in a community and engage with others, but it is a process of "self-objectification" and "self-extension." Patočka's second movement, like the first, has modalities of inauthenticity and incompleteness: "Existence in this entire realm is an interested one. This is the realm of the average, of anonymity, of social roles in which people are not themselves, are not existence in the full sense... [and] are reduced to their roles."[37] The idea that one's work can reduce a person to an object of mere productivity leads him to identify certain ways of working as dehumanizing. Patočka is also concerned, as in the first movement, with the worker who works merely to sustain his bodily needs and who sees work as the main or only purpose of existence. In work, we might be capable of self-denial of instinctual-affective desires,[38] of deferring our instincts and subordinating ourselves to a work project, but we might still be unaware that work is not a full existence. For Patočka, there is a form of existence beyond work, and it requires self-awareness and reflection to overcome the objectifying pressures of work to arrive at "an existence that sees itself as existence,"[39] rather than merely seeing oneself within the functional role of productivity, where one exists as a cog-in-a-machine. The third movement of existence captures this world beyond

---

37 Patočka, *BCLW*, 151.
38 For Patočka, asceticism and self-denial are part of the transition from the first to second movement; while he does not elaborate at length on asceticism in *BCLW*, Gandhi's own self-denial practices might be put in this light: had Gandhi only worked to deny his bodily pleasures, he would not have achieved the third movement, an understanding of the self in the world where those measures of self-denial became political and brought other people together. It is in the second movement for Patočka where "purging oneself of the immediate, of the instinctual, is what asceticism makes self-conscious." *BCLW*, 159.
39 Patočka, *BCLW*, 151.

work, but without work, the first movement cannot be overcome nor the third movement achieved.

In applying this framework to Gandhi, it is necessary to observe several modes of work at stake over the course of his life. His first profession was as a British lawyer, and as already mentioned, he came to see this as an inauthentic mode of work. As depicted in Glass's *Satyagraha*, between this first career and becoming a full-time activist, Gandhi set up a self-sufficient farm in South Africa, calling it Tolstoy Farm in reference to the seminal inspiration that the writings of Leo Tolstoy played in shaping his views of the world.[40] Perhaps Glass's characterization of this phase in Gandhi's life in the libretto might be considered an appropriately evocative description of this transformative stage. In one line in the opera, Gandhi implores those helping him on the farm to change their relationship with work: "So act as the ancient of days old, performing works as spiritual exercise."[41] For Gandhi, this would be a reference to both the Hindu tradition of karma yoga as well as the Christian tradition of spiritual exercises, as he drew on both.[42] Tolstoy Farm in South Africa was a literal experiment in self-sustenance and self-rule, and from this 'work,' and (as Patočka would call it) his 'self-projection,' was initially grounded in the earth (literally in farming and spinning cotton), and later the work was projected into the sphere of both politics and spirituality.[43] Of course the farm was eventually not enough for Gandhi, and his politicization is depicted in Glass's opera as growing out of his reaction to being randomly and violently attacked in a racist incident.[44] After such a life-event, he came to see that the farm was not going to solve the problem of unjust colonial practices of racial segregation in South Africa. This form of 'work' could not confront such violence, and Gandhi eventually went on to do his 'spiritual exercises' on a political stage.

---

40 Gandhi most frequently cited Leo Tolstoy's *The Kingdom of God is Within You*. Gandhi recounts that he was "overwhelmed" by the book when he first read it. (See: *An Autobiography*, 137.)

41 Philip Glass and Candace DeJong, *Satyagraha*, libretto.

42 For an account of the political implications of Gandhi's religious syncretism, see: Bhikhu Parekh, *Gandhi's Political Philosophy* (Notre Dame: University of Notre Dame Press, 1989), 85–109.

43 Paraphrasing here from Patočka's previously quoted passage on the three movements, see above. Patočka, *BCLW*, 148.

44 Richard Attenboro's biographical film, *Gandhi*, uses a similar incident to explain the beginnings of his transformation away from being a lawyer, where he is thrown off a train for refusing to move to the appropriate car for non-whites (*Gandhi*, 1982: Columbia Pictures). This is recounted in Gandhi's *Autobiography* as well.

Despite leaving behind the farm, aspects of self-rule and self-sustenance stayed with Gandhi's movement and structured the way his political 'work' was done. On the farm, the early satyagrahis (the activists following Gandhi's satyagraha movement) learned how to do manual labor as a spiritual exercise that was valuable in-and-of itself; work was done because it was a self-sustaining activity that promoted self-rule and more work. While some of the labor also produced food, that was incidental to Gandhi's reasoning in setting up the farm, and it was more like what Bonhoeffer called a "community without a *telos*" (see previous chapter). It was meant to gather people together to do something together, where doing work for the sake of itself and being able to separate one's activities from the final results of action became the core of Gandhi's vision. This is also generally the way all activism has to begin, as results are so tenuously distant at the start of all movements and campaigns. No one knows what will happen once the political action is initiated, yet everyone within the community of action has to agree to start acting nonetheless, together in a frame of mind where action has no telos but itself, where it is worth doing in order to do it, intrinsically so.

It is helpful to illuminate this paradox by remembering that when Gandhi began his satyagraha program in South Africa, it was not 'reasonable' or 'logical' for him to believe that he could do away with British colonialism. It was hardly reasonable for him to believe he could get one British law on segregation changed. In order to undertake the humblest of his early campaigns, he had to renounce the idea that his actions would bear fruit in the immediate *or* long term, and to focus instead on the action itself.[45] What was the structure of appropriate action? Was the action fitting to the context? What message was the action sending? What was within the action that was morally worthy in-and-of-itself, with no other results? Was the action treating human beings as valuable ends in and of themselves? Gandhi wrote that this approach came directly from his reading of one part of the Hindu text of the *Bhagavad Gita*, a moment in the story where the warrior Arjuna hesitates on the battlefield when faced with the imperative to kill members of his own clan.[46]

---

45 In another famous instance, Robert Oppenheimer used this framework to understand his involvement as a scientist in developing the atomic bomb. See: James A. Hijiya "The *Gita* of J. Robert Oppenheimer," *Proceedings of The American Philosophical Society* 144, no. 2 (June 2000). Discussed below.

46 "The Message of the Gita," CWMG: VOL XLI; reprinted in Stephen Mitchell, ed., *Bhagavad Gita: A New Translation*, reprint ed. (New York: Harmony Books, 2002), 211–222.

There is a dialogue with the Hindu god Krishna about why he, Arjuna, should not hesitate, and why he should fulfill his duty as a warrior and 'renounce the fruits of his actions.' Krishna convinces Arjuna to act and to carry out his duty as a warrior, demonstrating how the renunciation of the fruits of one's actions (that is, the ability to give up one's fixation on final results) was necessary to make action valuable in-and-of-itself. Despite the violence that this entailed in the context of the particular story, Gandhi speaks of this moment as important for the development of his understanding of action, duty, and non-violence.[47]

This framework of renunciation, in turn, can motivate people beyond states of ambivalence when they sense their actions will indeed bear no fruit. This way of reasoning became for Gandhi another way of pointing to the intrinsic value of action itself, where one has to value it over and above its instrumental ends, therein motivating people to act in circumstances where the fruits of action are highly problematic and uncertain. In Arjuna's case, action meant killing his cousins and clan; in Gandhi's case, it meant starting a political campaign that involved uncertain ends, significant amounts of bodily pain, and ridicule by both his own people and the British authorities. Separating oneself from the ends and fruits of action is an act of detachment, and while paradoxical within a goal-oriented culture of results, it is liberating, perhaps in the third-movement sort of way Patočka would call 'existence becoming aware of its existence.' In Glass's *Satyagraha* libretto, the idea is expressed as potentially revolutionary: "with senses freed, the wise man should act, longing to bring about the welfare and coherence of the world. Therefore, perform unceasingly the works that must be done, for the man detached who labors on to the highest must win through."[48] Gandhi surely longed for the welfare and coherence of the world to come as a *result* of his actions, but this stance requires that one renounce the fruits of action in one's own lifetime, knowing that one does not have divine knowledge of the future, nor necessarily even fully accurate knowledge of what will come

---

47 Duty was central to Gandhi's philosophy, and also the basis for his questioning of the emerging paradigm of 'human rights,' including the drafting of the Universal Declaration of Human Rights. He famously asked why it was that there was not a universal declaration of duties. See Anthony Parel, "Gandhian Freedoms and Self-Rule," in *Gandhi's Experiments with Truth: Essential Writings by and about Mahatma Gandhi*, ed. Richard L. Johnson (Lanham: Lexington Books, 2006) 185.

48 Philip Glass and Candace DeJong, *Satyagraha*, libretto. For an in-depth discussion about detachment as a personal-political choice that links Gandhi with Stoic ideas, see Richard Sorabji, *Gandhi and the Stoics: Modern Experiments on Ancient Values* (Oxford: Oxford University Press, 2012).

from one person's attempt at action, duty, and responsibility. Therefore, detachment from labor and detachment from one's work in the world is necessary to reach a higher plain of existence, or what Patočka would call the third movement of existence.

This discussion directly evokes the question (from the introduction) about how the value of dissident action might be intrinsic to itself; its value may not depend upon instrumental objectives being realized within the span of a single lifetime. Gandhi turned to the *Bhagavad Gita* and the story of Arjuna and Krishna to make this point about his own political work: he tried to follow Krishna's advice to Arjuna that the point of battle is to be a good warrior, not to be tied to (and in the case of Arjuna) paralyzed by thoughts of the final or ultimate instrumental and objective results of the action. This is paradoxical because action (especially political action) is traditionally thought of as the means to an end, and the end as more important than the means. Gandhi reverses this traditional Machiavellian logic and argues throughout his life that the means are much more important, in particular the means of non-violence. Gandhi often suggests that violence will arise in contexts where the means and ends are separated; Gandhian nonviolence, by fusing the means and ends and collapsing the subject-object dichotomy, aims to sustain the integrity of the human being in contexts of violence, even if it asks the satyagraha activist to subject the integrity of his or her own body to the violence of another. When Patočka discusses movement, he fittingly describes how the relationship between the subject (the actor) and the object (the ends) is collapsed, it is the case that "all inner unification is accomplished by the movement itself, not by some bearer, substrate, or corporeity, objectively understood."[49] In this frame, the movement itself is the meaning of human existence, not the object toward which we move, and not the 'thing' at the end of the movement. The meaning resides in the moving subjectivity of human experience, or in musical terms, in the shared performance of the music, not the standing ovation at the end.

Within this framework, motion and work are a form of devotion for Gandhi, creating the willingness to stay in motion toward the truth; or in Patočka 's language, he sought to transcend the instrumentality of the

---

49 Patočka, *BCLW*, 147. In another passage, he explains: "what is distinctive about our attempt is our interpretation of movement; we understand it independently of the dichotomy between subject and object. That dichotomy presupposes on the one hand an objective world, complete, self-enclosed—and on the other hand a subject, perceiving this world." *BCLW*, 153.

second movement. This understanding of the intrinsic value of non-violent resistance is not dependent upon the political ends it may bring about, but for Gandhi is linked to an idea of living in truth:

> Without ahimsa [nonviolence] it is not possible to seek and find Truth. Ahimsa and Truth are so intertwined that it is practically impossible to disentangle and separate them. They are like the two sides of a coin... who can say, which is the obverse, and which is the reverse? Nevertheless, ahimsa is the means, Truth is the end... if we take care of the means, we are bound to reach the end sooner or later. When once we have grasped this point, final victory is beyond question.[50]

The "final victory" in the battle is not the "final" political battle, but comes in the war against the self's propensity for violence, which one can control in oneself through the pursuit of truth. Then, like two sides of the same coin, if one is really genuinely pursuing the truth in a nonviolent manner, then the pursuit of truth is itself nonviolent; it is supposed to be circular and not linear. Satyagraha is a force toward truth, where surely the troops are mobilized, but where the war is not against others (this would entail violence), but rather against the lack of truth in the self and in the world.

The Third Movement: Confrontation and Nonviolent War

A year after the well-known 1930 'salt march,' Gandhi was let out of the prison where he had been held as a punishment for organizing the march. He was allowed to negotiate with the British Viceroy about the issue of the salt tax, and on March 17, 1931, he addressed a large crowd in Bombay, describing the significance of the moment:

> We have developed a war mentality: we thought of war, we talked of war and nothing but war. Now we have to sing a completely different tune. We are in the midst of truce. With some of us, I know the very mention of the word truce sends a shiver through their bodies. That is because we had thought of nothing but war and had believed that there could be no

---

50   Gandhi, *From Yervada Mandir*, 12–13.

compromise. But that was not a position becoming a true Satyagrahi. The Satyagrahi whilst he is ever ready for fight must be equally eager for peace.[51]

The salt march was, by this description, a war. As he continues through the speech, Gandhi explains the specific nature of the compromise, and admonishes his followers not to be violent, but to be ready again to undertake more satyagraha movement if the government did not fulfill the agreement:

> But let no one forget that the settlement is provisional and the negotiations may break down at any stage. Let us therefore keep our powder ever dry and our armour ever bright. Failure should not find us napping, but ready to mobilize at the first command. In the meanwhile let us carry on the process of self-purification with greater vigour and greater faith, so that we may grow in strength day by day.[52]

The description of the salt march as 'war' and the need to "keep our powder ever dry and our armor ever bright" attests to the warrior mentality behind Gandhi's vision. Indeed, the language of war, battle, warriors, and fighting pervades his writings.[53] His use and understanding of 'war' was much more complicated than a colloquial understanding of two armies sent to kill and defeat one another; he used the language of war to describe many forms of justified confrontation. Gandhi wanted his followers to feel as if they were troops in an army, capable of destroying *things*, but willing to engage in practices meant to show their belief in the power of nonviolence through provoking violence in others. As he set out to destroy dehumanizing social traditions and repressive political systems, Gandhi had to ask his 'army' to put their bodies on 'the front line' of 'battle' to create forward movement toward change. The movement of the individual warrior and the movement of history became intertwined and mutually constitutive. Gandhi did in fact "make history" through engaging in this battle.

---

51 Gandhi, CWMG, Vol. 45: 305. Printed in *Young India* on March 19, 1931.
52 Gandhi, CWMG, Vol. 45: 306. Also quoted in Gene Sharp, *Gandhi Wields the Weapon of Moral Power* (Navjivan Trust, 1997 [1960]).
53 Farah Godrej, "Ascetics, Warriors, and a Gandhian Ecological Citizenship," *Political Theory* 40, no. 4 (August 2012), 437–465.

To keep his 'army' in forward motion towards a horizon that would have seemed impossible to reach when the campaigns were first begun as small protests in South Africa, Gandhi developed a system whereby the care of each satyagrahi for his own soul was a necessary prerequisite for achieving the discipline necessary to engage in the non-violent war that was satyagraha understood more generally. With this approach, one had to go to war against oneself before one was allowed to go to war for India; as described above, the ritual preparations for confrontation required satyagrahis to prove their own ability to exert self-discipline and self-control over their bodies, following Gandhi's belief that violence in the soul produced violence in the world through the actions of the body.[54] He ironically depended on violence, of course, and understood the 'natural' reaction to confrontation to be one of violence; if his satyagrahis were not attacked, his campaign would not be a performance of righteous warriors in battle, and they would not have gained the same degree of moral high ground through refusing to react to violence violently.

This puts the relationship between violence and nonviolence in Gandhi's thinking on paradoxical ground: he needed violence (and assumed people to be violent) while at the same time he sought to do away with violence in his own life and in the lives of his satyagrahi followers. The paradox of nonviolence being in mutual dependence with violence applies to the social-political and historical level as much as it applies to the satyagrahi as an individual: despite history's adoring remembrance of his non-violent tactics, Gandhi was attempting to turn something into nothing (to destroy a whole political system) by developing a way of thinking that enabled his followers to do nothing (not violently resist) when they would otherwise be inclined to do something (to fight back when attacked). In other words, he wanted British colonialism to disappear and becoming nothing, for people to rule themselves instead of being ruled by others, and when someone was inclined to return state-sponsored violence with their own violence, what Gandhi taught them was supposed to give them the ability to *force* themselves to do nothing. To have to force oneself to do nothing is to acknowledge that the default state of the human being is one of motion,

---

54 "The first act of destruction taught him that the Truth which was the object of his quest was not outside himself but within. Hence the more he took to violence, the more he receded from Truth. For in fighting the imagined enemy without, he neglected the enemy within." Gandhi, *From Yervada Mandir,* 8–9.

or as Patočka puts it: "Even a thinker meditating must assume a certain physical posture; even quieting down, negation of movement and dynamism, even interrupting the immediate thrust toward things, are physical accomplishments."[55] This follows from his assertion that "existence is movement," and that self-consciously controlling that movement is part of overcoming both the first and second "inauthentic" movements of existence. Confronting others by sitting still turns out to be no small endeavor.

If in Patočka's first movement one's body controls the self, and in the second movement it is systems and economies that control our minds and bodies through instrumental reason, then in the third movement we take back control of both body and mind together.[56] Taking back such control is a kind of nonviolent war to defeat the forces that dehumanize us. When Patočka takes up the problem of war in an essay entitled "Wars of the Twentieth Century and the Twentieth Century as War," he is trying ask why war becomes a meaningful act while it is also an "orgiastic" instance of violence.[57] Like Gandhi, he seems to insist that the warrior knows things and can think in a way that the non-warrior will not understand. Patočka wagers a disorienting observation: "the idea that war itself might be something that can explain, that has itself the power of bestowing meaning, is an idea foreign to all philosophies of history."[58] It was not going to be, however, foreign to his own philosophy of history, nor to his own comments about a "century and its deep addiction to war."[59] He wanted to take on the question of 'war's ability to explain' more directly than prior philosophies of history. In a few dense, elliptical and somewhat nonlinear pages in *Heretical Essays*, Patočka explores what it might mean to look at the phenomenon of war as part of the answer to larger philosophical questions. He begins by citing the work of those who have written about World War One and the experience of 'the front,' agreeing with the general idea that soldiers can return from the frontline experience with a sense of meaningfulness and an understanding of the world that those living in 'the day' and 'in peace' cannot begin to fathom.[60] He evokes the irony that war is usually

55 Patočka, *BCLW*, 43.
56 Patočka has a brief discussion of the pleasure-denying logic of ascetic practices. See note 38 above; *BCLW*, 159.
57 Patočka, *HE*, 113.
58 Patočka, *HE*, 120.
59 Patočka, *HE*, 120.
60 Ernst Jünger and Pierre Teilhard de Chardin.

waged to "save lives," but that it brings the soldiers to confront their proximity to death, where they can see through the pursuit of peace as partially false, and where the desire to "save lives" will continually launch more wars.[61] The soldier gains a different understanding, however, worth quoting at length because this is one passage where Patočka directly explains the categories of the third movement through the lens of war and confrontation:

Of those [soldiers] whom it sacrifices it demands, by contrast, endurance in the face of death. That indicates dark awareness that life is not everything, that it can sacrifice itself. That self sacrifice, that surrender, is what is called for. It is called for as something relative, related to peace and to the day. The frontline experience, however, is an absolute one. Here, as Teilhard shows, the participants are assaulted by an absolute freedom, freedom from all the interests of peace, of life, of the day. That means: sacrifice of the sacrificed loses its relative significance, it is no longer the cost we pay for a program of development, progress, intensification, and extension of life's possibilities, rather, it is significant solely in itself. This absolute freedom is the understanding that here something has already been achieved, something that is not the means to anything else... something above and beyond which there can be nothing. This is the culmination, this self-surrender which can call humans away from their vocations, talents, possibilities, their future. To be capable of that, to be chosen and called for in a world that uses conflict to mobilize force so that it comes to appear as a totally objectified and objectifying cauldron on energy, also means to overcome force.[62]

Patočka then details how the overcoming of everydayness shakes apart given understandings of the world, and points out how this also transforms the relationship between 'the enemy' and the 'sides' that participate in war: "the adversary is a fellow participant in the same situation, fellow discoverer of absolute freedom with whom agreement is possible in difference, a fellow participant in the upheaval... the solidarity of the shaken for all their contradiction and conflict."[63] In a later passage, he more fully develops the idea of "solidarity of the shaken" (the topic of the next chapter) as the only potential solution to a "humankind so

61 Patočka, *HE*, 129.
62 Patočka, *HE*, 129–130.
63 Patočka, *HE*, 131.

permeated and fascinated by the experience of war that the outlines of this history of our time can only be understood in its terms."[64]

The addiction to war has never stopped in the twentieth century, Patočka argues, as even forms of peace depend upon war, with the Cold War lingering in the background of his analysis as the primary example. He will insist that the solider who has experienced the force of war still knows more than the rest of us, and is also more free: "Those who are exposed to the pressure of the Force are free, far more free than those who are sitting on the sidelines."[65] This freedom is the freedom of the third movement, with all the second-movement attachments to instrumental objectives and quotidian everydayness of work broken by the frontline experience of war, and the "conversion" experienced in this context brings the soldier "to a level on which [he] can integrate finitude, situated-ness, earthliness, [and] mortality precisely into existence."[66] The soldier knows more intimately finitude and mortality, and thus "the transformation of the meaning of life... here trips on nothingness, on a boundary over which it cannot step, along which everything is transformed."[67]

While more will be elaborated in the next chapter about the relationship between 'solidarity of the shaken' and 'nothingness,' it is important to note that *Heretical Essays* ends with an evocation of *polemos*, a concept elaborated by Patočka in an earlier chapter but reconsidered in the last two paragraphs of the book through an invocation of Heraclitus's ancient Greek idea that war makes some free and others slaves, showing some to be human and others divine.[68] The ones who understand *polemos*, Patočka argues, are the ones who understand that adversaries "belong to each other in the common shaking of the everyday."[69] While the full import of these intricate ideas is too much to consider here, Patočka communicates the general impression that there are some types of war and confrontation that create meaning and others that destroy it; for the kind of confrontation that creates meaning, Patočka adopts the idea of *polemos* from both Heraclitus and Heidegger.[70] In its most basic sense, *polemos* in

---

64   Patočka, *HE*, 132.
65   Patočka, *HE*, 134.
66   Patočka, *BCLW*, 151.
67   Patočka, *HE*, 131.
68   Heraclitus, *Fragments: the Collected Wisdom of Heraclitus*, ed. Brooks Haxton (New York: Viking, 2001).
69   Patočka, *HE*, 136.
70   See Gregory Fried, *Heidegger's Polemos: From Being to Politics* (New Haven: Yale University Press, 2000) 26. As the editor to *Heretical Essays* notes, Patočka is relying on two fragments of Heraclitus in particular: (DK22 B80) "It is necessary to know war is common and right is strife

Greek refers to a confrontation, but for Patočka, it is a confrontation that leads to a common understanding, rather than being merely destructive. Therefore, it is the basis for 'solidarity of the shaken,' but also a different rehearsal of the third movement. In his own words from the second of the *Heretical Essays*:

> *Polemos* is at the same time that which constitutes the *polis* and the primordial insight that makes philosophy possible. *Polemos* is not the destructive passion of a wild brigand but is, rather, the creator of unity. The unity it founds is more profound than any ephemeral sympathy or coalition of interests; adversaries meet in the shaking of a given meaning, and so create a new way of being human—perhaps the only mode that offers hope amid the storm of the world: the unity of the shaken but undaunted.[71]

This 'new way of being human' (like the third movement) is to meet within 'the shaking of a given meaning,' (the shaking necessary to destroy the inauthenticity of the second movement) which is to say that all questions must be thrown open, all dogmas challenged, and the 'unity' that remains is a group of human beings in the realm of freedom searching for truth, thus the common grounding of both the *polis* and philosophy in a certain moment of history.[72] Life must move forward toward confrontation and the opening of meaning for such truths to be uncovered, and therein the 'third movement of human existence' requires the kind of confrontation that seems to be suggested by *polemos*, that is, "a task for all of life in its integrity."[73] Gandhi's paradoxically 'non-violent war' and 'peaceful battles' illuminate (if not also at times approach) what Patočka means when he describes how a moment of *polemos* can shape all aspects of life, perhaps representing the idea that you have not fully lived to the utmost of human existence until you have gone to war—though non-violent war might count. To live in truth via *polemos* is to understand one's finitude and the reality of being-toward-death, that is, the death that the soldier knows too well during every moment at the front. It also means

---

and that all things happen by strife and necessity." And: (DK22 B53) "War is the father of all and king of all, and some he shows as gods, others as men; some he makes slaves, others free." See *Heretical Essays*, 181.

71 Patočka, *HE*, 43.

72 For a detailed account of the connections between the third movement, *polemos*, and history in Patočka's work, see Marion Bernard, *Patočka et L'unité polémique du monde* (Peeters: Louvain-La-Neuve, 2016), especially 471–513.

73 Patočka, *BCLW*, 151.

being willing to confront the situation and face up to one's responsibility for that situation, and to do that under a 'common understanding' and in solidarity with others.[74]

Patočka's partial reversal of the moral platitude that 'war is bad' and 'peace is good' in the last pages of *Heretical Essays* might be some cause for consternation, but one of the things that Gandhi's life can demonstrate is that when one becomes self-aware of the finitude of one's bodily existence (enough to become detached from desire), and when instrumental-rational objectives are given up (renouncing the fruits of one's actions), and finally when a warrior's ethos is engaged to live life (the finale to what one might call Gandhi's 'three movements'), the solidarity that emerges is something that might approximate the solidarity of the front, where everyone is necessarily 'shaken' to the extreme. Patočka seems to be evoking the possibility that death is a very collective and common experience that can unite us radically, and the ones who have the best access to this knowledge are warriors. From them we should learn something about the collective task of solidarity: in the theatre of war, warriors live and confront each other's death and become willing to die for each other readily. The sense of meaninglessness and alienation that besets soldiers when they return to 'peacetime' is often put in terms of lost solidarity: they miss their comrades-in-arms more than anything else. This is to say that 'solidarity of the shaken' might be an extension of this wartime phenomenon, perhaps Patočka's exploration of a 'moral equivalent of war,' to use William James's expression without appropriating the substance of his argument.[75] Having decided against taking up arms to do violence, Gandhi nonetheless understood this solidarity intimately and thoroughly, recognizing the need to turn his followers into warriors in order for solidarity to hold amongst them all.

Gandhi also knew how to shake history apart at the seams to create that solidarity. His politics entailed destruction—in the very literal sense of the word: he wanted to demolish a structure—that of British colonialism—to make it collapse and wash away into the river of time, to fully negate its existence as a system of politics, economics, and cult-

---

74 This is also to say that Patočka's idea of being-toward-death is different from Heidegger's. Heidegger claims that one can only truly confront one's own death, a rather solitary task. Martin Heidegger, *Being and Time*, trans. Joan Stambaugh (Albany: SUNY Press, 1996) 219–246. See also Chapter Two.

75 William James, *William James: Essays and Lectures*, ed. Richard Kamber (Routledge, 2016 [1910]) 274–285.

ure.[76] His politics have been called anarchistic by some; from another angle of vision, he was nihilistic, at least in a technical sense of wanting to turn something into nothing.[77] He wanted a whole world and a whole way of doing things to go away—he "tripped on nothingness," to use Patočka's words—but he wanted to do that while condemning the violence that was directed towards individual human beings. He had an official 'constructive program' at the same time as he tried to shake apart colonialism, but history has not remembered this as well as his unmaking of the British Empire. What traditional historical narratives have also sidelined is how Gandhi's idea of 'victory' was much more complicated than achieving the one specific goal of Indian independence. Even after his 'success,' there are vestiges of colonialism (and other things Gandhi set out to destroy, like Hindu untouchability) that have persisted in India; if he were alive today, Gandhi would not look upon India and claim he had won any total and final victory. He would likely admonish his followers to continue the as-yet incomplete movement.[78]

This points to a larger problem within the discussion of all such 'movements' and the study of dissidence in general, one that Patočka would find equally problematic. The language of 'movement' is everywhere within analyses of dissidents in political science, especially under the frame of 'social movement theory.'[79] However, this research (some theoretical, some empirical), does not conceive of movement philosophically, but conceives of movements instrumentally, and the whole body of scholarship is about whether given actions (marches, demonstrations, social media posts, etc.) create political outcomes. Whatever might have been Gandhi's impressive success in dismantling British colonialism,

76 Farah Godrej, "Ascetics, Warriors, and a Gandhian Ecological Citizenship," *Political Theory* 40, no. 4 (August 2012): 437–465.

77 Chapter Four contains a longer description of political nihilism. That he had a 'romance with death' is Devji's argument. See *The Impossible Indian*.

78 Some of them have understood this, and continue his legacy of nonviolent action and social justice through programs in India. See the Navajivan Trust, http://www.navajivantrust.org, and the Gandhi Ashram at Sabarmati, http://www.gandhiashramsabarmati.org/en/.

79 As explained in the introduction, this large body of work is framed by instrumental and rationalist questions about the formation and outcomes of groups of people who identify politically or socially with an issue, act in the public sphere, and are called 'social movements' as a way to talk about the aggregation of preferences, principle-agent theory, and cost-benefit analyses. These economistic calculations of such group action, as hopefully already explained, are not the center of the questions at stake here, because I am arguing that Patočka helps to probe the intrinsic value of action and movement, not its instrumental consequences. For a review of the field, see: Donatella Della Porta and Mario Diani, eds., *The Oxford Handbook of Social Movements* (Oxford University Press, 2015).

and the thousands who came after him and successfully used nonviolent resistance to meet their political goals, it is possible that Gandhi would look at political actors who are obsessed with 'success' and argue that they missed the point of satyagraha, having misunderstood the relationship between means and ends. No one has to win or be successful vis-à-vis an opponent for their action to be "truth-force," and satyagraha was originally conceived by a small group of dissidents with little to no chance of success.[80]

For Patočka at the end of *Heretical Essays*, war is a truth-force; it is a way of coming to a deeper understanding of the meaning of human existence. His account is both pessimistic and optimistic: he suggests wars will continue as long as human life continues, and by the usual 'daytime' standard of 'war is bad,' this strikes the reader as pessimistic. War, however, is also the occasion for the type of solidarity where there is a "means by which this state is overcome."[81] War holds some truth that we need, a truth we might not be able to find elsewhere, and also holds within itself at least a partial resolution to its own paradox.[82] Gandhi's thought opens up the possibility that there might be war without violence, a type of *polemos* and confrontation where one can be a warrior, and be in proximity to death (and the wisdom that proximity brings), but where the forward movement of existence is not compromised by having to do violence to the bodies of others. For Patočka, *polemos* is also a highly constructive force, and when he first describes it (early in

---

80 Given the terrain of paradoxes at stake here, and the dependence of all things upon their opposites, it will perhaps not come as a surprise that part of the way Gandhi deconstructed the notion of 'success' (as framed in instrumental terms of achieving self-interest by a campaign) was to claim there was no place for 'defeat' either, further undercutting the need to call anything 'successful.' This depended on a turn to the theology of sacrifice and self-suffering: "For the quest of Truth involves *tapas*—self-suffering, sometimes even unto death. There can be no place in it for even a trace of self-interest. In such a selfless search for Truth nobody can lose his bearings for long. Directly he takes to the wrong path he stumbles, and is thus redirected to the right path. Therefore the pursuit of Truth is true bhakti (devotion). It is the path that leads to God. There is no place for cowardice, no place for defeat. It is the talisman by which death itself becomes the portal to life eternal." Gandhi, *From Yervada Mandir,* 5–6. In other words, death is not defeat.

81 Patočka, *HE*, 134.

82 An exploration of this aspect of war (a work influenced by Patočka) is Marc Crepon, *The Thought of Death and the Memory of War*, trans. Michael Loriaux (Minneapolis: University of Minnesota Press, 2013). Nicolas de Warren has also addressed topics of war and warriors in Patočka 's work: "He Who Saw the Deep: The Epic of Gilgamesh in Patočka's Philosophy of History," in Francesco Tava and Darian Meacham, eds., *Thinking after Europe: Jan Patočka and Politics* (London: Rowman & Littlefield International) 135–159; de Warren, N. "Homecoming. Jan Patočka's Reflections on the First World War," in Michael Staudigl, ed. *Phenomenologies of Violence* (Leiden: Brill, 2014), 207–243.

Heretical Essays, before he uses it in the context of war) it seems like the opposite of Gandhi's proposed destruction of a political-economic system, and more like what Gandhi called his 'constructive program' for building a new India. This arises in Patočka's discussion about how history came to be history:

> History arises and can arise only insofar as there is *arete*, the excellence of humans who no longer simply live to live but who make room for their justification by looking into the nature of things and acting in harmony with what they see—by building a *polis* on the basis of the law of the world which is *polemos*, by speaking that which they see as revealing itself to a free, exposed yet undaunted human (philosophy).[83]

Gandhi was perhaps an example of this kind of *arete* (human excellence), one kind of answer to Patočka's question about whether "historical humans are willing to embrace history."[84] While he was assassinated before he was able to build a new *polis* out of the fragments of decolonized India, he was a warrior of non-violence who understood living in contradiction and problematicity.[85]

The Aporia of War and History

When Patočka describes the larger purpose behind thinking philosophically about the movement of human existence, he argues that "only by starting out from these three fundamental lines, from understanding how they presuppose and negate each other mutually, can we... achieve a certain insight into the way in which these three strands (two movements governed by the Earth, a third breaking free of it) make up the overarching human movement we call history."[86] This is one bridge between his *Body, Community, Language, World* and *Heretical Essays in the Philosophy*

---

83 Patočka, *HE*, 43.
84 Patočka, *HE*, 118.
85 Gandhi's definition of a 'true' warrior: "Wherein is courage required—in blowing others to pieces from behind a cannon, or with a smiling face to approach a cannon and be blown to pieces? Who is the true warrior—he who keeps death always as a bosom-friend, or he who controls the death of others? Believe me that a man devoid of courage and manhood can never be a passive resister...[but] even a man weak in body is capable of offering this resistance. One man can offer it just as well as millions." Gandhi, *Hind Swaraj*, in CWMG X: 50.
86 Patočka, *BCLW*, 161.

of History: he contends that if one understands the way the body moves through the community, one's language and the world, one achieves some insight into a heretical philosophy of history. Or, as in Gandhi's case, one gets insight into a philosophy of existence that leads to heretical actions and the reshaping of history. The polyphonic composition that was Gandhi's life was movement within that "overarching human movement we call history." As discussed in the prior chapter about Bonhoeffer, this ability to move within history and think of oneself historically opens human existence to the possibility of dissidence, but in particular, to that form of dissidence that might otherwise seem hopeless and futile in light of vast power differentials, where in renouncing the fruits of one's actions one might break free of 'the Earth,' of that horizontal world that binds us, but that also gives us the ability to transcend our particularities and quotidian attachments.

Renouncing the fruits of one's actions, however, should not be overly romanticized. When Robert Oppenheimer witnessed the first test of the atomic weapon he had helped to design and build, his reaction was to think of the *Bhagavad Gita*.[87] He had taken this text seriously enough throughout his life to do his own translation from Sanskrit.[88] The line he evokes is from the moment in the story when the Hindu God Krishna fully shows himself (in his true form, not just in his human avatar) to the protagonist, Arjuna. This occurs in the narrative while they are discussing Arjuna's hesitation to kill his cousins. Along with a grandiose display of ostentatious power, Krishna declares that: "I am death, destroyer of worlds." When Oppenheimer saw the first mushroom cloud, this is what he later said (in an interview reflecting back) had come to his mind; he felt like he was becoming death and the destroyer of worlds.[89] The quotation from the *Bhagavad Gita*, as well as his later outspoken objections to the further use of nuclear weapons, are evidence of Oppenheimer's recognition of both his own enormous power and the general human ability to amass uncontrollable hubristic momentum through technological mastery. This recognition did not come without a cost: Oppenheimer's

---

87 Oppenheimer discussed his relationship with the Gita in the documentary film *The Day After Trinity: J. Robert Oppenheimer and the Atomic Bomb*, https://youtu.be/Vm5fCxXnK7Y, directed by Jon Else (1944; Santa Monica, CA.: Pyramid Films) aired 1981.

88 James A. Hijiya, "The *Gita* of J. Robert Oppenheimer," *Proceedings of The American Philosophical Society* 144, no. 2 (June 2000).

89 This is what Oppenheimer said. Other translations of the line from the Gita vary. See: *The Day After Trinity*.

security clearance was revoked during the McCarthy era. He was framed as a security risk for his pre-war associations with leftist organizations, and also came under suspicion for his resistance to the initiative to develop the hydrogen bomb.[90]

In a short essay entitled "The Heroes of Our Time," Patočka includes Oppenheimer as one the 'repentant scientists' who came to understand that the scientific work on nuclear technology undermined the possibilities for a human and moral existence.[91] For Patočka, the 'repentant scientists' were 'heroes' because they were willing to question the wisdom of putting such world-destroying power into human hands, as well as being heroic for their ability to make career-ending sacrifices in order to challenge given political realities and the momentum of destruction.[92] Historian James A. Hijiya argued that Oppenheimer used the *Bhagavad Gita* as a template for figuring out how to act when he did not want to act, turning to Arjuna's example in order to continue to build the bomb while he had grave doubts about what would happen afterwards. The story of Arjuna was a way to understand his duty to fulfill his role as a scientist-warrior in the context of defeating the Axis Powers, and this helped him set his doubts aside until after the war, when he then voiced his concerns about the destructive potential he had created.

As already described, this same moment from the *Gita* had a formative influence on Gandhi's political thought; he wrote about how this display of godly power, by convincing Arjuna to act and to carry out his duty as a warrior, had been a demonstration of how the renunciation of the fruits of one's actions and giving up a fixation on final results was necessary to make action valuable in-and-of-itself.[93] For Gandhi, this meant developing a program of nonviolent action; for Oppenheimer, it meant creating a violent weapon. There is a stark irony in these two men turning to the same passage in the same religious text, one to justify action through a political program of strict non-violence, the other to justify action through a scientific program of building a bomb that could violently destroy the entire world. This represents many paradoxical things, but perhaps what is most relevant to dissidents across time

90   Hijiya, "The *Gita* of J. Robert Oppenheimer."
91   Patočka, "Heroes of Our Time." « Les heros de notre temps » *Liberte et sacrafice : Ecrit politiques,* » trans. Erika Abrams, (Grenoble : Jerome Millon, 1990) 325–330.
92   Patočka, "Heroes of Our Time."
93   Gandhi, "The Message of the Gita," CWMG: VOL XLI; reprinted in Stephen Mitchell, ed., *Bhagavad Gita: A New Translation*, reprint ed. (New York: Harmony Books, 2002), 211–222.

and place is how human hubris develops in contexts of war, both violent and nonviolent war.

For both Gandhi and Oppenheimer, they could see that being a true warrior meant renouncing the fruits of one's actions and not fixating on instrumental ends. Through such renunciation and detachment, Oppenheimer became 'death, destroyer of worlds' as Gandhi too sought to destroy the world (of colonialism) with a certain amount of 'success.' Both confronted history, and that meant a full shaking of all given meanings, as well as shaking the political, social and cultural structures of the time. Yet Gandhi met his own end through the violence of an assassin who thought Gandhi was too persistent in keeping India and Pakistan as one country; Oppenheimer died as an embittered outcast from the government of the country he once thought he had saved. Oppenheimer believed that the US government would stop after a single use of the atomic weapon and after Hitler was gone; Gandhi thought the Muslims in India would also come to see nonviolence as more important than their own self-rule, and was surprised as the partition of India turned violent and destructive under his watch. Both Gandhi and Oppenheimer came to such conclusions in a frame of moral absolutism; such a stance emerged from an unflinching adherence to a *moral* goal at the end. They were hell-bent on *moral* success, even if they had understood the importance of renouncing instrumental ends.

Whether or not the *Bhagavad Gita* demands a renunciation of *moral* fruits as well as *instrumental* fruits of action is a question of Hindu theology beyond the scope of this discussion. Another question can be raised, however, about the nexus of heroism and dissidence and the nexus of Gandhi and Oppenheimer in light of Patočka's *polemos*: what is the relationship between moral discourse and political action? It is difficult to be a dissident without believing in one's own moral righteousness, as the entire enterprise of dissidence depends upon a firm personal stance towards a sense of right and wrong, and the seeming necessity for unwavering commitments. The solidarity created within groups of dissidents sometimes develops a similar unwavering quality: there is a kind of willingness to 'fight' to the death, as seen even in Gandhi's statement in the aftermath of the Salt March. While Gandhi might be a good illustration of the dynamics of war at stake in Patočka's idea of *polemos*, the unwavering kind of solidarity he advocated and practiced at the height of the success of his mass movement might not have been solidarity 'of the shaken.' When successful, he perhaps became less susceptible to 'the shaking' than at the beginning; once he had broken free of 'the Earth' and risen above his grounded attachments, his adherence to moral ends created a moral certainty that became a central part of his arguments, perhaps the new 'fruit' at the end of his march.[94]

'Solidarity of the shaken,' as will be explored in the next chapter, surely demands and depends upon Patočka's notion that humans are moral creatures and constituted through morality. But his suspicion about all forms of 'absolutism'—from absolute metaphysics to the absolutes of objective knowledge in science to the absolutist power of certain political arrangements—opens the possibility of questioning moral absolutism while remaining morally grounded. Gandhi's inability to see a type of moral 'rightness' in the views of those who opposed him might be an example of how moral absolutism can cloud certain truths; perhaps by the end of his *instrumentally* successful campaigns to free India, he held fast to a kind of moral absolutism about what 'self-rule' meant, limiting his ability to see the shaken-ness of minority positions.

If Patočka's idea of *polemos* is helpful, it might also push back against the epistemological absolutism that underpins such moral absolutism; with the lens of Patočka's *polemos*, it might be possible to assert that in war (violent or nonviolent) one can never really know the fruits of one's actions, let alone have those fruits to enjoy at the end. This would include the possibility that absolute moral knowledge might be inaccessible, so there remains a need to renounce (as a fruit) the knowledge of moral certainty as a form of epistemological absolutism.[95] In most dissident activities and campaigns, the full consequences of collective and individual actions simply cannot be known; the same holds for war. War unfolds as an epistemological drama about knowledge and its relationship to truth, and what the 'true warrior' knows at the end of Patočka's *Heretical Essays* is that the 'ends' or the 'fruits' of war cannot be known immediately, and sometimes can never be known; the form of truth accessible to the warrior is about the lack of truth, the fog of war.[96] Patočka's solidarity of the

---

94 This implies that it is possible to read Patočka's philosophy of history onto the history of an individual. When he discusses the relationship between myth and knowledge, it is a circular process always having to be redone and reexamined: "They will live in myth again," as Patočka, explains, (*Plato and Europe*, 88) and therefore earthly success might re-tie us to the 'earth' we had once escaped from. The case of the environmental activists, discussed in Chapter Five, explores this reattachment to the earth as a necessary grounding (if literally) against absolutisms.

95 This would be a strain of Augustinian thinking in Patočka; see Chapter Two.

96 This line of argument is influenced by Tim O'Brien's description of what war does to traditional (if unshaken) ideas of morality, knowledge, and truth: "For the common soldier, at least, war has the feel—the spiritual texture—of a great ghostly fog, thick and permanent. There is

shaken, the solidarity of the warriors, the solidarity of the warriors who understand, is the solidarity of those who know they do not know; it is Socratic. The warrior in *polemos* must renounce the fruits of one's actions, but perhaps more importantly, also must renounce the presumption of absolute knowledge as a type of fruit, including moral knowledge.

In a late interview after his security clearance was revoked, Oppenheimer responded to a question by saying he was no longer 'close enough to know or judge' an issue of nuclear security.[97] This might be part of the Platonic and Socratic repentance that Patočka would admire: he came to know that he did not know. Yet if it was the full 'repentance' of the repentant scientist, it would not only be that he did not know state secrets without a security clearance, but that he was also suggesting that he did not understand how the arms race, and the addiction to war that the hydrogen bomb represented, had meaning in the wider swath of history. Only in being close to war, right up in the face of war, can one begin to know—and even then, war changes and becomes something different in the midst of the movements of human existence, the movement of history, and with the passage of memory into time. Not only can one war have little resemblance to other wars, but nor is any particular war's meaning constant; as time passes, even the same war comes to be narrated differently by both soldiers and historians. Looking backward but trying to live in forward motion, the meanings and truths ascribed to wars will continually shift.

It is not entirely clear whether or not Oppenheimer's repentance was deep enough for him to properly symbolize Patočka's desire for a scientist capable of giving up his power and hubris. Or, to use Bonhoeffer's words from the previous chapter, trying to estimate such inner thoughts would amount to guessing on a matter of "the purity of the heart" that "only God can judge."[98] If he was repentant, following Patočka's hope that he was, then the end of his life might represent a moment of Platonic *aporia*, where he came to know that he 'did not know' in the larger

---

no clarity. Everything swirls. The old rules are no longer binding, the old truths no longer true. Right spills over into wrong. Order blends into chaos, love into hate, ugliness into beauty, law into anarchy, civility into savagery. The vapors suck you in. You can't tell where you are, or why you're there, and the only certainty is overwhelming ambiguity. In war you lose your sense of the definite, hence your sense of truth itself, and therefore it's safe to say that in a true war story nothing is ever absolutely true." Tim O'Brien, *The Things They Carried* (New York: Houghton Mifflin Harcourt, 2009) 78.

97   J. Else, *The Day After Trinity*.
98   See Chapter Two, note 95.

sense, and where that not-knowing could lead to further questions and further examination. This would have entailed 'solidarity of the shaken' with those comrades-in-arms who understood that we cannot understand what the atomic bomb really and fully did, and who also understand that part of the reason one has to give up the fruits of one's actions is because we cannot *know* those fruits. To claim we know would be hubris, and inhuman, and would deny the idea that existence is movement, and movement existence, and that the river of life is always moving beyond our ability to grasp it. In the river of such historical movement—the river that Heraclitus claimed we could not step into twice—we will never fully know the fruits of the warrior's actions.[99] Patočka's *polemos* and the third movement, the integrated apotheosis of human movement-as-existence, is the un-concealment of war's *aporia*: for this, it is not just solidarity that will do, but it must be solidarity 'of the shaken.'

---

99   Heraclitus, *Fragments: the Collected Wisdom of Heraclitus*, ed. Brooks Haxton (New York: Viking, 2001).

Chapter Four
Solidarity of the Shaken: in Conversation with Atomic Activism

In the aftermath of the atomic explosions in Hiroshima and Nagasaki in 1945, those documenting the event took photographs of nuclear heat shadows. Outlines of objects and human bodies were marked on brick and concrete surfaces by the blast's heat. Most captions describe the shadows of bodies as having been left behind by those who had been 'vaporized.'[1] The eeriness of these images evokes something different than traditional war photographs of injured bodies, general destruction, and decimated buildings. The simple outlines and the word 'vaporize' suggest that not only can our modern technological weapons kill us in a few seconds, but they might instantly turn our cells and flesh into an entirely different arrangement of molecules that can disappear into thin air.[2] This goes beyond 'ashes to ashes and dust to dust.' The suggestion of these photographs is that there is not even that much—no ashes and no dust, simply nothing left at all. If we think a short distance beyond

---

1   Photos are available in the online archive of the Hiroshima Peace Memorial Museum, http://hpmmuseum.jp/. These generalizations about the captions arose through a variety of internet searches, including "Hiroshima, nuclear, shadow, vaporization, image." This showed that many different websites, in the pattern of a meme of sorts, had adopted this labeling for these historical images. The websites included many newspapers and reputable museums (like the Hiroshima Peace Museum) as well as other less formal uses of the photographs by individuals on personal websites and travel sites.

2   There seems to be an internet debate about the scientific possibility of actual vaporization in these circumstances with the particular weapon that was used. I have no expertise to confirm the validity of the debate, and it is the use of the word 'vaporize' in captions (and in the imaginations of the viewers) that is of interest here. Even if actual vaporization of human bodies did not occur that day, and something else resulted in the markings, 'vaporization' can easily be imagined, and that idea creates the subsequent thoughts about annihilation that matter for this argument.

the frame of the photographs, we realize that only a few bodies were next to hard surfaces and able to leave behind an eerie shadowy mark; tens of thousands were annihilated and disappeared into thin air, quite literally.

The two words 'annihilation' and 'nihilism' come from a common Latin root: *nihil*, or 'nothing.' To annihilate something is to turn it into nothing. To adopt a fully nihilistic view about the world means believing the world is a type of nothingness. A milder form of nihilism is the rejection of moral norms and social conventions. In a more technical philosophical sense, nihilism entails the rejection of metaphysical explanations of the universe. To look at the photographs of nuclear shadow-bodies requires thinking about our potential for nothingness in physical, social, philosophical, and spiritual terms. Norman Mailer offers a summary of the issues this creates in his 1957 essay "The White Negro":

> Probably, we will never be able to determine the psychic havoc of the concentration camps and the atom bomb upon the unconscious mind of almost everyone alive in these years. For the first time in civilized history, perhaps for the first time in all of history, we have been forced to live with the suppressed knowledge that the smallest facets of our personality or the most minor projection of our ideas, or indeed the absence of ideas and the absence of personality could mean equally well that we might still be doomed to die as a cipher in some vast statistical operation... our psyche was subjected itself to the intolerable anxiety that death being causeless, life was causeless as well, and time deprived of cause and effect had come to a stop.[3]

It is not a distant stretch of the imagination to look at the shadow-body photographs and see that time stopped at ground zero, vaporizing human life into cause-less-ness and meaninglessness. Before the height of his career as a political activist in the United States, Mailer recognized in the late 1950s that his generation existed within this framework

---

3   Norman Mailer, "The White Negro," *Dissent*, (Fall 1957), https://www.dissentmagazine.org /online_articles/the-white-negro-fall-1957. Mailer became a kind of unofficial spokesman for the 1960s dissident generation in the United States, an editor at *Dissent* magazine and author of many fictional and nonfictional books that tried to capture the zeitgeist of the 1960s and beyond. He participated in the dissidence of this highly activist decade, ran for office (and lost), protested on the steps of the Pentagon in 1968 (and in many other places), and wrote about his experiences along the way. See: J. Michael Lennon, *Mailer: A Double Life*, (New York: Simon and Schuster, 2013).

of "psychic havoc" wrought by the nihilism and potential annihilation of the atomic situation. By the 1960s in the US, however, it seemed like everywhere there was activism: the civil rights movement, the women's rights movement, protests against the Vietnam war, students challenging university administrations, and a diffuse counterculture movement spawned out of the 'hipster culture' of the 1950s. (This was the main topic of Mailer's essay; the description of the bomb was only the prelude.) There is therefore a paradox in Mailer's rather meaning-filled and activist life-in-motion, especially when thought about in light of his concerns in the 1950s about meaninglessness and life coming to a stop. Annihilation and then nihilism (forces of nothingness and stillness) were followed by the rise of so much activism (forces of motion) that a generation defined itself by its desire to change the world through street protests.

What might Patočka say to this? His philosophy took aim at various forms of indifference as a kind of human sickness of stillness, and being indifferent to the world and ignoring the good and evil in the world was for Patočka a way of being less-than-human. As already suggested in prior chapters, his own activism arose out of his ideas about overcoming indifference through living in truth, caring for the soul, and confronting 'the everyday' to become involved in history. Someone like Mailer participated in history through both reflection and action, becoming part of a larger activist conversation that frequently evoked images of atomic destruction; as the examples below will demonstrate, citing the atomic bomb was common logic for most 1960s activists, not just Mailer. It was as if the first step to being a dissident (about any issue) required dwelling for a few moments in nuclear nothingness, recognizing how the atomic situation was a fundamental challenge to the human ability to find meaning in history and human life, but how it therefore also offered a reason for developing ways to confront nihilism and despair through political action.

Patočka's ideas can shed light on this paradoxical dynamic of nihilism, meaninglessness, and activist politics, especially his idea of 'solidarity of the shaken.' If something fundamental changes about the world when we have to worry about being vaporized instantaneously by the products of our own technological scientific innovations, and if the lingering threat of nuclear annihilation throughout the Cold War was the shaking of the world—if quite literally—this might also have created a form of solidarity that kept people in motion towards new political possibilities that aimed to make life more 'meaningful' and less politically nihilistic than it was before the atomic blast cast its peculiar shadows.[4] Following Patočka through his notions of 'shakenness' and 'solidarity' reveals how a sense of meaninglessness can be partially overcome by keeping history in motion through constant Socratic confrontation, which in turn gives rise to dissident politics. In examining Patočka's vision for 'solidarity of the shaken,' it also becomes easier to look at the nuclear heat shadows and see how the human body actually did put up enough resistance to change the color of the concrete background, and this was something, not nothing.

To illuminate these dynamics, an in-depth description of 'solidarity of the shaken' is followed below by an exploration of several texts of activism from the 1960s that help to illustrate this complex concept. In the interests of focusing on how 'solidarity of the shaken' will resonate with activists across time and place, this will be a thematic overview that puts Patočka's ideas into conversation with the activists' texts, but not a detailed historical account of what gave rise to each text. Each is a well-known document that became part of the historical narrative of the 1960s in the United States, and the history of this era is thoroughly analyzed elsewhere. What is important to focus on here is how these statements all attempted to capture the zeitgeist of the atomic situation, each articulating the self-understanding of those participating in a confrontation with history. Each text is also meant to represent some aspect of the pre-political thinking that 'solidarity of the shaken' might give rise to, and thus to characterize the forms of dissidence that help expand aspects of Patočka's ideas. The texts were chosen among many other possibilities, and the selection was justified by thematic fit with specific concepts.

The first is Mario Savio's speech "An End to History," where he calls on his fellow students at Berkeley to recognize the difference between genuinely historical understandings and the a-historical structure of university bureaucracies, showing how becoming aware of oneself in light of history, including the ability to historicize one's own thoughts and actions in order to understand others and articulate mutual understanding, is a necessary condition of solidarity. The second is Paul Tillich's *Shaking of the Foundations*, a sermon addressing the nuclear situation and the relationships between meaning, meaninglessness, and nihilism,

---

4   Elaine Scarry has argued in a compelling way how we might make ourselves worry again in such a way that changes American politics. In *Thermonuclear Monarchy: Choosing Between Democracy and Doom,* she is worried about the lack of worry about nuclear weapons, and the degree to which the weapons undermine democratic institutions. (W.W. Norton and Co., 2014).

demonstrating a way of thinking oneself out of human hubris by under-standing the relationship between solidarity and living in truth as based upon humility, where one uses the methods of philosophy not to gain power and mastery over others, but instead to acknowledge that 'shaking foundations' is potentially dangerous and therefore requires moral restraint. The third is the "Russell-Einstein Manifesto," a statement of scientists in 1954 as they tried to convince the public of the harms of radiation and nuclear testing, illuminating how scientists thoroughly seeped in rationalism can nonetheless be self-aware enough to begin to transcend the boundaries of techno-science that so worried Patočka and other heirs of Heidegger's and Husserl's concern about the "crisis" of the scientific world view.[5] This awareness then helps them become capable of problematizing the relationship between human subjectivity and scientific objectivity in order to formulate a shared understanding about the spiritual emptiness of some scientific and technological understandings of the world. The fourth is the Port Huron Statement, a political manifesto of the Students for a Democratic Society, where they tried to define a new type of politics in the shadow of their belief that they might be "the last generation in the experiment with living,"[6] and where they understood that they had to shake away indifference to move toward a conception of freedom through the bonds of solidarity that could overcome individual powerlessness.

Together these four documents are meant to provide a fruitful terrain for unpacking Patočka's complicated but compelling idea of 'solidarity of the shaken.' Such juxtapositions, however, are not meant to argue that Patočka's conception of freedom (or rationality, philosophy, or history) exactly matches the perspectives of these authors, but rather to say that Patočka's questions about shaken-ness, freedom, and solidarity can be useful in asking new questions of these familiar texts. This conversation uses Patočka's categories to show the degree to which anyone anywhere can attempt to step outside of his or her own preconceived ideas about the world, asking whether we can examine more thoroughly the "place" of our being-in-history, while also staying in motion towards

---

5   Edmund Husserl, *The Crisis of European Sciences and Transcendental Phenomenology*, trans. David Carr (Evanston: Northwestern University Press, 1970); Martin Heidegger, *The Question concerning Technology* (New York: Harper & Row, 1977); Patočka, "The Dangers of Technicization in Science according to E. Husserl and the Essence of Technology as Danger according to M. Heidegger," in Kohák, *Selected Writings*, 223–238.
6   "Port Huron Statement," (New York: Students for a Democratic Society, 1962) 4. Hereafter abbreviated as "PHS."

future possibilities that might more fully realize our humanity as morally constituted in solidarity with others. Whatever action might flow out of thinking along with Patočka's idea of 'solidarity of the shaken' would, furthermore, require acknowledging that the freedom which arises through dissidence is not from gaining political power, but rather (to return to Havel's idea) is part of seeking 'the power of the powerless' (see Chapter One), where the individual is liberated through reconstituting his or her relationship with others. 'Solidarity of the shaken' is not only a social concept, therefore, but a philosophical one, as it can break apart accepted meanings by showing how even small acts of dissent are powerful enough to cause layers of self deception to fall away from engrained ideologies. This type of liberation can be dangerous in a variety of senses, so such action also humbly requires a recognition of the human inability to know and control every outcome of action, as discussed above in Chapter Three.

Shaking Everydayness: Patočka's Vision

To understand what Patočka means by the human condition of being 'shaken,' it is useful to start with his conception of the opposite of shaken-ness, which then illuminates what being 'shaken' can potentially mean. If one is not shaken, for Patočka, in a basic sense one is bored. He has a more specific and deeper meaning in mind, however, that goes beyond the lack of readily accessible amusement: "Boredom is not something negligible, a 'mere mood,' a private disposition, but rather the ontological condition of a humanity which has wholly subordinated its life to everydayness and its anonymity."[7] To subordinate a life to "everydayness" means to be primarily concerned only with oneself and one's own biological survival, therein being caught up in the various mechanical accouterments of technological civilization, unable to see beyond oneself towards transcendent, spiritual or higher-order concerns about the meaning of human life. One is 'bored' in a larger ontological sense (that is, the boredom pervades an entire being and existence) even if one feels sufficiently entertained by technological objects and material things in the immediate present. Ontological boredom arises because we are not searching for the meaning of what we are doing. Or, when

---

7   Patočka, *Heretical Essays*, 112.

searching for that meaning, there is not much meaning there to find. This idea, however quotidian (and boring) it might seem in our own time as technological gadgets overtake our lives in too many (boring) ways, for Patočka, he was able to put boredom into the same breath as the rather more dramatic frameworks of "metaphysical experience" and Hiroshima:

> Boredom does not retreat but rather forces its way to the forefront... in the form of compulsory recreation, it becomes one of the characteristic metaphysical experiences of our age (while others include the experience of combat and Hiroshima). What else does it mean, this gigantic Boredom which cannot be covered up even by the immense ingenuity of modern science and technology...?[8]

Patočka also explains how understanding this boredom is necessary to critically reflect on the problems of techno-science and automation (see Chapters One and Five), and he laments that there is something about this "gigantic boredom" that "turns today's mystery into tomorrow's common gossip and triviality."[9] As this passage suggests, boredom should be a question and a phenomenon of problematicity, an occasion to ask if we want to transcend nihilism and find meaning in life, just as much as Hiroshima and the World Wars challenged us to find meaning in meaninglessness. (See more on Paul Tillich's use of this phrase, below.) Patočka's evocation of modern boredom arises in the context of discussing the meaning of war, and the degree to which "war is the full fruition of the revolt of the everyday."[10] It would be going too far to say that Patočka sees war as arising because we want to overcome boredom, but it would perhaps be more consistent with his thoughts to say that war is one of those things that shakes us out of the trap of everydayness, making it harder to become bored in the larger ontological sense (see Chapter Three). War forces us to the 'front,' either literally or metaphorically, and puts us face-to-face with death, which is another way of forcing one to ask questions about the meaningfulness of one's life.[11]

While Patočka does not explicitly reference in this passage which war he might be thinking of (he lived through several), it is helpful to evoke

---

8   Patočka, *Heretical Essays*, 114.
9   Patočka, *Heretical Essays*, 114.
10   Patočka, *Heretical Essays*, 113.
11   Pierre-Étienne Schmit, "'Going to War Itself": J. Patočka and the Great War," *Le philosophoire* 2 (2017): 135–168.

how, in the lead-up to World War One, there was rhetoric (and perhaps propaganda) arguing that war was a good and necessary aspect of life that kept forces of vitality alive in political communities.[12] Referencing this, in the beginning of Erich Maria Remarque's anti-war novel *All Quiet on the Western Front*, the school boys are in a rather 'boring' classroom setting, well-organized and ordered; when the talk of war begins, the level of excitement and energy exponentially increases, and they go running out the door enthusiastically to sign up for 'the front.' Remarque is surely mocking their exuberance, but this is part of what Patočka is evoking in turn: war can pull us out of 'the everyday' and our 'gigantic' ontological boredom, but it is a rather dangerous way of doing that, as it is linked to the 'orgiastic' element of human life, and perhaps many other unpredictable human impulses.[13] (See discussion of *polemos* in Chapter Three).

While war might be one way to shake an individual out of boredom and everydayness, 'history' is also an important part of 'solidarity of the shaken,' and Patočka's 'history' includes war, but also includes many other less violent means of opening new possibilities for finding meaning. He develops 'solidarity of the shaken' out of an interpretation of history:

> History arises from the shaking of naïve and absolute meaning in the virtually simultaneous and mutually interdependent rise of politics and philosophy. Fundamentally, history is the unfolding of embryonic possibilities present in this shaking.[14]

History is constituted for Patočka by both politics and philosophy, and history, philosophy, and politics together become capable of shaking

---

12 The centenary celebrations of World War One were an occasion to reflect upon this conversation about the civilian enthusiasm for the war. For one journalistic summary, see Pierre Purseigle, "The Tragedy of Consent," *The Telegraph*, http://i.telegraph.co.uk/multimedia /archive/02750/Inside_The_First_W_2750680a.pdf. For some of the philosophical implications for how this influenced Patočka, see: C. Sternad, "Max Scheler and Jan Patočka on the First World War," *Labyrinth. An International Journal for Philosophy, Value Theory and Sociocultural Hermeneutics* 19, no. 1 (2017): 89–106.

13 "To shake the everydayness of the fact crunchers and routine minds, to make them aware that their place is on the side of the front and not on the side of even the most pleasing slogans of the day which in reality call to war, whether they invoke the nation, the state, classless society, world unity, or whatever other appeals, discreditable and discredited by the factual ruthlessness of the Force, there may be." Patočka, *Heretical Essays*, 134–136.

14 Patočka, *Heretical Essays,* 77.

naïve meanings and creating new possibilities for human action. While war is one form of politics that might temporarily pull us out of our everydayness, dissident politics in general also has potential for shaking our routines and boredom, as does the perpetual questioning of philosophy. When Patočka offered a more substantive definition of 'solidarity of the shaken,' it included the philosophical task of finding deeper understandings of the world, and he emphasized doing this alongside others:

> The means by which this state [of war] is overcome is the solidarity of the shaken; the solidarity of those who are capable of understanding what life and death are all about, and so what history is about... The solidarity of the shaken is the solidarity of those who understand. Understanding, though, must in the present circumstances involve not only the basic level, that of slavery and freedom with respect to life, but needs also entail an understanding of the significance of science and technology, of that Force we are releasing.[15]

To overcome boredom and everydayness, then, one has to come together with others who understand history, or this particular conception of history-as-shaking, and find solidarity with those who are willing to question the problems of science, technology, and the 'force' of war. While that much is somewhat clear, these lines occur within the last few pages of Patočka's *Heretical Essays in the Philosophy of History*, and lead up to a conclusion that is somewhat less clear. His final references in *Heretical Essays* are to Heraclitus's *polemos* and human conflict (see Chapter Three), and he ends with a question about possibly reevaluating the meaning of both the history of Western civilization and the meaning of human history in general. The implication seems to be that he wants to keep history moving by shaking those meanings that are held fast as truth and orthodoxy by historians themselves, but there are no clear practical descriptions of where or how to begin this process, apart from asking philosophical questions.

Patočka's linkage of solidarity, understanding, and "that Force we are releasing" through science and technology are, however vague, questions that the atomic situation demanded. There were those that 'got it' and understood, like Mailer and his concern with generational "psychic havoc," and there were those who persisted in their everydayness and

---

15   Patočka, *Heretical Essays*, 134–136.

dismissed the problem, those who "learned to stop worrying and love the bomb," to borrow the subtitle of Stanley Kubrick's nuclear film *Dr. Strangelove*.[16] Those 'who understood' had solidarity with each other in their insistence on worrying about the implications of science and technology. 'Shakenness' became a counter-force to "the Force," drawing people together to take action:

> The solidarity of the shaken shaken in their faith in the day, in 'life' and 'peace'—acquires a special significance, especially in the time of the releasing of Force. Force released is that without which 'day' and 'peace,' human life defined by a world of exponential growth, cannot exist.[17]

What Patočka means here, exactly, is open to some interpretation, given the ambiguity and abstraction of the language. If the "force released" is both science and technology in general, and the atomic force in particular, and those who are "shaken" are in a more enlightened state than those who are not, then releasing the force has paradoxically created a kind of enlightenment by shaking the faith of those who would otherwise ignore the problem. Sometimes historical catastrophe wakes people from a very deep slumber, and that has historical significance in a way that cannot be wholly condemned as merely bad or unfortunate. Patočka is also not an anti-war pacifist (see below, part IV).[18] He, like everyone living in the nuclear age, could see how technology and science had created exponential growth—in both population and (in some places) the daily material comfort of that population—and by another argument, the threat of the force of war also created peace, even if that peace was the strained particularities of 'Cold War peace.' The constructive possibilities

---

16 *Dr. Strangelove, or, How I Learned to Stop Worrying and Love the Bomb*, directed by Stanley Kubrick (1964; Columbia Pictures).

17 Patočka, *Heretical Essays*, 135.

18 One of Patočka's clearest statements in regard to the importance of being willing to fight a war when necessary is his commentary on the Munich agreement with Germany in the lead-up to World War Two, where Czech leaders went along with the appeasement of Hitler and decided not to fight. Patočka perceived that his people were willing to fight and sacrifice, but their leaders were not, and accused them smallness and cowardice. Had they fought, Patočka claimed, "Czechoslovakia as a Central European state with a consistently enacted democracy, rigidly defended and resolved to go to the last extreme, could have played a respectable role in the middle of the European crisis. Such a Czechoslovakia could, even in the event of defeat and military catastrophe, have gathered moral energy for the future, so that in later times it would not be a mere plaything in the hands of the superpowers of the postwar era... Who does not fight back ends badly." Patočka, "What are the Czechs," in Jan Bažant, Nina Baržantova and Frances Starn, eds. *The Czech Reader* (Durham: Duke University Press, 2010), 426–428.

in this seemingly destructive context, however, become clearer when Patočka says more about how it creates a new form of solidarity among those willing to say 'no':

> All the forces on whose basis alone can humans live in our time are potentially in the hands of those who so understand. The solidarity of the shaken can say 'no' to the measures of mobilization which make the state of war permanent. It will not offer positive programs but will speak, like Socrates' *daimonion*, in warnings and prohibitions. It can and must create a spiritual authority, become a spiritual power that could drive the warring world to some restraint, rendering some acts and measures impossible.[19]

The idea of a force that speaks in warnings and prohibitions, one that might become a spiritual power that produces restraint on the world's warring parties, and one that seeks to make certain measures of mobilization impossible, is an idea that opens up comparisons to anti-nuclear activists and the voices of the 1960s generation. These activists made their entrée into history by evoking their own understanding of death, destruction, and the dangers of permanent war. The 'positive programs' they suggested were mostly ignored, and they could also only speak in warnings and prohibitions, but by landing somewhere near truth in their modalities of activist speech, they developed a kind of solidarity of the shaken that was also a way of living in truth. Whether or not they drove the world (at least in part) to "some restraint" is another question, but through looking at their texts through this lens, Patočka's notion of 'solidarity of the shaken' can be given more tangible substance and clarity.

Becoming an Historical Being: Mario Savio's "An End to History"

Patočka's concern with the philosophy of history is represented throughout his work, not just in *Heretical Essays on the Philosophy of History*. This book represents, however, one of his most coherent later works that presents a semi-systematic view on what history is, under what conditions humans become historical beings, and how history might relate to the

---

19   Patočka, *Heretical Essays*, 135.

human ability to move toward moral consciousness and moral action. As referenced in the introduction, the 'heresy' of the 'heretical' in the title is multifaceted. Commentators have variously described the heresies, and within Patočka's essays themselves there are several indications that he wants to use phenomenology to challenge traditional historical accounts, but that he also wants to (perhaps heretically) diverge from Husserl and Heidegger in important ways at the same time as deploying a phenomenological methodology.[20] As described above, what Patočka is constantly pushing against is the idea of 'everydayness' and the propensity to take the world as it is, rather than questioning as problematic what one sees, hears, and believes. One aspect of the heresy of the heretical, however, is how he asserts that this process of questioning is what history *is*. To be 'shaken' and to be 'historical' are phenomenologically parallel in his definitions. According to Patočka, we entered into history as a human species when we became willing to confront and shake given meanings; history-as-shaking was the origin of human consciousness. If we follow Patočka's idea that "history is the unfolding of embryonic possibilities present in this shaking,"[21] then we can begin to see why interpretations of history can themselves shake up history politically. Karl Marx was one example of this, where his famous political manifesto begins with an interpretation of history, but Patočka does not directly address Marx, likely for historical-political reasons of his own situation in a Communist state, and does not agree with the Marxist sense of history as a totality.[22] Instead, he concerns himself with those major ruptures where philosophy and politics together became historically self-aware and therein changed the direction of history and historical action. He uses the emergence of the Greek *polis* and the beginning of Christianity as his main two examples.[23] These were moments when

---

20 See Introduction and note 12.

21 Patočka, *Heretical Essays,* 77.

22 After the preface, the first section of Marx's *Communist Manifesto* begins: "The history of all hitherto existing society is the history of class struggles." Karl Marx & Frederick Engels. *The Marx-Engels Reader* (New York: Norton, 1978), 473. To apply the theory noted in the introduction, from Leo Strauss's essay *Persecution and the Art of Writing*, one might be able to go so far as to say Patočka was really critiquing Marxism in a hidden way without ever mentioning it, to avoid being controversial but to speak to those who could read between the lines. Given his later willingness to be controversial, take risks and sacrifice, however, the interpretation of which 'interpretation of history' he was using and critiquing could go either way. Ultimately there are multiple heresies and multiple possibilities.

23 Patočka, *Heretical Essays*, in chapters 1–3 and throughout the argument. He stays distant from Marx's example of the "historical" clashes between the proletariat and the bourgeoisie.

humanity reconceived of the past and future at the same time, creating a rupture in everydayness.

One question that emerges in applying Patočka's ideas to the activism of the 1960s is whether this notion of rupture holds for atomic activism. Does a certain conception of history change in this era, including the way self-aware actors think philosophically and choose to 'act historically' in the political arena? In "An End to History," Mario Savio answers this question affirmatively, imploring his fellow student activists to change their understanding of history in the context of the Free Speech Movement (FSM) at Berkeley in 1964. This document is a transcript of a speech Savio gave when the FSM first came together to protest against university administration rules designed to limit student speech on campus. He talks about the differing perspectives of the students and the university bureaucracy on the events of the day:

> In our free-speech fight at the University of California, we have come up against what may emerge as the greatest problem of our nation—depersonalized, unresponsive bureaucracy... As a bureaucrat, an administrator believes that nothing new happens. He occupies an a-historical point of view... we held a sit-in on the campus. We sat around a police car and kept it immobilized for over thirty-two hours. At last, the administrative bureaucracy agreed to negotiate. But instead, on the following Monday, we discovered that a committee had been appointed, in accordance with usual regulations, to resolve the dispute. Our attempt to convince any of the administrators that an event had occurred, that something new had happened, failed. They saw this simply as something to be handled by normal university procedures... The same is true of all bureaucracies. They begin as tools, means to certain legitimate goals, and they end up feeding their own existence. The conception that bureaucrats have is that history has in fact come to an end. No events can occur now that the Second World War is over which can change American society substantially.[24]

Savio's diagnosis of the problem of bureaucracy follows the sense that 'history' includes the belief that something can, will, and should change about human institutions as times change. For him, bureaucracy, as an

24 Mario Savio, "An End to History," http://www.fsm-a.org/stacks/endhistorysavio.html. Published originally in *Humanity, an Arena of Critique and Commitment,* No. 2 (December 1964).

emblematic product of rationalism and systematic logic, is a symptom of the problem of techno-science and the need for a predictable and structured outcome to human interaction; this rationalization of human interaction objectifies the human participants, and once rendered into objects, the possibilities for spontaneous action become highly limited. A kind of everydayness sets in, as "usual regulations" pervade all aspects of life, and where the shaking of those meanings seems to be impossible, and so history seems to stop. To identify that stoppage at the end of World War Two, as Savio does, is much like Mailer's reference to the atomic bomb at the beginning of his essay about hipster dissent; there is a recognition that something happened at that moment that changed everything, and Savio is challenging what he apparently sees as the bureaucratic interpretation of that event as having settled everything. Savio argued instead that this moment in time must be understood as a moment of rupture, of history being put into motion. As he continues later in the speech, he therefore reinterprets the events of World War Two, arguing that new events can and will occur thereafter, and in saying this, he himself becomes part of the relationship between history and action. His speech and actions 'made it' into the 'history books.'[25]

Both Patočka and Savio see a linkage between understanding mechanized systems and understanding how history comes to a standstill; they also see how the philosophical task of asking questions becomes ineffective and stultified when any institution claims that history has ended or stopped. Savio goes on to explain how this has an impact on political action, and how he, as an activist, wants to convince other students to recognize their place in the forward motion of history. He tries to convince them to understand not just their moral obligation to shake up the bureaucracy, but also their obligation to each other through a form of solidarity:

> Most people who will be put out of jobs by machines will not accept an end to events, this historical plateau, as the point beyond which no change occurs... All of us must refuse to accept history's final judgment that in America there is no place in society for people whose skins are dark. On campus students are not about to accept it as fact that the university has ceased evolving and is in its final state of perfection, that students and

---

25 See Chapter 5, below, "Heretical Metaphysics of Historicity."

faculty are respectively raw material and employees, or that the university is to be autocratically run by unresponsive bureaucrats.[26]

Losing jobs to machines was another example of mechanism and technology having dehumanizing effects. Racism was for Savio the best example of the lack of solidarity, and he linked the problem of racism and the problem of bureaucracy to common roots, to the autocratic system and the attitude that 'we proceed by standard procedures as we are.' He went on to describe what students were doing to put history into motion again:

> Students have begun not only to question but, having arrived at answers, to act on those answers. This is part of a growing understanding among many people in America that history has not ended, that a better society is possible, and that it is worth dying for… America is becoming ever more the utopia of sterilized, automated contentment. The 'futures' and 'careers' for which American students now prepare are for the most part intellectual and moral wastelands. This chrome-plated consumers' paradise would have us grow up to be well-behaved children. But an important minority of men and women coming to the front today have shown that they will die rather than be standardized, replaceable and irrelevant.[27]

At the end of his speech, Savio turns to the language of 'the front' as a form of willing confrontation; he also turns to notions of sacrifice as being a necessary element of activism; he critiques automated contentment, and would likely agree with Patočka's idea that, "to reach the point when all who are capable of understanding would feel inwardly uncomfortable about their comfortable position, that is a meaning that can be reached beyond the human peak of resistance to Force, its very overcoming."[28] For affluent American college students in the 1960s, they surely did reach a point where they recognized their own comfort as something uncomfortable in light of the problems of the world, from racism to war to university bureaucracies. (A similar description of the transition from comfort to being purposefully uncomfortable is made in the Port Huron Statement, discussed below.) By the time of Savio's statement in 1964, the Vietnam anti-war movement had not developed

---

26   Savio, "An End to History."
27   Savio, "An End to History."
28   Patočka, *Heretical Essays*, 135.

its full momentum, but one can sense that if it had, Savio would probably have agreed with the flavor of Patočka's idea that "[h]umankind will not attain peace by devoting and surrendering itself to the criteria of everydayness and of its promises."[29] For Savio, the 'front' was still a metaphor, but an important one that was a key to getting beyond the false promise of 'everydayness,' trying to move toward a horizon where people do not have to be standardized, replaceable, and irrelevant. If people were so replaceable, the shadows of Hiroshima would not be nearly so scary and disturbing.

Solidarity and Humility: Tillich's "Shaking of the Foundations"

As discussed in the prior chapter, after the first test explosion of a nuclear weapon, Robert Oppenheimer thought of the *Bhagavad Gita*: "Now I am become death, destroyer of worlds."[30] References to apocalyptic spiritual texts in association with the mushroom cloud did not end there. When Paul Tillich, a German protestant theologian who emigrated to the US during World War Two, gave a sermon in 1955 on "The Shaking of the Foundations" and addressed the problem of the atomic situation, he began by quoting those sections in the Bible that describe a ruined earth and total destruction in the books of Jeremiah and Isaiah: "the mountains shall depart and the hills be removed,"[31] "the sown land lies a desert and the towns are razed,"[32] "the whole land shall be desolate. And for this shall the earth mourn and the heavens above be black."[33] Given that nuclear blasts cause radioactive rain that is indeed black, and are powerful enough to remove whole hills and hillsides, the fact that the towns were razed seems to be the least of many parallels.[34] Tillich cites these passages and then states what he sees as the new truth:

---

29 Patočka, *Heretical Essays*, 135.
30 *The Day After Trinity: J. Robert Oppenheimer and the Atomic Bomb*, directed by Jon Else (1944; Santa Monica, CA.: Pyramid Films), aired 1981, https://youtu.be/Vm5fCxXnK7Y
31 Isiah, 54:10. Quoted in Paul Tillich, *The Shaking of the Foundations* (United States: Wipf & Stock Publishers, 2012) 1.
32 Jeremiah, 4:23-30.
33 Jeremiah, 4:23-30.
34 "In one of the later books, Second Peter, it says that 'the heavens will vanish with a crackling roar, and the elements will melt with fervent heat, the earth also and the works therein shall be burnt up.' This is no longer vision; it has become physics." Paul Tillich, *The Shaking of the Foundations*, 3.

There was a time when we could listen to such words without much feeling and without understanding. There were decades and even centuries when we did not take them seriously. Those days are gone. Today we must take them seriously. For they describe with visionary power what the majority of human beings in our period have experienced, and what, perhaps in a not too distant future, all mankind will experience abundantly. 'The foundations of the earth do shake.' The visions of the prophets have become an actual, physical possibility, and might become an historical reality.[35]

As Tillich further discusses the implications of the atomic situation, he focuses on the key difference between the Biblical passages and the current historical situation: in the Bible, it is God who causes the destruction. In the nuclear age, it is human beings who do it, assuming God-like power to destroy creation. This is problematic for Tillich:

Out of the fertile soil of the earth a being was generated and nourished, who was able to find the key to the foundation of all beings. That being was man. He has discovered the key which can unlock the forces of the ground, those forces which were bound when the foundations of the earth were laid. He has begun to use this key. He has subjected the basis of life and thought and will to his will. And he willed destruction... The greatest triumph of science was the power it gave to man to annihilate himself and his world.[36]

Tillich's suspicion of the scientific enterprise and human hubris is hardly masked; he and Patočka would agree on the scariness of what techno-science has done in producing our means of self-destruction and self-annihilation. He and Patočka would not see themselves out of the problem in quite the same way, however, despite the Christian resonances in many of Patočka's ideas (see Chapter Two). For Tillich, he ends his meditation by creating a fork in the road, as if we have two theological choices to emerge from the mess we have created:

But if the foundations of this place and all places begin to crumble, cynicism itself crumbles with them. And only two alternatives remain—de-

---

35   Tillich, *Shaking of the Foundations*, 2–3.
36   Tillich, *The Shaking of the Foundations*, 4

spair, which is the certainty of eternal destruction, or faith, which is the certainty of eternal salvation... For the earth always carries its end within it. We happen to live in a time when very few of us, very few nations, very few sections of the earth, will succeed in forgetting the end. For in these days the foundations of the earth do shake. May we not turn our eyes away; may we not close our ears and our mouths! But may we rather see, through the crumbling of a world, the rock of eternity and the salvation which has no end![37]

This direct turn toward notions of God's eternity in the face of earthly calamity is not a surprising response for a Christian theologian and minister. A new form of death is yet another way of getting to eternal salvation.[38] Death for Patočka is somewhat more complicated than this, however, as his idea of death contains a relationship to finding meaning in life (see Chapter Two). The notion of eternity is important to him, but for Patočka it is not a rock; the religious formulation of eternity as a "rock" represents a final destination, a stillness and an end, so it would be inconsistent with his theory of motion and perpetual problematicity. He would agree with Tillich that the atomic bomb is an occasion to begin searching for meaning, but the relationship between that search and a final 'whole' understanding of the world through "eternal salvation" is not where Patočka would look to find answers. Instead, he turns to notions of perpetually-created meaning through living, perhaps living in truth:

Meaning will never be simply given or won once and for all. It means that there emerges a new relation, a new mode of relating to what is meaningful; that meaning can arise only in an activity which stems from a searching lack of meaning, as the vanishing point of being problematic, as an indirect epiphany... the constant shaking of the naïve sense of meaningfulness is itself a new mode of meaning, a discovery of its continuity with the mysteriousness of being and what-is as a whole."[39]

---

37 Tillich, *The Shaking of the Foundations*, 11.
38 Some religious groups want the apocalypse to come sooner, so to be saved sooner, and they support nuclear weapons. See: M. Cook, "Christian Apocalypticism and Weapons of Mass Destruction," in S. Hashmi and Steven Lee, eds., *Ethics and Weapons of Mass Destruction: Religious and Secular Perspectives* (Cambridge: Cambridge University Press, 2004).
39 Patočka, *Heretical Essays*, 61.

This perspective would push back against Tillich's insistence on eternal salvation in "Shaking of the Foundations," but it is not wholly incompatible with Tillich's larger body of work, as the search for 'the meaning within meaninglessness' was the hallmark phrase of Tillich's philosophical-theological account in *Courage to Be*.[40] Patočka would likely not disagree with his argument until Tillich's final chapter of *Courage to Be*, where he outlines the 'God above God' as a metaphysical solution to this search.[41] For Patočka, the search seems to go on indefinitely, towards a horizon where we can imagine God there, but all the while knowing that this is not a place where we as mere humans can arrive at definitively. Our participation in an image of eternity can be proximate and historical, but for Patočka, never final and permanent.

Yet at the end of this sermon about 'shaking,' Tillich does something more akin to Patočka when he asks about the prophets, about those who have told of the doom that God's wrath and the nuclear situation will bring. In this frame, he asks an illuminating variant of the dissident's question:

> But is it a sign of patriotism or of confidence in one's people, its institutions and its way of life, to be silent when the foundations are shaking? Is the expression of optimism, whether or not it is justified, so much more valuable than the expression of truth, even if the truth is deep and dark? Most human beings, of course, are not able to stand the message of the shaking of the foundations. They reject and attack the prophetic minds, not because they really disagree with them, but because they sense the truth of their words and cannot receive it... I have always felt that there might be a few who are able to register the shaking of the foundations— who are able to stand this, and who are able, above all, to say what they know, because they are courageous enough to withstand the unavoidable enmity of the many.[42]

Tillich argues here that there are a few people who understand, a few who can bear the truth, a few who do not run away from the truth, and a few who are thus called to end the silence about the nature of the shaking. All this is phenomenologically consistent with the self-understandings of dissidents and activists, including Patočka's notion of 'solidarity

---

40 Paul Tillich, *The Courage to Be* (New Haven: Yale University Press, 1952).
41 Tillich, *Courage to Be*, 171.
42 Tillich, *The Shaking of the Foundations*, 8.

of the shaken.' Tillich is referencing the prophets in this passage, who he thinks now need to be taken more seriously in their descriptions of how the earth is being shaken apart.[43] But he also moves on to discuss the scientists and their paradoxical role in how prophecy has unfolded in modernity:

> Science is atoning for the idolatrous abuse to which it has lent itself for centuries. Science, which has closed our eyes and thrown us into an abyss of ignorance about the few things that really matter, has revealed itself, has opened our eyes, and has pointed, at least, to one fundamental truth—that 'the mountains shall depart and the hills shall be removed,' that 'earth shall fall down to rise no more,' because its foundations shall be destroyed.[44]

By "idolatrous abuse," Tillich seems to mean that science has given man the illusion that he is God and is omnipotent vis-à-vis the natural world because of his ability to use the scientific method to harness the forces of the earth. The atonement here seems slightly ironic; by producing nuclear weapons through processes of coming to understand the mechanics of God's universe, the scientists, by making the given world match the apocalyptic horrors of biblical prophecy, have shown that the Bible is more correct (in a literal descriptive sense) than previously thought. Even if this irony played out to demonstrate the accuracies of the prophets, Tillich does not think this has made the world a better place. To him, the situation has been a reiteration of the common historical theme of human hubris with a predictably disastrous ending:

> But man is not God; and whenever he has claimed to be like God, he has been rebuked and brought to self-destruction and despair. When he has rested complacently on his cultural creativity or on his technical progress, on his political institutions or on his religious systems, he has been thrown into disintegration and chaos; all the foundations of his personal, natural and cultural life have been shaken. As long as there has been human his-

---

43 Another possible interlocutor here, difficult to include because of space constraints, would be Erich Fromm's delineation of "The Prophets and the Priests," a description of the difference between those who are able to dissent against convention (he calls them the prophets) and "the priests" who uphold conventions. Fromm, *On Disobedience, Or Why Freedom Means Saying 'No' to Power* (New York: Harper Perennial, 2010) 13–40.

44 Tillich, *The Shaking of the Foundations*, 5–6.

tory, this is what has happened; in our period it has happened on a larger scale than ever before. Man's claim to be like God has been rejected once more; not one foundation of the life of our civilization has remained unshaken.[45]

While Tillich seems convinced that the atomic situation marks an historical era of considerable self-destruction, he manages to end the sermon on an optimistic note by dissecting the implications of the relationship between the shaking of the foundations, cynicism, and our ability to be self-reflective.[46] In the end, cynicism is overcome by the shaking, like Patočka's history of problematicity, and similar to how 'solidarity of the shaken' overcomes grandiose ontological boredom. Patočka's 'boredom' and Tillich's 'cynicism' have a lot in common. As Tillich writes:

> There is scarcely one thing about which we may not be cynical. But we cannot be cynical about the shaking of the foundations of everything! I have never encountered anyone who seriously was cynical about that. I have seen much cynicism, particularly among the younger people in Europe before the war. But I know from abundant witnesses that this cynicism vanished when the foundations of the world began to shake at the beginning of the European catastrophe. We can be cynical about the end only so long as we do not have to see it, only so long as we feel safety in the place in which our cynicism can be exercised.[47]

Being able to see the end, to see death, is an experience of a new beginning and a way to pull us out of the safety of cynicism. The difficult business of telling people they are going to die, however, poses risks

---

45   Tillich, *The Shaking of the Foundations*, 6.
46   To contextualize this idea, Tillich writes: "Is it humanly possible to face the end cynically? There are certainly some among us who are cynical toward most of that which men create and praise. There are some among us who are cynical about the present situation of the world and the leaders of the world. We may be cynical, of course, about the true motives behind all human action; we may be cynical about ourselves, our inner growth and our outer achievements. We may be cynical about religion and about our Churches, their doctrines, their symbols and their representatives..." "How much of our lives consists in nothing but attempts to look away from the end! We often succeed in forgetting the end. But ultimately we fail; for we always carry the end with us in our bodies and our souls. And often whole nations and cultures succeed in forgetting the end. But ultimately they fail too, for in their lives and growth they always carry the end with them. Often the whole earth succeeds in making its creatures forget its end, but sometimes these creatures feel that their earth is beginning to grow old, and that its foundations are beginning to shake." Tillich, *The Shaking of the Foundations*, 10.
47   Tillich, *The Shaking of the Foundations*, 10.

for those who voice the warnings and admonitions. When referencing those who speak the truth about death, Tillich describes the prophets as Socrates-like characters, endangered by those who would like to stay in their chains of cynicism: "No man with a prophetic spirit likes to foresee and fore-say the doom of his own period. It exposes him to a terrible anxiety within himself, to severe and often deadly attacks from others, and to the charge of pessimism and defeatism on the part of the majority of the people."[48] Tillich's vision of a prophet speaking the truth comes to sound much like the Platonic vision of the philosopher telling the truth to those in the cave, which in turn comes to sound like the activist who is in danger of being attacked by those to whom he speaks the truth. The assassinations of prophet-like political activists in the United States in the 1960s are etched on collective memory as much as the decade's activism: John F Kennedy, Robert Kennedy Jr., Martin Luther King Jr., and Malcom X. They had more hopeful messages than prophesizing doom and death, by and large, and they were trying to counter cynicism and boredom for a whole generation. Such confrontation and shaking of the foundations were not taken lightly; it was dangerous.

The Repentant Scientists

The collection of Patočka's essays in *Freedom and Sacrifice* includes a short piece entitled "The Heroes of Our Time." As discussed in Chapter Three, one of Patočka's four examples is "The Repentant Atomic Scientists: Oppenheimer and Sakharov."[49] Dedicating only two paragraphs to his explanation, Patočka connects their "heroism" to their ability to sacrifice their social position, their jobs, and their identity as scientists for the greater good of others. Patočka claims that they realized the total destructiveness of the power they had harnessed, while also being willing to speak out against their own life's work as a warning to others. Patočka sees their actions as 'repentance' for their sins of having helped to create the scientific tools that could one day lead to the destruction and annihilation of the planet. Oppenheimer and Sakharov were not the only scientists involved in atomic projects who later showed such repentance and felt obligated to warn humanity about not just about the dangers of

---

48 Tillich, *The Shaking of the Foundations*, 8.
49 Patočka, *Libertad y Sacrificio*, trans. Ivan Ortega Rodriguez (Salamanca: Ediciones Sígueme, 2007) 345.

the weapons themselves, but also the dangers of nuclear radiation (the understanding of which was initially much more limited than it is now). Examining additional examples of such 'repentance' can help expand the sense of Patočka ideas, while also illuminating the degree to which nuclear scientists in the 1950s helped create a form of 'solidarity of the shaken.'

One such example is the "Russell-Einstein Manifesto." In 1955, a group of scientists and intellectuals gathered at the town of Pugwash in Nova Scotia, Canada, and issued a statement calling for an end to all war.[50] The manifesto advocates a pacifist position in response to the nuclear threat, and became the basis for an organization now called The Pugwash Conferences, which still works to promote disarmament, conflict resolution, and international agreements that limit the use of weapons of mass destruction.[51] The Pugwash Conferences were one of the earliest organizations doing this type of work, and now they are part of a much larger anti-nuclear movement that is global and widely supported. While Patočka would not agree that their pacifist position would ever be successful in ending war, the ontological claims in the manifesto about the relationship of nuclear war to human life show a shift in understanding that helps to illuminate how 'solidarity of the shaken' could inform the paradoxes of the nuclear age. While war did not get abolished as Einstein and his colleagues hoped it would, the appeal they made to the universality of bodily health as a species-wide (and thus global) concern has significant implications for all dissident movements, in particular the continuing anti-nuclear movement and the environmental movement (see Chapter Five). If, for Patočka, war reveals the shakenness of the human situation, and if that shakeneness can be the grounding for solidarity, then the emplacement of the human body within sites of vulnerability and fragility matters for how the relationship of war and solidarity changed in the nuclear age; one does not have to be in a war zone to be physically shaken by, and vulnerable to, nuclear war, as radiation spreads everywhere. The 'repentant scientists' who produced this manifesto were some of the first to see the political implications of this scientific reality. They saw human 'shakenness' as much more literal and physical than Patočka's more abstract historical and metaphorical notion, but they nonetheless would agree that the diffused consequences

---

50 "Russell-Einstein Manifesto," July 9, 1955, http://pugwash.org/1955/07/09/statement
    -manifesto/.
51 "About Pugwash," accessed Dec. 28, 2019, https://pugwash.org/about-pugwash/.

of this type of war could have as its corollary a diffused type of global solidarity through the recognition of how the fragility of the human body can shape political consciousness.

Patočka wrote about the phenomenology of the human body in the philosophical terms of 'corporeity,' often under the influence of French philosopher Maurice Merleau-Ponty.[52] To speak of corporeity was a way of unpacking how humans are 'emplaced' in the world in particular situations and contexts, never fully able to transcend the circumstances of their body (see Chapter Three). The background to this discussion was how the relationship between the human spirit and the human body was an ancient philosophical question, and through the traditional lenses of Plato, Christianity, and some of their heirs, the body was initially 'philosophized' as part of the particular, local, varied site of heterogeneity, symbolizing the changing non-universal aspects of different human lives. This was thought to be in contrast to the spirit or the soul, which was traditionally thought of as the universal, global, and unchangeable aspect of humanity that we have in common with everyone everywhere. One impact of modern science upon philosophy, and one reason why science is accused of atheism, is that biology, chemistry, and modern medicine discovered universal and species-wide systems that apply to all bodies everywhere. Politically, therefore, references to the common bodily characteristics of the 'biological human species' could then become calls to reject personal and local attachments in favor of universal concerns common to all human bodies, and this is what the Russell-Einstein Manifesto did. The former traditional understanding was reversed within their 'scientific' paradigm, and implicitly, in such a framework, 'the spirit' becomes a less important, less universal, and more particular (and thus subjective) aspect of human existence.

While Patočka had his worries about this aspect of modern science, the 'repentant scientists' were fully within this paradigm, and tried to use the idea of biological universality not only to transcend global religious differences (and different interpretations of 'spirit'), but also to reinforce the obvious point that human life without a healthy body is not possible anywhere, and thus one's local 'emplacement' near a nuclear

---

52 While there are many works of Merleau-Ponty's that Patočka would have been thinking of, his central work is *Phenomenology of Perception*. For further commentary on the philosophical relationship, see E. Evink, "Surrender and Subjectivity: Merleau-Ponty and Patočka on Intersubjectivity," *Meta: Research in Hermeneutics. Phenomenology and Practical Philosophy*, V, no. 1 (2013): 13–28.

test site emitting excess radiation (or other types of technologically-produced toxins) would change the fate of one's particular, individual life quite dramatically.[53] Yet instead of that particular illness of that particular body pushing it farther from the universals shared with other people, and thus farther from some general shared metaphysical condition, they also pointed out how, in the nuclear age, that illness becomes global and universal. Radiation from nuclear testing was deposited in the whole earthly atmosphere; while the effect is initially more intense near explosion sites, it diffuses and comes to impact everyone's body in a similarly tragic way, as all cells everywhere mutate and become prone to cancer. The scientists could then claim that the one thing that pulls us outside of all localities, cultures, and particularities, and moves us towards universal solidarity with all of humanity, is indeed the body's universality. They thought they should ground efforts toward solidarity and political change, therefore, on the biology of the species, and on the body's fragility and susceptibility:

> We are speaking on this occasion, not as members of this or that nation, continent, or creed, but as human beings, members of the species Man, whose continued existence is in doubt. The world is full of conflicts; and, overshadowing all minor conflicts, the titanic struggle between Communism and anti-Communism. Almost everybody who is politically conscious has strong feelings about one or more of these issues; but we want you, if you can, to set aside such feelings and consider yourselves only as members of a biological species which has had a remarkable history, and whose disappearance none of us can desire.[54]

For the scientists, the "biological human species" was endangered, and therefore should have been prioritized as more important than nation, creed, and ideology. Now, more than half a century later, in an age when science and the universal biology of the species are taken for granted, this does not seem all that revolutionary. But the human reckoning with

---

53 In another similar statement on this idea, Albert Schweitzer used his platform as a Nobel Laureate and made a speech in 1957 about the long-term effects of radiation on the human body. His main concern was the continued testing of hydrogen bombs, perpetuating the release of radiation into the earth's atmosphere. His "A Declaration of Conscience" was broadcast on April 24, 1957, https://www.wagingpeace.org/a-declaration-of-conscience/. The printed version was originally published in *Saturday Review*, May 18, 1957. Schweitzer won the Nobel Prize for his humanitarian work setting up a hospital in Africa; he was doctor, a philosopher, and a musician.

54 "Russell-Einstein Manifesto."

the mechanisms and processes of science was, as Patočka's concerns with techno-science demonstrated, a raw and open question in the time after World War Two. Worries abounded about whether the universality of the human spirit was overshadowed by scientific and biological formulations, and there was real concern about whether science and religion might be reconciled. Patočka's response was to advocate reigning in the scientists with a kind of self-sacrificing morality, including a reemphasis on the spirit of being, and thus identifying Oppenheimer and Sahkarov as heroes because he understood their stance as representing a willingness to question what they had previously believed and to sacrifice positions of authority in order to do so.

Einstein and his colleagues had a somewhat different response, where it was not so much the science itself that was the problem, but what the politicians did with the science. The manifesto acknowledged the possibility of total destruction that could be brought about by nuclear war and radiation, and then declared that war (not science) was what should be questioned:

> Here, then, is the problem which we present to you, stark and dreadful and inescapable: Shall we put an end to the human race; or shall mankind renounce war? People will not face this alternative because it is so difficult to abolish war. The abolition of war will demand distasteful limitations of national sovereignty. But what perhaps impedes understanding of the situation more than anything else is that the term 'mankind' feels vague and abstract. People scarcely realize in imagination that the danger is to themselves and their children and their grandchildren, and not only to a dimly apprehended humanity. They can scarcely bring themselves to grasp that they, individually, and those whom they love are in imminent danger of perishing agonizingly.[55]

Raising awareness about nuclear weapons, following this logic, was meant to bring people to see themselves in solidarity with others in 'mankind,' and therefore to try to end 'mankind's' self-destructive practice of war. But there is also a recognition within this statement that 'mankind' and humanity had become too distant and intangible, too 'vague and abstract' to prompt action. Einstein and his colleagues wanted to bridge this abstraction, and to achieve such understanding and solidarity, they

55   "Russell-Einstein Manifesto."

thought it would take an act of imagination, of projecting a possibility not previously conceived:

> We have to learn to think in a new way. We have to learn to ask ourselves, not what steps can be taken to give military victory to whatever group we prefer, for there no longer are such steps; the question we have to ask ourselves is: what steps can be taken to prevent a military contest of which the issue must be disastrous to all parties?... No one knows how widely such lethal radio-active particles might be diffused, but the best authorities are unanimous in saying that a war with H-bombs might possibly put an end to the human race. It is feared that if many H-bombs are used there will be universal death, sudden only for a minority, but for the majority a slow torture of disease and disintegration.[56]

Learning to think in a new way about war, sovereignty, the body, and the relations of human beings to one another is no small task. Einstein's theory of relativity could change all of science and the way people thought about the physical world, so why not change entirely the way people thought about war? Was not the atomic bomb a moment of opportunity for such a change in thinking? This was clearly ambitious, even if it might also have been naïve. What they were asking for was a new conversation about the collective understanding of the world, with the hope that a new solidarity would flow from that understanding. What he was asking for was what Patočka would call a "*metanoesis* of historic proportion," a conversion or changing of the mind (*metanoesis*) about an entire view of the world:

> The possibility of a *metanoesis* of historic proportions depends essentially on this: is that part of humanity which is capable of understanding what was and is the point of history, which is at the same time ever more driven by the entire positioning of present day humanity at the peak of techno-science to accept responsibility for meaninglessness, also capable of the discipline and self-denial demanded by a stance of uprooted-ness in which alone a meaningfulness, both absolute and accessible to humans, because it is problematic, might be realized?[57]

---

56 "Russell-Einstein Manifesto."
57 Patočka, *Heretical Essays,* 75–76. *Metanoesis* is a 'change of mind' or 'conversion,' but also has a connotation of being a type of repentance where one is able to think about what one previously thought, then change the course of thinking. This paragraph appears in the Czech

Einstein and his colleagues accepted responsibility for some of the meaninglessness the bomb had brought about, and they were able to see themselves in the context of history, to "understand the point of history," and they came forward with their manifesto trying to shake apart the prior meaning of war and conflict, uprooting themselves and dissenting against nuclear weapons as an atonement and repentance for having created them. Patočka might see their call for a new way of thinking as akin to how 'solidarity of the shaken' emerges from a conversion of historical thinking, and would likely agree with the Socratic spirit behind calling for new ideas and new questions about the implications of ever-more powerful nuclear weapons like the hydrogen bomb.

Patočka did not, however, unlike Einstein, think war was something that would ever end. He makes this clear in his discussion of the idea of *polemos* (see Chapter Three). He would have disagreed with the point on the horizon that Einstein chose to aim for (the end of war), and also might have seen Einstein's explanation of the problem as too facile and too easy. For Patočka, war arises from mysteries about the world we are probably not fully capable of understanding, and he would probably avoid seeking absolute answers. Perhaps in the case of war, "we are dealing only with the uncovering of meaning that can never be explained as a thing, which cannot be mastered, delimited, grasped positively, and dominated, but which is present only in the seeking of being... thus it is this mystery that expresses itself in the shaking of naively accepted meaning."[58] Part of Patočka's critique of techno-science was that the answers it produced could be too formulaic and too simple. Ending all war everywhere to prevent atomic destruction was a clear and simple answer, but perhaps too clear. Patočka would have seen Einstein as retaining naïve meanings in his understanding of the world, and would have called for such ideas to be shaken apart. He might have said that war cannot be "mastered, delimited, grasped positively and dominated," even if the scientists wanted it to be that way. War is one of those things we cannot see the bottom of, leading us to ask, with Patočka, "is not the infinite depth of reality possible only because we cannot see its bottom, and is not just that a challenge and an opportunity for humans in their reach for meaning...?"[59]

version of *Heretical Essays* (from which Kohák's English translation derives) but does not appear in the version of the text that Patočka wrote in German. See Patočka, J. *Péče o duši III*, eds. I. Chatvik and P. Kouba (Prague: Oikoymenh, 2002) 81, 584.

58 Patočka, *Heretical Essays*, 77.
59 Patočka, *Heretical Essays*, 75.

Like the end of Tillich's sermon on nuclear weapons, the Russell-Einstein Manifesto presents a dramatic fork in the road between salvation and destruction in its conclusion. The future is framed as a stark choice:

> There lies before us, if we choose, continual progress in happiness, knowledge, and wisdom. Shall we, instead, choose death, because we cannot forget our quarrels? We appeal as human beings to human beings: Remember your humanity, and forget the rest. If you can do so, the way lies open to a new Paradise; if you cannot, there lies before you the risk of universal death.[60]

Such binary formulations are good at getting people's attention, though rarely does reality confine itself to two categories so tidily. Since the writing of this document, 'humanity' has been able to carry on for many more decades without salvation *or* destruction. War has not ended, but neither has the world. We have perhaps remembered *some* of our humanity, but by no means have we forgotten the rest of our particular differences of class, race, nation, and creed. While the Russell-Einstein Manifesto is a noble statement in search of world peace that helped give grounding to the 'solidarity of the shaken' of today's anti-nuclear activists, through Patočka's categories, it can be seen that this manifesto still suffered from tinges of absolutism, where the 'fog of war' was naïvely denied through using a lens of excess scientific clarity. The contrast and synthesis suggest that we all should feel 'shaken' in a bodily sense by the universal presence of nuclear radiation in our common earthly atmosphere, and should therefore find ourselves in a kind of nuclear kinship and solidarity with all the peoples of the earth, but even with that knowledge, and even with that solidarity, there is no clear and tidy way to "fix" the medical-technological-political problem created by the atomic situation.

Politics, Freedom, and Indifference: The Port Huron Statement

When the Students for a Democratic Society (SDS) came together at a convention in 1962 in Port Huron, Michigan, to draft what they called

---

60 "Russell-Einstein Manifesto," July 9, 1955, http://pugwash.org/1955/07/09/statement -manifesto/.

an "Agenda for a Generation," they did so in light of the atomic situation, claiming that they might be "the last generation in the experiment with living."[61] They were a group of college students from throughout the United States who wanted to articulate the shape of a crisis, and political action became their way of seeking deeper meaning in light of the nearness of atomic death. They wanted to propose a vision for what the 'New Left' could become as a political movement in the future, and the lengthy document goes into considerable detail about specific policy issues, social justice concerns, an institutional analysis of university bureaucracy, and various political interpretations of the Cold War and decolonization. The authors referenced the atomic situation frequently, and while with hindsight their concerns about death and destruction might seem like a touch of youthful melodrama, their statement reveals a sincere response to the tensions and contradictions manifested in the world around them. They saw indifference in the context of crisis, apathy in the midst of fear, and they experienced all the attendant paradoxes of trying to do something when it seemed impossible to do anything as a mere college student.

In the midst of this, however, they offered a vision that Patočka would find quite familiar. They seemed to demonstrate that the combination of living in truth, care of the soul, confrontation, and solidarity of the shaken was capable of creating the activist impetus towards a new political vision. Politics became the exercise of philosophy, a way of bridging theory and practice in order to act, and their mode of solidarity recognized both the fragility and humility of individuals, but also the potential for imagining a new world on the horizon through cooperation with others. By the end of their narrative, there is a sense that their ideas, when put into practice with a genuine sense of self-sacrifice and a willingness to engage the world beyond the self, could create political action that was in itself capable of creating meaning in a world where meaninglessness had become a predominant force of indifference. Their dissident politics, on this measure, was a method of addressing nihilism and atomic annihilation together.

Most of this depended, in the end, on being able to look at the world in such a way to reveal things as new and different, taking apart what 'everydayness' had taken for granted. Beginning with the structure of the university, where they found themselves emplaced, they moved toward

---

61 PHS, 4.

more general concerns, pointing out the absurdity and indifference created by their political situation:

> Look beyond the campus to America itself... The desperation of people threatened by forces about which they know little and of which they can say less; the cheerful emptiness of people 'giving up' all hope of changing things; the faceless ones polled by Gallup who listed 'international affairs' fourteenth on their list of 'problems' but who also expected thermonuclear war in the next few years: in these and other forms, Americans are in withdrawal from public life, from any collective effort at directing their own affairs.[62]

This general withdrawal from public affairs was something the students felt had limited their own political freedom as activists. The general indifference amounted to a wall of silence and passivity difficult to break through. In a democracy, if the general population is entirely indifferent to politics, in some basic sense an individual is not free to engage in politics by him or herself, even if one feels far from indifferent. Democracy (of the modern non-Athenian type) is based upon majority rule, political parties, community groups, and ratios of parliamentary representation that make it virtually impossible for merely one individual citizen voice to "count." A single political leader, with no one to vote for her or him, cannot come into power. One person can be heard, however, as a single voice in his or her own words through the channels of the media, but that, too, often depends upon whether the message is properly 'crowd-sourced' or 'shared' with others. Now that we count 'page views' and 'likes,' this is perhaps somewhat more obvious than it was previously. Figures like Martin Luther King Jr. and Gandhi seem to represent strong individual voices who carried a message that was very much their own, but leaders and activists of this sort could not have done anything without the other people who were convinced by their message and came out in the streets to agree with them. So the Port Huron students understood that in their democracy, they were not free when those around them were indifferent, because no one can do anything alone (politically-speaking) in a democracy. Dissidents in authoritarian societies often seem much more like lone voices in the wilderness of conformity—Havel's "handful of isolated maniacs"—but as discussed in Chapter One, they themselves

---

62 PHS, 11.

attested that they could not have done what they did without that handful, without others to confirm that their sense of being 'maniacal' was at least ironically shared and reciprocated. Indeed, one cannot have solidarity with oneself.

This is a banal point, of course, to say that politics is collective, but rarely do we think of our freedom as being inhibited if others do not join us in our endeavors. Part of what a rights-based discourse does is to obscure this point; if I have a right to do something, and no one is going to stop me from doing it, then am I not free to do it? The answer to this in the political arena depends on what the 'it' is. Am I free to launch a general strike? Am I free to start my own political movement? When it comes to certain forms of political action, a single individual is not at all free to do those things alone, democracy or no democracy. The way that Patočka theorizes 'indifference' and 'boredom,' however, captures his idea of freedom as something that requires at least some intersubjective understanding with other people to enable common action. "Solidarity of the shaken is the solidarity of those who understand," he writes, and that understanding is an understanding of each other that overcomes indifference, challenges tradition and everydayness, and shakes the world into a higher form of self-awareness through interaction with others.

Probing the sources of indifference in any society is therefore one of the first steps toward being able to dissent, and even prior to that, in being able to understand other people enough to communicate the importance of certain political causes to them in such a way that allows joint action. What causes a person to step away from politics in an authoritarian society like Patočka's is clear enough: they fear repercussions by the police and authorities for doing and saying things that are against the official ideology or that threaten the established power structure. In an open democracy, the sources of indifference and apathy can also be anxiety, but these anxieties are much more hidden and obscured, and it becomes difficult to transform indifference into political action.

In the context of 'atomic activism' in the US in the 1960s, unmasking anxieties in order to overcome indifference and create solidarity was a general way of describing what many activist movements did, including the Civil Rights Movement, the anti-war protests, and the women's movement. The Port Huron Statement was one of the clearest and most thorough articulations of this relationship between atomic anxiety, indifference, and activism. This document shows how the atomic situation was used rhetorically to highlight the urgency of all matters—from social justice, war, meaninglessness, and the structure of the economy. When one took nuclear annihilation seriously, the pathways for dissidence and activism capable of overcoming indifference opened up towards other terrains of possibility. Patočka's description of what the "shaking of accepted meaning" did historically is also an apt description of what the students were doing:

> In accepting responsibility for themselves and others[,] humans implicitly pose the question of meaning in a new and different way. They are no longer content with the bondage to life itself, with subsistence as life's content... thus the result of the primordial shaking of accepted meaning is not a fall into meaninglessness but, on the contrary, the discovery of the possibility of achieving a freer, more demanding meaningfulness.[63]

Whether or not the students found this "freer, more demanding meaningfulness" in their political endeavors cannot be answered definitively for every participant, but this kind of vision seems like it was a significant part of their stated goals in their manifesto, as they were clearly attempting to "accept responsibility for themselves and others" by confronting political meaninglessness. What we can learn from the statement of the SDS corroborates what we can learn from Patočka in conversation with Tillich, Savio, and Einstein's scientists: overcoming indifference requires historical awareness, a critical view of the social-political system, the ability to enter into critical dialogue with tradition, and a humble awareness of the imminence of death. Looking at several specific examples from the Port Huron Statement can demonstrate how these elements of pre-political awareness come together.

First, the students describe the apathy and indifference, giving it a name and specific characteristics:

> Our work is guided by the sense that we may be the last generation in the experiment with living. But we are a minority – the vast majority of our people regard the temporary equilibriums of our society and world as eternally-functional parts. In this is perhaps the outstanding paradox: we ourselves are imbued with urgency, yet the message of our society is that there is no viable alternative to the present... America rests in national stalemate, its goals ambiguous and tradition-bound instead of informed

---

63 Patočka, *Heretical Essays*, 63.

and clear, its democratic system apathetic and manipulated rather than 'of, by, and for the people.'[64]

Then, they identify those problems and the context whereby they began to see something wrong with the picture of the world given to them by adults and tradition:

> We are people of this generation, bred in at least modest comfort, housed now in universities, looking uncomfortably to the world we inherit... As we grew, however, our comfort was penetrated by events too troubling to dismiss. First, the permeating and victimizing fact of human degradation, symbolized by the Southern struggle against racial bigotry, compelled most of us from silence to activism. Second, the enclosing fact of the Cold War, symbolized by the presence of the Bomb, brought awareness that we ourselves, and our friends, and millions of abstract 'others' we knew more directly because of our common peril, might die at any time. We might deliberately ignore, or avoid, or fail to feel all other human problems, but not these two, for these were too immediate and crushing in their impact, too challenging in the demand that we as individuals take the responsibility for encounter and resolution.[65]

After diagnosing the core problems as bigotry and the bomb, they combine their observations about apathy with an analysis of the political landscape, arriving at a description of how their imaginations are 'blunted' by the acceptance of impenetrable institutions:

> The fact that each individual sees apathy in his fellows perpetuates the common reluctance to organize for change. The dominant institutions are complex enough to blunt the minds of their potential critics, and entrenched enough to swiftly dissipate or entirely repel the energies of protest and reform, thus limiting human expectancies. Then, too, we are a materially improved society, and by our own improvements we seem to have weakened the case for further change.[66]

Understanding that 'material improvement' does not represent an entirely fulfilled human life, they go on to describe how the Port Huron

---

64 PHS, 4.
65 PHS, 3.
66 PHS, 4.

Statement is meant to articulate an understanding of common challenges and problems, and is one part of the larger task of seeking human dignity through human autonomy:

> The search for truly democratic alternatives to the present, and a commitment to social experimentation with them, is a worthy and fulfilling human enterprise, one which moves us and, we hope, others today. On such a basis do we offer this document of our convictions and analysis: as an effort in understanding and changing the conditions of humanity in the late twentieth century, an effort rooted in the ancient, still unfulfilled conception of man attaining determining influence over his circumstances of life.[67]

With humility and a sense of a forever-retreating horizon of complexity, they then outline their method:

> We have no sure formulas, no closed theories... A first task of any social movement is to convince people that the search for orienting theories and the creation of human values is complex but worthwhile. We are aware that to avoid platitudes we must analyze the concrete conditions of social order. But to direct such an analysis we must use the guideposts of basic principles. Our own social values involve conceptions of human beings, human relationships, and social systems.[68]

They assert that the empirical and "concrete conditions of social order" are not the only necessary analysis, but an examination of "human beings, human relationships and social systems," must also be included. Subjective and intersubjective philosophical questions, therefore, are seen as equally necessary as empirical questions. Such an analysis calls for making a bridge between philosophical questions and practical questions, between abstract ideas and beings-in-the-world as they are. When they move in a philosophical direction to define and redefine "man" in this world, they challenge the techno-scientific world-view of humanity:

> We regard men as infinitely precious and possessed of unfulfilled capacities for reason, freedom, and love. In affirming these principles, we are

---

67   PHS, 5.
68   PHS, 6.

aware of countering perhaps the dominant conceptions of man in the twentieth century: that he is a thing to be manipulated, and that he is inherently incapable of directing his own affairs. We oppose the depersonalization that reduces human beings to the status of things—if anything, the brutalities of the twentieth century teach that means and ends are intimately related, that vague appeals to 'posterity' cannot justify the mutilations of the present.[69]

From this conception of human beings, they arrive at a number of assertions about what politics will look like at the end of this inquiry, and what sort of solidarity might arise out of a new understanding:

In a participatory democracy, the political life would be based in several root principles: that decision-making of basic social consequence be carried on by public groupings; that politics be seen positively, as the art of collectively creating an acceptable pattern of social relations; that politics has the function of bringing people out of isolation and into community, thus being a necessary, though not sufficient, means of finding meaning in personal life.[70]

If meaning in one's own life can be found through politics, this is what will eventually overcome 'ontological boredom,' and so the students have much in common with Patočka's conceptions and concerns.

The hope that politics might be a way to bring people out of isolation by helping them find shared meanings sounds like many things Patočka described within the idea of 'solidarity of the shaken,' including his diagnosis of the problem of indifference, his concern about techno-science, and his vision of politics and dissidence as valuable for their intrinsic ability to give meaning to life, over and above the instrumental gain from any particular policy change. "A person of spirit," Patočka writes, "always understands, and that understanding is no mere observation of facts, it is not 'objective knowledge,' even though a free person must also master objective knowledge and integrate it with what matters and what is subordinate."[71] The students were attempting, on Patočka's terms, to be persons of spirit, acting in amplitude and not balance. Even so, the Port Huron Statement presents many 'objective facts' about the economic,

69 PHS, 6.
70 PHS, 7–8.
71 Patočka, *Heretical Essays*, 134.

military, and political conditions of the 1960s, and the document goes on for fifty pages; these quotations are only from the first five pages. Rereading it in a different era, however, it comes across as an example of how a politics of meaning was partly constructed out of the atomic situation. Believing that one might be "the last generation" in any human experiment, by extrapolation, could become an equivalently compelling occasion for activism. Or, as Patočka would say, "the solidarity of the shaken is built up in persecution and uncertainty,"[72] and such solidarity emerges to address the anxieties and alienation of the time. In light of the interrelated dangers of nuclear annihilation and nihilism, the students' version of 'solidarity of the shaken' sought to overcome indifference through various modalities of political action, perhaps knowing what Patočka meant when he said that "humankind will not attain peace by devoting and surrendering itself to the criteria of everydayness and of its promises."[73] As the students asked themselves: "if these anxieties produce a developed indifference to human affairs, do they not as well produce a yearning to believe there is an alternative to the present, that something can be done to change circumstances in the school, the workplaces, the bureaucracies, the government?"[74]

As dissidents and activists go forward to address such tasks, Patočka would have them see the world as formed with the potentials of nihilism and annihilation, but also filled with possibilities for confrontation and action, where anyone can (and must) continue to ask questions about meaning: "Humans cannot live in the certitude of meaninglessness. But does that mean that they cannot live with a sought for and problematic meaning? That precisely this life in a problematic context is part of meaningfulness in an authentic sense, not in a privative or a dogmatic one? Perhaps Socrates knew this..."[75]

---

72 Patočka, *HE*, 135.
73 Patočka, *HE,* 135.
74 PHS, 4.
75 Patočka, *HE*, 75.

Chapter Five
Shipwrecked Existence: in Conversation with Environmental Activism

In 2014, journalist Joe Duggan asked climate scientists to write hand-written letters about their feelings. A website and blog called "Is This How You Feel?" then publicized the letters as a new way to discuss the dangers of climate change.[1] A survey had recently concluded that ninety-seven percent of climate scientists had come to agreement about the human origins of the atmospheric carbon dioxide that produces the greenhouse effect and global warming.[2] Yet after so much research and scientific agreement, and still so little political progress in addressing the problem, asking scientists about their feelings was meant to open a new dimension of the problem, something beyond charts, graphs, and numbers. Dozens of well-established scientists from around the world responded to the request, many confessing that they were not accustomed to the strange task of writing about their feelings. They used adjectives not usually found in scientific studies: discouraged, dismayed, cautiously hopeful, terrified, sad, optimistic, overwhelmed, and tired. There are descriptions of how frustrating it is that policy makers and the general public still doubt the validity of their research. There are expressions of hope and optimism that as human beings, we will become capable of fixing the problems we have created. Then there is this:

---

[1] "Is This How You Feel?" http://www.isthishowyoufeel.com/this-is-how-scientists-feel.html.

[2] John Cook, Dana Nuccitelli, Sarah A Green, Mark Richardson, Bärbel Winkler, Rob Painting, Robert Way, Peter Jacobs and Andrew Skuce, "Quantifying the consensus on anthropogenic global warming in the scientific literature," *Environmental Research Letters* 8, No. 2 (15 May 2013). Related website: http://theconsensusproject.com. A summary of the controversy it generated: Gayathri Vaidyanathan, "How to Determine the Scientific Consensus on Global Warming," *Scientific American* (July 24, 2014). https://www.scientificamerican.com/article/how-to-determine-the-scientific-consensus-on-global-warming/.

Sometimes I have this dream. I'm going for a hike and discover a remote farm house on fire. Children are calling for help from the upper windows. So I call the fire brigade. But they don't come, because some mad person keeps telling them that it is a false alarm. The situation is getting more and more desperate, but I can't convince the firemen to get going. I cannot wake up from this nightmare.[3]

Despite all of their knowledge and their feelings of panic, scientists do not know how to convince the firemen to get going; they cannot make those in charge of emergencies take action on the emergency that is climate change. The nightmare is perpetual because people are dying in real time from the effects of climate change, but the false alarm persists in the minds of too many, aided and abetted by powerful social, economic and political forces.

The authors of the Port Huron Statement (see previous chapter) thought it possible that nuclear weapons might make them the "last generation with the experiment of living."[4] While the threat of nuclear annihilation has not gone away, climate change has also shown itself to be another force capable of producing a shaken and disrupted 'last generation' in a slower-moving frame. The changes in the earth's atmosphere and the rising of the seas will one day make the present world unrecognizable, and each generation will become the 'last' to know some aspect of the natural world: today we might be the last to know coral reefs, children today might be the last to know polar bears in the wild, and in each geographical location, there will be a 'last generation' to know a particular crop yield, a particular sort of winter, or that particular sort of spring day. From now on, there will always be a last generation in the experiment of living *in this way*. Whether 'living in this way' is good or bad will depend entirely upon where a person happens to have been born, or where they have been thrown into the world in a random location by an accident unrelated to their own choices. For each community that climate change eventually transforms, however, there will nonetheless be some choice about how to respond responsibly, and how to become part of the fire brigade that finally "get[s] going."

There are resources to understand this type of political transformation in Patočka's categories. To follow the previous chapters, 'responding

---

3   Stefan Rahmstorf, "Is This How You Feel?"
4   See Chapter Four.

responsibility' is related to living in truth, caring for one's soul, confronting the political and economic establishment, and seeking solidarity with others whose lives have been shaken apart by irreversible ecological transformations. In other words, each of Patočka's main ideas can be used to examine the phenomenon of environmental activism. Inserting his categories into what has become a vast, diverse, and sometimes contradictory set of practices and discourses will not resolve all the paradoxes at stake, but perhaps more humbly, putting his ideas into conversation with a few selected environmental activists can offer additional examples of how Patočka's thinking can be relevant for finding new ways to think about the contemporary world of dissidence and activism. If Patočka stated in the *Plato and Europe* lectures that we are all on "a ship that necessarily will be shipwrecked,"[5] then his ideas also might be one way to ask important questions about both the nihilism created by the degradation of the planet and the frustration created by the incapacity of global political systems to respond to the emergency.[6]

Conversations about climate change (and all the attendant scientific, economic and political arguments) are deeply connected to philosophical problems regarding the human relationship to nature. Patočka's dissertation and first book was entitled *The Natural World as a Philosophical Problem*.[7] 'The natural world' in his philosophical gaze in 1936 referred to a specific problem in Husserl's philosophy, and did not correspond precisely to what we mean when we say 'the environment' today.[8] Yet when

---

5   Patočka, *Plato and Europe*, 2.
6   The production of books about the environmental crisis has rapidly increased in pace in the last several years, across many different academic disciplines, and the words of warning have been flowing much faster than any concrete policy change, so many authors want to represent their work as a way to raise awareness and get people to 'do something.' In this crowded field, I cannot pretend that putting one more set of concepts into the sphere of discussion will make any more political action happen, however unfortunate that is. As with the prior chapters, however, the more modest aim here is to show how some of Patočka's ideas might reveal forms of thinking about how to stay in motion in the difficult and frustrating circumstances currently facing environmentalists, or, in other words, how to sustain dissidence in unsustainable times.
7   Jan Patočka, *The Natural World as a Philosophical Problem*, trans. Erika Abrams, eds. Ivan Chvatík and L'ubica Ucník (Evanston: Northwestern University Press, 2016).
8   Patočka's original theorization of 'the natural world' in his 1936 text dealt with the categories of 'natural' life that were prior to history, as well as attendant problems about the concepts of 'world' and 'nature' in the work of Husserl and Heidegger as related to the original state of being human prior to historical consciousness. Within this technical debate, the divide between humanity and nature was at stake, where some of the questions revolved around the degree to which the 'natural world' existed prior to human categories, human words, and human concepts used to interpret and describe that world. In this frame of questioning, the human domination of nature was not material, but philosophical, and he describes

read in light of the categories and concepts already discussed about Patočka's work, especially techno-science and absolutism, the 'philosophical problem' of the 'natural world' in his early work seems to raise important questions he developed later about politics. For the purposes of this analysis, the title of his first book provides the occasion to ask what sort of philosophical problem the natural world is for activists and dissidents today, and how conceptions of the natural world necessarily underpin the political choice to become an environmentalist. Asking such questions can also lead towards a synthesis of Patočka's ideas about types of pre-political thinking that might continue to matter in the future of global activism more generally.

In the end, what environmental activists are trying to do requires a new form of solidarity that matches the scope and extent of the climate change problem; Patočka's solidarity of the shaken, as it is built upon the architecture of living in truth, caring for the soul, and confrontation, might be a form of solidarity capable of reaching more corners of the shrinking and warming earth. Together, these concepts reveal something about the dynamics of nihilism and alienation as well, where activist responses to impending doom might not save the entire planet, but nonetheless might be capable of saving the individual from total meaninglessness through providing a way to overcome alienation from nature. This chapter will therefore give a sketch of Patočka's philosophical ideas about some aspects of 'nature,' and then turn to contemporary cases of environmental activism, each chosen as an example of 'those who

---

philosophical conversations about the possibilities of an 'objective reality' outside of human thought, and the debate about the degree to which humans are capable of stepping outside of their own realities and situations to think about how they think and see what is "naturally" given (the question of Husserl's epoché). This was one of Husserl's questions later taken up by Heidegger, so as a dissertation, Patočka's work was largely concerned with interpreting the texts of these philosophers. When he later went back and revised and commented upon his own work and asked whether the question still mattered, he then ventured some abstract applications that led him to doubt parts of his initial thesis, but also came to see the wider applicability of the question about understanding the human relationship towards nature more generally. When seen in light of his comments about the exploitation of the earth by technoscience and forms of absolutism in politics and economics in other writings, it is not quite enough to say he was fully an environmentalist in our contemporary sense, but it is enough to say that he found the then-present general understanding of the human relationship to nature as problematic and potentially exploitative of the intrinsic value of the natural world. Some recent scholarship has also taken up these questions in his work: O. Stanciu, "Nature et monde naturel dans la pensée de Jan Patočka," *Alter. Revue de phénoménologie* 26 (2018): 47–64; K. Novotný, «Leben und Natur. Zur frühen Phänomenologie der natürlichen Welt bei Jan Patočka," *Acta Universitatis Carolinae Interpretationes* 7, no. 1 (2017): 11–29.

understand.'[9] These activists 'get it' in a way Patočka would appreciate, and they help illuminate what might be a stake in developing a political theory based on Patočka's ideas.

The Natural World as a Philosophical Problem

In 1970, Patočka revisited his 1936 argument in *The Natural World as a Philosophical Problem*, adding extensions and elaborations to his earliest philosophical work. While in 1936 he had set out to address how human beings are torn between the 'natural world' and the 'rational scientific and technological world,' in 1970 he noted that he had underestimated the degree to which this problem was connected to the problem of movement, living in truth, and the meaning of existence.[10] Like most of his writings during the last decade of his life, he expressed how he thought he had not gone far enough in his youth to realize the full implications of the crisis of meaning in modernity.[11] He also regretted that his initial approach to the problem was too 'other-worldly,' and he argued that he "had not [in 1936] yet understood that the method advocated there does not lead to concrete human life in the world, in society and in history."[12] After this self-critique, Patočka goes on to suggest that finding meaning in such a 'concrete life' should be one reason we examine 'nature.' This should be done, he argues, through understanding human life in terms of the three movements of existence (see Chapter Three).

Patočka goes on to relate the third movement of existence to the problem of the natural world by rehearsing much of what is already in the lectures of *Body, Community, Language, World*, but then he adds a series of assertions about the relationship between nature, movement, existence and the earth:

---

9   See prior chapter on the relationship between solidarity of the shaken and 'those who understand.'

10 Patočka, *The Natural World as a Philosophical Problem*, 160–165. Hereafter abbreviated "NWPP."

11 A good contextualization of Patočka's ideas about the natural world and its relationship to the problem of meaning and the structure of scientific rationalism can be found in Lubica Ucník, *The Crisis of Meaning and the Life-World: Husserl, Heidegger, Arendt, Patočka* (Athens: Ohio University Press, 2016). Ucník's other essays on the problem of rationalism and mathematization in Patočka's work have informed the range of questions raised in this chapter. See bibliography for a complete list.

12 Patočka, *NWPP*, 160.

Existence as movement is related to the great powers which shape the nat-ur-al-ity of nature prior to all singular objects, first and foremost the earth as the first immobile referent of all movement and as the power holding sway over all things bodily… the corporeality of all motion keeps before our eyes the fact that, insofar as we move, take action, and in so acting understand at once ourselves and things, we are part of nature, *phusis*, the all-embracing world.[13] When interested and occupied above all with human relations and social functions, living in and for work, organization, struggle and competition, we tend to forget this natural aspect and, at the same time, our relationship to the all-embracing *phusis*.[14]

It can be seen here that for Patočka in 1970, work, organization, struggle, and competition are part of the second movement, an inauthentic and not-fully-realized movement of existence. To overcome the second movement, he advocates a return to the first movement in order to reach the third, a return that necessary involves a return to nature *and the earth*:

The movement of anchoring or sinking roots, which grounds the other two [movements], is, however, most suitable to remind us of this suprem-acy of *phusis* [nature] in the whole of life. In fact, all of our actions, in-cluding precisely work and struggle, take place solely on the basis of this instinctive-affective prime motion, which constitutes so to say the ostinato of life's polyphony.[15]

If the earth is the ostinato of life's polyphony, where the ostinato is the stubborn rhythm in a piece of music that constantly repeats itself,[16] (a favorite of composer Phillip Glass, see Chapter Three), and polyphony is the vast variation within the history of individual lives, then for Patoč-ka, the earth and nature are not just the beginning of existence-as-move-ment, but they are the constant rhythm that holds together the disparate variations of human movement. Connected back to the first motion of the earth, all of the human movements emanating from the earth share

---

13 *Phusis* is the ancient Greek word for "nature." It is a cognate with the verb "to grow." For more on Heidegger's evolving use of the word, from which Patočka is drawing upon, see: "Nature and *phusis*," *A Heidegger Dictionary*, ed. Michael Inwood (Oxford: Blackwell Publishing, 1999).
14 Patočka, *NWPP*, 163, 165.
15 Patočka, *NWPP*, 165.
16 "A continuously repeated melodic or rhythmical figure or phrase," in "ostinato, adj. and n.," Oxford English Dictionary Online, accessed February 25, 2017, http://www.oed.com/view /Entry/133156.

this common rhythm, suggesting a radical equality between all those on the earth that exist in polyphonic movements, but together face finitude and death, another ostinato integrated with earthliness:

> In the last movement, the true movement of existence, the point is to see myself in my ownmost human essence and possibility—in my "earthliness" which is, at the same time, a relationship to being and to the universe... And this presence of the world is what makes it possible too for us to see ourselves in the world, to see our connection and our dependence, the "part" we play in the world. Human life thus experienced in festive rapture retains a glint of the suprahuman, the divine. In this light, it is then easier to take up our lot, which is an indispensable part of the world, though the most arduous and most finite of all—the lot of a mortal being.[17]

Here is another integration of the horizontal and the vertical modalities of thinking (see Chapter Two): the glint of the superhuman, the upward glance, integrates the banalities of horizontal worldly existence into a festive rapture that makes mortality on earth easier to endure.

These 1970 additions to *The Natural World as a Philosophical Problem* were written, by Patočka's own account, in a hurry and under the duress of the post-1968 political climate in Czechoslovakia. As he explained in an afterward to the first French translation in 1976, it was for this reason that the 1970 text had not been included with the French translation.[18] The newest English translation, however, includes the 1970 text. These passages, therefore, by Patočka's own account, do not contain a systematic and fully coherent description of how his ideas about the relationship between scientific rationality, humans, the natural world, and the earth had evolved since 1936. These are evocations and suggestions of larger ideas, and not fully elaborated; there are no examples given. What can be taken away, however, and what is relevant for thinking through the problem of environmental activists and their relationship to the natural world, is that Patočka suggests a connection between the earth, earthliness, sinking roots, and grounding (first-movement categories) and the possibilities for realizing the third movement of ultimate possibility; he makes circular what appeared in *Body, Community, Language, World* as more linear. By his 1970 account, we do not just move away from the

---

17 Patočka, *NWPP*, 175–176.
18 Patočka *NWPP*, 182.

earth and away from the first movement, but the earth and the human being's place within nature is circularly integrated into the third movement. The three movements of existence, with this added analysis of the earth, almost 'come full circle' in a literal sense. This integration is therefore related to the full realization of existence:

> The third movement of existence... discovers here a fundamental dimension of the natural world, a dimension which is not given, which escapes both perception and recollection, eludes objective identification, and yet essentially determines this world.[19]

This is a challenging idea (and a challenging sentence), because Patočka seems to be asserting that there is a dimension of the natural world that is not immediately given to us, that escapes both perception and recollection, eludes objective identification, but *determines* the world.

While this "dimension" seems therefore to sit in a hard-to-reach vacuum, it is, among many things Patočka did not fully elaborate, nonetheless a philosophical problem that can give some hint at the problem of meaning within a nihilistic world, as arriving at the third movement implies at least a partial overcoming of nihilism. (To follow the architectural metaphor used in earlier chapters, this might be the secret room in the Patočka house, the one without a door.) Even if it is merely an empty space, even if it might take "a festive rapture [that] retains a glint of the suprahuman" to figure out what exactly this dimension of meaning might be, the wager here is that like Gandhi and Bonhoeffer, who might have reached what Patočka would call a 'third-movement' of existence through their political action and historical self-awareness, so too do environmental activists represent a way of reaching the third movement through their understanding of the natural world, especially through their movement within that world towards the preservation of our "earthliness" (if quite literally).

The textual ground here is too uncertain to make any rigid claims of absolute equivalence between Patočka's fragmented thoughts and the structure of human action within any particular environmental movement, but if framed in light of Patočka's three movements of existence,

---

19 Patočka, *NWPP*, 180. This is at the very end of the 1970 addendum, and he does seem to suggest that this 'sphere' is what he has been trying to clarify in the preceding pages, that is, the sphere where the third movement and the natural world come together, but the language is a sketch and only abstractly evocative.

then environmental activists return to the earth and the first movement in order to attain the third movement, and in so doing, they seek to dwell within the contradiction posed by Patočka's original question about the natural world in 1936: what is to be done about the gap between the natural world as it appears to human experience and the natural world as it is rationalized by scientific categories? In this question, then, it is possible to reflect upon the nihilism implied by the earth's pending destruction, because to defend the earth, to defend the natural world against the ravages of technology and absolutist rationality, is to find the third movement, the culmination of human existence, in the political action of being an environmentalist.[20] So Patočka's claims are evocative and suggestive, providing an occasion for asking questions about the implications of his other ideas for this particular form of activism.

Like the other forms of political action discussed in prior chapters, this too requires a certain mode of living in a truth, the care of the soul, the confrontation of given realities, and the solidarity of the shaken. In this case, the activist might also confront a moment of 'existential recognition,' where the radical equality of the human relation to the earth (as the origin of the first movement) renders one aware of our common emplacement, with everyone else on earth, on a "ship that must necessarily be shipwrecked," where *together* we paddle on rising seas to the ostinato of a common original rhythm. But like Camus's Sisyphus, we might imagine ourselves nonetheless 'happy' in this realization that we must paddle into eternity, as we find the "solidarity of those who understand,"[21] and our sense of place is radically extended and enlarged, the entire earth becoming our home.[22] This might be something like what Patočka means by the "movement... that determines the world."[23] Or it might not be. But perhaps the only way to explore the secret room of

---

20 "In the third movement, it becomes apparent that I can open myself for being in yet another way, that I can modify this bondage to the particular and transform my own relationship to the universe." *NWPP*, 175.

21 See *NWPP*, 187: "Without acceptance, there is no human existence; man is not only thrown into reality, he is also accepted, he is thrown as accepted; acceptance is part of thrownness. This is why the bliss of being accepted, though it is not a simple veil, a screen marring the true perspective of the origin, is what it is only on the basis of anxiety; it is an anxious and ambivalent bliss." The environmental activist is 'happy' (by Camus's sense) because the divide between the natural world as given naively and the natural world as scientifically rationalized is overcome within a community of people who understand likewise and accept (if anxiously) their common shipwrecked existence.

22 Albert Camus, *The Myth of Sisyphus and Other Essays*, trans. J. O'Brien (New York: Vintage Books, 1955).

23 Patočka, *NWPP*, 180. As quoted above.

solidarity-in-understanding is to re-describe the rooms that border it in light of the relationship between human movements and nature.[24] A discussion of Patočka's concepts will therefore be interwoven below with an exploration of the types of environmental activism that Patočka might find revealing of certain deeper truths about human existence and our relationship to nature.

Living in the Truth of Myth

If Patočka were to gaze upon the world of environmental activism today, he would likely be most drawn to those approaches that focus on the human dimension of the crisis, where the path of movement toward the future requires acknowledging new truths about the human relationship to nature and human beings' relationships to one another. Among the many truths it is necessary to confront in order to move forward in the context of the environmental crisis today, Patočka would be interested in at least these three: firstly, the problem of embodiment, where the movement of the human body through the world now requires confronting the truth that the environment is polluted, carcinogenic, and down to the level of micro-plastics in the rain, infused with the detritus of human production that endangers the health and movement of our bodies; secondly, the problem requires confronting an economics of supposedly unending capitalist growth, where humans have become mere components of a vast machine they have little control over; and thirdly, he would likely argue that there is a problem concerning the relationship between truth and myth, where writing new narratives about the human relationship to nature is necessary, but where old, shadowy ideas stubbornly do not give way. While there are inevitably more applications of his ideas to the question of how to 'live in truth' as an environmentalist, these three set the stage for discussing the wider implications and applications of his approach.

The embodied truth of the environmentalist's perspective in light of Patočka's world-view would have to take into account that "existence as movement... is essentially bodily. The corporeality of existence is not

---

24 Derrida, in *The Gift of Death*, discusses some of Patočka's ideas about death as surrounding a different kind of secret; I agree with him that the structure of the un-articulated should be sought, though the contents of the political 'secret' of Patočka's work as interpreted here is quite different than Derrida's.

only part of its situatedness, part and parcel of the situation in which we always find ourselves; all our activity and creativity as well, our affectivity and our comportment are bodily."[25] (See Chapter Three for prior discussion.) If Patočka is right about the bodily origins of all creativity, to defend our creativity we have to defend our bodies, and here he seems to mean creativity in a wider sense than just artistic creativity, but rather the larger ability of humans to "create" things in the world, including material things through physical labor, the reproduction of the species, and art as well. Given such a view of human movement and existence, the protection of the body is paramount, and so living in truth as an environmentalist would require seeing all the ways our bodies are harmed through the human destruction of the natural world. The truth at stake now seems relatively straightforward, but it has taken many decades to gain acceptance that human-induced changes to the earth will have a radical impact on the human body, coming as pollution, poisonous chemicals, radioactivity, the extinction of animals related to our food supply (pollinating bees most especially), and dangerous weather that will change our body's likelihood of survival.[26] One of the earliest works of environmentalism, Rachel Carson's *Silent Spring*, pointed out how the use of chemicals and pesticides harmed various species and ecosystems and also endangered human health.[27] Many of the chemicals she wrote about have since been banned, but not all of them, and this remains a campaign platform for many environmental organizations.[28] There is a growing amount of data about how cancer rates are much higher in polluted areas, as well respiratory diseases that also lead to early death.[29] The activist's defensive war against these forms of pollution of the

---

25 Patočka, *NWPP*, 163.
26 See McKibbon, *Oil and Honey*, discussed below. This is also to say that by looking at it in this way, environmental politics are no longer an example of a 'post-material' value in the sense Ronald Inglehart described them in his early work; the destruction of the earth is rather 'material' at this point, impacting the ability of people to survive in a basic way and garner 'materials' to do that. The connection between environmental change, the food shortages in the Middle East, and the Arab Spring makes this case. See: Caitlin E. Werrell, Francesco Femia, and Anne-Marie Slaughter, "The Arab Spring and Climate Change" (Center for American Progress, 2013).
27 Rachel Carson, *Silent Spring* (Houghton Mifflin Harcourt, 2002).
28 See for example the Environmental Working Group, www.ewg.org.
29 World Health Organization International Agency for Research on Cancer, https://www.iarc.fr/cards_page/iarc-research/. Over one hundred research papers produced by this UN agency are concerned with the link between cancer and environmental contaminants world-wide. Many cancer research centers in many countries have similar programs.

atmosphere by carbon and chemical emissions is therefore also a war against the poisoning of the human body.

The violence done against the body as a result of environmental degradation makes physical what the transcendentalists argued was spiritual; to someone like Thoreau, without enough fresh air, the care of the soul was not possible, but modern science has now demonstrated that without enough fresh air, the care of the body is no longer possible either.[30] At a certain point death becomes inevitable in the short term for those who cannot escape the contaminants, and these are also frequently the poor and marginalized populations who are forced to live near the worst waste sites.[31] So for activists, defending the universality of bodily health becomes important, especially in socially unequal circumstances. This requires, as Gandhi knew quite well, a necessary politicization of the body. Gandhi published newspaper articles about the state of his body during his efforts at fasting and celibacy; the border between public and private was broken down, and people could understand that politics had a direct impact on his body, on their own bodies, and that there was physical discomfort, illness, and pain as a result of a political situation (see Chapter Three).

Today, the unwillingness of politicians to regulate certain atmospheric emissions has a direct impact on millions, if not billions, of human bodies. Thanks to Einstein and other nuclear scientists (see Chapter Four), this sort of understanding was reached about the bodily harm done by the radiation released from nuclear testing, and after strange cancers began appearing in populations close to the tests sites, and the scientific understandings of radiation advanced, this resulted in changes in global policy about nuclear testing.[32] While it did not decrease stockpiles of nuclear weapons, it did help to diminish the repeated explosions

---

30 Henry David Thoreau, *Walden* (Yale University Press, 2006 [1854]).
31 The subfield of 'environmental justice' addresses these types of situations. In the United States, the environmental justice movement first gained recognition for highlighting the placement of toxic waste sites and garbage dumps in poor minority communities. The Bhopal disaster in India, where thousands died as a result of a leak at a pesticide plant in 1984, galvanized another well-known early environmental justice movement, and now the concept is widespread and used throughout the world. The research and literature are growing rapidly, but two limited examples: David Schlosberg, *Defining Environmental Justice: Theories, Movements, and Nature* (Oxford University Press, 2009) and Gordon Walker, *Environmental Justice: Concepts, Evidence and Politics* (London: Routledge, 2012).
32 International Nuclear Test Ban Treaties were negotiated in 1963 (limited) and 1996 (complete). For the current issues surrounding these treaties, including debates about their relative effectiveness, see: Sverre Lodgaard and Bremer Maerli, eds., *Nuclear Proliferation and International Security*, (London: Routledge, 2007).

that polluted the atmosphere and led to the deaths of radiation victims.[33] For each type of chemical that may cause cancer or another disease, environmentalists hope the successful aspects of this story might be repeated, and there have been certain successes, though many of the pollutants that cause major health problems have not yet been regulated globally in the same way as nuclear testing. Environmental activists have taken from Gandhi already his principles of asceticism and the idea that we must make do with less consumption and less waste;[34] they also might take from Patočka the notion that both the body and the earth are our home in equal measure, and defending the body usually always seems more urgent. Whether this is survival, narcissism, or both, does not really matter: if it makes us sick, we have a stake in stopping it. The problem for environmental activism is telling the story that connects the specific illness to the specific body, and establishing causation between the chemical and the cancer. The truth of causation can be easily contested, and demands for proof and facts can thwart many campaigns. Large companies that sell pollutants often have financial resources that vastly exceed those of activist organizations, and when contesting truths turns into an expensive legal battle to get substances banned, it is often the companies that win.

That is why, to evoke the second aspect of 'living in truth' that environmentalists engage, Patočka's early thoughts on the dangers of the economic machine propelled by war and technology are still painfully relevant today. Even though they would use different words to describe the problem, most environmental activists today see human alienation from the natural world as caused by the rationalistic forces of economic production. The global economy has changed the way humans live, work, and breathe; the chemical makeup of the earth's atmosphere has changed as a result of the 'rational' processes of such economic production, where 'economic growth' is treated as an unquestioned 'good,' and pollution and environmental destruction have long been thought of as only 'externalities,' or mildly unfortunate side-effects of 'good and necessary growth.' 'Economic sciences' are still based on a type of 'rationality,'

---

33 One of the most well-known campaigners who helped bring about this awareness was Albert Schweitzer. See: "A Declaration of Conscience," *Saturday Review* XL (May 18, 1957): 17–20. Also see: David K. Goodin, "Schweitzer Reconsidered: The Applicability of Reverence for Life as Environmental Philosophy," *Environmental Ethics* 29, no. 4 (2007): 403–421.

34 Farah Godrej, "Ascetics, Warriors, and a Gandhian Ecological Citizenship," *Political Theory* 40, No. 4 (August 2012): 437–465.

however, and are still driving the actions of individuals, firms, and nation-states towards many perceived 'goods' few want to abandon: development, prosperity, status, and comfort. Even if 'rational' climate scientists push back against the 'rationality' of the economic logic, the failures to convince certain audiences of the dangers of climate change points to a problem somewhere beyond facts and beyond rationality, towards a terrain where competing rationalities and attachments to myths need to be further investigated. A 'fact' is a phenomenon just as much as a 'myth' is a phenomenon, so phenomenology has a way of revealing and uncovering why supposedly 'rational' humans become attached to, and enamored with, both myths and facts, sometimes losing the ability to tell them apart. Unmasking and revealing why and how 'science' is not taken very seriously in certain economic, political, ideological, and cultural spaces, therefore, is something a critical phenomenological gaze like Patočka's can begin to uncover.

In many political and cultural spaces today, one sort of science (climate science) has seemingly lost (or never fully gained) an authoritative voice, whereas another sort of science (economic science) carries on authoritatively as *the* path towards 'the good.' The activists and dissidents that seek to slow the production of the sources of climate change (fossil fuels and greenhouse gasses) face this cultural challenge of 'competing sciences' every day in their work. Climate activists often try to use 'scientific rationality' to compete against stronger forms of attachment to 'economic rationality.' This approach only sometimes works. While politicians in some countries are willing to listen to scientific data of certain kinds and at certain moments, both 'sciences' are still in tension, and the case of climate change has shown that there is a limit to the acceptance of 'facts' and 'data' when the resulting conclusions are in tension with other more deeply held beliefs and world views (perhaps based on 'myths') about the meaning of prosperity, comfort, status, power, and economic success.

Explaining attachments to myths and the sources of world-views about nature has become a central part of what environmental activism has had to do to counter economic rationality. While a full examination of the public debates about the myths and facts of climate science is beyond the scope of this account, if it can be said that 'climate science' has been turned into a type of 'myth' in the arena where climate-change denial has power, and thus this 'science' does not have social acceptance and political authority in this particular realm, a world-view like Patočka's that is suspicious of absolute rationality (and at times science itself...) can illuminate these paradoxes of belief and disbelief in a way that rationalized cost-benefit analysis cannot.[35] Patočka takes myths seriously, and absorption in myth is a common human phenomenon for him, one that we cycle in and out of as we do philosophy and pursue truth. As previously quoted, he believes that "philosophy is reflection. At the moment when reflection breaks through, when people awaken, this does not mean they stop falling back into slumber. They will live in myth again."[36] Pursuing the 'scientific truth' of climate change and its interaction with economic rationality has necessarily involved this cycle of myths and truths being not just intertwined, but in constant dialectical motion vis-à-vis one another, where the 'truth' will continually have to confront the 'myth,' over and over again in a frame of Socratic questioning. And so, on a similar course, environmental activists and climate scientists will necessarily also have to proceed.

'Rationalistic' and 'scientific' views of politics have tried to explain the denial of climate change rationally, in the terms of a collective action problem, where it is 'irrational' to give up personal advantages for the sake of 'the common,' and so the 'tragedy of the commons' ensues.[37] In certain legal spaces, part of the tragedy is averted by legislation and making harmful practices illegal or 'more rational,' as well as giving subsidies for environmentally-friendly behavior to make some environmentally-friendly actions more 'rational,' or offering 'carbon offsets' as a kind of 'rational' payment scheme.[38] This 'rational' approach has not, however, solved the larger global existential problem of averting the emergency: beliefs and commitments that are deeper than science have prevailed in enough political communities that large-scale international cooperation has been ineffective.[39] This has shown that we might live in the same

---

35 There is a body of social psychology research about "beliefs in climate change" that is largely based on positivist and rationalistic assumptions. For one example, a meta-analysis that examines over a hundred separate studies, see: Matthew Hornsey, J., Emily A. Harris, Paul G. Bain, and Kelly S. Fielding, "Meta-analyses of the Determinants and Outcomes of Belief in Climate Change," *Nature climate change* 6, no. 6 (2016): 622–626. Many of these studies conclude that political ideology has a more important role in "determining beliefs" than knowledge of scientific facts.

36 Patočka, *Plato and Europe*, 88.

37 Garrett Hardin, "Tragedy of the Commons," *Science* 162, Issue 3859 (Dec. 13 1968): 1243–1248, DOI: 10.1126/science.162.3859.1243. This original article was followed by the creation of a subfield of study in political science and sociology. See: "The Garrett Hardin Society," http://www.garretthardinsociety.org.

38 For one example, see Kate Ervine, "The Politics and Practice of Carbon Offsetting: Silencing Dissent," *New Political Science* 34, no. 1 (2012): 1–20.

39 Debates about the recent Paris Climate Agreement highlight this dynamic. For one example, see: Robert Falkner, "The Paris Agreement and the new logic of international climate politics," *International Affairs* 92, no. 5 (2016): 1107–1125.

territorial world with others—the earth—but we also live in entirely different worlds of belief from each other. In such a context, whether or not minds can be changed by living in truth and caring for the soul, or by questioning and shaking apart given meanings through 'solidarity of the shaken,' might be related to how the human community survives the impacts of climate change.

To 'live in truth' in the midst of climate change's contradictory realities, therefore, requires recognizing the 'truth of myth,' to evoke a contradiction, and the degree to which myth holds meaning for human life in a way scientific rationality might not hold meaning. As Patočka observes:

> Myth penetrates the secrets of human life with admirably deep clairvoyance. So sharp is its sight that it calls for assuagement, and it is assuaged by the narrative form, the mock history transposing it into the past... Once we understand the intention of myth, we realize that it does not only see clear in man's present reality, but also contains a standpoint, an attitude, an openness for the future in which we disclose our own-most possibility.[40]

In understanding a similar conundrum, some environmental activists have been trying to rewrite the founding myths of civilization, in particular Western civilization's attachment to rationality and progress through economic production and 'growth' paradigms. This is what is at stake in reinterpreting *Genesis* as a call to stewardship, rather than dominion (see below.) The task of rewriting myths, however, is perhaps more difficult than scientific research, as myths are diffused through the long and complicated sinews of culture and history. 'The truth of myth,' however absurd that phrase sounds from a scientific and rational viewpoint, has to be acknowledged, and to use Patočka's word, assuaged, because myth can be a connection between "mock history" and the possibilities of "openness for the future." Certain myths are open to the future, and others are not, and openness to the future, in Patočka's vision, means uncovering the "intention of myth" in order to disclose reality to ourselves. Most cultures have original founding myths that define the human relationship to the earth and in turn define a human relationship to a territorial home and a place on earth. How environmental activists

---

40 Patočka, *NWPP*, 176.

choose to "assuage" such myths, therefore, has much to do with their successes and failures to 'live in truth.'

The Earth as Our Common Home

Patočka argues in *Heretical Essays* that "for all the vast production of the wherewithal of living, human life remains homeless... The greatest homelessness, however, is in our relation to nature and to ourselves," where humans have "lost contact with that ground beneath their feet... thereby... they also gave up their own selves, their distinctive place among all that is."[41] His idea of homelessness in relation to nature arises within his discussion of the problems of techno-science, where he also critiques the "orgiastic brutality" of modern war, and evokes his concern with "all that vanishes in the face of modern voluntary and enforced mobility, the gigantic migrations which by now affect nearly all the continents."[42] His conclusion to this discussion is not optimistic, and he describes how "humans are thus destroyed externally and impoverished internally, deprived of their 'ownness,' of that irreplaceable I."[43] Finding a home and a sense of home in nature thus becomes part of how Patočka sought to address the existential nihilism of modern homelessness, where the problem of 'home' becomes the ground to finding grounding, so-to-speak, in the common ground one finds with others on earth.[44]

Within the environmental movement today, it is something of a truism to argue that the first "environmentalists" who were most "at home on earth" were indigenous peoples living outside of Europe prior to colonization. This argument refers to both nomadic and settled groups in Africa, Asia, and the Americas, and focuses on the ways such cultures

---

41   Patočka, *Heretical Essays*, 113. He states that he is drawing from Hannah Arendt in this passage. Arendt discusses cosmic homelessness in both *Origins of Totalitarianism* and *The Human Condition*.

42   Patočka, *HE*, 115–116.

43   Patočka, *HE*, 117.

44   Patočka articulates a social and intersubjective conception of 'home' in *Natural World as a Philosophical Problem,* 81: "The concrete home, this place of common will and safety where my own will plays an important but only partial role, arises first in mutual help; home is not, as it may perhaps appear on the ground of purely individual constitution, a simple hub of personal satisfaction and security but rather a shared center of safety... So it is in this modality of cooperation that actual homeliness, actual closeness with something real, true certainty within what-is—the certainty that we understand and are understood (or that we can understand and be understood)—comes to be."

cultivated the natural world and saw the earth as the common home of all peoples, including ancestors and progeny alike.[45] While it is an over-generalization to label all indigenous groups in this way, as some were (and are) better stewards of the earth than others, there are many good examples of contemporary indigenous cultures where the descendants of early indigenous societies have engaged in many environmentally-friendly practices for many generations, and continue to do so in the name of cultural norms that see it as necessary to cultivate the earth as a common home for all peoples. Many of these societies also see it as a spiritual obligation to their gods and ancestors to actively engage in tending to this larger 'home.'[46] Archeological evidence, historical evidence, and ethnographic research within existing indigenous communities has shown that the truism has much truth within it, and environmentalists believe, therefore, that the contemporary industrialized world has much to learn from indigenous practices. In recognition of this link, even the United Nations has developed bridges between its programs to support indigenous communities (which are some of the poorest and most marginalized on earth today) and its world-wide environmental program, recognizing how indigenous knowledge and concepts might inform enlightened environmental policy at the global level.[47]

There is an aspect of this discussion that does more than just praise indigenous world-views, but also critiques and blames Christian religions for environmental destruction. Such arguments point to the original sources of disrespect for the earth in European colonization, the development of capitalism through colonization, and the propagation of Christian ideas through missionary practices alongside colonization

---

45 This linkage emerges in both policy studies and cultural studies more generally. A few representative examples: George J. Dei, Budd L. Hall, and Dorothy Goldin Rosenberg, *Indigenous Knowledges in Global Contexts: Multiple Readings of Our World* (Toronto: University of Toronto Press, 2000); D. Michael Warren and Kristin Cashman, *Indigenous Knowledge for Sustainable Agriculture and Rural Development* (International Institute for Environment and Development, Sustainable Agriculture Programme, 1988); Anne Ross, Kathleen Pickering Sherman, Jeffrey G. Snodgrass, Henry D. Delcore, and Richard Sherman, *Indigenous Peoples and the Collaborative Stewardship of Nature: Knowledge Binds and Institutional Conflicts*, (New York: Routledge, 2016); Julian Kunnie and Nomalungelo Ivy Goduka, eds. *Indigenous Peoples' Wisdom and Power: Affirming our Knowledge through Narratives*, (Burlington: Ashgate Publishing, Ltd., 2006); Alan Bicker, Roy Ellen, and Peter Parkes, *Indigenous Environmental Knowledge and Its Transformations: Critical Anthropological Perspectives*, (London: Routledge, 2003).

46 See for example: Roger S. Gottlieb, *This Sacred Earth: Religion, Nature, Environment*, (London: Routledge, 2004).

47 The United Nations Environment Program explicitly addresses indigenous issues, see: "Indigenous Peoples and their Communities," https://www.unenvironment.org/civil-society-engagement/major-groups-facilitating-committee-and-regional-facilitators/indigenous.

(many which sought to convert indigenous peoples to various forms of Christianity).[48] The doctrinal focus of these arguments is often the passages in the book of *Genesis*, where God tells man "be fruitful and multiply, and fill the earth and subdue it, and have dominion over the fish of the sea, over the birds of the air, and over every living thing that moves on the earth."[49] Those Christians who read this in a certain way, where human "dominion" over the earth was seen as a human right and a Christian right, are blamed for setting in motion the exploitation of the earth for human development that eventually created climate change, because within this argument, if such 'dominion' was a God-given right of believers, then the entirety of the earth (plants, animals, oceans, rivers, and forests) was seen to be there *for* humans, not for itself. When nature only has instrumental value and not intrinsic value, it is exploited. Furthermore, if in the processes of economic and cultural colonization, there was any indigenous population that pushed back against that Christian understanding of 'dominion,' they were subjected to forced conversion to the 'proper' belief system, or in many cases, extermination and genocide.[50] Again, ample evidence provides many examples of this having occurred, and so also through this more tragic and destructive reality, indigenous peoples and the environment remain connected; they were simultaneously and duly exploited, and thus today, the need arises to simultaneously and duly protect them through the attempt to rectify past wrongs and clean up the harms done to both human communities and their natural environments.[51] A 'common home,' in this light, there-

---

48 For a description of both the guilt of Christianity and the potential to reform the Christian vision in an earth-friendly way, see: E.M. Conradie. *Christianity and Earthkeeping: In Search of an Inspiring Vision* (Vol. 16. African Sun MeDIA, 2011).

49 Bible, King James Version, *Genesis* 1:28. In some of the King James Versions, the word "fill" is translated with the slightly more eco-friendly "replenish." See: Peter Harrison, "Subduing the Earth: Genesis 1, Early Modern Science, and the Exploitation of Nature," *Journal of Religion* 79, No. 1 (Jan. 1999) 86–109.

50 Jens Meierhenrich, *Genocide: A Reader* (New York: Oxford University Press, 2014). (This includes chapters on indigenous peoples); Jennifer Huseman and Damien Short, "'A Slow Industrial Genocide': Tar Sands and the Indigenous Peoples of Northern Alberta," *The International Journal of Human Rights* 16, no. 1 (2012): 216–237; Laura Westra, *Environmental Justice and the Rights of Indigenous Peoples: International and Domestic Legal Perspectives*, (New York: Routledge, 2012); Daniel Brook, "Environmental Genocide: Native Americans and Toxic Waste," *American Journal of Economics and Sociology* 57, no. 1 (1998): 105–113.

51 The UN's "2030 Agenda for Sustainable Development" has a subsection on "Indigenous Peoples and the 2030 Agenda," https://www.un.org/development/desa/indigenouspeoples /focus-areas/post-2015-agenda/the-sustainable-development-goals-sdgs-and-indigenous. html and UN General Assembly Document (A/RES/70/1). For a history of the campaigning that led to this inclusion, see Matthew Rimmer, "The World Indigenous Network: Rio+ 20,

fore means the protection of both humans and the natural world, where to care for one is to care for the other, much like in some indigenous cosmologies, where the earth and nature are seen as animate aspects of the community enabling the flourishing of all species.[52]

The UN programs on environmental sustainability that draw from indigenous experience are one place where this linkage between human rights and the protection of the natural world is turned into policy practice, but one of the most ironic rehearsals of the environmentalist argument about finding a 'common home' in recent times came from the head of the Catholic Church, Pope Francis. In his encyclical *Laudato Si,* "On Care for Our Common Home," he asked his followers to treat the earth as a "common home" for all peoples, while simultaneously pointing out how the Christian account of creation in *Genesis* had been misread for a *very long* time.[53] Pope Francis has been trying to convince Catholics that they have a spiritual obligation to see the earth as a locus of stewardship, not dominion, as "an inadequate presentation of Christian anthropology gave rise to a wrong understanding of the relationship between human beings and the world."[54] He not only implies that the founding myth of the Christian faith community has been misinterpreted, but also argues that since the industrial revolution and the full development of Western civilization's obsession with progress, material goods, and the exploitation of the earth, the wrong vision of nature has been at work:

> Often, what was handed on was a Promethean vision of mastery over the world, which gave the impression that the protection of nature was something that only the faint-hearted cared about. Instead, our "dominion" over the universe should be understood more properly in the sense of responsible stewardship.[55]

In what Patočka might call a 'metanoia of historical proportion,' Pope Francis made this argument while coming to echo what indigenous peoples had been saying for many generations about how to treat the

Intellectual Property, Indigenous Knowledge and Sustainable Development," in *Indigenous Intellectual Property*, ed. M. Rimmer (Edward Elgar Publishing, 2015).

52 John A Grim, ed. *Indigenous Traditions and Ecology* (Cambridge: Harvard University Press, 2001).

53 Papa Franceso, *Enciclica Laudato Si*. "On Care for Our Common Home." Vatican Press, 2015. (Abbreviated hereafter *"Laudato Si."*)

54 *Laudato Si* §116.

55 *Laudato Si* §116.

earth as a common home. He not only rejected the 'dominion' justification for the earth's exploitation, but also called for the development of a philosophy of "integral ecology," recognizing that the confrontation of techno-science and its attendant capitalist-industrialist practice would require an adjustment in the church's philosophical understanding of the natural world.[56] He seemed to see, as Patočka had in *Heretical Essays*, that environmental problems were, among other things, problems of cosmic homelessness and human alienation from nature.[57]

He includes in his descriptions much that Patočka would agree with: a critique of human hubris and techno-science,[58] a critique of the propensity of scientific rationalism to absolutize the world, and a critique of all types of economic practices that objectify and exploit human beings.[59] He comes in the end to advocate a new kind of politics combined with a recognition of human conscience in order to address the intertwined problems of our alienation from the natural world,[60] the earth's destruction by economic systems and the growth of poverty and inequality,[61]

---

56 Frances's idea of 'integral ecology' combines his religious understanding with the research field of political ecology, which began in the 1970s and 1980s as a subfield dedicated to examining how politics and environmental issues interact with ideas about nature. This is now a growing field of study with its own identity and broad scope. For one guide to a now vast literature, see: Thomas Perreault, Gavin Bridge and James McCarthy, eds. *Routledge Handbook of Political Ecology* (New York: Routledge, 2015).

57 Patočka, *HE*, 113.

58 *Laudato Si* §104: "nuclear energy, biotechnology, information technology, knowledge of our DNA... have given those with the knowledge, and especially the economic resources to use them, an impressive dominance over the whole of humanity and the entire world. Never has humanity had such power over itself, yet nothing ensures that it will be used wisely, particularly when we consider how it is currently being used." §105: "we stand naked and exposed in the face of our ever-increasing power, lacking the wherewithal to control it. We have certain superficial mechanisms, but we cannot claim to have a sound ethics, a culture and spirituality genuinely capable of setting limits and teaching clear-minded self-restraint."

59 *Laudato Si* §106: "Human beings and material objects no longer extend a friendly hand to one another; the relationship has become confrontational. This has made it easy to accept the idea of infinite or unlimited growth, which proves so attractive to economists, financiers and experts in technology. It is based on the lie that there is an infinite supply of the earth's goods, and this leads to the planet being squeezed dry beyond every limit."

60 *Laudato Si* §112: "We have the freedom needed to limit and direct technology; we can put it at the service of another type of progress, one which is healthier, more human, more social, more integral... [like when] the desire to create and contemplate beauty manages to overcome reductionism through a kind of salvation which occurs in beauty and in those who behold it."

61 *Laudato Si* §190: "Where profits alone count, there can be no thinking about the rhythms of nature, its phases of decay and regeneration, or the complexity of ecosystems which may be gravely upset by human intervention. Moreover, biodiversity is considered at most a deposit of economic resources available for exploitation, with no serious thought for the real value of things, their significance for persons and cultures, or the concerns and needs of the poor."

and the need to reshape political systems to be responsive to human communities rather than global corporations and profit-seeking.[62] This all entails as well a "cultural revolution," and he asks his followers to refuse to participate in the current social, economic and political practices that destroy our common home.[63] Like Patočka in *The Natural World as a Philosophical Problem*, Pope Francis also makes a lengthy argument about the degree to which the human body, in its emplacement on the earth, is integrated with other biological systems. Air, water, land, plants, and animals all co-determine what it is for people to be human beings, to engage in life projects, to be healthy, and to live within communities.[64] He expresses political frustrations that the goals of Rio Summit in 1992 have not been realized, acknowledging that the horizon of potentially effective international cooperation to realize goals of environmental sustainability has been retreating ever more quickly, seemingly harder to reach than it was a generation ago.[65] Given all this, his 'integrated ecology' requires care of the body, care of the soul, and care of the earth, as well as a specific sort of politics, because the body is integrated with the biological processes of the earth as well as social and political systems.

In order to become more integrated with the earth and to overcome alienation and homelessness, Francis had many policy recommendations, but he also recognized that reinterpreting the founding myth of Christian civilization in *Genesis* was a necessary part of the overall response. Rewriting founding myths is something that ecologically-minded theologians have been calling for long before *Laudato Si*, but the effort of the Catholic Church to catch up is notable given the position of power and prestige held by the Pope.[66] He clearly argues

---

62 *Laudato Si* §161: "Doomsday predictions can no longer be met with irony or disdain... The effects of the present imbalance can only be reduced by our decisive action, here and now. We need to reflect on our accountability before those who will have to endure the dire consequences." §189: "Politics must not be subject to the economy, nor should the economy be subject to the dictates of an efficiency-driven paradigm of technocracy."

63 *Laudato Si* §113–114: "All of this shows the urgent need for us to move forward in a bold cultural revolution."

64 *Laudato Si* §10; *Laudato Si* §138–139: "When we speak of the "environment," what we really mean is a relationship existing between nature and the society which lives in it. Nature cannot be regarded as something separate from ourselves or as a mere setting in which we live. We are part of nature, included in it and thus in constant interaction with it. Recognizing the reasons why a given area is polluted requires a study of the workings of society, its economy, its behaviour patterns, and the ways it grasps reality."

65 *Laudato Si* §166–167.

66 Rewriting the founding myth of civilization as it relates to the human relationship with the environment has been suggested by various theologians, for one early example see: Sean McDonagh, *To Care for the Earth: A Call to a New Theology* (Santa Fe: Bear and Co., 1986). The

that to interpret *Genesis* to say that "man" has "dominion" over the natural world requires denying something to future generations, because it requires ranking all of earth's creation on a hierarchy with man at the top, therefore able to exploit the animals, the trees, the oceans and the rivers for immediate use, which then makes it impossible to leave the 'natural world' intact for future generations to enjoy. To think about *Genesis* in a different way is therefore a path to understanding the present world in a different light:

> Once we start to think about the kind of world we are leaving to future generations, we look at things differently; we realize that the world is a gift which we have freely received and must share with others. Since the world has been given to us, we can no longer view reality in a purely utilitarian way, in which efficiency and productivity are entirely geared to our individual benefit. Intergenerational solidarity is not optional, but rather a basic question of justice, since the world we have received also belongs to those who will follow us.[67]

If the dominion argument is replaced with a stewardship argument, then "to rule over" becomes "to care for," with the connotation that part of that care is the preservation of non-human aspects of the natural world as valuable. This raises the question of whether Pope Francis's vision of nature remains, in the tradition of Christianity, a kind of usable anthropocentric value with humans on the top of the hierarchy—where non-human entities are valuable "gifts" because they can be used by humans, or whether Francis's vision is trying to push the theological terrain to a notion of eco-centric intrinsic value—that is, seeing animals and plants as being valuable intrinsically, in and of themselves, unrelated to the human ability to use them. By saying he does not want a "purely utilitarian" view of the natural world to prevail, he is at least trying to question presuppositions about the human relationship to nature that have prevailed in his faith community for generations, if not centuries.

Patočka also analyzes the story of *Genesis* within his 1970 revisions to the *Natural World as a Philosophical Problem*, by some measure calling for

---

central chapter is called "A New Story," where he integrates findings of modern science with a new way to tell the story of human creation, combining Christian ideas with those of indigenous cultures in the Philippines. The Yale Forum on Religion and Ecology, http://fore.yale.edu/, has also been a center of research and projects related to ecology and cosmology.

67 *Laudato Si* §159.

a reinterpretation of this founding myth for the post-nuclear world.[68] When Patočka discusses *Genesis*, he does so in the context of developing a deeper understanding of the third movement of existence as a mode of breaking free from the bondage of the second movement through recognition of mortality and responsibility.[69] *Genesis* is evoked alongside terms of devotion, confrontation, solidarity, and self-surrender, where Patočka seems to argue for a life that moves towards 'free possibility,' where thanks to the recognition of mortality (i.e. finding death in the garden) we can take up a new responsibility for an integrated life, one that is not anthropocentric, but rather cosmocentric and luminocentric:

> In this new attitude, confronting finitude does not mean self-attachment, binding and relating everything we encounter to our accepted, obdurate self. This confrontation has now the meaning of devotion... This means: life in self-surrender, life outside oneself, not a mere solidarity of interests but a total reversal of interest—I no longer live in that which separates and encloses, but rather in that which unites and opens... This turn is not accompanied by a loss of the world but, on the contrary, by its full discovery... the world here lives more deeply, a cosmocentric and luminocentric life.[70]

This seems to suggest that the confrontation with finitude and death (what we gained in leaving the garden) can be a more general path towards devotion, including an assumption that the world can be united and open, that solidarity is a total reversal of (perhaps private) interests, and thus the "turn" to a "new attitude" can mean the possibility of living a "cosmocentric" existence that is not solipsistically enclosed. If we find a way to counter "our accepted, obdurate self," then we care for our soul in the context of caring for the world and the others within it, and under a framework of solidarity that might be able to cross generations:

> Life given in dedication is, in a certain sense, everlasting. Not that human mortal finitude is eliminated and replaced by the fruits of the tree of life. But the life that gives itself up lives outside itself, and the authenticity of this "outside itself" is attested precisely by what it gives itself up to. It thus begets a community of those who understand each other in surrender and

---

68 Patočka, *NWPP*, 176–179.
69 Patočka, *NWPP*, 178.
70 Patočka, *NWPP*, 178.

devotion, and, through the negation of separate centers, cement a fellow-ship of dedication, a fellowship in devoted service, which transcends every individual... their transcending into a chain of beings united not merely by an external link, of beings which are not mere islands of life in a sea of objectivity, but for whom things and objects emerge from the ocean of being in the service of which they commune. The third movement of existence... discovers here a fundamental dimension of the natural world.[71]

While Patočka's language is abstract and without examples, he starts with the fruits of the tree of life and mortality, references to *Genesis*, but then he moves to language that evokes his ideas about "the third movement," (see Chapter Three) where the individual transcends a former sense of self for a new vision of reality. His language also seems to evoke a sense of 'solidarity of the shaken,' as a community forms in "surrender and devotion," where "those who understand each other" are united in a "fellowship of dedication" with "a chain of beings." He makes the "sea of objectivity" seem like it is an inauthentic place, cites the third movement as needing to come back to the natural world, and then a few sentences later the essay ends, without further elaboration.

What might be clearer than the details of this particular (and particularly abstract) passage is how Patočka saw it as necessary, in the larger frame of the argument, to address both the interpretation of the creation myth *and* the problem of the natural world as a philosophical problem *together*, in the same analysis, and that these issues were, for him as for Pope Francis, intertwined.[72] The papal encyclical is notable as a statement by a Christian religious leader who is willing to question the traditional formulation of the *Genesis* myth alongside an exploration of the details of climate change science in significant detail, also advocating political

---

71 Patočka, *NWPP*, 179.
72 Had Patočka had a longer and more detailed space to work out this problem, there is a vague sense that he might have put together more firmly the turn out of the garden, a moment of dissenting against the rules via sin, with a description of a kind of third movement moment of transformation. But this is not entirely clear in the text, and it is from the use of similar words, not the clarity of the argument, that this comes across; it is a poetic similarity, not a logical one. This would need to be explored further in a more technical and detailed analysis along-side Patočka's other theological reflections. For further commentary on Patočka's theological thinking, see: M. Kočí, "Metaphysical Thinking after Metaphysics: A Theological Reading of Jan Patočka's Negative Platonism," *International Journal of Philosophy and Theology* 79, no. 1-2 (2018): 18–35. The relationship between the expulsion from the garden and Patočka's politics (via Dostoevsky) is also discussed here: Jozef Majernik, "Jan Patočka's Reversal of Dostoevsky and Charter 77," *Labyrinth: An International Journal for Philosophy, Value Theory and Sociocultural Hermeneutics* 19, no. 1 (2017): 26–45.

objectives aiming at greater international cooperation and specific forms of local governance.[73] To frame this as a problem of "creating a common home" situates Francis in the light of Patočka's intertwined categories of caring for the soul, living in truth, and solidarity of the shaken, where Francis would take 'shaken' to mean not just those who are awakened by historical and philosophical knowledge, but those who are also shaken in their vulnerability to poverty, pollution, and the destruction of their homes. It also opens the question of whether, on this axis, Pope Francis could be categorized as a 'repentant theologian,' to extend Patočka's idea of the 'repentant scientist' to another category. (See previous chapter) *Laudato Si* exhibits at least a partial metanoia that is repentant for at least some parts of the clash between the Christian and indigenous worlds,[74] and would be consistent with Patočka's ideas of care of the soul and solidarity of the shaken, while also acknowledging that in the era of climate change, the natural world has become a new type of philosophical problem.

What both Pope Francis and Patočka understood was how myths penetrate quite deeply into the soul of human existence, and meanings, like feelings, are generally not the terrain of scientific discourse. Theologians, first within indigenous cosmologies, and now with Pope Francis, are more aware of this dynamic than are natural scientists. This matters for climate change. If 'living in scientific truth' has not been enough to get the fire brigade moving, the wager of Pope Francis and other theologians is that understanding the relationship between caring for the earth and caring for the soul might create more urgency, and this will require a reconsideration of the founding myths of the 'dominion' civilizations, including reassessing our relationship to the history of myths and the myths of

---

73 In more recent statements, Francis has suggested adding "environmental sin" to the Church's catechism, and further debate has emerged about the degree to which his encyclical has had an impact on Catholics and the wider world. See: "Audience with Participants in the 20th World Congress of the International Association of Penal Law, 15.11.2019," accessed Jan. 3, 2020, http://press.vatican.va/content/salastampa/en/bollettino/pubblico/2019/11/15/191115j. html. For a study about whether the encyclical has changed views of Catholics, see: Maibach, E., Leiserowitz, A., Roser-Renouf, C., Myers, T., Rosenthal, S. & Feinberg, G. *The Francis Effect: How Pope Francis Changed the Conversation about Global Warming* (George Mason University and Yale University. Fairfax: George Mason University Center for Climate Change Communication, 2015); G. Marshall, "Pope's Climate Essay Won't Convince Trump, It Didn't Even Work on Catholics," May, 26 2017, https://www.climatechangenews.com/2017/05/26 /popes-climate-essay-wont-convince-trump-didnt-even-work-catholics/.

74 Pope Francis invited indigenous leaders to a synod on the destruction of the Amazon rainforest in October 2019 to attempt to collaborate on responses, demonstrating his awareness of the problem.

history.[75] Thinking of the future generations, or so Francis claims, can make us think differently now; thinking about a new version of the future is related to thinking about a new version of the past. What happens in the future, therefore, depends upon which type of history prevails in the present. Environmental activists have also been trying to change the meaning of the natural world and the human relationship to the earth by asking us to understand ourselves in light of a new history and new sense of historicity. Rewriting myths is part of the solution, but so too is rewriting our sense of time, reconceiving of the relationship between past, present and future. It is, furthermore, within myths and story telling (the "narrative form" Patočka suggests) where our sense of time is cultivated, where meaning and narrative are ascribed to what would otherwise be the empty ticking of the clock and the empty boxes of the calendar.[76]

The Heretical Metaphysics of Historicity

When Erazim Kohák, a Czech environmental philosopher who was inspired by Patočka's work (and who has translated several of his works into English), was writing about how different philosophies have made distinctions between humans and animals, he wrote that "recent philosophy, seeking in historicity a substitute for the spirituality it has lost, has been loath to recognize the temporality of animal life."[77] In the footnote, he cites a nineteenth century debate about the shifting relationship between conceptions of nature and conceptions of history, referencing how it was previously argued that because of their awareness of time

---

75 One interesting point of comparison: Charles Mann, *1491: New Revelations of the Americas Before Columbus* (New York: Vintage Books, 2006). Mann argues that the Amazon rainforest might not be 'natural,' but the remains of a cultivated garden planted by natives before the arrival of the Spanish conquistadors. His argument has generated controversy about the potential environmental implications of rewriting the account of European colonization to the status of 'myth' rather than 'fact.' In his view, the Spanish did not conquer a pre-industrial primitive culture, but rather disease wiped out an advanced and sophisticated civilization before Europeans ever witnessed its extent and size. This is an example of the kind of rewriting of origin myths at stake in environmentalism. The 'fact' at stake is the pre-colonization population numbers in the Americas; an acrimonious debate exists about whose fact is a fact and whose fact is a myth. For an account of the debate, see: C. Mann, "1491," *Atlantic Monthly* 289, no. 3 (2002): 41–52.

76 For a more detailed discussion of Patočka's concepts of time, see P. Kouba, "Time in 'Negative Platonism,'" in *The Phenomenological Critique of Mathematisation and the Question of Responsibility*, eds. L. Učník, I. Chvatík, A. Williams (Springer: 2015): 79–88.

77 Kohák, *Embers and the Stars: A Philosophical Inquiry into the Moral Sense of Nature* (Chicago: University of Chicago Press, 1984) 75.

and history, humans were said to be separate from nature, categorically different from plants and animals, and in this separateness and difference, could have dominion over the earth. Kohák critiques this worldview because it led to a mode of thinking where it was believed that animals and plants had no sense of time—it was said that they could not recognize the passage of time, nor was it believed that they could become bored in the midst of time's passing—and these ideas of human distinctiveness from animals thus became dependent upon a fundamental misunderstanding of animals themselves.[78] Kohák dismisses the idea that plants and animals have no temporality as absurd, giving several examples of growing plants and industrious animals, and stating that "the lives they live are so clearly purposive, leaving their tracks on a past and projecting into a future."[79] He then describes the difference between the time of the clock (mechanical time) and the time of the seasons (natural time) and expresses his desire to be firmly in the context of the latter, not the former, and states that "the temporality of clocks is inherently absurd, meaningless, if taken as reality itself."[80] He then concludes that plants, animals, and humans are all within a natural time that has a moral structure, and while each species has a different purpose, he concludes:

> What is crucial is that humans, whether they do so or not, are capable of encountering a moment not simply as a transition between a before and an after but as the miracle of eternity ingressing into time. That, rather than the ability to fashion tools, stands out as the distinctive human calling. Were it not for humans who are able to see it, to grieve for it and to cherish it, the goodness, beauty, and truth of creation would remain wholly absorbed in the passage of time and pass with it. It is our calling to inscribe it into eternity.[81]

This act of inscription is, on his account, present in everyday actions within human life, and is not just the act of writing (one form of inscription) but also the act of finding a place within the world to write oneself into nature.

---

78 Much emerging scholarship on the inner lives of animals makes links with environmental ethics. See for example, Amy J. Fitzgerald and Linda Kalof, eds., *The Animals Reader: The Essential Classic and Contemporary Writings* (Oxford: Berg, 2007).

79 Kohák, *Embers and the Stars*, 76. See also: Peter Wohlleben, *The Hidden Life of Trees: What They Feel, How They Communicate—Discoveries from a Secret World* (Berkeley: Greystone Books, 2016).

80 Kohák, *Embers and the Stars*, 78.

81 Kohák, *Embers and the Stars*, 85.

This is also a description of the human being at the intersection of the horizontal and the vertical modalities of existence (see Chapter Two) who understands that, as Kohák writes in a later chapter, "it is as eternal that humans constitute history—and as historical that they become aware of eternity. Only a philosophy which does justice to the morality of being human can do justice to its historicity as well."[82] If eternity is the vertical modality of life, and history the horizontal modality, at their intersection is morality. While his initial reference to "contemporary philosophy using historicity to replace spirituality" was developed towards a critique of Marxist conceptions of historicity, in this later passage he reintegrates morality and historicity through a conception that seems to be drawn almost directly from Patočka's analysis of 'eternity and historicity,' which, as discussed in Chapter Two, conceives of eternity as within history and at the intersection of horizontal and vertical modalities of existence.[83] Kohák continues: "If there is an answer humans can give to the vertigo of history it is in the recognition of the eternity which intersects time and gives it meaning. Historicity then, as depth and horizon, is a gift of eternity, not its contradiction."[84]

To speak of the temporal conceptions of the bees and the beavers in the same breath as notions of eternity and historicity is Kohák evoking Patočka through examples that Patočka himself never gave. This also illustrates several key questions necessarily asked by environmentalists: how are we to do things for future generations that none of us will ever personally benefit from, and how do we justify those actions as important for eternity (and continued human existence into eternity) and our historicity (as important for what future generations will say about our now, our present, when they look back at us as historians)? Environmentalism has to be justified somewhere between eternity and historicity as a moral problem, reimagining not just the future, but also the future's conception of the past, the future's past that happens to be our present. Kohák and Patočka do not seriously flirt with the idea of human extinction (they speak seriously of our existence into eternity), but one recently conceived environmental organization calls itself Extinction Rebellion, and in its mission statement describes how human temporality—the relationship between the future, present and past—must be rearranged in order to undertake the moral fight against climate change:

---

82 Kohák, *Embers and the Stars*, 174.
83 Patočka, *Éternité et historicité,* trans. Erika Abrams (Paris: Éditions Verdier 2011).
84 Kohák, *Embers and the Stars*, 175.

Our world is in crisis. Life itself is under threat... We hear history calling to us from the future... It's a future that's inside us all—located in the fierce love we carry for our children, in our urge to help a stranger in distress... And so we rebel for this, calling in joy, creativity and beauty. We rise in the name of truth and withdraw our consent for ecocide, oppression and patriarchy. We rise up for a world where power is shared for regeneration, repair and reconciliation. We rise for love in its ultimate wisdom. Our vision stretches beyond our own lifespan, to a horizon dedicated to future generations and the restoration of our planet's integrity. Together, our rebellion is the gift this world needs. We are XR [Extinction Rebellion] and you are us.[85]

In further descriptions of their "Principles and Values" (see Preface), the references to how a sense of historicity and a particular sense of time become an impetus for political action to save the earth are reiterated throughout: "this is the time"; "this is what destiny feels like"; "time is broken and buckled"; "to everything there *was* a season"; "times of crisis can be times when life is lived transcendently, for a purpose beyond the self"; "to be in unity with each other and with the life-source, call it the spirit, call it the divine"; "the extinction of the living world is our suicide." They also argue that the contract between the generations is broken, and that protest is therefore "life in rebellion for life.[86]

This is also a vision that articulates the need to live in truth ("tell the truth is the first demand"), to care for the soul ("nothing more sacred than protecting the spirit deep within all life"), to confront established politics and economics ("a pathological obsession with money and profit is engineering this breakdown"), and to find solidarity of the shaken ("we are fighting for our lives and if we do not link arms, we will fail").[87] Those who wrote this website in the UK were probably unaware of Jan Patočka the Czech philosopher.[88] The overlap of ideas, however, seems

---

85 "The Truth," Extinction Rebellion, https://rebellion.earth/the-truth/about-us/.

86 "Why We Rebel," Extinction Rebellion, curated by Jay Griffiths with XR UK Vision team, https://rebellion.earth/the-truth/about-us/.

87 "Why We Rebel," Extinction Rebellion.

88 Extinction Rebellion presents itself on its website as a leaderless organization that is not hierarchically arranged, and the content of the website is attributed to a group of people from a particular moment in the formation of the organization, and it invites anyone to freely use and disseminate the content ("you are us," etc.). It therefore seemed against the spirit of their endeavor to try to interview "the writer" of the statement about philosophical sources to ask them if they knew Patočka. People with advanced philosophy degrees end up in all types of variously unrelated jobs, and the statement seems philosophically well-informed, quoting

to confirm that there is something substantive to the idea of the times having a spirit, a zeitgeist where from multiple unconnected entities, a spiritual thread emerges, and in multiple voices, a sense of what history will remember about this moment in time becomes "inscribed into eternity," to use Kohák's phrase. Extinction Rebellion set about articulating why they were taking political action, and it happens to partially map onto those aspects of Patočka's thinking that now seem most relevant to contemporary dissidents. Could this mean that our common historicity seems to inscribe a common vision into 'the now,' demonstrating something about how humans currently exist between the vertical and horizontal, between eternity and historicity, paddling to the ostinato of a common rhythm on the earth's rising seas?

In less conjectural terms, as the authors of the manifesto state near the end, spirituality will continue to matter in this entire pursuit, in part because our sense of traditional spirituality and metaphysics has (in Kohák's terms) been at least partly replaced by historicity. An environmental activist can always explain *for whom* they are doing what they are doing, and it is usually some higher idea beyond themselves, and often contains references to history and one's sense of place within history (the more technical word "historicity" referring to this internal sense).[89] There is a kind of historicity within environmentalism that speaks in a liturgy of 'the future generations,' 'the time to act is now,' and the need to 'sacrifice for the children.' For Extinction Rebellion, history 'calls from the future,' from outside of our own time, like a divinity calls from a different temporal horizon irrupting into human life. History also judges, like God judges, and environmental activists often claim that history will judge us harshly if we do not do something *very soon*.[90] Historicity, in this frame, is represented by these concrete references to time, history, and the future generations, and has become a bridging metaphysics seeking

---

Gandhi and evoking other ideas from the history of dissidence, so I could also be underestimating the breadth and depth of the author's or authors' knowledge. The larger point of quoting this is phenomenological not genealogical; this statement is a phenomenon that appeared in the world and the ideas presented in that phenomenon are resonant with ideas of Patočka's, and the goal of this exposition is to reveal such similarities.

89 For a general background on the development of the idea of historicity within phenomenology, see: C. Guignon, "History and historicity," *A Companion to Phenomenology and Existentialism* (2006): 545–558. See also: M. Heidegger, *Being and Time*, "The Basic Constitution of Historicity" (§74).

90 This is a core line of argument in Greta Thurnberg's activism, for example. See: G. Thunberg, *No One Is Too Small to Make a Difference* (Penguin, 2019); G. Thunberg, "Our house is on fire." *The Guardian* 20 (2019).

to unite people across cultures, religions, places, and languages. It is also an example of moving towards 'solidarity of the shaken,' the solidarity that Patočka wrote about as being almost synonymous with history itself: "History arises from the shaking of naïve and absolute meaning in the virtually simultaneous and mutually interdependent rise of politics and philosophy. Fundamentally, history is the unfolding of embryonic possibilities present in this shaking"[91] (see Chapter Four).

The shaking, the solidarity, and the rise of politics and philosophy are all intertwined and mutually constitutive aspects of making history. Environmentalists, on this logic, prescribe a new understanding of history while engaging in solidarity of the shaken to create a new form of politics, and this maps onto Patočka's ideas, at least on the abstract level, but also shows how there is a notion of historicity (and a self-conscious awareness of one's place in history) that constitutes a substitute for traditional metaphysics while also giving rise to dissident politics. The evocations of history and historicity by environmental activists are also metaphysical in so far as the idea of history is used to create common higher principles into which both moral categories and political action then become structured: it is *wrong* to harm the opportunities of future generations; it is *good* to care for all of creation so that everything can exist into the future; it is *good* to cooperate across the borders of sovereign states so that history will judge you more kindly, and so on. This is a moral discourse.

If the vertical gaze of human life points toward metaphysics as an external reference point, as a set of ideas seen outside of time and outside of ourselves, there is an irony at stake to say that one's (extra-territorial a-historical) 'metaphysics' is constituted through a sense of historicity that is grounded and rooted in a time and in a place. 'Metaphysics of historicity' is a logically contradictory idea, as rationality would have it that something historical cannot be metaphysical, and metaphysics is by definition outside of the historically particular. But while rationality cannot explain it, the metaphysical discourse of historicity appears as a phenomenon alongside environmentalists as they seek to rewrite the founding myths of the Promethean civilization they are fighting against. That the future generations will suffer, that history will judge, that we are in a time "of now" when we can do something to act, that our action will make a difference: are these facts, or are these myths? Or are they myths (read:

91   Patočka, *Heretical Essays,* 77.

a new creation story) that the scientific facts demand? There is a burning house, the children are screaming, the fire brigade will not come, so what story do you tell the firemen to inspire movement? If the metaphysics of history has any meaning, one would tell the firemen that they will be condemned by history if they do not act into history's unfolding possibilities; that they are on the grand stage of history with a large attentive audience watching them; that it is necessary to suspend their suspicion that it is a false alarm, but they also need to ignore the hunch that they might not make it in time; that climate change is, to use Kohák's words, "eternity ingressing into time," and that they are the humans who can be "inscribed into eternity" for doing something that might one day 'go down in history,' where an account of their actions might make it into the sacred text known as 'the history books.' In telling this story, the process of inscribing eternity into historicity is unveiled, history is given metaphysical qualities, and if the firemen come to 'believe in history,' as others 'believe in God,' then this story becomes a way to inscribe meaning onto the potential meaninglessness of a nihilistic human life where we regret 'doing nothing' but still find it so difficult to 'do something.'[92]

---

92 In Christian doctrine, but also in certain aspects of Judaism, Islam and other religions, history already has metaphysical qualities because it is said to have been preordained by God; that line of reasoning, however, is absent from the claims of most environmentalists, where 'history' and 'future generations' stand alone as having metaphysical properties without any direct reference to a divinity. The case of Pope Francis is of course an exception, see above. Augustine's *City of God* is usually cited as the fullest articulation of the Christian vision of the intertwinement of history and divinity, where God predestined all events, but where the Christian must nonetheless exercise free will in response to God's call as it is written into historical events, and thus the relationship of metaphysics to historicity is a topic within Christian theology; see for example, Emil L. Fackenheim, *Metaphysics and Historicity* (Milwaukee: Marquette University Press, 1961). Another use of 'history' and historicity to replace metaphysics (and nullify divine history) occurs within Marxism, where traditional divinity is removed from the equation of historical progress, but where the materialist historical battle between the bourgeoisie and the proletariat is something that followers are supposed to believe in (perhaps worship in a sense), and 'history' becomes an unquestioned idea representing a determined and determining aspect of ontology, epistemology and therefore politics. Patočka (and Kohak's appropriation of Patočka) does not embrace the Marxist sense of history (their idea is not deterministic or rigid in a Marxist sense, and a person stepping into history can create a rupture, contingency and unpredictability), though they do not completely abandon the Christian sense, even if they are secularizing the concept to via Heidegger's notion of historicity. The Christian idea of 'kairos,' the seizing of the moment by stepping into a call of action given by God in history, is relevant to dissidence and Bonhoeffer (see Chapter Two), who arguably combined both the Christian ideas of preordained history and kairos with a secular sense of 'doing things for the coming generations.' The use of historicity as a metaphysical idea and force in environmental activism arguably rejects both the Marxist and the Christian sense, so represents a new example of politicized historicity, and this is perhaps just the beginning of a much longer exposition needed to fully validate and explain these differences and what they mean for contemporary politics in light of past ideas.

For the fire brigade, the culminating plea might be to tell them that their life will have meaning if they go, and so they might go, quite voluntarily, without any coercion, incentives, or payments.

The meaning given to this life when it embraces action does not come from seeking or reaching final results or the indicators of empirical thresholds, as the results will appear only sometime beyond the span of human mortality; while history is calling from the future, the future is not here yet, and the *final* results of climate change will never be seen or experienced by anyone living today. As a result, environmentalism is action without a *telos*, without any absolute final results that will be definitively known; it is action that is only process, only questions, only problematicity, directed toward only intermediary phenomenon, not finalities.[93] Framing history as a semi-divine call from the future, then, makes sense in light of Patočka's concerns about other less Socratic forms of history:

> Modern civilization suffers not only from its own flaws and myopia but also from the failure to resolve the entire problem of history. Yet the problem of history may not be resolved, it must be preserved as a problem... The question is whether historical humans are still willing to embrace history.[94]

Environmentalists seem to embrace a sort of history that will always be "preserved as a problem," or more specifically, preserved as a metaphysical problem. Perhaps as a result, environmentalism will continually regenerate itself as a form of political action precisely because it does not depend upon final ends, but instead draws sustenance from being an inscription of meaning onto human lives that might have otherwise

---

93 The idea of a 'politics of possibilities' has some affinities with William Connolly's ideas of a 'politics of becoming.' He uses the climate change problem within several examples, especially when discussing the tragic dimensions of collective political action where "the lesson is that you must act forward in a world replete with uncertainty, sensitive to possible ways in which old habits may be out of touch with new developments." *A World of Becoming* (Durham: Duke University Press, 2011) 156–57. That climate change might be an 'emergent system' capable of changing other systems (175) is probably related to how activists see their own process of human becoming. 'Existential recognition' might be one partial antidote to what Connolly theorizes as 'existential resentment' and 'existential gratitude,' but to expand on the details of these similarities would be a different more extensive discussion. Turning to continental philosophy in order to expand the bounds of political theory, especially in regards to existential issues about the relationship between self and other, is a project we probably share, but in different ways.

94 Patočka, *HE*, 118.

just been vaporized, or been lost to objectification, or been disappeared towards "no-man's lands" of bureaucracy or economic rationality, thrown somewhere beyond history.[95] With and within history, "life in rebellion for life" makes sense.[96] And as Camus argued in *The Rebel*, "rebellion cannot exist without a strange form of love... Real generosity toward the future lies in giving all to the present. Rebellion proves in this way that it is the very movement of life... Its purest outburst, on each occasion, gives birth to existence... All of us, among the ruins, are preparing for a renaissance beyond the limits of nihilism. But few of us know it."[97]

Solidarity of the Shaken and Existential Recognition

At the end of Max Weber's pessimistic account of the origins of capitalist economics in the *Protestant Ethic and the Spirit of Capitalism*, he predicts that the "iron cage" of capitalism will keep its worker-prisoners in a state of frenzied production "until the last ton of fossilized coal is burnt."[98] By some recent calculations, if all the remaining oil and coal is extracted from the earth and burnt, the planet will be devastated; this is the rationale for protesting against further extraction in places like the Tar Sands of Alberta, as well trying to stop the construction of pipelines that facilitate such extraction.[99] Weber's admonition suggests that he might agree that the natural world is a philosophical problem because of its relationship to death: in the name of a type of economic 'survival' that 'depends' upon extracting those fossil fuels, the overall 'survival' of the species is put at risk.[100] Those who believe that the

---

95 This was Mario Savio's worry in the speech "End of History," discussed in Chapter Four, where he was concerned that a sense of history would hit a dead end in a bureaucratic tunnel of nothingness.

96 See "Extinction Rebellion: About Us," quoted above.

97 Albert Camus, *The Rebel*, trans. A. Bower (New York: Vintage, 1956), 304–305.

98 "The Puritan wanted to work in a calling; we are forced to do so. For when asceticism was carried out of monastic cells into everyday life, and began to dominate worldly morality, it did its part in building the tremendous cosmos of the modern economic order. This order is now bound to the technical and economic conditions of machine production which today determine the lives of all the individuals who are born into this mechanism, not only those directly concerned with economic acquisition, with irresistible force. Perhaps it will so determine them until the last ton of fossilized coal is burnt." Max Weber, *The Protestant Ethic and the Spirit of Capitalism*, trans. Talcott Parsons, (New York: Charles Scribner's Sons, 1958 [1905]) 181.

99 Bill McKibbon, "Do the Math," in *Oil and Honey: The Education of an Unlikely Activist* (New York: Macmillian, 2013); http://math.350.org/.

100 Patočka takes up the argument presented in *Protestant Ethic and the Spirit of Capitalism* in *Heretical Essays* as he is telling the story of the transition from a spiritual understanding of nature to

capitalist growth paradigm can go on forever have actually abandoned the first principles of scarcity that founded the discipline of economics, as they imagine that even after the last ton of fossilized coal is burnt, we could still be speaking of 'economic growth' in terms of a 'healthy economy' and more production. Environmental activists who go against the growth paradigm might be said to be returning economics to the original sense of 'economizing,' that is, limiting consumption in light of scarce resources in the name of human survival.[101] Remembering Weber helps to ask the question of whether the momentum of the capitalist machine is now unstoppably self-propelled by the world-wide desire to appear as one of the 'chosen ones' of economic-consumerist existence; what we can buy gives us social status, and that might have become more important than life itself. Weber could see a century ago that such a cultural-economic force might result in the iron cage of flattened and objectified human existence, but also in the irreversible pollution of the air inside that cage. Environmental activists are asking whether it is possible to redirect the machine of capitalism before that last ton of coal is burnt and no one can breathe anymore.

In this formulation, the natural world is a philosophical problem because it is a problem of the scope and extent of the possibilities for human action to be undertaken on a species-wide terrain in the name of species-wide survival. This type of action, as environmentalists know, must be undertaken jointly by people who might be radically different from each other in a myriad of ways, but who feel forced to find a way to share the experience of common vulnerability and mortal finitude. As already suggested, both as an idea and a practice, Patočka's 'solidarity of the shaken' might be a helpful way to look at the problem of species-wide cooperation. As already discussed in Chapter Four, and to quote again

---

an economic understanding of nature (*HE*, 111–112). Though he does not cite Weber directly, he asserts: "So many spiritual themes ultimately conjoined in giving rise to an unspiritual, wholly 'practical,' secular and material conception of reality as an object to be mastered by our mind and hands." (*HE*, 112) Then he moves to the related ideas of Kierkegaard and Durkheim, and a further critique of techno-science and anthropocentrism.

101 De-growth economics arguably began with the Club of Rome report in 1972, *The Limits of Growth*. Patočka cites this report in *Heretical Essays* when he is addressing the problem of 'decadence' in modern technological civilization. (*HE*, 95) Current work challenging the growth paradigm is growing; see for example: Robert Ayres, *Turning Point: End of the Growth Paradigm* (Routledge, 2014); Stephen J. Purdey, *Economic Growth, the Environment and International Relations: The Growth Paradigm* (Routledge, 2010). Matthias Schmelzer, "The Growth Paradigm: History, Hegemony, and the Contested Making of Economic Growthmanship," *Ecological Economics* 118 (2015): 262–271; Samuel Alexander, "Planned Economic Contraction: The Emerging Case for Degrowth," *Environmental Politics* 21, no. 3 (2012): 349–368.

here, 'solidarity of the shaken' requires coming together in a common understanding with others, but notably also entails recognition of the human hubris at stake in using science and rationality to unleash a force we might not be able to control:

> The solidarity of the shaken is the solidarity of those who understand. Understanding, though, must in the present circumstances involve not only the basic level, that of slavery and freedom with respect to life, but needs also entail an understanding of the significance of science and technology, of that Force we are releasing.[102]

Patočka writes this in the context of war and 'the front-line experience,' and the destructiveness of this 'force,' even though he is not specific, was probably both trench warfare and nuclear war, with the whole problem of modernity wrapped together with the unending momentum of the Cold War. Without these wars, it is also possible that the post-WWII economic machine might not have ever fully launched as it did.[103] The wars of Patočka's twentieth century have not entirely ended, and the capitalist growth economy and the war economy remain interconnected. "The war machine" is a concept in circulation today, extending the idea of the 'military-industrial complex' that concerned the activists of the 1960s (see Chapter Four), and as the work of Hardt and Negri argues, this machine seems capable of continually regenerating itself in new forms.[104] Patočka's evocative and less specific ideas about 'the force' would not be in radical disagreement with this contemporary thesis about the war machine, as he acknowledged that the war-like "attack on nature" is probably a direct result of the "industrial age:"

> The humans of the industrial age are incomparably more powerful and have at their disposal a far greater reservoir of energy than humans of earlier ages... They live in an incomparably greater social density and can make use of it to intensify their attack on nature to force her to yield ever

---

102 Patočka, *Heretical Essays*, 134–136.
103 Patočka links war and his critique of techno-science in *Heretical Essays*, 113–115. Also see: O. Stanciu, "The Great War as a 'cosmic event.' Jan Patočka and the experience of the frontline," *Revue philosophique de la France et de l'étranger* 143, no. 4 (2018): 507–524.
104 Michael Hardt and Antonio Negri, *Empire* (Cambridge: Harvard University Press, 2006); Michael Hardt and Antonio Negri, *Multitude: War and Democracy in the Age of Empire* (New York: Penguin Random House, 2005).

more of the energy they intend to integrate in the schemata of their calculations.[105]

This is an image of the industrial human who has used technology and its calculations to harness ever more power and energy, who attacks nature to "force her to yield" ever more energy, where the unending pursuit for that last ton of coal is done for the sake of power and power alone.[106] If this is the 'force' the wars of the twentieth century and the industrial age have unleashed, it is relevant that one of Patočka's answers to war is the 'solidarity of the shaken:'

> The means by which this state [of war] is overcome is the solidarity of the shaken; the solidarity of those who are capable of understanding what life and death are all about, and so what history is about... only one who is able to grasp this, who is capable of conversion, of metanoia, is a spiritual person.[107]

If in Chapter Three it was argued that Patočka's concept of war might be taken more broadly than just armies clashing on the battlefield, and rather represented a larger human process of confrontation, then it seems straightforward to say that there is a war going on between those destroying the earth and those trying to defend it.[108] The "spiritual per-

---

105 Patočka, *HE*, 95.

106 Patočka uses here a metaphor ("to force her to yield") that was later used by ecofeminists who made comparisons between the treatment of the earth and the rape of women, connected as well to the usage of 'mother earth' to describe the common human relationship to the earth using feminine pronouns. It would require a longer study beyond the scope of this work to trace the possibilities for a comparison between some of Patočka's formulations and the development of early feminist thinking about nature, but scholarship has already been done tracing the rape metaphor throughout various aspects of environmentalism. See, for example: Andree Collard and Joyce Contrucci. *Rape of the Wild: Man's Violence against Animals and the Earth* (Bloomington: Indiana University Press, 1989); Gudmarsdottir, S. (2010). "Rapes of Earth and Grapes of Wrath: Steinbeck, Ecofeminism and the Metaphor of Rape," *Feminist Theology*, 18(2), 206–222.

107 Patočka, *Heretical Essays*, 134–136. His definition of "spiritual person" from his earlier essay is also helpful to remember here. See: Patočka, "Spiritual Person and the Intellectual," *Living in Problematicity, ed. and trans. Eric Manton,* (Praha: Oikoymenh, 2007) 51–70. The wider political senses of his 'spiritual person' are discussed here: J. Homolka, "Jan Patočka's Non-Political Politics," *Acta Universitatis Carolinae Interpretationes* 7, no. 1 (2017): 130–146.

108 Like other movements seeking to change laws and the practices of the political establishment, environmental activists have long been engaged in confrontational practices of civil disobedience where they put their bodies in harm's way in order to create a violent reaction or arrests that will garner the attention of the media, lawmakers and the general public. Some of this has included the destruction of public and private property, such as depicted

son" today, in the context of the war to defend the earth, is the engaged environmental activist who is trying to get the fire brigade to respond to the emergency of climate change. Patočka's definition of such a person also recognizes that a certain stance towards mathematics and science ("the schemata of calculations") is necessary to "understand" this possibility of conversion. A spiritual person is capable of mastering "objective knowledge and integrating it with what matters and is subordinate," and "spiritual authority" is that which could "drive the warring world to some restraint."[109]

If Patočka's ideas are generally applicable to many historical processes where the momentum of modernity needs to be checked and 'restrained,' then the question becomes whether 'solidarity of the shaken' would be a pathway to begin to transform the relationships within this ongoing war between the environmental activists, the passive and indifferent citizen populations, the technocratic elites, the capitalists burning the coal, and the various political bodies choosing to regulate or subsidize related human actions. If such solidarity and mutual understanding can be a "restraint," according to Patočka, it will be so because some realize they are "parasites on the sidelines who live off the blood of others," and "those who are capable of understanding would feel inwardly uncomfortable about their comfortable position."[110] The role of the scientists and experts is also at stake: "To achieve thereby that component of the spirit, the 'technical intelligentsia,' primarily researchers and those who apply research, inventors and engineers, would feel a waft of this solidarity and would act accordingly."[111] The researchers' feelings matter; the climate scientists who 'feel like' children are burning alive and being sacrificed by the unresponsive fire brigade are a necessary part of the process to "shake the everydayness of the fact crunchers and routine minds" and create a "spiritual conversion."[112]

---

in Edward Abbey's novel *Monkey Wrench Gang* and further developed by the organization Earth First. Edward Abbey, *Monkey Wrench Gang* (New York: Harper Perennial, 2006 [1975]). Earth First, www.earthfirst.org. This type of activism engages in a 'war' against the machines and infrastructure being used to 'attack nature,' doing things like sabotaging bulldozers to prevent construction, and at times standing in front of bulldozers to prevent work from being done. This is, by and large, framed as a defensive war, a battle to protect and to prevent harm from being done, implicitly asking the perpetrators of the industrial age to stop their attack on nature.

109 Patočka, *HE*, 135.
110 Patočka, *HE*, 135.
111 Patočka, *HE*, 136.
112 Patočka, *HE*, 136.

By one reading of Patočka's framework, the scene seems to be ripe for such solidarity: the climate scientists are in solidarity with activists, both activists and scientists are being backed up by spiritual authorities like Pope Francis and other religious leaders who are willing to rewrite the myths of civilization, and activists are painfully aware that "what history is about" is actually a metaphysical problem of species survival (see prior section). This is a spiritual confrontation in progress, and perhaps the sort of clash Patočka would say creates meaning out of nihilism and could be eternally perpetuated into the future. It might not be possible to 'win' definitively, as the confrontation will always happen within a retreating horizon, but it seems like the 'understanding' and action might be sustained across borders and across generations with something like the solidarity of the shaken. It might even be possible to say that it has already spanned generations, if the first flowering of environmentalism is identified with the 1960s and 1970s, when Rachel Carson's *Silent Spring* and other early work first appeared.[113]

Yet, from another view, the metanoia-conversion-existential revolution has seemed extremely slow.[114] There seems to be something still missing, and what seems like an otherwise fertile ground for solidarity has not exactly produced a mass revolution in human behavior or political institutions. The proximate culprits have already been mentioned: profit-seeking corporations, status-seeking consumerism, attachment to the Christian 'dominion' lifestyle, and political ideologies supported by (and formed from) all of these forces. But in the spirit of Patočka's

---

113 Rachel Carson, *Silent Spring* (Houghton Mifflin Harcourt, 2002). The movement that began in the middle of the twentieth century to increase awareness about the dangers of environmental degradation has been sustained and continually grown in size, scope and seriousness in multiple forums around the world. Efforts by activists and scientists to change the public understanding of climate change have already succeeded in shifting the zeitgeist during the last several decades. While the political will to change the legal framework of regulation has not yet caught up with scientific awareness, environmental issues are taken seriously by the public in a way they were not fifty years ago. Being an 'environmentalist' at one point in history meant being part of a small fringe movement; 'environmental issues' are now a mainstream subject of study, a regular part of political discourse, and a regular topic of media discussion. Those who deny climate change and the problems of environmental degradation are considered the 'fringe' in many parts of the world, reversing the prior balance of opinion. See, for example, Marco Armiero and Lise Sedrez, eds., *A History of Environmentalism: Local Struggles, Global Histories* (London: Bloomsbury Academic, 2014).

114 See note 37 in the Introduction. "Existential revolution" was a term used by Havel in *Power of the Powerless* to describe how modern politics might be transformed, where the "intrinsic locus can only be human existence in the profoundest sense of the word. It is only from that basis that it can become a generally ethical—and, of course, ultimately a political—reconstitution of society."

assertion that mere facts are never enough to understand the universal horizon of human experience,[115] there are certain environmental activists who have demonstrated that really what is at stake is a problem embedded within cultural attachments to a certain mode of human relations, where the problem is that people cannot recognize certain other people *as people*. The philosophical problem of the natural world might have turned into, in the end, a philosophical problem of intersubjective human relations and recognition, or as it is sometimes phrased in philosophy, 'the problem of The Other.'[116] Patočka's ideas surrounding 'solidarity of the shaken' might be able to illuminate this in a way that will not provide any immediate solution, but clarifies the slowness that seems to be confounding and frustrating environmental activists and climate scientists alike.

The question might be posed as such: what if the failure at stake is actually that we are unable to see and understand other human beings as human beings like ourselves, where we cannot conjure ourselves as part of a larger species at all, let alone imagine ourselves as part of nature as a whole, and yet, *we are pretending that we can*? What if, in other words, we have a philosophical problem with the both the natural world *and* the human world, but we use the former to deny the latter, conceiving of these as separate problems, pretending in a theatrical way that we have a sense of intersubjective understanding with others, or that we can empathize with others, when in fact we do not have any such an understanding, and are also severely inhibited in trying to create such an understanding? If some part of this conjecture might be true, and this type of thinking infects environmentalism, then the frustrated exhortations about how glaciers are melting faster than the glacial pace of political change might be explained by unmasking the theatrics of this self-deception. Or, to use Platonic terms, the shadows we are watching dance on a cave wall, thinking they are reality, need to be critically examined, even if these ideas are very dear to the heart. Perhaps the shadows

---

115 See note 133 below.
116 The problem of 'the other' in Patočka's work is discussed both in terms of his method of asubjective phenomenology and his understanding of intersubjectivity. For examples of this conversation, see: E. Evink, "Horizons and Others: Gadamer, Levinas, Patočka." *American Catholic Philosophical Quarterly* 84.4 (2010): 727–46; J. Čapek, "Oneself through Another: Ricœur and Patočka on Husserl's Fifth Cartesian Meditation." *Meta: Research in Hermeneutics, Phenomenology, and Practical Philosophy* Vol. IX, No. 2, December 2017: 387–415; J. Čapek, "Intersubjectivity and Self-awareness in Husserl and Patočka." *The Journal of Speculative Philosophy* 33, no. 3 (2019): 512–526. See also note 144 below.

will not dance in a different way like we want them to, even though it seems possible, because they are shadows of unreality.

Patočka's 'solidarity of the shaken' asks us to ask about Plato's problem of self-deception in relation to solidarity, as it implicitly asks us to ask if "the understanding" of those who "understand what life and death are about" is actually impossible at certain distances. It also asks us to ask, perhaps most controversially, if crying out about extinction, annihilation, universal death, and species destruction—the tropes of today's environmentalist discourse—makes us, as humans, hate each other more than we ever have. Or, at the least, this discourse might significantly obstruct ahimsa and Gandhi's truth-as-love, even as 'Extinction Rebellion' quotes Gandhi's truth-as-love in its mission statement. This potential hatred is not 'nature as a philosophical problem,' but 'The Other' as a philosophical problem, which in turn creates political and material problems not yet fully recognized. Climate change might have inadvertently helped us find the limits of intersubjectivity, that is, the limits of our human ability to mutually understand each other, and posed to us the Socratic question of how we can know what we do not know.

The environmental organization 350.org can demonstrate this problem phenomenologically in a way Patočka might appreciate. Begun by writer Bill McKibbon and a group of students at Middlebury College in the United States, the organization strives to connect climate change activists throughout the world through a platform of online communication, joint days of action, and networked campaigns. In their own words, they seek to "hold our leaders accountable to the realities of science and the principles of justice,"[117] and to take actions to try to return carbon particulate rates in the atmosphere to three hundred and fifty parts per million.[118] In existence since 2008, their common global campaigns have produced a line of communication between those in wealthy countries and those people in impoverished areas of the world most impacted by climate change. The website is both a campaign toolbox and a repository of photographs of activists involved in coordinated global days of action,

---

117 From 350.org website: "We believe that a global grassroots movement can hold our leaders accountable to the realities of science and the principles of justice. That movement is rising from the bottom up all over the world, and is uniting to create the solutions that will ensure a better future for all."

118 This was an amount cited by scientist James Hansen in January 2008 as 'livable' for the human species. "Target atmospheric CO2: Where should humanity aim?" *Open Atmospheric Science Journal* (2008), vol. 2, 217–231.

where different groups around the world all came together to do similar protests on the same day.

In his book *Oil and Honey*, McKibbon gives an account of setting up the organization and how they conducted the campaign against the Keystone Oil Pipeline in the United States. One part of this was a show called 'Do the Math.'[119] He and other activists travelled by bus throughout the country to try to communicate the numbers of climate science in a stage-friendly way. They called it a 'road show,' and McKibbon recounts rehearsing with professional actors, screen writers, and producers who volunteered their time. They used the repository of photographs from activists around the world to show the connections between people on various continents, emphasizing how actions on one side of the earth impact human lives on the other side. They also presented the science and numbers to demonstrate what would happen if the remaining fossil fuel reserves of the earth were burned into the atmosphere and Weber's vision came true.

The audience for the road show would have varied in different cities in the United States, but it was presumed that most people drove their cars to hear the show and went home to houses warmed or cooled by some form of fossil fuels. One of the photographs used in one of McKibbon's later public presentations about *Oil and Honey* showed a sign being held up by an impoverished farmer reading: "What you do there impacts us here."[120] A few slides later, the pictures of farmer-activists in Bangladesh made the same point: they were involved with 350.org because it was the only channel of communication where they could say something directly to those people with the highest rates of carbon emissions who were having a tremendous impact upon their lives from tens of thousands of miles away. This communication, alongside a show about 'doing the math,' had been deliberately designed to produce a form of emotional catharsis in the audience, as any classic tragic stage performance should. It aimed to change the viewer's intersubjective relationship with the Bangladeshi farmer and others who might soon lose their homes under water. It was meant to force one to realize that weather is not just weather, and creating pollution is not a personal action but a political action impacting the whole global community. It was, on Patočka's terms, an attempt to create solidarity of the shaken.

---

119 Bill McKibbon, *Oil and Honey*.
120 Bill McKibbon, at a talk given at Boston College, April, 2016.

Putting the mathematics of scientific reports together with empathy-producing photography of empowered activists was aimed to educate about causation, perhaps changing the way people act both in their daily lives as they pollute, but also in their willingness to be political. This method of performance acknowledged that math and science are not enough to make the case, but nor could pictures of people half-a-world away in dire need motivate political action in a local context; both science and story-telling were needed. The road show did not create a congressional and legal revolution, but it was successful in showing that there is something about mere science by itself, in all its rational facts, figures and objective data, which cannot fully persuade one to change one's behavior. 'Do the Math' at 350.org, ironically given the title, is much closer to Havel's 'spiritual and existential' revolution than it is to any outcomes-based linear-causal mathematical approach.[121] The campaigners were relying on the fact that they know they are within a culture and society still culturally attached to its Cartesian inheritance (as Husserl predicted and Patočka elaborated on) that worships numbers and objective outcomes as 'scientific.' The professional stage managers who organized the tour were savvy to this much as they tried to make the math and science clear and palatable to any 'layman' in the audience, but they knew that numbers could not stand alone, and brought images of people from around the world as a form of narrative to tell a story. They knew that effective climate change activism needed to create intersubjective recognition and understanding across vast distances and differences of culture and economic conditions.

Whatever the other differences might have been between a wealthy American and a poor Bangladeshi farmer, the idea was that if they both recognize in each other the threat of death posed by climate change, then 350.org might have produced a form of 'existential recognition' that could ground political action on the trajectory of existentialist politics

---

121 As Havel writes in "Politics and Conscience," this is an example of "that which I called 'antipolitical politics,' [which] is possible and can be effective, even though by its very nature it cannot calculate its effect beforehand. That effect, to be sure, is of a wholly different nature from what the West considers political success. It is hidden, indirect, long-term, and hard to measure; often it exists only in the invisible realm of the social consciousness, conscience, and subconsciousness, and it can be almost impossible to determine what value it assumed therein and to what extent, if any, it contributes to shaping social development." *Open Letters*, 270. If we were to insert this into the multidimensional mathematics of Cantor sets or Goedel's incompleteness theorem or emergence theory (see Connolly, *A World of Becoming*, note above) then it might not be so ironic. For the sake of simplicity, I refer here to linear Cartesian systems that imply direct causation.

that cross state borders and represent a kind of 'solidarity of the shaken.' Existential recognition would require not a form of reciprocal (implying equality) and mutual (implying voluntary and consensual) recognition, but would imply rather the threat of species-wide death (call it 'really radical equality'). That is, the dual sense of existential might be evoked: it is both of an 'existent,' an existent that is alive and living (not an object) and therefore capable of dying, but it is also the same kind of 'existential' implied in the phrase 'existential threat,' as in, something that can kill and be killed.[122] Or, in Patočka's terms, existential recognition is the realization that we are on the same ship and exist together as human beings, but the ship can be sunk, killing us all, all at once. We 'recognize' each other in this common death, and therefore recognize our existences as tied together with each other now, as we live. The wealthy resident of lower Manhattan surely felt something like this existential recognition in thinking about other climate-threatened places during their own Hurricane Sandy.

Yet there is nothing mutual about the extent of resources the New Yorker had to deal with this threat when compared to the amount of resources the Bangladeshi farmer does not have. Calling this 'mutual recognition,' if mutual implies a kind of relational equality, would be too strong and too celebratory, hiding the tragic element in the encounter between the American in the audience and the photograph of the farmer. 'Existential recognition' is not a term Patočka uses, but seems to be within the spirit of his ideas, and helps overcome implications of mutual equality that other understandings of recognition depend upon.[123] In

---

122 The modalities of recognition at stake in activist and dissident organizations, including the idea of 'existential recognition,' are ideas more fully developed in my book, A. Brinton, *Philosophy and Dissidence in Cold War Europe*, (Palgrave, 2016) and in "Association and Recognition in Authoritarian Societies: A Theoretical Beginning," *European Journal of Political Theory* 11, no. 3, July 2012.

123 The development of the idea of 'existential recognition' in my prior work arose in response to a literature on recognition in philosophy and political theory that seemed to lack a way to adequately theorize forms of recognition outside of state-based and psychological approaches. Patočka informed some of this view, which was also built upon more recent work on the concept of recognition, including (though not an exhaustive list): Lash and Fetherstone, eds., *Recognition and Difference*, (London: Sage Publications, 2002); Patchen Markell, *Bound by Recognition* (Princeton: Princeton University Press, 2003); Paul Ricoeur, *The Course of Recognition*, trans. David Pellauer (Cambridge: Harvard University Press, 2005); Charles Taylor, *Multiculturalism and 'The politics of recognition': An Essay* (Princeton: Princeton University Press, 1992); Simon Thompson, *The Political Theory of Recognition: A Critical Introduction* (Cambridge: Polity Press, 2006); Nancy Fraser, "From Redistribution to Recognition? Dilemmas of Justice in a 'Post-Socialist' Age," *New Left Review*, no. 212, 68–93, 1995; Nancy Fraser, "Rethinking Recognition," *New Left Review*, 2000, no. 3, 107–120; Amy Gutmann, ed. *Multiculturalism:*

this example, it is recognized that even if all the wealthy Americans in the room listening to McKibbon and looking at the farmer gave up their fossil-fuel consuming activities tomorrow, the farmer will still get flooded out of his home. Sharing the common experience of human mortality remains, but the wealthy powerful person has the privilege of recognizing death in a different way, mainly postponing it with technology.[124] A vast chasm emerges, and so the hope of intersubjective understanding with the farmer is also shown to be elusive, and there is a recognition of a vast difference between these two members of a common species. The wealthy audience 'gets it' that they can never really 'get it'; they come to understand in a negative way that they will probably never have to experience what the farmer is experiencing, but their own carbon emissions are implicated in his homelessness, death, or both.

At this realization, the 'existential recognition' produced within that moment can turn in different directions, one of which might be the metaphysics of historicity, where action can then be done "in the name of history" or "in the name of the future generations" to help the situation and bridge the gap. This seemed to be McKibbon's hope. But it can also turn to nihilism, hopelessness, and no action whatsoever, becoming the boredom of forced indifference, where someone might write a check to 350.org in order to leave the room with slightly less embarrassment, but thereafter try to forget the occasion. It is necessary to be very sober, therefore, about what is not *necessarily* going to happen in the moment of existential recognition; it is not an outpouring of love for our common humanity in the fullness of empathy, because what the audience realizes is that they can never feel as the farmer feels, and they can never understand his interiority, what he is thinking, at such a distance; they can only really understand his destruction. The diffusion of responsibility for the destroyed and sinking ship shows distant existences to be intertwined, but also reveals radical difference. Acknowledging this Socratic limitation, however, opens up the possibility of what *could* happen if existential recognition were multiplied exponentially throughout a world of concerned people who "understand what life and death are about," to use

---

Examining the Politics of Recognition (Princeton: Princeton University Press, 1994); Axel Honneth, *Struggle for Recognition: The Moral Grammar of Social Conflicts,* trans. Joel Anderson (Cambridge: Polity Press, 1995).

124 For one contemporary account that is skeptical of the ability of technology to fix environmental problems in a broader egalitarian way, see: Ozzie Zehner, *Green Illusions: The Dirty Secrets of Clean Energy and the Future of Environmentalism*, (Lincoln: University of Nebraska Press, 2012).

Patočka's words. There is a different political import of saying 'we do not know' instead of saying 'we know how he feels;' the latter might be the shadow on the wall, the former closer to the truth.

350.org might be the farmer's only feasible way to participate in anything political related to climate change, given his lack of political power and Bangladesh's lack of power to control the carbon emissions of other countries. The wealthy American in McKibbon's audience may have a hundred ways to 'do something' to stop his or her life from creating carbon emissions, to pressure politicians to enact reforms, perhaps to run for office. The power differentials are enormous, and within this kind of activism there is an attempt to create a bridge between two extremely different human beings as an existential *recognition* of a common situation *on earth*. That we share a common home is a key aspect of that fragile bridge, and so too is coming to 'act in the name of history,' but it might be more important to admit what neither side knows about the other. 350.org makes it possible for the farmer to say something and act as a result of this shaken-ness—he has already taken part in the global campaign they organized that produced the photograph—and his hope might be that the campaign makes someone on the other side of the earth more likely to act as well, but he can never really know if what he does has any effect. The wealthy American can join *the same* campaign to address the eerie gap of disorientation produced by realizing they will never understand the situation of those they affect by their actions, and this might close the gap with a sense of solidarity based on *not knowing* how the farmer feels. The campaign creates a Socratic moment when *both sides* realize that climate change has opened the possibility of *seeing* universal homelessness, universal history, universal alienation from nature, and universal death, but when through such visions, individuals realize there is radical inequality in the potentials for *experiencing and knowing* these things in an embodied way. Even if the wealthy can postpone these calamities of homelessness for the foreseeable future, while the poor cannot, it is nonetheless revealed that the situation of this radical difference *exists*. This seems miniscule and a bit obvious, but it might be more than it appears at first glance.

As climate change advances into its new realities, most people will want to (if they can) run away from the forces of homelessness, alienation, and death, unless it is depicted on the safety of a movie screen, where such plots seem eternally popular. It is necessary to ask, therefore, whether in real life the wealthy will also come to run away from those *people* most likely to experience these forces, and in so doing, expand the gap of global intersubjective misunderstanding. The obligation a wealthy American has to the Bangladeshi farmer might be moral, and capable of creating political engagement through organizations like 350.org, but as the global normative universe currently stands, that obligation is not legal or social, and so running away is still very much an option. History could change this, and environmental activists want it changed, but it has not changed yet. If Patočka would have us take seriously other people's myths and other people's subjective consciousness in relation to their intersubjective relationships with us, then we should think it quite possible that the glimpse into a world where we are 'in it together' produced by the 350.org presentation might have been utterly terrifying for a wealthy person, a kind of horror movie unfolding in real life. So even though two very different people can be shaken together and in some kind of solidarity through the existential recognition produced by campaigns about climate change, the fear engendered might make the otherness of the other that much more profound. Geographical distance has been collapsed by global media and the internet, without which 350.org and many environmental organizations would not be possible, but more 'information' might mean more reasons for fear, not fewer, and reasons for fearing *people*, not just natural disasters.[125]

The beginning of the realization that we do not know what we thought we already knew, if we return to the moment of turning toward truth in Plato's cave, is *dangerous* on Plato's account. It is when Socrates is killed for showing the light of truth. There is debate about how to count the number of environmentalists killed each year, but it is at least in the hundreds.[126] Fear, in the history of human experience, becomes easily intertwined with hatred; most wars reveal both fear and hatred, as well as encouraging both. The more fearful a person, the more likely they

---

125 Havel's comments in an interview (in the burgeoning internet age of 2008 and quoted in the introduction) are relevant here: "'To live in truth'... does not mean just the possession or communication of information. Because information, like a virus, circulates in the air so one person may absorb more and another one less. Truth, however, is a different matter because we guarantee it with our own self. Truth is based on responsibility. And that is an imperative that is valid in every age... of course we no longer live under totalitarian pressure—but *that doesn't mean we've won.* We still need what I refer to as an 'existential revolution,' even though it might look different in different places." Václav Havel, interview by Adam Michnik, "After the Velvet, an Existential Revolution?," *Central European Forum Salon*, November 20, 2008, http://salon.eu.sk/en/archiv/801.

126 "Enemies of the State? How Governments and Businesses Silence Land and Environmental Defenders." Global Witness Report. July 30, 2019, https://www.globalwitness.org/en/campaigns/environmental-activists/enemies-state/.

are to be violent; Gandhi knew this as he trained non-violent warriors to conquer their fears before they were allowed onto the 'battlefield' of nonviolence.[127] If Patočka's ideas about 'solidarity of the shaken' arose alongside his thoughts about war, especially in *Heretical Essays*, then so too might an application of the idea require acknowledging that one of the deeper truths about human existence revealed by both war and the solidarity of the shaken is that fear shuts down intersubjective understanding, and then the demonization of others becomes facile and habitual for the human species, and so war begets war. This might be a return to a banal boring everydayness, but it nonetheless needs to be acknowledged: telling everyone the world is going to end has consequences far beyond being accused of a false alarm, as fear may also make people turn inward, devote their resources to only those nearest and dearest, digging themselves into the fortifications of the familiar, where they build their ramparts from the profits of their economic rationality and bid others to stay away. Or, in other words, whole populations might already be voluntarily enacting the xenophobic prelude to war as a response to their simmering dread about the possibilities of climate change.[128]

The wonder of Patočka's evocative thoughts on the unfolding of 'heretical history,' though, is that he sees within certain moments in history a possibility of rupture in the prior banal ways of proceeding, "where life is no longer its sole purpose but where there is a possibility of living for something else, [where] lies a rupture that is not merely quantitative." He then describes how the work of Hannah Arendt inspired him to see the existential aspects of politics, the *polis*, and the public sphere interwoven:

> In the contradiction between its self-enclosed generative privacy and the will to public openness there is already a continuity, generated and maintained by free human activity. This new human possibility is based on mutual recognition of humans as free and equal, a recognition which must

---

127 "Qualifications and Training of a Satyagrahi," in *Selected Works of Mahatma Gandhi Volume Five Voice of Truth* (Ahmedabad: Navajivan Publishing House, 1969) 154–165.
128 If framed in this way, Patočka's ideas take on a prescience if seen in light of the current French interest in "collapsologie," a discourse and movement reacting against mainstream environmentalism in favor of an approach that rejects technology and sees war and conflict over resources as imminent. See: Pablo Servigne & Raphaël Stevens, *Comment tout peut s'effondrer. Petit manuel de collapsologie à l'usage des générations présentes*, (Le Seuil, 2015). For a summary in English: Harrison Stetler, "'Collapsologie': Constructing an Idea of How Things Fall Apart," *New York Review of Books*, Jan 21, 2020.

be continually acted out, in which activity does not have the character of enforced toil, like labor, but rather of the manifestation of excellence, demonstrating that which humans can be in principle equal in competition with each other. At the same time that means living fundamentally not in the mode of acceptance but of initiative and preparation, ever seeking the opportunity for action, for the possibilities that present themselves; it means a life in active tension, one of extreme risk and unceasing upward striving in which every pause is necessarily already a weakness for which the initiative of others lies in wait.[129]

If every pause is one that will see the problem of climate change get worse, and every pause will be taken advantage of by those who are not regulated and checked by moral principles, then this is an unceasing struggle with everything at stake. Patočka's notion of recognition hinges here on the ability of recognition to reveal the free equality between all human beings, but is intimately connected with the ability to live a 'life in active tension' within situations of 'extreme risk.' While he starts with Arendt's ideas, he circles back after this passage to notions of the home, and homelessness, and how "political life draws its free possibilities from the home and its work, the home in turn cannot exist without the community which not only protects it but gives it meaning."[130] He acknowledges that he sounds like he is describing a warrior's life, but then turns to saying that freedom is the main point, and the political person is free in a way a warrior is not, and a certain sense of freedom is revealed in moments of historical rupture:

> Nothing of the earlier life of acceptance remains in peace; all the pillars of the community, traditions, and myths are equally shaken, as are all the answers that once preceded questions, the modest yet secure and soothing meaning, though not lost, is transformed... Humans cease to identify with it, myth ceases to be the word on their lips. In the moment when life renews itself, everything is cast in a new light. Scales fall from the eyes of those set free...[131]

He then identifies this idea of historical rupture, again relying on Arendt, with "the renewal of life's meaning in the rise of political life." On this

---

129 Patočka, *HE*, 37–38.
130 Patočka, *HE*, 38.
131 Patočka, *HE*, 40.

track, the proper response to living through a moment of historical rupture is to shake old ideas using philosophical questions, but then to exercise freedom through doing politics. Could it then be imagined, via Patočka's categories, that climate change has made us freer than we have ever been, if also enacting an eerie sense of potentially violent freedom? Responding to it, and living a life of "initiative and preparation," would then open the opportunity of embracing "the practical effort to inwardly act against those life-structures which force existence into a situation incompatible with its character as a free possibility."[132]

However abstract Patočka's ideas might seem, his understanding of 'solidarity of the shaken' seems to answer the question of whether or not we can escape to freedom from Weber's iron cage, and it seems he would answer in the affirmative, in part because he sees politics as a process of possibilities: if we shake apart traditional understandings, if we come together in solidarity with others, and in that understanding realize that we are 'at the front' of a perpetual war (metaphorical or otherwise), then we are capable of being historical, responsible, and free:

If one of the two basic possibilities is the possibility of breaking free of the dependence on [mere, everyday] life and on the contrary linking that life to something free, something capable of accepting responsibility and respecting responsibility, that is, the freedom of others, will it not then become necessary to explain precisely history, that is, the most basic human achievement, from this dimension of human being... history, this domain of changing social being of humans, the terrain of traditions in which we establish continuity with our achievements... by rejecting or by continuing, the social being of humans can manifest itself as essentially free, accessible to us 'objectively' to the extent that we can retrospectively note what of it has been transmuted into firmly set facts, but cannot reduce it to those facts alone.[133]

---

132 Patočka, *NWPP*, 177.
133 Patočka, *HE*, 154. This concern with "facts" reiterates what was already there for Patočka in 1936 in *The Natural World as a Philosophical Problem*: "the naïve world can never be fully explained by the principles of the world of mathematical natural science with its conception of the universe as the totality of relations. For the positivist thinker, as we have seen, the world is a totality of facts. A fact is an independent relation, comprehensible in itself, which can to this extent be isolated from the whole. The world, conceived as a totality of facts, contains only realities; the laws governing the occurrence of these realities, for example, are not themselves facts. The natural world, as we have described it, is neither a fact for a totality of facts in this sense—if for no other reason, because it is, as universal horizon, the circle of possibilities on the basis of which alone real determinate facts can be apprehended." *NWPP*, 83.

Here Patočka seems to suggest that humans are free to create history by rejecting or continuing certain social relationships and the corresponding relationship to certain facts. How climate change will change the facts of social relationships is not yet settled enough to discern which parts of the present struggles will become 'history' and which parts will be forgotten, but if Patočka's idea is that history is a set of social relationships that underpin freedom as an achievement, human beings are free to write history by rewriting social relationships, that is, if they choose to.[134] Being and existing in history is our choice; whether "humans are willing to embrace history"[135] is a question, not a given. Weber does not present his iron cage as a choice; it is part of the inevitable march of capitalistic rationality. Patočka's notion of history as the "shaken certitude of pre-given meaning" can lead to the 'solidarity of the shaken' and therein *a choice* to resist the 'rule of everydayness' and 'the force' that otherwise might *seem to* imprison us in inescapable logics of technological progress and alienation from nature, but actually do not.[136]

This freedom comes back to the problem of meaning, and how those who find each other in the solidarity of the shaken and the 'solidarity of those who understand' will see that "a meaning can be reached beyond the human peak of resistance to Force."[137] Or as Havel argued: "When Jan Patočka wrote about Charter 77, he used the term 'solidarity of the shaken.' He was thinking of those who dared resist impersonal power and to confront it with the only thing at their disposal, their own humanity."[138] Finding one's own humanity, finding meaning in history, and resisting impersonal power in a bid for freedom are deeply intertwined in this vision.[139] The philosophical problem of the natural world is, on this account, a deeply human problem of freedom and responsibility, where the crisis lies within the dynamics of recognition and misrecognition, and where environmental activism unveils the necessarily

---

134 This passage also calls for a longer analysis of how Patočka mixes Heideggerian notions of historicity with overtones of Hegelian ideas of history-as-freedom, but this is unfortunately beyond the scope of this discussion.

135 Patočka, *HE*, 118.

136 Patočka, *HE*, 118.

137 Patočka, *HE*, 135–136.

138 Havel, "Politics and Conscience," in *Open Letters,* 271.

139 P. Lom. "East Meets West—Jan Patočka and Richard Rorty on Freedom: A Czech Philosopher Brought into Dialogue with American Postmodernism." *Political theory* 27, no. 4 (1999): 447–459. As a conclusion to his argument distinguishing Rorty and Patočka, Lom argues that Patočka's view of freedom and responsibility is ahead of its time vis-à-vis the environment and technology.

human problem of intersubjective misrecognition embedded into discourses of 'nature.' While some scholarship in environmental studies rightly critiques the centering of 'humanity' in analyses and discussions as too anthropocentric, it is now clear that the rivers, oceans, the animals, and plants unfortunately cannot save themselves.[140] As Kohák had pointed out, it is humans who can inscribe meaning onto these aspects of the natural world in order to *recognize* them as intrinsically valuable, not instrumentally exploitable, and thus come to embrace the politics, history, philosophy, and theology willing to do something to save our common home.[141] It is only *some* humans who are *free* to do this, since those powerful (and wealthy) enough to have created the Anthropocene have, in another sense, enslaved those without their same power.[142] In the totality of the Anthropocene, the power of the powerless can only be harnessed by those humans willing to confront other more powerful humans *on behalf of* the non-human species and entities of the earth now so fully under an inescapable dominion.

Faring Forward, Voyagers

The original problem that Patočka was addressing in *The Natural World as a Philosophical Problem* concerned Husserl's philosophical category of "the natural world," and in Husserl's phenomenology at that time, this was a reference to the world that was 'naturally' given before human analysis rendered everything into words, concepts, labels, and constructed human categories and narratives; Patočka often called it the 'naïve' world, and stated that one aim of his philosophy was to get beyond this naiveté by "elucidating the manner in which man exists in and relates to his world—at what fundamental levels and in what acts of subjectivity

---

140 One example, among many, calling for a paradigm shift away from anthropocentrism using philosophy, in a journal dedicated to this effort: F. Ferrando. "The Party of the Anthropocene: Post-humanism, Environmentalism and the Post-anthropocentric Paradigm Shift." *Rel.: Beyond Anthropocentrism* 4 (2016): 159. See also: E. Shoreman-Ouimet and Helen Kopnina. *Culture and Conservation: Beyond Anthropocentrism* (Routledge, 2015).

141 Kohák, "Human Rights and Nature's Rightness," in R. Cohen and A. Tauber, eds., *Philosophies of Nature: The Human Dimension. In Celebration of Erazim Kohák* (Dordrecht: Kluwer Academic Publishers, 1998). The other essays in this volume are also relevant to this point.

142 The term 'anthropocene' now designates an era where nothing is beyond human reach and manipulation, so in this frame it is a totality, and those humans who have power to control the world (other people, animals, plants, waterways, oceans, forests, atmosphere, etc.) do in some sense enslave all those without the power to defend themselves.

this relationship is established."[143] To establish a "relationship" with the world through "acts of subjectivity" was part of an effort to follow up with Husserl's concern about whether or not preconceptions and the given categories of thinking in the human mind can (or cannot) be set aside in order to see the world objectively and transcendentally in a scientific way. Yet saying that the world can be established through "acts of subjectivity" might also be another way to say that one's sense of the world cannot be established solely through acts of objectivity, and that preconceptions (such as myths) can never be fully transcended.[144] The "natural world" to the modern post-scientific gaze, at least on this logic, *has to be* a world constructed out of human categories, with an architecture that was built on preconceptions and cultural narratives. Patočka could see how one's architecture of preconceptions about nature could lead to actions of domination or stewardship, thoughts of reverence or exploitation, and relationships of utility, hatred, or love. While the 'forces' of modernity had not been kind to nature, he still saw choices, possibilities, and problematicity; prior conceptions of the world mattered for making all choices, including political choices, because it was possible to question those conceptions through a certain form of philosophy, politics and history, what Patočka called *polemos*.

In making the choice to become an environmental activist, this account would suggest that the questions of existential recognition, intersubjectivity, and the metaphysics of historicity can be interlinked through the problem of sustainability, but in a double sense: this is 'sustainability' in the sense of sustaining political motivation to campaign for the 'sustainability' of life on earth. Whatever happens, this campaign will need to go on, quite literally, forever. Activist campaigns of any sort cannot be sustained forever (or even for a shorter, prolonged time) on merely instrumental ends; they must also have intrinsic value that binds together members of a community with one another through the spirit

---

143 Patočka, *NWPP*, 53.
144 What 'the subject,' 'subjectivity,' and 'intersubjectivity' mean for Patočka in comparison to other philosophers of phenomenology is an ongoing scholarly conversation that discusses his view as being one of 'asubjective phenomenology' or anti-subjectivist phenomenology. This is a technical discussion showing how Patočka does not quite fit into traditional philosophical categories and concepts of subjectivity, and how he avoids a completely subjectivist stance by insisting that the self is constituted through interaction with the other in a given world. How this contrasts with other views in phenomenology is more fully elaborated here: R. Barbaras, *Jan Patočka: Phenomenologies asubjective et existence* (Paris: Association Culturelle Mimesis, 2007) and James Mensch, *Patočka's Asubjective Phenomenology: Toward a New Concept of Human Rights* (Würzburg: Königshausen und Neumann, 2016). See also note above, 116.

of forward motion. Common moral and normative commitments that go beyond instrumental objectives and provide respective communities with forms of recognition are key to sustaining causes and campaigns over decades and generations.

The economic logic of individualism may yet prevail, and the planet and capitalism may go towards destruction with Weber's last ton of fossilized coal, but part of the 'success' of several decades of environmental activism lies within its ability to be sustainable in-and-of-itself, harnessing the intrinsic value of all life, aiming itself toward rewriting the way humans think about the natural world for future generations and future histories, making the dissidence itself intrinsically valuable and therefore probably perpetual. This is a type of politics that is not based on the 'objectivity' of measurements and confirmed positivist outcomes, and it is largely aimed toward a future that no single person alive today will ever actually glimpse or measure. It requires faith and trust that history is indeed calling from the future, and also requires acting as if, in this moment of history, we can act for action's sake, and dissent for dissent's sake, therein overcoming nihilism, annihilation, or both. In T. S. Eliot's words: "So Krishna, as when he admonished Arjuna/ On the field of battle./ Not fare well,/But fare forward, voyagers."[145] We are not faring well, but we can surely fare forward.

If the politics of existential recognition within environmental activism can rearrange the relationship between objectivity and subjectivity in such a way to create a community more capable of sustained political activism that fares forward, it depends in this case on the assumption that the natural world is as much a philosophical, narrative, and mythological problem as it is a scientific and numeric problem; it is not one or the other, but it is both. When Patočka evokes the natural world as a philosophical problem alongside the scientific problem of knowing the world, one can see environmental activism as a response to nihilism—and in particular, the sort of nihilism created by the market, its rationality, and how the market transforms human beings into cogs in the machines of production and consumption who are incapable of understanding each other. A nihilistic view would hold that Weber's iron cage will only get stronger until the last ton of fossilized coal is burnt, and then the end of the world will surely come about, minimally the end of the world

---

145 T. S. Eliot, *Four Quartets*. In: T. S. Eliot, *Collected Poems 1909–1962* (New York: Harcourt, Brace & World, 1970) 195, 197.

of living *like this*, but also potentially the end of living at all, including mass extinctions, the shortening of life spans through the health-related impacts of burning fossil fuels, and if bees die off, the potential loss of food sources on which we survive. To be an environmental activist, however, is to say 'no' to letting the iron cage win, it is to say 'no' to nihilism, to say 'yes' to human life shared with the life of other living beings, including the poor and marginalized in countries other than our own, as well as the plants and animals with whom we *should* live a mutually dependent and integrated life. It is to recognize that both hatred and love will flow from this stance.

The 'meaning' of the natural world has changed as climate change science has advanced and activism has continued, and the climate change debate will continue to be a debate over changing meanings.[146] Facts can exist independently of meanings, and information can float about unconnected from truth, but facts have to *mean something* to *someone* in order for action to occur. Patočka gives us the insight that existential meaning must precede movement in the realm of human political action, creating a space where meanings are repeatedly contested by both new myths and new truths. He sees the phenomenology of meaning as the retreating horizon of modernity, and the problem of meaning as the future horizon of his own work that was cut short by his own political action and his own death.[147] Activists that carry on in the face of certain failure plumb the existential terrain of politics, but also a different notion of truth and meaning. If "human life in all its forms is a life of truth, admittedly finite, but engaging our responsibility no less rigorously," as Patočka asks, then "does not *finite* truth, thoroughly distinct from truth *relative* to something other than itself, mean an everyday struggle against the erring, illusions, and obduracies which go along with it, and in which man attempts to relinquish himself?"[148]

---

146 If changing language is an indication of changing meanings, the number of new words and phrases coined within the environmental movement during the last several decades has been given as one testament of this. See: Martinez-Alier et. al. "Between Activism and Science: Grassroots Concepts for Sustainability Coined by Environmental Justice Organizations." *Journal of Political Ecology* 21: 19–60.

147 See prior discussion of the role of meaning in Patočka's late work, and especially in Učník, *The Crisis of Meaning and the Life-world* (2016) and the chapter on Patočka.

148 Patočka, *NWPP*, 190.

Epilogue: Political Distress and Underground Books

Czech novelist Bohumil Hrabal wrote a story about a worker in a total-itarian state who was responsible for destroying printed materials no longer allowed to exist. In *Too Loud a Solitude*, the worker labors by him-self in a dark basement, where truckloads of books and papers marked for destruction are offloaded. The worker is then responsible for put-ting them into a compression machine to create pallets that are later hauled away and put into an incinerator. Drinking beer from morning until night, instead of shoveling the printed materials quickly into the hydraulic press, he endeavors to do two things: to save the few select books he can (his apartment is entirely filled with books and there is almost no longer any place to sleep), and for those he cannot save, he tries to make sure the books are shown a magnanimous and dignified death. He creates pallets of installation art with the soon-to-be destroyed books, newspapers and reproductions of disallowed art; some pallets are thematic, others arranged by genre. From scraps of books and papers slated for destruction, he creates new art, with the knowledge that what he makes will soon be incinerated.[1]

Apart from his boss, some ex-girlfriends, and another group of work-ers at the new incineration factory he visits later in the story, the only other character in the story is a philosophy professor from the Comenius archives. This professor comes to the worker's cellar looking for the the-atre reviews, but also asking after whatever other special finds the worker

---

1 Bohumil Hrabal, *Too Loud a Solitude*, trans. Michael Henry Heim, Harvest in Translation (Bos-ton: Houghton Mifflin Harcourt, 1992). Kindle.

has saved for him, mostly philosophy books. After every question and exchange, the professor gives the worker a continuous stream of tips, dropping ten crown notes his way, ostensibly for his beer supply and in exchange for the books. It is implied that the professor is one of the few who understands why the protagonist does not just incinerate the books, but also why he makes works of art no one will ever see and why the effort is nonetheless worthwhile.

At the time depicted in the story (before 1989), there would have been only one well-known philosophy professor in Prague who worked at the Comenius archives as his 'day job,' while at night writing and leading philosophy seminars, also underground, like the worker, also in an attempt to artistically repackage the history of Western philosophy, also living with the likelihood that no one would ever see his work if the political situation worsened. Patočka is not named in the story by Hrabal; the story is a work of fiction. Patočka did, however, spend many years working at the Comenius archives, and of course had strong sympathies with those in the underground who were trying to save the intellectual life of their country, even when that effort seemed hopeless and it looked as if all the books might be destroyed anyway. In the story, the philosophy professor comes by regularly, beginning conversations about books that might inspire a new outlook on the bleakness of the present situation, even if everything seems to be on the verge of death; he also generously finances the drinking fund that keeps this all going. Hrabal's character seems like a humble tribute to Patočka, an unnamed symbolic and indirect reference. To contemplate this uncertain literary allusion, therefore, is to imagine Patočka there in Hrabal's story, giving tips to those in the underground who are lonely, alienated, and frustrated by the political distress of their day, but who nonetheless love their books.

In Plato's *Apology*, after Socrates is condemned to death, he asks those in attendance at the trial to look after his sons when he dies: "reprove them, as I have reproved you, for not caring about that for which they ought to care, and thinking that they are something when they are really nothing. And if you do this, my sons and I will have received justice at your hands."[2] If Socrates had been able to live longer, he would have taught his sons to live in humility, to understand that they are "nothing,"

---

2 Plato, *Apology*, 42a. Translation B. Jowett (http://classics.mit.edu/Plato/apology.html). See also the translation of Thomas West: "And if they are reputed to be something when they are nothing, reproach them just as I did you: tell them that they do not care for the things they should, and that they suppose they are something when they are worth nothing. And if you do

and to care for what ought to be cared for. If Patočka's death has been called Socratic in form, then part of the parallel is also in content: even though he died, he nonetheless left behind wisdom about how to humbly acknowledge the limits of human existence while at the same time providing an imperative to care for that which ought to be cared for, that which makes existence meaningful. Like the worker in the story, books (and the history of philosophy, art and culture they represent) ought to be cared for, even when it seems certain the past will be destroyed by the zealots of the present, and even when, for the worker, 'care' means only a magnanimous burial. On Socrates' account, 'care' would amount to a concern about justice, where justice requires a certain kind of politics, and where politics is a matter of caring for the balance between the waring elements of the soul.

In Hrabal's story, the underground worker loses his sense of purpose and meaning once he comes to the realization he will be replaced by automatic machines and younger, more efficient systems of paper destruction. After he has been let go from his job because his method is not sufficiently rational, efficient, and systematic, he returns late one night to the underground paper press, packages himself up with selections of symbolically-appropriate books, climbs in, and turns on the compressor with these thoughts in his head:

> I will follow Seneca, I will follow Socrates, and here, in my press, in my cellar, choose my own fall, which is ascension, and even as the walls press my legs up to my chin and beyond, I refuse to be driven from my Paradise, I am in my cellar and no one can turn me out, no one can dismiss me. A corner of the book is lodged under a rib, I groan, fated to leave the ultimate truth on a rack of my own making, folded in upon myself like a child's pocket knife..."[3]

Death by compression arises from the overall pressure of the entire political-economic-cultural situation, all of which together squeezes life away and brings him to believe that the only path for self-created meaning, the only path for choice, is to be the agent of his own death. The situation has brought him to believe that choosing one's own fall is to turn a fall

---

these things, we will have been treated justly by you, both I myself and my sons." *Four Texts on Socrates*, (Cornell: Cornell University Press, 1998) 97.

3   Bohumil Hrabal, *Too Loud a Solitude*, trans. Michael Henry Heim, Harvest in Translation (Boston: Houghton Mifflin Harcourt, 1992), 95. Kindle.

into an ascension, to remain in the paradise of his books and his artwork through his own agency. Self-inflicted violence lets him leave behind the ultimate truth of his own myth that he himself made; it is a recovery of lost agency at the same time as it requires believing that 'I am really nothing,' and therefore the heir of, the son of, a Socratic understanding of the world.[4]

The hopelessness, futility, and inanity of many dissident endeavors, as well as the violence it will bring upon one's body and soul, is already articulated in Plato's account of Socrates and the cave. As argued at the outset of this book, many modern acts of political self-sacrifice will structurally and symbolically retell the story of Socrates and the Platonic cave. The line between suicide and self-sacrifice has been explored differently in prior chapters, and turning to Hrabal here is not meant to make an assertion about which conceptual framework (Havel, Bonhoeffer, Gandhi, or Patočka) is more (or less) accurate or morally excusable. Nor is this to say that reading Patočka's work will necessarily inspire such actions. To read his work, however, and to saturate oneself in his ideas and concepts, is to experience Patočka dropping ten crown notes as donations to a certain different kind of drinking supply: if it is not the literal alcoholic flow, then by the end of his life, Patočka assumed his readers were thirsty for answers to the question of how to confront political distress and the loss of meaning in modern life. He told them to open philosophy books. This would also *therefore* save philosophy books from destruction, because reading books is to incorporate a book in one's own memory and life, giving the book itself continued life. Philosophy is saved when it is lived, that is, lived by being practiced within a human life and courageously kept in motion through new eras and challenges. At the same time, philosophy books might help to address a small piece of one's own distress. Perhaps the one parallel with actual alcoholic drink, to arbitrarily extend the metaphor, is the modicum of courage that the supply of certain philosophy can bring: when it is drunk, even and especially in excess, somehow dissident political action, however offensive to "the authorities," might become more possible, and so then one can author oneself away from authority and into "history."

Had Patočka lived longer and been able to turn towards writing a philosophical phenomenology of meaning—the project he hinted at

---

4   Patočka's own son was quite involved politically, the extent of which as has been revealed by the recent publication of the secret police files kept on Patočka himself. See: Petr Blazek, ed., *"Kéž je to všecko ku prospěchu obce!" - Jan Patočka v Statni Bezpecnosti* (Praha: Academia, 2017).

in his last essay about Dostoevsky[5]—philosophy might not have been the only element of such a work, even if it would have had to have been a central component of a multi-layered, three-dimensional, existentially heavy, and artistically composed pallet representing a cellar-bound life. In a phenomenology of meaning, Patočka might have attempted to narrate his composed pallet as an antidote to the kind of nihilism suffered by Hrabal's protagonist. It is implied that had Hrabal's worker been allowed to continue doing the work he had been doing, and had he not been cut off from this artistic endeavor of composing hopelessly beautiful pallets, he would not have entirely lost hope. However pointless and inane his job might have seemed, the story is about losing the ground of meaning by losing the ground beneath one's ability to do one's own work, whatever that might be. Dissidents forced into the underground and out of a world where they receive recognition from the larger society and culture for their work, might instead turn to 'solidarity of the shaken' as a possible form of human connection. In Hrabal's story, this was the bond between the philosopher and the worker: they could see across a class divide, across age, across educational levels, and found the solidarity of 'those who understand' through the beauty, shaken-ness, and fragility of the human relationship to books.

5   Patočka, "On Masaryk's Philosophy of Religion," translated by Jiří Rothbauer et al. in L. Hagedorn and J. Dodd, eds., *Religion, War and the Crisis of Modernity: A Special Issue Dedicated to the Philosophy of Jan Patočka*, The New Yearbook of Phenomenology and Phenomenological Philosophy XIV (New York: Routledge: 2015), 95–135.

Bibliography

Abbey, E. *Monkey Wrench Gang*. New York: Harper Perennial, 2006.

Ackerman, P. and DuVall, J. *A Force More Powerful: A Century of Nonviolent Conflict*. New York: St. Martin's Press, 2000.

Adorno, T. and Horkheimer, M. *Dialectic of Enlightenment*. Edited by G.S. Noerr. Translated by Jephcott. Stanford: Stanford University Press, 2002.

Allen, D. *The Philosophy of Mahatma Gandhi for the Twenty-First Century*. Lanham: Lexington Books, 2008.

Alexander, S. "Planned Economic Contraction: The Emerging Case for Degrowth." *Environmental Politics* 21, no. 3 (2012): 349–368.

Arato, A. *Civil Society, Constitution, and Legitimacy*. Landam: Rowman and Littlefield, 2000.

Arendt, H. *Between Past and Future*. New York: Penguin Books, 1993.

Arendt, H. *Crises of the Republic*. New York: Harcourt Brace Jovanovich, 1969.

Arendt, H. *The Human Condition*. Chicago: University of Chicago Press, 1958.

Arendt, H. *On Revolution*. New York: Viking Press, 1963.

Arendt, H. *On Violence*. New York: Harcourt Brace & World, 1969.

Arendt, H. *Origins of Totalitarianism*. New York: Harvest Book, 1973.

Aristotle. *The Complete Works of Aristotle,* The Revised Oxford Translation. Edited by Jonathan Barnes. Princeton: Princeton University Press, 1984.

Armiero, M. & Sedrez, L. *A History of Environmentalism: Local Struggles, Global Histories*. London: New York: Bloomsbury Academic, 2014.

Attenborough, Richard, dir. *Gandhi*. 1982; New Dehli, India: Columbia Pictures. DVD.

Augustine of Hippo, *City of God*. Peabody, Mass.: Hendrickson Publishers, 2009.

Ayres, R. *Turning Point: End of the Growth Paradigm*. New York: Routledge, 2014.

Ballantyne, T., & Burton, A. *Bodies in Contact: Rethinking Colonial Encounters in World History*. Durham: Duke University Press, 2005.

Barbaras, R. *Jan Patočka: Phenomenologies asubjective et existence*. Paris: Association Culturelle Mimesis, 2007.

Barbaras, R. *Le mouvement de l'existence: Études sur la phenoménologie de Jan Patočka*. Chatou: Les Éditions de la Transparence, 2007.

Barbaras, R. *L'ouverture du monde: Lecture de Jan Patočka*. Chatou: Les Editions de La Transparence, 2011.

Barnett, V.J. *Theologian of Resistance: The Life and Thought of Dietrich Bonhoeffer*. New York: Fortress Press, 2016.

Bartlett, R. V., and W. F. Baber, *Consensus and Global Environment Governance: Deliberative Democracy in Nature's Regime.* Cambridge, MA: The MIT Press, 2015.

Bauman, Z. *Modernity and the Holocaust.* Ithaca, NY: Cornell University Press, 1989.

Bažant, J. and N. Baržantova and F. Starn, eds., *The Czech Reader.* Durham, NC: Duke University Press, 2010.

Benhabib, S. "The Strange Silence of Political Theory: Response." *Political Theory* 23, no. 4 (1995).

Bergen, D. L. *Twisted Cross: The German Christians.* Chapel Hill: University of North Carolina Press, 1996

Berkowitz, R., J. Katz and T. Keenan, *Thinking in Dark Times: Hannah Arendt on Ethics and Politics.* New York: Fordham University Press, 2010.

Berman, S. "Civil Society and the Collapse of the Weimar Republic," *World Politics* 49, no. 3 (April 1997): 401–429.

Bernard, M. "Patočka and Plato: The Idea of a Politics of the Soul." *Revue de métaphysique et de morale* 3 (2017): 357–370.

Bernard, M. *Patočka et l'unité polémique du monde.* Louvain-La-Neuve: Peeters, 2016.

Bicker, A, R. Ellen, and P. Parkes. *Indigenous Environmental Knowledge and its Transformations: Critical Anthropological Perspectives.* London: Routledge, 2003.

Biemel, W. *Die Welt des Menschen, die Welt der Philosophie: Festschrift für Jan Patočka.* Haag: M. Nijhoff, 1976.

Blazek, P. editor, *"Kéž je to všecko ku prospěchu obce!" - Jan Patočka v. Statni Bezpecnosti.* Prague: Academia, 2017.

Blecha, I. *Jan Patočka a ohlas fenomenologie v ceske filosofii.* Olomouc: Univerzita Palackeho, 1995.

Bolton, J. *Worlds of Dissent: Charter 77, The Plastic People of the Universe, and Czech Culture under Communism.* Cambridge, MA: Harvard University Press, 2012.

Bonhoeffer, D. *The Complete Dietrich Bonhoeffer Works.* Vol. 6, *Ethics.* New York: Fortress Press, 2005.

Bonhoeffer, D. *The Complete Dietrich Bonhoeffer Works.* Vol. 8, *Letters and Papers From Prison.* New York: Fortress Press, 2010.

Bonhoeffer, D. *The Complete Dietrich Bonhoeffer Works.* Vol. 16, *Conspiracy and Imprisonment 1940–1945.* New York: Fortress Press, 2006.

Bonhoeffer, D. *Ethics.* Edited by E. Bethge; Translated by N.H. Smith. New York: Macmillan, 1955.

Bonhoeffer, D. *Letters and Papers from Prison: The Enlarged Edition.* Edited by E. Bethge. Translated by R. Fuller and F. Clark. New York: Touchstone, 1997.

Bonhoeffer, D. *Sanctorum Communio (The Communion of Saints).* New York: Harper and Row, 1963.

Bozóki, A. "Preparing for the Revolution: Hungarian Dissident Intellectuals before 1989." *Baltic Worlds* 2, no. 1 (2009): 41–46.

Bradatan, C. *Philosophy, Society and the Cunning of History in Eastern Europe.* London: Routledge, 2012.

Bradatan, C., and A Serguei. *Dying for Ideas: the Dangerous Lives of Philosophers.* New York: Bloomsbury, 2015.

Bradatan, C., and A. Serguei, *In Marx's Shadow: Knowledge, Power and Intellectuals in Eastern Europe and Russia.* Lanham: Lexington Books, 2010.

Brinton, A. "Association and Recognition in Authoritarian Societies: A Theoretical Beginning." *European Journal of Political Theory* 11, no. 3 (2012): 324–347.

Brinton, A. *Philosophy and Dissidence in Cold War Europe.* London: Palgrave-MacMillan, 2016.

Brinton, A. "Vaclav Havel's Civil Society," in *Key Concepts in Václav Havel's Core Vocabulary: Analyses and Implications*. David Danaher and Kieran Williams, eds., Prague: Karolinum Press, Forthcoming.

Brook, D. "Environmental genocide: Native Americans and Toxic Waste." *American Journal of Economics and Sociology* 57, no. 1 (1998): 105–113.

Bugajski, J., and M. Pollack, *East European Fault Lines: Dissent, Opposition, and Social Activism*. Boulder: Westview Press, 1989.

Butler, J. *Notes Toward a Performative Theory of Assembly*. Cambridge MA: Harvard University Press, 2015.

Cajthaml, M. *Europe and the Care of the Soul. Jan Patočka's Conception of the Spiritual Foundations of Europe*. Nordhausen: Verlag Traugott Bautz, 2014.

Camus, A. *The Myth of Sisyphus and Other Essays*. Translated by J. O'Brien. New York: Vintage International, 1991.

Camus, A. *The Rebel*. Translated by A. Bower. New York: Vintage, 1956.

Čapek, J. "Intersubjectivity and Self-awareness in Husserl and Patočka." *The Journal of Speculative Philosophy* 33, no. 3 (2019): 512–526.

Čapek, J. "Le devoir de l'homme envers lui-même." *Tumultes* 1 (2009): 351–370.

Čapek, J. "Oneself through Another: Ricœur and Patočka on Husserl's Fifth Cartesian Meditation." *Meta: Research in Hermeneutics, Phenomenology, and Practical Philosophy* Vol. IX, No. 2, December 2017: 387–415.

Carson, R. *Silent Spring*. New York: Houghton Mifflin Harcourt, 2002.

Chernus, I. *Nuclear Madness: Religion and the Psychology of the Nuclear Age*. New York: SUNY Press, 1991.

Chvatík, I. "The Responsibility of the 'Shaken.'" In *Jan Patočka and the Heritage of Phenomenology: Centenary Papers*. Dordrecht: Springer, 2011: 263–279.

Chvatík, I. "Solidarity of the Shaken." *Telos* 94 (1993): 163–166.

Chvatík, I., and Abrams, E. eds. *Jan Patočka and the Heritage of Phenomenology:* New York: Springer, 2010.

Chvatík, I., L. Ucnik, and A. Williams, *'Jan Patočka's Care for the Soul' in the 'Nihilistic' World*. Proceedings of the 41st Annual Meeting of the Husserl Circle, 2010.

Chvatík, I., L. Ucnik, and A. Williams, *The Phenomenological Critique of Mathematisation and the Question of Responsibility: Formalisation and the Life-World*. New York: Springer, 2014.

Ciocan, C. ed. *Jan Patočka and the European Heritage*. Special issue, *Studia Phenomenologica. Romanian Journal for Phenomenology* VII (2007).

Cohen, J. L., and A. Arato, *Civil Society and Political Theory*. Cambridge, MA: MIT Press, 1992.

Cohen, R. and A. Tauber, eds., *Philosophies of Nature: The Human Dimension. In Celebration of Erazim Kohák*. Dordrecht: Kluwer Academic Publishers, 1988.

Collard, A. and J. Contrucci. *Rape of the Wild: Man's Violence against Animals and the Earth*. Indiana University Press, 1989

Connolly, W. E. *The Augustinian Imperative: A Reflection on the Politics of Morality*. New York: Sage Publications, 1993.

Connolly, W. E. *The Fragility of Things: Self-organizing Processes, Neoliberal Fantasies, and Democratic Activism*. Durham: Duke University Press, 2013.

Connolly, W. E. *A World of Becoming*. Durham: Duke University Press, 2011.

Conradie, E.M. *Christianity and Earthkeeping: In Search of an Inspiring Vision*. Vol. 16. Stellennosch: African Sun MeDIA, 2011.

Cook, J. and Dana Nuccitelli, Sarah A. Green, Mark Richardson, Bärbel Winkler, Rob Painting, Robert Way, Peter Jacobs, and Andrew Skuce. "Quantifying the Consensus on Anthropogenic Global Warming in the Scientific Literature." *Environmental Research Letters* 8, no. 2 (2013): 024024.

Cook, M. "Christian Apocalypticism and Weapons of Mass Destruction," in S. Hashmi and S. Lee, eds., *Ethics and Weapons of Mass Destruction: Religious and Secular Perspectives.* Cambridge: Cambridge University Press, 2004.

Crépon, M. *The Thought of Death and the Memory of War.* Translated by M. Loriaux. Minneapolis: University of Minnesota Press, 2013.

Cripps, E. *Climate Change and the Moral Agent: Individual Duties in an Interdependent World.* Oxford: Oxford University Press, 2013.

Cronin, M. "Crossing the Elbe or Why We Need a New Culture of Dissidence." *European Journal of English Studies* 17, no. 2 (2013): 136–148.

Dahrendorf, R. *Reflections on the Revolution in Europe.* New York: Random House, 1990.

Dalton, D. *Mahatma Gandhi: Nonviolent Power in Action.* New York. Columbia University Press, 1993.

Danaher, D. *Reading Václav Havel.* Toronto: University of Toronto Press, 2015.

Davis, S. H. and A. Wali. *Indigenous Views of Land and the Environment.* Vol. 188. Washington, DC: World Bank, 1993.

Declève, H. *Profils de Jan Patočka: hommages et documents.* Bruxelles: Publications des Facultés universitaires Saint-Louis, 1992.

Della Porta, D. and M. Diani, eds. *The Oxford Handbook of Social Movements.* Oxford: Oxford University Press, 2015.

Dei, G. J., B. L. Hall, and D. G. Rosenberg. *Indigenous Knowledges in Global Contexts: Multiple Readings of Our World.* University of Toronto Press, 2000.

Derrida, J. *The Gift of Death.* Translated by D. Willis. Chicago: University of Chicago Press, 1995.

Devji, F. *The Impossible Indian: Gandhi and the Temptation of Violence.* Cambridge: Harvard University Press, 2012.

De Warren, N. "He Who Saw the Deep: The Epic of Gilgamesh in Patočka's Philosophy of History." (2016): 135–159.

De Warren, N. "Homecoming. Jan Patočka's Reflections on the First World War," ed. M. Staudigl *Phenomenologies of Violence,* Chapt. 10, 207–243. Leiden: Brill, 2014.

Đilas, M. *The New Class: An Analysis of the Communist System.* New York: Frederick A. Praeger, 1957.

Dodd, J. *Crisis and Reflection: An Essay on Husserl's Crisis of the European Sciences.* Dordrecht: Kluwer Academic Publishers, 2004.

Dodd, J. "Jan Patočka's Philosophical Legacy." *The Oxford Handbook of the History of Phenomenology* (2018): 396.

Dodd, J. *Violence and Phenomenology.* London: Routledge, 2009.

Drakulić, S. *How We Survived Communism and Even Laughed.* New York: Harper Collins, 1993.

Drummond, J. J., & Lester E. E. *Phenomenological Approaches to Moral Philosophy: A Handbook.* Dordrecht and Boston: Kluwer Academic Publishers, 2002.

Dubček, A. *Hope Dies Last: Autobiography of Alexander Dubček.* Translated by J. Hochman. New York: Kodansha International, 1993.

Duicu, D. *Phénoménologie du mouvement: Patočka et l'héritage de la physique aristotélicienne.* Paris: Hermann, 2014.

Einstein, A. "The Russell-Einstein Manifesto." [1955] In *Scientists in the Quest for Peace. A History of the Pugwash Conferences.* Cambridge, MA: The MIT Press, 1972. 137–140. Also accessed here: http://pugwash.org/1955/07/09/statement-manifesto/

Eliot, T. S. *Collected Poems 1909–1962.* New York: Harcourt, Brace & World, 1970.

Else, J. *The Day After Trinity: J. Robert Oppenheimer and the Atomic Bomb*. Pyramid Films, 1981.

Erikson, E. *Gandhi's Truth: On the Origins of Militant Nonviolence*. New York: Norton & Co., 1993.

Erikson, R. *Complicity in the Holocaust: Churches and Universities in Nazi Germany*. Cambridge: Cambridge University Press, 2012.

Ervine, K. "The Politics and Practice of Carbon Offsetting: Silencing Dissent." *New Political Science* 34, no. 1 (2012): 1–20.

Evink, E. "Horizons and Others: Gadamer, Levinas, Patočka." *American Catholic Philosophical Quarterly* 84.4 (2010): 727–46.

Evink, E. "Surrender and Subjectivity: Merleau-Ponty and Patočka on Intersubjectivity," *Meta: Research in Hermeneutics. Phenomenology and Practical Philosophy*, Vol. I (2013): 13–28.

Fackenheim, E.L. *Metaphysics and Historicity*. Milwaukee: Marquette University Press, 1961.

Falk, B. J. *The Dilemmas of Dissidence in East-Central Europe*. Budapest: Central European University Press, 2003.

Falk, B. J. "Resistance and Dissent in Central and Eastern Europe: An Emerging Historiography." *East European Politics and Societies*, Vol. 25 (2011): 318.

Falkner, R. "The Paris Agreement and the New Logic of International Climate Politics." *International Affairs* 92, no. 5 (2016): 1107–1125.

Fanon, F. *The Wretched of the Earth*. Translated by R. Philcox. New York: Grove Press, 2005.

Fedorowicz, J. "Polish Independent Culture in the Era of Glasnost." *Uncaptive Minds* 1, no. 2 (1988).

Fehér, F., A.Heller and G. Markus. *Dictatorship Over Needs*. Oxford: Basil Blackwell, 1983.

Feil, E. *Glauben lernen in einer Kirche für andere: der Beitrag Dietrich Bonhoeffers zum Christsein in der Deutschen Demokratischen Republik*. Gütersloh: Chr. Kaiser, Gütersloher Verlagshaus, 1993.

Ferrando, F. "The Party of the Anthropocene: Post-humanism, Environmentalism and the Post-anthropocentric Paradigm Shift." *Rel.: Beyond Anthropocentrism* 4 (2016): 159–174.

Findlay, E. F. *Caring for the Soul in the Postmodern Age: Politics and Phenomenology in the Thought of Jan Patočka*. Albany, NY: State University of New York Press, 2002.

Fink, E., J. Patočka, M. Heitz and B. Nessler. *Eugen Fink und Jan Patočka. Briefe und Dokumente 1933–1977*. München: Karl Alber, 1999.

Fitzgerald, A. and L. Kalof, eds., *The Animals Reader: The Essential Classic and Contemporary Writings*. Oxford: Berg, 2007.

Forti, S., and Hanafi, Z. *The New Demons: Rethinking Power and Evil Today*. Stanford: Stanford University Press, 2014.

Foucault, M. *Discipline and Punish: The Birth of the Prison*. Translated by A. Sheridan. New York: Vintage Books, 1995.

Francis, P. *Laudato si: On care for our common home*. Vatican: Our Sunday Visitor, 2015. https://w2.vatican.va/content/francesco/en/encyclicals/documents/papa-francesco _20150524_enciclica-laudato-si.html

Fraser, N. "Rethinking Recognition." *New Left Review* 3 (2000): 107–120.

Fraser, N., and A. Honneth. *Redistribution or Recognition? A political-philosophical dialogue*. London: Verso, 2003.

Fried, G. *Heidegger's Polemos: From Being to Politics*. New Haven: Yale University Press, 2000.

Fromm, E. *On Disobedience, Or Why Freedom Means Saying 'No' to Power*. New York: Harper Perennial, 2010.

Frogneux, N. *Jan Patočka. Liberté, existence et monde commun.* Argenteuil: Le Cercle Herméneutique, 2012.

Gadamer, H. *Truth and Method.* Translated by J. Weinsheimer and D. Marshall. New York: Continuum, 2002.

Gan, B. *Violence and Nonviolence: An Introduction.* London: Rowman and Littlefield, 2013.

Gandhi, M.K. *The Collected Works of Mahatma Gandhi.* 100 vols. Delhi: Publication Division, Ministry of Information and Broadcasting, Government of India, 1958–1994. Accessed online: https://www.gandhiheritageportal.org/the-collected -works-of-mahatma-gandhi.

Gandhi, M.K. *From Yervada Mandir: Ashram Observances.* Translated by Valji Govindji Desai. Ahmedabad: Jinanji Desai, 1991.

Gandhi, M. K. *Gandhi: An Autobiography. The Story of My Experiments with Truth.* Boston: Beacon Press, 1993.

Gandhi, M. K. *Non-Violent Resistance (Satyagraha).* New York: Dover, 2012.

Gandhi, M. K. *Satyagraha in South Africa.* Madras: S. Ganesan, 1928.

Gandhi, M. K. *Selected Works of Mahatma Gandhi Volume Five: Voice of Truth.* Ahmedabad: Navajivan Publishing House, 1969.

Ganguly, D., and J. Docker, *Rethinking Gandhi and Nonviolent Relationality: Global Perspectives.* London: Routledge, 2007.

Garton Ash, T., and A. Roberts. *Civil Resistance and Power Politics: The Experience of Nonviolent Action from Gandhi to the Present.* Oxford: Oxford University Press, 2009.

Garton Ash, T. *The File.* New York: Random House, 1997.

Garton Ash, T. *The Magic Lantern.* New York: Vintage Books, 1993.

Gasché, R. *Europe, or The Infinite Task: A Study of a Philosophical Concept.* Stanford: Stanford University Press, 2009.

Gasché, R. "Patočka on Europe in the Aftermath of Europe." *European Journal of Social Theory* 21, no. 3 (2018): 391–406.

Gellner, E. *Conditions of Liberty: Civil Society and its Rivals.* New York: Penguin, 1994.

Geremek, B. "Civil Society Then and Now." *Journal of Democracy* 3, no. 2 (1992): 3–12.

Geremek, B. *The Idea of a Civil Society.* Durham: National Humanities Center, 1992.

Germain, R. and M. Kenny, *The Idea of Global Civil Society: Politics and Ethics in a Globalizing Era.* New York: Routledge, 2005.

Gides, D. *Pacifism, Just War and Tyrannicide: Bonhoeffer's Church-World Theology and his Changing Forms of Political Thinking and Involvement.* Eugene: Pickwick Publications, 2011.

Glass, P., and C. DeJong, *Satyagraha Libretto.* New York: Tanam Press, 1983.

Global Witness Report. "Enemies of the State? How Governments and Businesses Silence Land and Environmental Defenders." July 30, 2019. Viewed January 10, 2020. https://www.globalwitness.org/en/campaigns/environmental-activists/enemies-state/.

Godrej, F. "Ascetics, Warriors, and a Gandhian Ecological Citizenship," *Political Theory* 40, no. 4 (August 2012): 437–465.

Godrej, F. "Nonviolence and Gandhi's Truth: A Method for Moral and Political Arbitration," *The Review of Politics* 68, No. 2 (Spring, 2006): 287–317.

Goetz-Stankiewicz, M. *Goodbye, Samizdat. Twenty Years of Czechoslovak Underground Writing.* Evanston: Northwestern University Press, 1992.

Goetz-Stankiewicz, M. and P. Carey, *Critical Essays on Václav Havel.* New York: G.K. Hall and Co., 1999.

Goodin, David K. "Schweitzer Reconsidered: The Applicability of Reverence for Life as Environmental Philosophy." *Environmental Ethics* 29, no. 4 (2007): 403–421.

Gottlieb, R. *This Sacred Earth: Religion, Nature, Environment.* New York: Routledge, 2004.

Green, C. *Bonhoeffer: A Theology of Sociality*. Grand Rapids: Eerdmans Publishing Company, 1999.

Green, C. and G. Carter, *Interpreting Bonhoeffer: Historical Perspectives, Emerging Issues*. Minneapolis: Fortress Press, 2013.

Gregor, B. and J. Zimmerman, *Bonhoeffer and Continental Thought: Cruciform Philosophy*. Indianapolis: Indiana University Press, 2009.

Grim, J. ed. *Indigenous Traditions and Ecology*. Cambridge, MA: Harvard University Press, 2001.

Gubser, M. *The Far Reaches: Phenomenology, Ethics and Social Renewal in Central Europe*. Stanford: Stanford University Press, 2014.

Gudmarsdottir, S. "Rapes of Earth and Grapes of Wrath: Steinbeck, Ecofeminism and the Metaphor of Rape." *Feminist Theology*, 18(2), (2010): 206–222.

Guénoun, D. *About Europe: Philosophical Hypotheses*. Translated by C. Irizarry. Stanford: Stanford University Press, 2013.

Guenther, L. *Solitary Confinement: Social Death and its Afterlives*. Minneapolis: University of Minnesota Press, 2013.

Guignon, C. "History and Historicity." *A Companion to Phenomenology and Existentialism* (2006): 545–558.

Guistino, C. M., C.J. Plum, and A. Vari, *Socialist Escapes: Breaking Away from Ideology and Everyday Routine in Eastern Europe, 1945–1989*. Brooklyn: Berghahn Books, 2015.

Gutmann, A. *Multiculturalism: Examining the Politics of Recognition*. Princeton: Princeton University Press, 1994.

Habermas, J. *The Structural Transformation of the Public Sphere*. Translated by T. Burger. Cambridge: The MIT Press, 1989.

Habermas, J. *Theory of Communicative Action*. Boston: Beacon Press, 1984.

Habermas, J. *Toward a Rational Society: Student Protest, Science, and Politics*. Translated by J. Shapiro. Boston: Beacon Press, 1970.

Habermas, J. *Truth and Justification*. Translated by B. Fultner. Cambridge: MIT Press, 2003.

Hagedorn, L. "'Christianity Unthought'—A Reconsideration of Myth, Faith, and Historicity." In *The New Yearbook for Phenomenology and Phenomenological Philosophy*. New York: Routledge, 2015: 49–64.

Hagedorn, L. *Tschechische Philosophen im 20. Jahrhundert – Klima, Rádl, Patočka, Havel, Kosik*. München: Deutsche Verlags-Anstalt, 2002.

Hagedorn, L. and J. Dodd, eds., *Religion, War and the Crisis of Modernity, A Special Issue Dedicated to the Philosophy of Jan Patočka. The New Yearbook of Phenomenology and Phenomenological Philosophy XIV*. New York: Routledge, 2015.

Hagedorn, L. and Y. Raynova, eds., *The Heretical Perspectives of Jan Patočka (1907–1977)*. Vienna: Axia Academic Publishers, 2018.

Hagedorn, L. and H. Reiner Sepp, eds. *Andere Wege in Die Moderne: Forschungsbeiträge zu Patočka's Genealogie der Neuzeit*. Würzburg: Konigshausen and Neumann, 2006.

Hagedorn, L. and M. Staudigl, eds. *Über Zivilisation und Differenz: Beiträge zu einer politischen Phänomenologie Europas*. Vol. 18. Würzburg: Königshausen and Newmann, 2008.

Hansen, J. "Target Atmospheric CO2: Where Should Humanity Aim?" *The Open Atmospheric Science Journal* 2, (2008): 217–231.

Haraszti, M. *The Velvet Prison: Artists Under State Socialism*. Translated by K. Landesmann. New York: Basic Books, 1987.

Hardin, Garrett. *Tragedy of the Commons*. Washington D.C.: American Association for the Advancement of Science, 1968.

Hardt, M. and A. Negri. *Empire*. Cambridge, MA: Harvard University Press, 2006.

Hardt, M. and A. Negri. *Multitude: War and Democracy in the Age of Empire*. London: Penguin Random House, 2005.

Harrison, P. "Subduing the Earth: Genesis 1, Early Modern Science, and the Exploitation of Nature." *Journal of Religion* 79, no. 1 (1999): 86–109.

Hashmi, S. and S. Lee, *Ethics and Weapons of Mass Destruction: Religious and Secular Perspectives*, Cambridge: Cambridge University Press, 2004.

Hauerwas, S. *Performing the Faith: Bonhoeffer and the Practice of Nonviolence*. Grand Rapids: Brazos Press, 2004.

Havel, V. *Art of the Impossible*. Translated by P. Wilson. New York: Fromm International, 1994.

Havel, V. *Disturbing the Peace*. Translated by P. Wilson. New York: Vintage, 1990.

Havel, V. *The Garden Party and Other Plays*. New York: Grove Press, 1993.

Havel, V. "Interview by Adam Michnik, After the Velvet, an Existential Revolution?" *Central European Forum Salon*, November 20, 2008. http://salon.eu.sk/en/archiv/801.

Havel, V. "A Joint Session of the U.S. Congress, Feb. 21, 1990." Archive of the Vaclav Havel Library, document 35359.

Havel, V. *Letters to Olga*. Translated by P. Wilson. New York: Alfred Knopf, 1988.

Havel, V. *Living in Truth*. London: Faber and Faber, 1986

Havel, V. *Open Letters*. Edited by P. Wilson. New York: Vintage, 1992.

Havel, V. "Power of the Powerless, 1978." Archive of the Vaclav Havel Library, document 35781.

Havel, V. "Speech: The Onassis Prize for Man and Mankind, May 24, 1993." Archive of the Vaclav Havel Library, document 35480.

Havel, V. "A Speech by Mr. Vaclav Havel [at] the Academy of Humanities and Political Science October, 27 1992." Archive of the Vaclav Havel Library, document 36020.

Havel, V. *Summer Meditations*. Translated by P. Wilson. New York: Vintage, 1992.

Havel, V. *To the Castle and Back*. New York: Alfred A. Knopf, 2007.

Hegel, G. W. F. *Grundlinien der Philosophie des Rechts*. Berlin: Verlag Ullstein, 1972.

Hegel, G. W. F. *Phenomenology of Spirit*. Translated by A.V. Miller. Oxford: Oxford University Press, 1977.

Hegel, G. W. F. *Philosophy of Right*. Translated by S.W. Dyde. Amherst: Prometheus Books, 1996

Heidegger, M. *Being and Time*. Translated by J. Stambaugh. New York: SUNY Press, 1996.

Heidegger, M. *Basic Writings*. New York: Harper Perennial, 2008.

Heidegger, H. *The Question concerning Technology*. New York: Harper & Row, 1977.

Heidegger, M. *Sein und Zeit*. Warsaw: De Gruyter, 2006.

Heitz, M. and B. Nessler, eds., *Eugen Fink und Jan Patočka. Briefe und Dokumente 1933–1977*. München: Karl Alber, 1999.

Heller, Á. "The End of Communism," *Thesis Eleven*, no. 27, 1990.

Heller, Á. and F. Fehér. *Eastern Left, Western Left. Totalitarianism, Freedom and Democracy*. New Jersey: Humanities Press, 1987.

Heneka, A. *A Besieged Culture. Czechoslovakia Ten Years after Helsinki*. Stockholm-Vienna: The Charta 77 Foundation, 1985.

Heraclitus, *Fragments: the Collected Wisdom of Heraclitus*. Edited by Brooks Haxton. New York: Viking 2001.

Hijiya, J. A. "The 'Gita' of J. Robert Oppenheimer." *Proceedings of the American Philosophical Society* 144, no. 2 (2000): 123–167.

Hirschman, A. O. "Exit, Voice and the Fate of the German Democratic Republic." *World Politics* 45, no. 2 (1993): 173–202.

Hladky, V. *Zmenit sam sebe. Duchovni cviceni Pierra Hadota, pece o sebe Michela Foucaulta a pece o dusi Jana Patocky.* Cerveny Kostelec: Pavel Mervart, 2010.

Homolka, J. "Jan Patočka's Non-Political Politics." *Acta Universitatis Carolinae Interpretationes* 7, no. 1 (2017): 130–146.

Honneth, A. *Freedom's Right: The Social Foundations of Democratic Life.* Translated by J. Gahahl. New York: Columbia University Press, 2014.

Honneth, A. *Reification: A New Look at an Old Idea.* Oxford: Oxford University Press, 2012.

Honneth, A. *Struggle for Recognition: The Moral Grammar of Social Conflicts.* Translated by J. Anderson. Cambridge: Polity Press, 1995.

Horkheimer, M. and T. Adorno. *Dialectic of Enlightenment.* Translated by E. Jephcott. Stanford, CA: Stanford University Press, 2002.

Hornsey, J.M., E.A. Harris, P. G. Bain, and K. S. Fielding. "Meta-analyses of the Determinants and Outcomes of Belief in Climate Change." *Nature climate change* 6, no. 6 (2016): 622–626.

Horvath, R. "'The Solzhenitsyn Effect': East European Dissidents and the Demise of the Revolutionary Privilege." *Human Rights Quarterly* (2007): 879–907.

Howard, V. R. *Gandhi's Ascetic Activism: Renunciation and Social Action.* Albany: State University of New York Press, 2013.

Hrabal, B. *Too Loud a Solitude.* Translated by Michael Henry Heim. New York: Houghton Mifflin Harcourt, 1990.

Humphrey, M. *Ecological Politics and Democratic Theory: The Challenge to the Deliberative Ideal.* London: Routledge, 2007.

Husema, J. and Short, D. "A Slow Industrial Genocide: Tar Sands and the Indigenous Peoples of Northern Alberta." *The International Journal of Human Rights* 16, no. 1 (2012): 216–237.

Husserl, E. *The Crisis of European Sciences and Transcendental Phenomenology.* Translated by D. Carr. Evanston: Northwestern University Press, 1970.

Inwood, M. ed., *A Heidegger Dictionary.* Oxford: Blackwell Publishing, 1999.

Isaac, J. C. *Arendt, Camus and Modern Rebellion.* New Haven: Yale University Press, 1994.

Isaac, J. C. "The Strange Silence of Political Theory." *Political Theory* 23, no. 4 (1995): 636–52.

James, W., *William James: Essays and Lectures.* Edited by Richard Kamber. New York: Routledge, 2016.

Japhy, J. and E. Swyngedouw, *The Post-political and Its Discontents: Spaces of Depoliticisation, Spectres of Radical Politics.* Edinburgh: Edinburgh University Press, 2014.

Johnson, R. L., *Gandhi's Experiments with Truth: Essential Writings by and About Mahatma Gandhi.* Lanham, MD: Lexington Books, 2006.

Judt, T. "The Dilemmas of Dissidence: The Politics of Opposition in East-Central Europe." *Eastern European Politics and Societies* 2 (1988): 185–240.

Judt, T. *Past Imperfect.* Berkeley: University of California Press, 1992.

Kantůrková, E. *My Companions in the Bleak House.* New York: Woodstock, 1987.

Karfík, F. "Jan Patočka a Problém Filosofie Dějin ke kontextu Kacířských esejů." *Reflexe* 50 (2016).

Karfík, F. *Unendlichkeitwerden durch die Endlichkeit: Eine Lectüre der Philosophie Jan Patočka's.* Würzburg: Königshausen and Newmann, 2008.

Keane, J. *Democracy and Civil Society.* London: Verso, 1988.

Keane, J. *Global Civil Society?* Cambridge: Cambridge University Press, 2003.

Keane, J. *The Power of the Powerless: Citizens against the State in Central-Eastern Europe.* New York: M.E. Sharp, Inc., 1985.

Keane, J. *Václav Havel: A Political Tragedy in Six Acts.* London: Bloomsbury, 1999.

Kearney, R. "Poetics and the Right to Resist: Patočka's Testimony." *International Journal of Philosophical Studies* 2, no. 1 (1994): 31–44.

Keck, M. and K. Sikkink, *Activists Beyond Borders*. Ithaca: Cornel University Press, 1998.

Kenney, P. *A Carnival of Revolution: Central Europe 1989*. Princeton: Princeton University Press, 2002.

Kershaw, I. *Popular Opinion and Political Dissent in the Third Reich, Bavaria 1933–1945*. Oxford: Oxford University Press, 1983.

Khagram, S., J. Riker, J. and K. Sikkink, *Restructuring World Politics: Transnational Social Movements, Networks, and Norms*. Minneapolis: University of Minnesota Press, 2002.

King, M. E. *Gandhian Nonviolent Struggle and Untouchability in South India: The 1924–25 Vykom Satyagraha and Mechanisms of Change*. Oxford: Oxford University Press, 2015.

Kis, J. *L'Égale Dignité : Essai sur les fondements des droits de l'homme*. Paris: Seuil, 1989.

Kis, J. *Politics as a Moral Problem*. Budapest: Central European University Press, 2009.

Kis, J. « Quelques idées pour l'opposition hongroise. » *Esprit*, 2 (1983).

Kluback, W. *The Essential Reinhold Niebuhr: Selected Essays and Addresses*. Edited by William Kluback, Vol. 21, No. 3, (1987): 187–189.

Kočí, M. "The Experiment of Night: Jan Patočka on War, and a Christianity to Come." *Labyrinth: An International Journal for Philosophy, Value Theory and Sociocultural Hermeneutics* 19, no. 1 (2017): 138–155.

Kočí, M. "Metaphysical Thinking after Metaphysics: A Theological Teading of Jan Patočka's Negative Platonism." *International Journal of Philosophy and Theology* 79, no. 1-2 (2018): 18–35.

Kočí, M. "Sacrifice for Nothing: The Movement of Kenosis in Jan Patočka's Thought." *Modern Theology* 33, no. 4 (2017): 594–617.

Kočí, M. *Thinking Faith after Christianity: A Theological Reading of Jan Patočka's Phenomenological Philosophy*. New York: State University of New York Press, 2020.

Kohák, E. *Cultural Identity and Global Humanity in Czech Philosophy*. Prague: Filosofia, 2008.

Kohák, E. *Embers and the Stars: A philosophical inquiry into the moral sense of nature*. Chicago: University of Chicago Press, 1984.

Kohák, E. *Jan Patočka Philosophy and Selected Writings*. Chicago: University of Chicago Press, 1989. Kołakowski, L. "Theses on Hope and Hopelessness," *Survey* 17, no. 3 (1971): 80.

Kołakowski, L. *Main Currents of Marxism: Its Origins, Growth, and Dissolution*. Translated by P.S. Falla. Oxford: Oxford University Press, 1981.

Kołakowski, L. *Metaphysical Horror*. Chicago: University of Chicago Press, 2001.

Kołakowski, L. *Toward a Marxist Humanism. Essays on the Left Today*. Translated by J. Zielonko. New York: Grove Press, 1968.

Kołakowski, L. and S. Hampshire, *The Socialist Idea. A Reappraisal*. New York: Basic Books, 1974.

Konrád, G. *Antipolitics: An Essay*. Translated by R. Allen. New York: Harcourt Brace Jovanovich, 1984.

Konrád, G. *A Guest in my own Country: A Hungarian Life*. Translated by J. Tucker. New York: Other Press, 2002.

Konrád, G. "To Cave Explorers from the West." *Dissent* 35 (1988): 463–466.

Kopecky, P. and C. Mudde, *Uncivil Society: Contentious Politics in Post-Communist Europe*. London: Routledge, 2003.

Kostrezewa, R. ed. *Between East and West. Writings from "Kultura."* New York: Hill and Wang, 1990.

Kotkin, S. *Uncivil Society: 1989 and The Implosion of the Communist Establishment*. New York: Modern Library, 2009.

Kouba, P. "Time in 'Negative Platonism.'" In *The Phenomenological Critique of Mathematisation and the Question of Responsibility*, New York: Springer, 2015: 79–88.

Krapfl, J. "Boredom, Apocalypse, and Beyond: Reading Havel through Patočka." *East European Politics and Societies* 32, no. 2 (2018): 278–284.

Kubrick, S., dir. *Dr. Strangelove, or, How I learned to stop worrying and love the bomb.* Columbia Pictures, 1964.

Kumar, K. *Ideas and Ideals of 1989.* Minneapolis: University of Minnesota Press, 2001.

Kundera, M. *The Unbearable Lightness of Being.* Translated by M.H. Heim. New York: Harper and Row, 1984.

Kunnie J. and Nomalungelo I. Goduka, eds., *Indigenous Peoples' Wisdom and Power: Affirming Our Knowledge through Narratives.* Burlington, VT: Ashgate Publishing, 2006.

Kuroń, J. *Revolutionary Marxist Students in Poland Speak Out: 1964–1968.* New York: Merit Publishers, 1968.

Kusin, V. *From Dubcek to Charter 77. A study of 'normalization' in Czechoslovakia 1968- 1978.* New York: St. Martin's Press, 1978.

Kusin, V. *Intellectual Origins of the Prague Spring.* Cambridge: Cambridge University Press, 1971.

Laignel-Lavastine, A. *Esprits d'Europe : autour de Czesław Miłosz, Jan Potočka, István Bibó.* Paris: Calmann-Lévy, 2005.

Laignel-Lavastine, A. *Jan Patočka : L'Esprit de la dissidence.* Paris: Michalon Le Bien Commun, 1998.

Lash, S. and M. Fetherstone. *Recognition and Difference.* London: Sage Publications, 2002.

Leghissa, G. and M. Staudigl. *Lebenswelt und Politik.* Würzburg: Königshausen und Neumann, 2007.

Lehman, S. *Der Horizont der Freiheit: Zum Existenzdenken Jan Patočkas.* Würzburg: Königshausen und Neumann, 2004.

Leufer, D. "A Ship Bound to Shipwreck: Jan Patočka's Philosophy of History." Doctoral thesis, KU Leuven, October 2018.

Leufer, D. "The Wound Which Will Not Close: Jan Patočka's Philosophy and the Conditions of Politicization." *Studies in East European Thought* 69, no. 1 (2017): 29–44

Levinas, E. *Entre Nous: Thinking of the Other.* Translated by M.B. Smith. London: Continuum, 1998.

Levinas, E. *Otherwise than Being, or, Beyond Essence.* Translated by A Lingis. Pittsburgh: Duquesne University Press, 1998.

Levinas, E. *Totality and Infinity: An Essay on Exteriority.* Translated by A. Lingis. Pittsburgh: Duqesnes University Press, 1969.

Lodgaard, S. and B. Maerli, eds., *Nuclear Proliferation and International Security.* New York: Routledge, 2007.

Lovelock, J. *Gaia: A New Look at Life on Earth.* Oxford: Oxford University Press, 2000.

Lom, P. "East Meets West—Jan Patočka and Richard Rorty on Freedom: A Czech Philosopher Brought into Dialogue with American Postmodernism." *Political theory* 27, no. 4 (1999): 447–459.

Maggini, G. "Europe's Janus Head: Jan Patočka's Notion of Overcivilization." *Epoche* 19, no. 1 (2014): 103–125.

Maibach, E., A. Leiserowitz, C. Roser-Renouf, T. Myers, S. Rosenthal and G. Feinberg. *The Francis Effect: How Pope Francis Changed the Conversation about Global Warming.* George Mason University and Yale University. Fairfax, VA: George Mason University Center for Climate Change Communication, 2015.

Mailer, N. "The White Negro." *Dissent* (1957). Retrieved from: https://www. dissentmagazine.org/online_articles/the-white-negro-fall-1957.

Majernik, J. "Jan Patočka's Reversal of Dostoevsky and Charter 77." *Labyrinth: An International Journal for Philosophy, Value Theory and Sociocultural Hermeneutics* 19, no. 1 (2017): 26–45.

Mann, C. *1491: New Revelations of the Americas Before Columbus.* New York: Vintage Books, 2006.

Mann, C. "1491." *Atlantic Monthly* 289, no. 3 (2002): 41–52.

Mantena, K. "Another Realism: The Politics of Gandhian Nonviolence." *American Political Science Review* 106, no. 2 (2012): 455–470.

Manton, E. "Ideology and the Politics of the "Chorismos": Patočka's Critique of Ideology." *Topics in Feminism, History and Philosophy, IWM Junior Visiting Fellows Conferences* 6 (2000). Retrieved from: http://www.iwm.at/wp-content/uploads/jc-06-08.pdf.

Marcuse, H. *One Dimensional Man.* Boston: Beacon Press, 1964.

Markell, P. *Bound by Recognition.* Princeton: Princeton University Press, 2003.

Markell, P. "Tragic Recognition: Action and Identity in Antigone and Aristotle." *Political Theory* 31, no. 1 (2003): 6–38.

Martinez-Alier, J. "Between Activism and Science: Grassroots Concepts for Sustainability Coined by Environmental Justice Organizations." *Journal of Political Ecology* 21 (2014): 19–60.

Marx, K. and F. Engels, *The Marx-Engels Reader.* New York: Norton, 1978.

Mastny, V. ed. *East European Dissent Vol.1, 1953–64 and Vol. 2, 1965–1970.* New York: Facts on File, 1972.

Matustík, M. J. *Postnational Identity: Critical Theory and Existential Philosophy in Habermas, Kierkegaard, and Havel.* New York: Guilford Press, 1993.

Matynia, E. *Performative Democracy.* Boulder, CO: Paradigm Publishers, 2009.

May, T. *Nonviolent Resistance: A Philosophical Introduction.* Cambridge: Polity, 2015.

McCarthy, R. M. and G. Sharp. *Non-Violent Action: A Research Guide.* New York: Garland Publishing, 1997.

McDermott, K. and S. Matthew. *Revolution and Resistance in Eastern Europe: Challenges to Communist Rule.* New York: Berg, 2006.

McDonagh, S. *To Care for the Earth: A Call to a New Theology.* Santa Fe, NM: Bear and Co., 1986.

McKibbon, B. *Oil and Honey: The Education of an Unlikely Activist.* New York: Macmillian, 2013.

Melançon, J. "Jan Patočka's Sacrifice: Philosophy as Dissent." *Continental philosophy review* 46, no. 4 (2013): 577–602.

Meierhenrich, J. *Genocide: A Reader.* Oxford: Oxford University Press: 2014.

Mensch, J. R. *Patočka's Asubjective Phenomenology: Toward a New Concept of Human Rights.* Würzburg: Königshausen und Neumann, 2016.

Merleau-Ponty, M. *Phenomenology of Perception.* Translated by C. Smith. London: Routledge, 2002.

Merleau-Ponty, M. *The Primacy of Perception and other Essays on Phenomenological Psychology, the Philosophy of Art, History and Politics.* Evanston: Northwestern University Press, 1964.

Merleau-Ponty, M. *The Visible and the Invisible followed by Working Notes.* Edited by Claude Lefort. Translated by Alphonso Lingis. Evanston: Northwestern University Press, 1969 [2001].

Merlier, P. *Autour de Jan Patočka.* Paris: L'Harmattan, 2010.

Michnik, A. "After the Velvet, an Existential Revolution?" *Central European Forum Salon.* (2008): Feb. 10, 2017.

Michnik, A. *The Church and the Left.* Translated by D. Ost. Chicago: University of Chicago Press, 1993.

Michnik, A. *Letters from Prison and Other Essays.* Translated by Maya Latynski. Berkeley: University of California Press, 1985.

Mihajlov, M. *Moscow Summer.* New York: Farrar, Straus and Giroux, 1965.

Mihajlov, M. *Underground Notes.* Translated by M.M. Ivusic. Kansas City: Sheed, Andrews, and McMeel, 1976.

Mill, J. S. *On Liberty.* London: Penguin Books, 1974.

Miłosz, C. *Captive Mind.* Translated by J. Zielonko. New York: Vintage, 1951.

Miri, S, Robert Lake, Tricia Kress. *Reclaiming the Sane Society.* Boston: Sense Publishers, 2014.

Mitchell, S. *Bhagavad Gita: A New Translation.* New York: Harmony Books, 2002.

Mlynář, Z. *Night Frost in Prague.* London: Hurst and Co., 1980.

Mlynář, Z. *Voices of Czechoslovak Socialists.* London: Merlin Press, 1977.

Moore, C. "Heretical Conversations with Continental Philosophy: Jan Patočka, Central Europe and Global Politics." *British Journal of Politics and International Relations* 11, no. 2 (2009): 315–331.

Moore, C. and C. Farrands, *International Relations Theory and Philosophy: Interpretive Dialogues.* London: Routledge, 2010.

Naess, A. *Gandhi and Group Conflict. An Exploration of Satyagraha. Theoretical Background.* Oslo: Universitetsforlaget, 1974.

Nellen, K. and P. Pithart and M. Pojar, eds. *Schriften zur tschechischen Kultur und Geschichte.* Stuttgart: Klett-Cotta, 1992.

Němec, J. and D. Soucek, eds. *Bibliografie 1928–1996 Jan Patočka.* Prague: Oikoymenh, 1997.

Niebuhr, R. "Death of a Martyr," *Christianity and Crisis*, no. 5, June 25, 1945.

Nielsen, K. B., R. Wüstenbrg, and J. Zimmermann, *A Spoke in the Wheel: The Political in the Theology of Dietrich Bonhoeffer.* München: Gütersloher Verlaghaus, 2013.

Novotny, K. *La genèse d'une hérésie. Monde, corps et histoire dans la pensée de Jan Patočka.* Paris: Vrin: 2013.

Novotný, K. "Leben und Natur. Zur frühen Phänomenologie der natürlichen Welt bei Jan Patočka." *Acta Universitatis Carolinae Interpretationes* 7, no. 1 (2017): 11–29.

Obrien, T. *The Things They Carried.* New York: Houghton Mifflin Harcourt, 2009.

Osborne, R. *Anarchy and Apocalypse: Essays on Faith, Violence and Theodicy.* Eugene: Cascade Books, 2010.

Ost, D. *Solidarity and the Politics of Antipolitics: Opposition and Reform in Poland Since 1968.* Philadelphia: Temple University Press, 1990.

Palouš, M. "Jan Patočka's Socratic Message for the Twenty-First Century." In *Jan Patočka and the Heritage of Phenomenology*, Berlin: Springer Dordrecht, 2011: 163–174.

Palouš, M. "The Parallel Polis after 12 Years." *Cordozo Studies in Law and Literature* 2, no. 1 (1990): 53–59.

Palouš, M. *The Solidarity of the Shaken. Jan Patočka's Legacy in the Modern World.* Washington: Academica Press, 2019.

Pantham, T. "Thinking with Mahatma Gandhi: Beyond Liberal Democracy." *Political Theory* 11, no. 2 (1983): 165–188.

Parekh, B. C. *Colonialism, Tradition, and Reform: an Examination of Gandhi's Political Discourse.* Newbury: Sage Publications, 1989.

Parekh, B. C. *Gandhi's Political Philosophy: a Critical Examination.* Notre Dame: University of Notre Dame Press, 1989.

Parel, A. "Gandhian Freedoms and Self-Rule," in *Gandhi's Experiments with Truth: Essential Writings by and about Mahatma Gandhi.* Edited by Richard L. Johnson. Lanham, MD: Lexington Books, 2006.

Patil, V.T. *Mahatma Gandhi and the Civil Disobedience Movement: A Study in the Dynamics of the Mass Movement*. Delhi: Renaissance Pub. House, 1988.

Patočka, J. *Aristote, ses devanciers, ses successeurs*. Translated by E. Abrams. Paris: Librairie Philosophique, 2011.

Patočka, J. *Body, Community, Language, World*. Edited by James Dodd. Translated by E. Kohák. Chicago: Open Court, 1998.

Patočka, J. "Čím je a čím není Charta 77," in Sebrané spisy [Collected Works] vol. 12. Praha: Oikoymenh, 2006: 428–30.

Patočka, J. "Co můžeme očekávat od Charty 77?" in Sebrané spisy [Collected Works] vol. 12. Praha: Oikoymenh, 2006: 440–4.

Patočka, J. *Die Bewegung der menschlichen Existenz*: Edited by Klaus Nellen and Jiří Němec. Stuttgart: Klett-Cotta, 1991.

Patočka, J. *Éternité et historicité*. Translated by E. Abrams. Lagrasse: Verdier, 2011.

Patočka, J. *Heretical Essays in the Philosophy of History*. Translated by Erazím Kohák. Chicago: Open Court, 1996.

Patočka, J. "Intellectuals and opposition." Translated by F. Tava and D. Leufer. In D. Meacham & F. Tava, *Thinking after Europe*, 2016.

Patočka, J. *An Introduction to Husserl's Phenomenology*. Translated by E. Kohák. Chicago: Open Court, 1996.

Patočka, J. "K záležitostem Plastic People of the Universe a DG 307" ["On the Matters of The Plastic People of the Universe and DG 307"]. In Sebrané spisy [Collected Works] vol. 12. Praha: Oikoymenh, 2006: 425–427. Translated by Paul Wilson as "The Planetary Game," *Ethos*, Vol. 2, Nr. 1 (1986): 15.

Patočka, J. "Kacířské eseje o filosofii dějin," in Sebrané spisy [Collected Works] vol. 3. Praha: Oikoymenh, 2002: 13–131. Translated by Erazím Kohák as *Heretical Essays in the Philosophy of History*. Chicago: Open Court, 1996.

Patočka, Jan. "Kolem Masarykovy filosofie náboženství" [Around Masaryk's Philosophy of Religion]. In Sebrané spisy [Collected Works] vol. 12. Praha: Oikoymenh, 2006: 366–422. Translated by Jiří Rothbauer et al. as "On Masaryk's Philosophy of Religion," in L. Hagedorn and J. Dodd (eds.). *Religion, War and the Crisis of Modernity (The New Yearbook for Phenomenology and Phenomenological Philosophy, vol. XIV)*. London: Routledge 2015: 95–135.

Patočka, J. *L'art et le temps*. Translated by E. Abrams. Paris: P.O.L., 1990.

Patočka, J. *Le monde naturel comme problème philosophique*. Translated by J. Danek and H. Declève. La Haye: M. Nijhoff, 1976.

Patočka, J. *L'Europe après l'Europe*. Translated by E. Abrams. Lagrasse: Verdier, 2007.

Patočka, J. *Libertad y Sacrificio*. Translated by Ivan Ortega Rodriguez. Salamanca: Ediciones Sígueme, 2007.

Patočka, J. *Liberté et sacrifice. Ecrits politiques*. Edited and translated by E. Abrams. Grenoble: Millon, 1990.

Patočka, J. *L'idée de l'Europe en Bohême*. Edited and translated by Erika Abrams. Grenoble: Millon, 1991.

Patočka, J. *Living in Problematicity*. Edited and translated by Eric Manton. Prague: Oikoymenh, 2007.

Patočka, J. *The Natural World as a Philosophical Problem*. Translated by E. Abrams. Edited by I. Chvatík and L. Ucník. Evanston: Northwestern University Press, 2016.

Patočka, J. *Plato and Europe*. Translated by P. Lom. Stanford: Stanford University Press, 2002.

Patočka, J. "Platón a Evropa," in Sebrané spisy [Collected Works] vol. 2. Praha: Oikoymenh, 1999. 149–355.

Patočka, J. *Sebrané spisy sv.1, Péče o duši I* (Vol. 1) [Collected Works. Volume 1, Care of the Soul I] Eds. I. Chvatík and P. Kouba. Praha: Oikoymenh, 1996.

Patočka, J. *Sebrané spisy sv.2, Péče o duši II* (Vol. 2) [Collected Works. Volume 2, Care of the Soul II] Eds. I. Chvatík and P. Kouba. Praha: Oikoymenh, 1999.

Patočka, J. *Sebrané spisy sv.3, Péče o duši III* (Vol. 3) [Collected Works. Volume 3, Care of the Soul III] Eds. I. Chvatík and P. Kouba. Praha: Oikoymenh, 2002.

Patočka, J. "Two Charter 77 Texts." Translated by Erazím Kohák in *Jan Patočka Philosophy and Selected Writings*. Chicago: The University of Chicago Press, (1989): 340–347.

Patočka, J. "What are the Czechs," in J. Bažant, N. Baržantova and F. Starn, eds. *The Czech Reader*. Durham, NC: Duke University Press, 2010: 419–428.

Patočka, J. and L. Hagedorn and H.R. Sepp, *Texte, Dokumente, Bibliographie*. München: Karl Alber, 1999.

Perreault, T., G. Bridge, and J. McCarthy, *Routledge Handbook of Political Ecology*. New York: Routledge, 2015.

Pettman, R. *Intending the World: A Phenomenology of International Affairs*. Melbourne, Australia: Melbourne University Press, 2008.

Pirro, R. *The Politics of Tragedy and Democratic Citizenship*. New York: Continuum, 2011.

Plato. *The Collected Dialogues of Plato: Including the Letters*. Bollingen Series LXXI. New Impression Edition. Eds. E. Hamilton, H. Carnes, and L. Cooper. Princeton: Princeton University Press, 2005.

Plato. *Four Texts on Socrates*. Edited by T. West. Ithaca: Cornell University Press, 1998.

Pollack, D. and J. Wielgohs, *Dissent and Opposition in Communist Eastern Europe: Origins of Civil Society and Democratic Transition*. Burlington, VT: Ashgate, 2004.

Pontuso, J. *Václav Havel: Civic Responsibility in the Postmodern Age*. Oxford: Rowan and Littlefield, 2004.

Popescu, D. *Political Action in Václav Havel's Thought: The Responsibility of Resistance*. Lanham: Lexington Books, 2012.

Přibáň, J. *Dissidents of Law: On the 1989 Revolutions, legitimations, fictions of legality and contemporary version of the social contract*. Hampshire: Ashgate Publishing, 2002.

Purdey, S.J. *Economic Growth, the Environment and International Relations: the Growth Paradigm*. New York: Routledge, 2010.

Rabanus, C. *Jan Patočkas Phänomenologie interkulturell gelesen*. Nordhausen: Traugott Bautz, 2006.

Rasmussen, L. *Dietrich Bonhoeffer: Reality and Resistance*. Nashville: Abingdon Press, 1972.

Renton, D. *Dissident Marxism: Past Voices for Present Times*. New York: Zed Books, 2004.

Richir, M. and E. Tassin,eds. *Ján Patočka: philosophie, phénoménologie, politique*. Grenoble: J. Millon, 1992.

Ricoeur, P. *The Course of Recognition*. Translated by D. Pellauer. Cambridge, MA: Harvard University Press, 2005.

Ricoeur, P. *History, Memory, and Forgetting*. Translated by K. Blamey and D. Pellauer. Chicago: University of Chicago Press, 2004.

Ricoeur, P. "Jan Patočka: A Philosopher of Resistance," *The Crane Bag* 7, no. 1 (1983): 116–118.

Ricoeur, P. *Oneself as Another*. Chicago: University of Chicago Press, 1995.

Rimmer, M. "The World Indigenous Network: Rio+ 20, Intellectual Property, Indigenous Knowledge and Sustainable Development." *Indigenous Intellectual Property*. Cheltenham: Edward Elgar Publishing, 2015.

Risse, T., Ropp, S., & Sikkink, K. *The Power of Human Rights: International Norms and Domestic Change*. Cambridge: Cambridge University Press, 1999.

Ritter, M. *Into the World: The Movement of Patočka's Phenomenology*. New York: Springer, 2019.

Rocamora, C. *Acts of Courage: Václav Havel's Life in Theatre*. Hanover: Smith and Kraus, 2004.

Rorty, R. "The Seer of Prague." *New Republic* 205, no. 1 (1991): 35–39.

Ross, A., K. P. Sherman, J. G. Snodgrass, H. D. Delcore and R. Sherman. *Indigenous Peoples and the Collaborative Stewardship of Nature: Knowledge Binds and Institutional Conflicts*. New York: Routledge, 2016.

Ryback, T. *Rock Around the Bloc. A History of Rock Music in Eastern Europe and the Soviet Union*. New York: Oxford University Press, 1990.

Şan, E. "Corporéité et existence: Patočka, Merleau-Ponty, Maine de Biran." *Studia Phænomenologica*, 12, no. 1 (January 2012): 133–156.

Sartre, J. P. *Existentialism and Human Emotions*. Translated by B. Frechtman and H.B. Barnes. New York: Carol Publishing, 1993.

Savio, M. "An End to History." Speech, Berkeley, CA, December 2, 1964.

Scarry, E. *Thermonuclear Monarchy: Choosing Between Democracy and Doom*. New York: W. W. Norton and Co., 2014.

Schell, J. *Unconquerable World: Power, Nonviolence, and the Will of the People*. New York: Metropolitan Books, 2003.

Schlosberg, D. *Defining Environmental Justice: Theories, Movements, and Nature*. Oxford: Oxford University Press, 2009.

Schmelzer, M. "The growth paradigm: History, hegemony, and the contested making of economic growthmanship." *Ecological Economics* 118 (2015): 262–271.

Schmit, P. "'Going to War Itself': J. Patočka and the Great War." *Le philosophoire* 2 (2017): 135–168.

Schock, K. *Unarmed Insurrections: People Power Movements in Non-Democracies*. Minneapolis: University of Minnesota Press, 2005.

Schöpflin, G. *Censorship and Political Communication in Eastern Europe: A Collection of Documents*. New York: St. Martin's Press, 1983.

Schöpflin, G. and N. Wood, *In Search of Central Europe*. Lanham: Rowman & Littlefield, 1994.

Schweitzer, A. "A Declaration of Conscience," *Saturday Review* (May 18, 1957): 17–20.

Scott, J. C. *Domination and the Arts of Resistance: Hidden Transcripts*. Yale: Yale University Press, 1990.

Scrogin, K. "The War on Concepts: The Thought of Jan Patočka and the War on Terror." *Kritike* 2, no. 1 (2008): 68–78.

Servigne P. and R. Stevens. *Comment tout peut s'effondrer. Petit manuel de collapsologie à l'usage des générations présentes*. Paris: Le Seuil, 2015.

Ševčík, M. and V. Zuska, *Mytus a umeni v pojeti Jana Patocky*. Prague: Karolinum, 2014.

Ševčík, M. and V. Zuska, *Negace a afirmace v Patockove koncepci umeleckeho dila*. Prague: Karolinum, 2012.

Sharp, G. *From Dictatorship to Democracy: A Conceptual Framework for Liberation*. Boston: Albert Einstein Institution, 2010.

Sharp, G. *Gandhi Wields the Weapon of Moral Power*. Ahmedabad: Navjivan Trust, 1997 [1960].

Shore, M. *The Ukrainian Night: An Intimate History of Revolution*. New Haven: Yale University Press, 2018.

Shoreman-Ouimet, E. and H. Kopnina. *Culture and Conservation: Beyond Anthropocentrism*. New York: Routledge, 2015.

Šimečka, M. *The Restoration of Order. The Normalization of Czechoslovakia.* Translated by A. G. Brain. London: Verso, 1984.

Skilling, H. G. *Charter 77 and Human Rights in Czechoslovakia.* London: George Allen & Unwin, 1981.

Skilling, H. G. *Samizdat and an independent society in Central and Eastern Europe.* Columbus: Ohio State University Press, 1989.

Skilling, H. G. and P. Wilson. *Civic Freedom in Central Europe. Voices from Czechoslovakia.* New York: St. Martin's Press, 1991.

Sokol, J. *Philosophie als Verpflichtung: Über Ethik, Menschenrechte, Bildung und Politik.* Heidelberg: Manutius Verlag, 2014.

Solzhenitsyn, A. *The Gulag Archipelago: An Experiment in Literary Investigation.* Translated by T.P. Witney. New York: Harper and Row, 1973.

Sorabji, R. *Gandhi and the Stoics: Modern Experiments on Ancient Values.* Oxford: Oxford University Press, 2012.

Stanciu, O. "The Great War as a 'cosmic event.' Jan Patočka and the experience of the frontline." *Revue philosophique de la France et de l'étranger* 143, no. 4 (2018): 507–524.

Stanciu, O. "Nature and the Natural World in the Thought of Jan Patocka." *Revue de Phénoménologie,* no. 26 (2018): 47–64.

Staudigl, M. *Phenomenologies of Violence.* Leiden: Brill Academic Publisher, 2013.

Sternad, C. "Max Scheler and Jan Patočka on the First World War." *Labyrinth. An International Journal for Philosophy, Value Theory and Sociocultural Hermeneutics* 19, no. 1 (2017): 89–106.

Stetler, H. "'Collapsologie': Constructing an Idea of How Things Fall Apart," *New York Review of Books.* Jan. 21, 2020.

Strauss, L. *Persecution and the Art of Writing.* Chicago: University of Chicago Press, 1988.

Students for a Democratic Society, "Port Huron Statement." New York: Students for a Democratic Society, 1962.

Šustrová, P. "Different Legacies of Dissent," *Uncaptive Minds* 7, no. 3 (1994).

Sunstein, C. R. *Why Societies Need Dissent.* Cambridge: Harvard University Press, 2003.

Suu Kyi, A. *Freedom from Fear and Other Writings.* London: Penguin, 1991.

Suu Kyi, A. *Letters from Burma.* London: Penguin, 1996.

Suvák, V. "The Essence of Truth (aletheia) and the Western Tradition in the Thought of Heidegger and Patočka." *Thinking Fundamentals, IWM Junior Visiting Fellows Conferences* 9 (2000).

Sviták, I. *The Czechoslovak Experiment. 1968–1969.* New York: Columbia University Press, 1971.

Szakolczai, A. "Thinking Beyond the East-West Divide: Foucault, Patočka, and the Care of the Self." *Social Research* 61, no. 2 (1994).

Szelényi, I. and G. Konrád, *The Intellectuals on the Road to Class Power.* Translated by A. Arato and R. Allen. New York: Harcourt Brace Jovanovich, 1979.

Szulecki, K. "Hijacked Ideas: Human Rights, Peace, and Environmentalism in Czechoslovak and Polish Dissident Discourses." *East European Politics and Societies* 25, no. 2 (2011): 272–295.

Tahmasebi-Birgani, V. *Emmanuel Levinas and the Politics of Non-violence.* Toronto: University of Toronto Press, 2014.

Tamás, G.M. "Legacy of Dissent. Irony, Ambiguity, Duplicity," *Uncaptive Minds* 7, no. 2 (1994).

Tardivel, E. *La Liberté au Principe: essai sure la philosophie de Patočka.* Paris: Librairie Philosophique Vrin, 2011.

Tardivel, E. "La subjectivité dissidente. Etude sur Patočka," *Studia Phænomenologica*, no. 7 (2007): 435–463.

Tassin, E. and M. Richir, eds., *Jan Patočka: philosophie, phénoménologie, politique*. Grenoble: Million, 1993.

Tava, F. *The Risk of Freedom: Ethics, Phenomenology and Politics in Jan Patočka*. Translated by J. Ledlie. New York: Rowman and Littlefield, 2015.

Tava, F. and D. Meacham, eds. *Thinking After Europe: Jan Patočka and Politics*. London: Rowan and Littlefield, 2016.

Taylor, F. *The Great Lie: Classic and Recent Appraisals of Ideology and Totalitarianism*. Wilmington: Intercollegiate Studies Institute, 2011.

Taylor, C. *Multiculturalism and "The Politics of Recognition": an Essay*. Princeton: Princeton University Press, 1992.

Thomas, P. *Marxism & Scientific Socialism: From Engels to Althusser*. New York: Routledge, 2008.

Thompson, S. *The Political Theory of Recognition: A Critical Introduction*. Cambridge: Polity Press, 2006.

Thoreau, H. D., *Walden*. New Haven: Yale University Press, 2006 [1854].

Thunberg, G. *No One Is Too Small to Make a Difference*. London: Penguin, 2019.

Tietz, C. *Theologian of Resistance: The Life and Thought of Dietrich Bonhoeffer*. Translated by V. Barnett. New York: Fortress Press, 2016.

Tillich, P. *Courage to Be*. New Haven: Yale University Press, 2000.

Tillich, P. *Shaking of Foundations*. New York: Charles Scribner's Sons, 1955.

Tolstoy, L. *The Kingdom of God Is Within You*. Translated by C. Garnett. New York: Cassell Publishing, 1894.

Tolstoy, L. *Writings on Civil Disobedience and Non-Violence*. Translated by A. Maude. Philadelphia: New Society Publishers, 1987.

Torpey, J. *Intellectuals, Socialism, and Dissent. The East German Opposition and Its Legacy*. Minneapolis: University of Minnesota Press, 1995.

Tucker, A. *The Philosophy and Politics of Czech Dissidence from Patočka to Havel*. Pittsburg: University of Pittsburgh Press, 2000.

Učník, L. *The Crisis of Meaning and the Life-world: Husserl, Heidegger, Arendt, Patočka*. Athens: Ohio University Press, 2016.

Učník, L. "Esse Or Habere. To Be Or To Have: Patočka's Critique Of Husserl And Heidegger." *Journal of the British Society for Phenomenology* 38, no. 3 (2007).

Učník, L. "Jan Patočka: From the Concept of Evidence to the Natural World and Beyond." *The Phenomenological Critique of Mathematisation and the Question of Responsibility* 76 (2015): 31–42.

Učník, L., I. Chvatík, and A. Williams, eds. *Asubjective Phenomenology: Jan Patočka in the Broader Context of his Work*. Nordhausen: Verlag Traugott Bautz, 2015.

United Nations, "2030 Agenda for Sustainable Development." https://www.un.org /development/desa/indigenouspeoples/focus-areas/post-2015-agenda/the-sustainable -development-goals-sdgs-and-indigenous.html.

United Nations Environment Programme, "Indigenous Communities and Their Communities." https://www.unenvironment.org/civil-society-engagement/ major-groups-modalities/major-group-categories/indigenous-peoples-and.

Vaculík, L. *A Cup of Coffee with My Interrogator*. Translated by G. Theiner. London: Readers International, 1987.

Vaculík, L. "Two thousand words to Workers, Farmers, Scientists, Artists, and Everyone," in Gale Stokes, editor, *From Stalinism to Pluralism*. New York: Oxford University Press, 1991.

Varsamopoulou, E. "Three Movements of Life: Jan Patočka's Philosophy of Personal Being." *The European Legacy,* July 2007: 12(5).

Veeravalli, A. *Gandhi in Political Theory: Truth, Law and Experiment.* Surrey: Ashgate, 2014.

Walker, G. *Environmental Justice: Concepts, Evidence and Politics.* New York: Routledge, 2012.

Warren, D.M. and K. Cashman. *Indigenous Knowledge for Sustainable Agriculture and Rural Development.* Report of the International Institute for Environment and Development, Sustainable Agriculture Programme, 1988.

Weber, M. *The Protestant Ethic and the Spirit of Capitalism.* Translated by Talcott Parsons. New York: Charles Scribner's Sons, 1958 [1905].

Werner-Müller, J. *What is Populism?* Philadelphia: University of Pennsylvania Press, 2016.

Werrell, C.E. and Francesco Femia, and Anne-Marie Slaughter, "The Arab Spring and Climate Change." Report of the Center for American Progress, 2013.

Westra, L. "Environmental Justice and the Rights of Indigenous Peoples: International and Domestic Legal Perspectives" *Journal of Environmental Law* 21, no. 2 (2009): 385–387.

Williams, Kieran. *The Prague Spring and Its Aftermath: Czechoslovak Politics, 1968–1970.* Cambridge: Cambridge University Press, 1997.

Wilson, P. *Civic Freedom in Central Europe. Voices from Czechoslovakia.* New York: St. Martin's Press, 1991.

Wohlleben, P. *The Hidden Life of Trees: What They Feel, How They Communicate—Discoveries from a Secret World.* Vancouver: Greystone Books, 2016.

Wolin, R. *The Politics of Being: The Political Thought of Martin Heidegger.* New York: Columbia University Press, 1990.

Zantovsky, M. *Havel: A Life.* New York: Grove Press, 2014.

Zehner, O. *Green Illusions: The Dirty Secrets of Clean Energy and the Future of Environmentalism.* University of Nebraska Press, 2012.

Index